CANON LAW SOCIETY
OF AMERICA

PROCEEDINGS
OF
THE FORTY-FIFTH
ANNUAL CONVENTION

SAN FRANCISCO, CALIFORNIA
OCTOBER 10-13, 1983

Canon Law Society of America
Washington, D.C. 20064

ISBN: 0-943616-22-0

TABLE OF CONTENTS

ADDRESSES

MAJOR SEMINARS

SEMINARS

MISCELLANEA

CANON LAW AS AN INSTRUMENT
FOR ECCLESIAL REFORM:
AN HISTORIC PERSPECTIVE

JAMES A. BRUNDAGE

Last January Pope John Paul II promulgated the new Code of Canon Law; next month, at the end of the *vacatio legis* on November 27, that code will come into full force and effect. During the twenty-four years since Pope John XXIII (1958-1963) announced a new code that would incorporate the changes in the Church's law made by the Second Vatican Council, this Society and its members have devoted much time, labor, and reflection to the code revision. As successive drafts of sections of the code appeared, members of this Society have spent countless hours analyzing, criticizing, and debating the new law. You have advised bishops and members of the Code Commission about the strengths and weaknesses of the draft versions and have suggested improvements in them. Not all of your suggestions were welcomed, to be sure; many good ones did not find their way into the final redaction of the code. But you have made your mark in the process and your efforts, I think, have not been in vain. The new code might well have been quite different without the efforts that members of this organization put into the consultation phase of code revision.[1]

The promulgation of the new code this year marks the end of one process and the beginning of another. Now canonists in the United States and throughout the world must implement the new law and apply both its words and its principles to the needs of real people in the real world. As professional canonists the members of this Society will elaborate a jurisprudence.

We must be clear about one thing from the outset: no statement or restatement of law, no matter how elegant and formally satisfying, has anything other than intellectual significance unless or until it is applied with insight, empathy, and understanding to the people and situations that it is supposed to order and regulate. The measure of the new code's success or failure will be its impact on individuals and society. That impact lies in your hands: as canonical practitioners—judges, advocates, procurators and administrators—you are the servants of the law and you also represent those whom the law governs. History's verdict on the new code will be a judgment on how well you implement that code. You have a dual mandate: on the one hand you are obliged to be faithful to the principles that the code embodies; and on the other hand you have an

[1] In addition to private consultations with bishops and members of the Code Commission, the Society and its members have contributed numerous published notes and articles to the public discussion of the code revision. Many of these are listed in Richard J. Cunningham, *An Annotated Bibliography of the Work of the Canon Law Society of America, 1965-1980* (Washington, D.C.: Canon Law Society of America, 1982).

1

obligation to apply those principles in ways that will serve the needs of those who choose to submit themselves and their affairs to the legal system of the code. These two obligations, in theory, should never conflict with one another. In practice the theory will often prove imperfect. Arriving at equitable adjustments between theoretical principles and practical needs is the essence of your task. This is the primary challenge, and the opportunity, that faces canonists now.

Canon law and the society we call the Church form what systems analysts would call a recursive feedback system. In other words, the law is one of a number of forces that play a role in shaping the ways in which members of the society behave. At the same time that law shapes behavior, the law itself, as it is framed and as it is applied, is molded by the actual and perceived behaviors of the members of the society. The interplay between the law, behavior, and perceptions of behavior is not a one-way street; influences flow in six directions simultaneously. But the traffic pattern is even more complex than this analogy suggests. Alterations in the economy, political institutions, social structure, and attitudes also result in changes in the canon law, either directly or at a second or third level in the feedback loop. No set of legal principles enunciated in any code, no matter how sophisticated, will function adequately if those who apply the principles to cases ignore these multiple interactions or pretend that they are of no consequence. The law is not something apart from society, nor is it a mechanism that functions independently of its time and place, its social and intellectual context.

The canonist must be aware of these interactions between law and society if she or he is to deal intelligently with the issues that implementation of the new code raises. Examples of potentially sensitive socio-legal issues will, I am sure, occur readily to each of us. Some obvious ones center around the academic freedom questions raised by episcopal mandates for teachers of theology;[2] around the possible labor relations implications of canon 1290; around the new retirement and pension provisions for pastors and bishops;[3] around the expanded authority of the national episcopal conferences;[4] around the practical consequences for litigants of the provisions for regional tribunals;[5] around the implementation of the new legislation on presbyteral councils[6] and pastoral councils.[7] Such a list could go on and on. The point is not that there are potential problem areas in the new code—that scarcely needs saying—but rather that

---

[2]Can. 810, § 1 and can. 812. All code citations, unless otherwise indicated, are to the canons in *Codex Iuris Canonici auctoritate Ioannis Pauli II promulgatus* (Città del Vaticano: Libreria Editrice Vaticana, 1983).

[3]Can. 402, § 2 and can. 538, §3.

[4]Can. 447-459; Bertram F. Griffin, "National Church Structures" in *Code, Community, Ministry: Selected Studies for the Parish Minister Introducing the Revised Code of Canon Law*, ed. James H. Provost (Washington, D.C.: CLSA, 1983), pp. 48-52.

[5]Can. 1423

[6]Can. 495-502; James H. Provost, "Presbyteral Councils" in *Code, Community, Ministry*, pp. 66-68.

[7]Can. 511-514.

2

canonists must devise solutions to those problems in the context of relationships between law and the community that are reciprocal, not unilateral. It is not only the task of canonists to implement the new code in ways that will serve the needs of individuals and society; canonists must in addition convince individuals and society to accept the principles that underlie the new code. This is a process of persuasion, not of command. The new code greatly reduces and simplifies the penal law of the 1917 code,[8] but even so it is difficult to see how many of the remaining penal provisions of the new code could ever be enforced as involuntary sanctions in American society.[9] The Church is a voluntary association, both in law and in fact, in this country. If Catholics are to submit their problems to canonical processes for review and disposition, they will have to be persuaded that the canon law, as set forth in the new code, holds out a plausible promise of furnishing equitable and acceptable solutions to their problems.

Canonists thus face a new era, not only because the law itself has changed, grown, and developed with the publication of the new code, but also because the relationship between the Church's law and the people of God has entered a new era—an era of voluntarism, an era in which canonists must rely upon persuasion, not penalties, to secure compliance with the decisions of the Church's courts.

There are elements of both continuity and innovation in this situation. There is continuity, after all, between the new code and the historical past of the Church's legal system; and there is innovation in many elements of the new code and in the new order of the relationship between Church, law, and society.

The present situation is unique, yet it is not entirely novel. Other generations of canonists have faced watershed situations, situations where a revision of existing canon law, coupled with changes in social circumstances, posed daunting challenges to the Church's lawyers. It may be helpful to look this evening at some of these past situations. Not, mind you, that you will find magic answers in these earlier situations to the problems of the present; but you can perhaps find other things that may be nearly as useful. For one thing it is comforting to know that others have faced similar problems and have survived the ordeal; in addition, the history of these earlier situations may suggest both some strategies that have worked in similar situations and other stategies whose past applications have been less successful than their proponents anticipated they would be. We can find things worth thinking about in failures as well as successes.

I should like to draw your attention to three specific moments in time: the promulgation of the *Liber Extra* by Pope Gregory IX (1227-1241) in 1234; the conclusion of the Council of Trent in 1563; and the promulgation of the old *Codex Iuris Canonici* in 1917. Each situation has similarities to the present; each has radical differences from the situation now; and each may suggest strategies for dealing with present circumstances.

[8]Bertram F. Griffin, "Ecclesiastical Sanctions" in *Code, Community, Ministry*, pp. 107-108.
[9]For a few examples see cann. 1337-1340, 1370, §§ 2-3, 1371, 1374-1376.

3

On September 5, 1234, Pope Gregory IX addressed the bull *Rex pacificus* to the teachers and students of canon law at the University of Bologna. The constitutions and decrees of his predecessors, the pope told them, had grown numerous and were circulating in competing versions in a multitude of different collections, while some important decisions were not to be found conveniently in any of the popular sources. On this account, Pope Gregory continued, he had directed his chaplain and penitentiary, Raymond of Peñafort, a Dominican friar, to collect the vagrant legislation into a single volume, to add the decrees of Gregory's own pontificate, to arrange the material in coherent order, and to prune away superfluous verbiage or irrelevant *dicta*, so that the meaning and intent of the laws should be clearly evident. Now that Raymond had done this, the pope concluded, the new version of the law was to be taught in the schools and used in the courts as the authoritative statement of the new law.[10]

Clearly what Gregory IX did 750 years ago in *Rex pacificus* bears more than a slight resemblance to what John Paul II did in *Sacrae disciplinae leges* in January of this year. Each pontiff published a new collection of law, each commanded that it be taught in the schools and used in the courts, each incorporated the acts of his predecessors and the constitutions of councils into the previously existing body of church law, each was acting in order to update a previously received system of canon law.[11] It is also obvious that there are important differences between the two situations. The *Liber Extra* that Gregory IX promulgated was intended to supplement the earlier law contained in Gratian's *Decretum*, not to replace. The 1983 *Codex Iuris Canonici*, on the other hand, expressly abrogates the 1917 *Codex*, as well as all contrary laws and customs, save for those that are expressly excepted from abrogation in the text of the new code.[12] The *Liber Extra* had been compiled essentially by one lone friar, with perhaps some secretarial help, in the course of about four years.[13] The 1983 code took six times as long to prepare and was the product of an international commission and battery of subcommissions, involving the labor ultimately of hundreds of experts and consultants, both men and women, clerical and lay.[14]

---

[10]Summarized from the text of *Rex pacificus* in *Corpus iuris canonici*, ed. Emil Friedberg, 2 vols. (Leipzig: B. Tauchnitz, 1879; repr. Graz: Akademische Druck- und Verlagsanstalt, 1959), 2:1-4.

[11]Text of *Sacrae disciplinae leges*, dated January 25, 1983, appears in *Codex Iuris Canonici* (1983), pp. vii-xiv.

[12]Can. 6, § 1.

[13]Johann Friedrich von Schulte, *Die Geschichte der Quellen und Literatur des canonischen Rechts*, 3 vols. (Stuttgart: F. Enke, 1875-1877; repr. Graz: Akademische Druck- und Verlagsanstalt, 1956; hereafter *QL*), 2:3-8; A. Van Hove, *Prolegomena ad Codicem iuris canonici*, 2d ed., Commentarium Lovaniense in Codicem iuris canonici, vol. 1, pt. 1 (Mechelen: H. Dessau, 1945), pp. 358-359; Alfons M. Stickler, *Historia iuris canonici Latini* (Torino: Libraria Pontificii Athenaei Salesiani, 1950), pp. 236-242; Gabriel Le Bras, Charles Lefebvre, and Jacqueline Rambaud-Buhot, *L'âge classique, 1140-1378: Sources et théorie du droit*, Histoire du droit et des institutions de l'église en Occident, vol. 7 (Paris: Sirey, 1965), pp. 235-243.

[14]The process is officially documented in the Commission's own periodical, *Communicationes* (Roma: Pontificia Commissio Codici Iuris Canonici Recognoscendo, 1969- ; in progress). English

The *Liber Extra* compressed within its covers roughly a century of ecclesiastical law-making and included the decrees and constitutions of two general councils, spanning the pontificates of twelve popes. The revised code takes account of the constitutions of one general council and the pontificates of seven popes over a span of sixty-six years. Although the number of canons and chapters in the two lawbooks is roughly similar (there are 1971 chapters in the *Liber Extra*, compared with 1752 canons in the new code), the *Liber Extra* is an appreciably longer work. The basic concept of the two lawbooks is quite different as well. The code attempts to digest a large body of law in a form created by the Commission that compiled it, while the *Liber Extra* for the most part reproduced the language of the original decretals and conciliar canons on which it was based. The code, in other words, is a restatement of conciliar and papal pronouncements, while the *Liber Extra* was much more like a casebook—a compilation of original sources rather than a reformulation of them.

But given that there are numerous and significant differences between the lawbook that canonists had to deal with in 1234 and the new code that they face today, both groups of canonists share some formidable problems. Let us, then, examine the problems that your predecessors faced and reflect on what they suggest to us.

Looking back over three quarters of a millenium, it seems to me that the canonists who worked with the new law of the *Liber Extra* in 1234 faced three challenges: first they had to implement a complex battery of organizational changes, mainly stemming from the reform legislation of the Fourth Lateran Council; second they needed to come to grips with a series of political problems that involved restructuring power relationships within the Church and also between the Church and secular society; and third they faced the intellectual challenge of creating a consistent system of jurisprudence and juristic principles that would enable them to interpret the new law and to integrate it with the previously existing system of canonistic jurisprudence.

First, of the problems in the Church's structure and discipline, perhaps the most pressing issue, and the one that the canonists dealt with least successfully, was clerical celibacy. For the previous century-and-a-half popes and councils had enunciated rules designed to enforce clerical celibacy, to ban clerical marriage, and the root out clerical concubinage. Recent legislation on all three matters was brought together in the *Liber Extra* and mechanisms for more effective enforcement of these rules were incorporated in the collection, notably the institution of episcopal visitation of parishes and religious houses. Despite an enormous investment of time and effort by conscientious bishops, however, success in enforcing the celibacy policy continued to elude the Church's jurists

---

summaries of these reports have appeared regularly in *Canon Law Abstracts* (Melrose, Scotland: Canon Law Society of Great Britain and Ireland, 1955-   ; in progress) since 1969. See also Pope Paul VI, "Allocution to the Commission for the Revision of the Code of Canon Law," *The Jurist* 26 (1966) 35-40, and J. Herranz, "L'apport de l' épiscopat à la nouvelle codification canonique," *L'année canonique* 23 (1979) 275-288.

and administrators for the next three hundred years. The canonists of the generations following 1234 also had to deal with a considerable body of new law concerning the administration of the sacraments; here they had partial success in implementing the new discipline. On one major issue, however, they met with nearly total failure: the new law incorporated in the *Liber Extra* sought to suppress clandestine marriages by requiring the publication of banns prior to marriage and by requiring that marriages be performed publicly in the presence of witnesses. Success in achieving these goals was minimal and clandestine marriage continued to present great practical problems until after the council of Trent. New legislation in the *Liber Extra* that required regular preaching by the parish clergy, reception of Communion at least once annually during the Easter time, and confession by the faithful on a regular basis was more successful.

The political and organizational problems that the *Liber Extra* posed for canonists revolved in large part around what we might call issues of Church and State. These issues involved the relationship between papal power and the power of the many European monarchies, notably the Empire. What were the limits on papal authority to forbid monarchs to interfere in the nomination or appointment of bishops or abbots? In what circumstances might the Church require the faithful to disobey commands of a secular ruler? What principles regulated power relationships within the Church itself? What rights did the pope enjoy to create and enforce law within the Church? How were his rights affected by the rulings of general councils? In cases of conflict between a council and a pope, which power should prevail? What rights did the pope have over bishops? What was the relationship of the college of cardinals to the pope? Was the pope obliged to consult the cardinals on major policy matters? If he did so, was be obliged to acquiesce in the views of the cardinals if they conflicted with his own? Likewise, what principles governed the relationship of bishops with their cathedral chapters?

These and numerous other issues raised, but not clearly settled, by the *Liber Extra* challenged the canonists of the mid-thirteenth century to devise sensible, workable solutions. Their success in doing so was very mixed, but the ingenuity of their efforts was certainly admirable. This was one of the great ages of canonistic creativity, of the application of the principles of the law to current problems in ingenious and sometimes very fruitful ways. The jurisprudence that the canonistic masters of the mid- and late-thirteenth centuries elaborated in response to some of these questions has been of basic importance ever since, not only for the internal power structure of the Church, but also for the philosophy of government in the West.

Third, the intellectual problems posed by the new legal order sketched out in the *Liber Extra* attracted the energies of some of the finest minds of the period. One has only to think, for example, of Cardinal Hostiensis (d. 1271),[15] Joannes

---

[15]On Hostiensis generally see Charles Lefebvre, "Hostiensis" in *Dictionnaire de droit canonique*, ed. R. Naz, 7 vols. (Paris: Letouzey et Ané, 1935-1965; hearafter *DDC*), 5:1211-1227. For

Andreae (1270-1348),[16] and Sinibaldo dei Fieschi (Pope Innocent IV, 1243-1254),[17] or such procedural writers as William of Drogheda (d. 1245),[18] and Bishop William Durand (d. 1296),[19] to appreciate the intellectual caliber of the men who devoted their efforts to the interpretation and implementation of the law of the *Liber Extra*.[20] Such men as these laid the foundations for the law of corporations, developed legal safeguards for the rights of the accused that we still use, and put together the fundamental concepts that underlie our notions of constitutional government—the rule of law, the theory of the limitations of sovereign power, the concepts that representation and consent of the governed are essential for the legitimate exercise of lawful authority.[21] In addition to the work of the jurists, the major theologians of the same generations— St. Thomas Aquinas, St. Bonaventure, and St. Albert the Great come readily to mind—also drew ideas and guidelines from the legal material in the *Liber Extra*, which was a basic source for their treatments of ecclesiology and political theory, but which also had a marked influence on many of their moral teachings.

particular aspects of his thought see especially Gabriel Le Bras, "Théologie et droit romain dans l'oeuvre d'Henri de Suse"in *Etudes historiques à la mémoire de Noël Didier* (Paris: Editions Montchrestien, 1960), pp. 195-204; Arturo Rivera Damas, *Pensamiento politico de Hostiensis: Estudio juridico-histórico sobre las relaciones entre el sacerdócio y el imperio en los escritos de Enrique de Susa,* Studia et textus historiae iuris canonici, vol. 3 (Zurich: Pas, 1964); John A. Watt, "The Use of the Term 'Plenitudo potestatis' by Hostiensis" in *Proceedings of the Second International Congress of Medieval Canon Law,* ed. Stephen Kuttner and J. Joseph Ryan, Monumenta iuris canonici C/1 (Città del Vaticano: S. Congregatio de seminariis et studiorum universitatibus, 1965), pp. 161-187; the same author's "The Constitutional Law of the College of Cardinals: Hostiensis to Johannes Andreae," *Mediaeval Studies* 23 (1971) 127-157; Brian Tierney, "Hostiensis and Collegiality" in *Proceedings of the Fourth International Congress of Medieval Canon Law,* ed. Stephan Kuttner, Monumenta iuris canonici, C/5 (Città del Vaticano: Biblioteca Apostolica Vaticana, 1976), pp. 401-409; and Clarence Gallagher, *Canon Law and the Christian Community: The Role of Law in the Church According to the Summa Aurea of Cardinal Hostiensis,* Analecta Gregoriana, A/8 (Roma: Universita Gregoriana, 1978).

[16]Guido Rossi, "Contributi alla biografia del canonista Giovanni d'Andrea," *Revista trimestrale di diritto e procedura civile* 11 (1957) 1451-1502; Stephan Kuttner, "Johannes Andreae and His Novella," *The Jurist* 24 (1964) 393-408; S. Stelling-Michaud, "Jean d'André" in *DDC* 6:89-92.

[17]Schulte, *QL* 2:91-94; Le Bras, Lefebvre, and Rambaud, *L'âge classique,* pp. 311-312; John A. Kemp, "A New Concept of the Christian Commonwealth in Innocent IV" in *Proceedings...Second International Congress of Medieval Canon Law,* pp. 155-159; Charles Lefebvre, "Sinibalde dei Fieschi" in *DDC* 7;1029-1062; and E. Amann in *Dictionnaire de theologie Catholique,* ed. A. Vacant, E. Mangenot, and others, 15 vols. in 30 (Paris: Letouzey et Ané, 1909-1950; hereafter *DTC*), 7/2:1981-1995.

[18]Le Bras, Lefebvre, and Rambaud, *L'âge classique,* p. 318; F. D. Logan, "Drogheda, William" in *New Catholic Encyclopedia,* 15 vols. (New York: McGraw-Hill, 1967; hereafter *NCE*), 14:924; D. Lindner, "Drogheda, William" in *Lexikon für Theologie und Kirche,* 2d ed., 14 vols. (Freiburg i/Br.: Herder, 1957-1967; hereafter *LThK*), 10:1131; H. G. Richardson, "Azo, Drogheda, and Bracton," *English Historical Review* 59 (1944) 22-47.

[19]Schulte, *QL* 2:144-156; Le Bras, Lefebvre, and Rambaud, *L'âge classique,* pp. 319-320; L. Falletti, "Guillaume Durand" in *DDC* 5:1014-1075; Stephen Kuttner, "William Duranti the Elder" in *NCE* 4:117; Alfons M. Stickler, "Durand v. Mende" in *LThK* 3:611.

[20]For brief biographical sketches of these and other major figures of the classical period of canon law see Le Bras, Lefebvre, and Rambaud, *L'âge classique,* pp. 306-324; J. A. Clarence Smith, *Medieval Law Teachers and Writers, Civilian and Canonist* (Ottawa: University of Ottawa Press, 1979), pp. 35-82; Van Hove, *Prolegomena,* pp. 467-495.

[21]Brian Tierney, "Medieval Canon Law and Western Constitutionalism," *Catholic Historical Review* 52 (1966) 1-17.

Thus the *Liber Extra* posed a challenge to several generations of jurists and theologians. A galaxy of thinkers responded to that challenge in ways that radically and permanently changed the contours of church government, introduced fundamental new ideas into political and ecclesiological thought, and gave rise to attitudes and beliefs that remain vitally important to Western thought today.

The creative response of the canonists of the late thirteenth and early fourteenth centuries to the challenges posed by the *Liber Extra* could not have been foretold, rationally at least, by someone looking at the new law in 1234. No necessary cause that I can discern obliged the canonists' response to take the form that it did. Their reaction to the new law was to seize the opportunities that it offered in order to rethink conventional doctrines and ideas. It was from this process that the most fruitful innovations of the classical period of canon law emerged. But it was equally possible that the canonists of the period could have refused the challenge, or could have dealt with the problems they faced by simply trying to fit the new law into the routines they had used in the past.

Just as the new law of the *Liber Extra* afforded the canonists of the thirteenth century an opportunity to rethink and restructure existing social and ecclesial institutions, so too the new law of the revised *Codex Iuris Canonici* offers canonists of this generation and their successors opportunities and incentives to rethink and restructure the existing state of affairs in the Church—if they are willing to reach out and grasp this chance. What the responses of our canonists may be and what results they may achieve are problematical. I can no more predict in 1983 what they will be than some predecessor of mine could have foretold in 1234 what the response of his generation would be to the opportunities presented by the *Liber Extra*. I can say, however, just as he might have said, that the opportunity is there for those who dare take it.

COUNCIL OF TRENT

A little more than three hundred years after the promulgation of the *Liber Extra*, the close of the Council of Trent in 1563 offered the Church and its canonists fresh sets of problems and opportunties. When that council finished its work after eighteen years of labor, it had substantially reworked many of the central features of earlier church discipline and government.[22] The council had created the nucleus of the Roman dicasteries as the basic operating divisions of the Church's central government.[23] It had made sweeping changes in

---

[22]On Trent and its achievements in general see Hubert Jedin, *Geschichte des Konzils von Trient*, 4 vols. (Freiburg i/Br.: Herder, 1949-1975); *Das Weltkonzil von Trient: Sein Werden und Wirken*, ed. Georg Schreiber, 2 vols. (Freiburg i/Br.: Herder, 1951).

[23]Hans Erich Feine, *Kirchliche Rechtsgeschichte*, 3d ed., vol. 1 (Weimar: Böhlaus, 1955), pp. 463-466; Van Hove, *Prolegomena*, pp. 398-405; Stickler, *Historia*, pp. 318-358; Paul Hinschius, *System des katholischen Kirchenrechts mit besonderer Rücksicht auf Deutschland*, 6 vol. (Berlin: J. Guttentag, 1869-1897), 1:391-497.

the law of marriage.[24] It had created the seminary system of priestly training.[25] The sum total of its achievement was a system of church government and ecclesiastical discipline that was to persist with only relatively minor alterations for three-and-a-half centuries and that is still, in the closing decades of the twentieth century, at the root of many of our notions about what the Catholic Church is and how it operates.

But the reform decrees of Trent did not translate themselves automatically or inevitably into operation. Reforming councils before Trent, after all, had more than once tried to revamp the Church's marriage law, its governmental system, its educational model, its judicial procuedures, and the like, but with little visible success. The reforms of Trent succeeded where earlier reform efforts had failed, in large part not only because the sixteenth-century Church found itself threatened by Lutheranism and Calvinism, but also because a host of talented and energetic post-Tridentine jurists fashioned appropriate tools to implement the policies that the Fathers of Trent had adopted.

Intellectual gifts of a high order and a keen sense for practical realities characterized many of the notable jurists who, in the generations following the close of the Council of Trent, translated its decrees and constitutions into working reality. The list is long and the names are perhaps less familiar than those of the classical canonists of the thirteenth century. I have in mind such figures as António Agustín (1517-1586),[26] Tomás Sanchez (1550-1610),[27] Anacletus Reiffensteul (1641-1703),[28] Zeger Bernhard Van Espen (1646-1728),[29] and Franz Schmalzgrüber (1663-1735);[30] nor should we forget Prospero Lambertini (1675-1758), who during the last two decades of his life was better known as Pope Benedict XIV.[31] The theologians of the period also had important insights into and comments upon the canonistic system of the period, notably Francisco Suarez (1548-1617)[32] and Cardinal Robert Bellarmine (1542-1621).[33] Under

---

[24]Feine, *Kirchliche Rechtsgeschichte*, pp. 483-484; Reinhard Lettmann, *Die Diskussion über die klandestinen Ehe und die Einführung einer zur Gültigkeit verpflichtenden Eheschliessungsform auf dem Konzil von Trient: eine kanonistische Untersuchüng*, Münsterische Beiträge zur Theologie, vol. 31 (Münster: Aschendorff, 1967); Adhémar Esmein, *Le mariage en droit canonique*, 2d ed., 2 vols. (Paris: Sirey, 1929-1935), 2:150-207; Hermann Conrad, "Das tridentische Konzil und die Entwicklung des kirchlichen und weltlichen Eherechtes" in *Das Weltkonzil von Trient* 1:297-324.

[25]Hinchius, *System* 4:501-525; Feine, *Kirchliche Rechtsgeschichte*, p. 481; *Das Weltkonzil von Trient* 1:293-294.

[26]Schulte, *QL* 3:723-728; K. Weinzerl, "*Augustín, António*" in *LThK* 1:211; E. Magnin, Antoine Augustin" in *DDC* 1:628-630; Cándido Flores Sellés, "Escritos ineditos de António Augustín," *Bulletin of Medieval Canon Law* (hereafter *BMCK*), n.s. 9 (1979) 84-88; Stephan Kuttner, "António Augustín's Edition of the Compilationes antiquae," *BMCL* 7 (1977) 1-14.

[27]Schulte, *QL* 3:737-738; *DDC* 7:864-870; *LThK* 9:307; *DTC* 14/1:1075-1085.

[28]Schulte, *QL* 3:154-155; *DDC* 7:547-548; *NCE* 12:212.

[29]Schulte, *QL* 3:704-707; *DDC* 5:457-461; *DTC* 15/2:2530-2531; *NCE* 5:543; Gustave Leclercq, *Zeger-Bernard Van Espen, 1646-1728, et l'autorité ecclésiastique*, Studia et textus historiae iuris canonici, vol. 2 (Zurich: Pas, 1964).

[30]Schulte, *QL* 3:160-161; *DDC* 7:888; *NCE* 12:1137-1138.

[31]Schulte, *QL* 3:503-510; *NCE* 2:278; *LThK* 2:177-178; *DTC* 2/1: 706-708.

[32]Schulte, *QL* 3:735-737; *DDC* 7:1094-1098; *NCE* 13:751-754.

[33]Schulte, *QL* 3:459-462; *DDC* 2:287-296; *NCE* 2:250-252; *DTC* 2/1: 560-599.

the leadership of such men as these, the canonists of the generations that followed Trent created a synthesis of the pre-Reformation law of the old *Corpus Iuris Canonici* with the new decrees of Trent and the flood of decisions that flowed from the newly-established Congregations that implemented the new order that the Tridentine Fathers had established.

The new synthesis that the canonists achieved during the late sixteenth, seventeenth, and early eighteenth centuries was reasonably well adapted to the needs of a Church living within the political and economic context of the *ancien régime*. The structures and the decision-making processes of the Roman Church by and large complemented the political system and the intellectual outlook of European rulers and ruling classes of that period. But the very success of the canonists who lived between the generation of António Agustín and the generation of Benedict XIV was paradoxically the weak point of the system that they fashioned. They tailored the canonistic institutions and juristic thought of the Church so closely to the measurements of an age of absolutism that their successors were to find it difficult, indeed very nearly impossible, to alter their jurisprudence and institutions to the needs of a society in the process of change. With the beginning of European industrialism and the social consequences that flowed from the new economic order, canonical structures and canonical thought found themselves increasingly out of phase with the changing political, economic, social, and intellectual climate. The canonists, whose adaptation to the old order had been so successful, found it difficult to accept the changes that came at an increasing rate in the Western world from the mid-eighteenth century onward. From roughly 1750 down to the end of the nineteenth century canonists were fighting a rearguard action to try to preserve the previous state of affairs, while the world around them was forging ahead in different directions. The conflict between a canonistic system adapted to an age of absolute monarchy and the needs of a Church during a period of rapid development of industrialized society, with all the changes that industrialization entailed in the restructuring of political and social institutions, became particularly strident during the decades that separated the American Civil War from the Spanish-American War.

Already during the First Vatican Council (1869-70), one bishop after another observed that the canon law was far advanced in disrepair. A revision of the law was urgently needed, the bishops declared, in order to cope with the problems of the Church and society. Some bishops felt that a revised and updated *Corpus Iuris Canonici* was needed that would be patterned on the model of the medieval *Corpus*, but reworked so as to excise obsolete decretals and expanded to include the decrees of Trent and Vatican I, as well as the voluminous body of more recent papal decrees and the decisions of the Roman dicasteries. Others argued that a new and more up-to-date approach was required. They argued for a codified restatement of the existing law that would modernize it; such a statement would be modeled on the civil law codes that one European nation after another had enacted since the Napoleonic Code of 1804. Despite differences in the approaches advocated, there was broad agreement that something had to be done urgently to bring canon law up to date and to make the law and the juristic system of the Church responsive to the new situation of the late nineteenth century.[34]

The existing law had become in considerable part obsolescent, as everyone agreed; there was doubt whether a good many of the older canons should any longer be regarded as still in force or not. And not only had there been a failure to keep pace with the changes in society, but canonistic scholarship itself had failed to meet the needs of the legal system. "As a result," a group of French bishops declared, "the study of canon law is entangled in a nearly infinite number of insoluble difficulties, there is vast room for controversies and lawsuits, thousands of people are beset by anxieties of conscience, and they are driven to hold the law in contempt." In short, the bishops concluded, "The laws are ruining us."[35]

1917 CODE OF CANON LAW

The response to these and other complaints from bishops, from canonists, and from other interested parties was slow to materialize. The move to consider the reform of canon law at the First Vatican Council in 1870 failed because of the abrupt close of the Council, following on the withdrawal of the French army from Rome and the occupation of the city by the forces of Victor Emmanuel. As a result the Council adjourned without taking action on canon law reform. It was not until 1904 that Pope Pius X (1903-1914) authorized Cardinal Pietro Gasparri to begin preparing a revision of canon law. Within a matter of weeks the decision was taken to depart from the previous patterns of ecclesiastical law revision and to cast the new law in the form of a code, modeled largely upon the recent examples of the Swiss Code (1881-1907) and the German Civil Code (1896).

The whole process of producing the new code was dominated by the formidable figure of Cardinal Gasparri. True, a commission of cardinals was named to oversee the work, suggestions for items to be included were solicited from bishops throughout the world, and expert consultors were named from various universities to advise on the project. But much of this was window dressing. From the beginning Gasparri was firmly in charge and he remained in control throughout. He prepared the basic outline that the new codification was to follow, he drafted the procedural rules for the various commissions and sub-commissions, he controlled the process of selecting commission members, and

---

[34]Giorgio Feliciani, "Il Concilio Vaticano I e il codificazione del diritto canonico," *Ephemerides iuris canonici* 33 (1977) 115-143, 269-289; Stephan Kuttner, "The Code of Canon Law in Historical Perspective," *The Jurist* 28 (1968) 132; Cardinal Pietro Gasparri cites the statements of a number of bishops on the matter in his preface to the 1917 *Codex Iuris Canonici*, annotated edition (New York: Kenedy, 1918), pp. xxviii-xxxi.

[35]Quoted in Gasparri, "Praefatio," p. xxix: "Hinc fit ut studium iuris canonici infinitis prope et inextricabilis difficultatibus implicetur, controversiis ac processibus latissimus locus pateat; et conscientiae mille anxietatibus angantur et in contemptum legis impellantur .... *orbruimur legibus*" (emphasis in the original).

he presided over the meetings of the various consultation groups. Gasparri himself acknowledged that he kept a tight grip on the proceedings; he added that without such close supervision and coordination, the preparation of the *Codex Iuris Canonici* might have taken twenty-five years. When we consider that the revision process that produced the 1983 code took twenty-four years, I think that we must give the cardinal full marks for a shrewd estimate. At the same time, Gasparri was also inclined to be a shade high-handed in abbreviating the discussion phase of the revision process. Thus, for example, he related in an address in 1934 that he had discovered early on that the experts in the plenary commission wanted to discuss in detail, and at what he clearly considered inordinate length, each canon of the proposed text. To forestall wordy, and doubtless wearying, meetings, Gasparri "suppressed" (his own words) the meetings of the plenary group. Instead he circulated printed drafts of proposed texts for written comments from the experts and required that they confine their observations to the margins of the printed drafts. Although he could not be quite so peremptory in dealing with the commission of cardinals, even there Gasparri kept his troops firmly in line.[36]

The basic text of the *Codex* was completed by mid-1914 and plans were made to promulgate it early the following year. The outbreak of World War I in August, 1914, followed by the death of Pius X later in the same month, delayed the process, however, and the new pope, Benedict XV (1914-1922), wished to consider the whole matter further. A final revision of the text was completed in 1916 and the code was formally promulgated on May 27, 1917, to take effect a year later.[37]

Some comparisons between the 1917 code and the 1983 code may be instructive. The 1917 code was largely Gasparri's; it would perhaps be an exaggeration to call it a one-man effort, but the cardinal's influence in its creation was paramount. The 1983 code, on the other hand, is the product of a more genuinely collegial process than was its predecessor. The aim of the 1917 code was to make canon law once more a workable system, in the sense that the code made it possible to determine with reasonable certainty what the law was and to foretell how it was supposed to operate in many different circumstances.[38]

The 1917 code was largely successful in achieving these goals. The 1917 code, moreover, was based upon a belief that it was useful, even essential, for the Church to centralize and consolidate its legal system. The 1983 code, in contrast, emphasizes diversification and a "new way of thinking" about these problems, to use Father Provost's words.[39] Symptomatic of this is the markedly

---

[36]See Kuttner, "Code of Canon Law," pp. 136-137, quoting from Gasparri's own account in *Acta Congressus Iuridici Internationalis VII saeculo a Decretalibus Gregorii IX et XIV a Codice Iustiniano promulgatis* (Roma: *** , 1937), 4:6-8.

[37]Benedict XV, *Providentissima mater ecclesia*, in *Codex Iuris Canonici* (1917), ed. cit., pp. xxxix-xlii.

[38]Gasparri, "Praefatio," pp. xxxv-xxxvi.

[39]James H. Provost, "Approaching the Revised Code" in *Code, Community, Ministry*, p. 15.

greater emphasis in the new code on local legislation molded to fit the needs of specific regions and the problems of particular societies.[40]

In short the two twentieth-century codes must be seen as products of their respective historical circumstances and as reactions against the perceived problems of the period preceding codification. The 1917 code responded to needs and perceptions that were largely set in place prior to the beginning of World War I. Its two major goals were to secure a systematized jurisprudence (in place of the canonistic chaos of the nineteenth century) and to centralize juridical processes and authority of the Church. These were by no means unworthy objects, but they carried with them significant dangers. One danger was that the canonistic system might become so rigid and inflexible that it would stifle growth and inhibit a healthy diversity of practice and the ability to adapt to changing situations. There was, in other words, a distinct danger that the 1917 code might become a legalistic girdle that would streamline the Church at the very real risk of strangling her. Prior to the Second Vatican Council, the resolution of problems through the Church's courts—almost exclusively marriage problems, as you know—was all too often a lengthy, expensive, and haphazard process, in which the needs and circumstances of the parties and the social context within which their problems arose were often ignored in favor of the mechanical application of a fistful of abstract formulae to issues that became progressively cloudier as the case continued and that often received no rigorous analysis at any point in the process.[41]

With all its faults and virtues—and both were real and significant—the 1917 code marked a watershed in the history of canon law. For the first time the whole of the Church's law was comprehensively summed up in a relatively brief compass, reduced to a set of lapidary formulae that claimed to state a series of basic, even eternal, principles, or at least strongly fostered that impression. I recall hearing a Scottish priest solemnly declare many years ago that "We should worship canon law"—by which he meant the 1917 code. If his theology was a trifle peculiar, he certainly caught the spirit of many other admirers of the 1917 code. Cardinal Gasparri's code breathed the spirit of triumphalism. It conceived of the Church as a static institution, *sine macula et ruga, semper et ubique immutabilis, per omnia saecula saeculorum.* The spirit of abstract legalism that permeated the 1917 code was intensely ahistorical, even antihistorical.[42]

But now the 1917 code, in its turn, is about to become another obsolete document, the concern of the historian rather than the practicing jurist. It will be supplanted a few weeks from now by a new code that is also the product of

[40]John A. Alesandro, "Particular Legislation" in *Code, Community, Ministry,* pp. 24-27.
[41]For well-analyzed examples under the 1917 code see John T. Noonan, Jr., *Power to Dissolve: Lawyers and Marriages in the Courts of the Roman Curia* (Cambridge, MA: Balknap Press, 1972), pp. 341-404.
[42]I have learned this in greater detail in the "Creative Canonist: His Role in Church Reform," *The Jurist* 31 (1971) 313-315.

a distinct moment in time, a new code that like the old one responds to at least some of the needs and perceptions of its historical period.

1983 CODE OF CANON LAW

Since the new code is the product of our own age, of the period whose views and prejudices we share, it may be useful to put it in perspective by trying a thought experiment. We can try to imagine what some future historian might have to say about the 1983 code when, at some future date, say late in the next century, she or he looks back at it, in turn, and tries to set it within its historical context. Such an historian may think that the 1983 code marks a modest reaction against some features of the 1917 code. Where the earlier code was relatively inelastic, the new code seeks to introduce a measure of flexibility. Where the old code prescribed a highly centralized order of church government and law, the new code allows a greater measure of regional variation and adaptation to new situations. Where the old code stressed the statics of the Church's structure, the new one pays some heed to its dynamics. My hypothetical successor might also remark that there is a great deal of continuity between the two codes; large chunks of the new code repeat provisions of the old one, either verbatim or with a few trivial cosmetic changes.[43]

[43]By way of illustration, some instances of identically worded provisions include:

1917 Code	1983 Code
can. 955, § 2	can. 1015, § 2
can. 960	can. 1020
can. 963	can. 1023
can. 1067, § 1	can. 1083, § 1
can. 1068, § 1	can. 1084, § 1
can. 1069, § 2	can. 1085, § 2
can. 1076, § 1	can. 1091, § 1
can. 1082, § 2	can. 1096, § 2
can. 1085	can. 1100
can. 1118	can. 1141
can. 1119	can. 1142

Many other canons of the code show only trivial changes in wording from the corresponding passages of the 1917 code, or merely incorporate changes in references from the old code to the new one. A few examples include:

1917 Code	1983 Code
can. 17 § 3:*Data* autem per modum sententiae iudicialis aut *rescripti* in re peculiari, vim legis non habet et ligat tantum personas atque afficit res pro quibus data est.	can. 16 § 3: *Interpretatio* autem per modum sententiae iudicialis aut *actus administrativi* in re peculiari, vim legis non habet et ligat tantum personas atque afficit res pro quibus data est.
can. 1038 § 1: Supremae tantum auctoritatis *ecclesiasticae* est authentice declarare quandonam ius divinum matrimonium *impediat* vel dirimat.	can. 1095 § 1: Supremae tantum *ecclesiae* auctoritatis est authentice declarare quandonam ius divinum matrimonium *prohibeat* vel dirimat.

I am inclined to think, however, that this imaginary future historian may not dwell at length on such matters as these. Rather, he or she is likely to be more interested in the question of what the canonists of the closing decades of the twentieth century and the opening decades of the twenty-first did with the 1983 code. Did they really try to exploit its possibilities, did it become in their hands a genuine instrument of renewal in the post-Vatican II Church? Or did they use the new code as a cloak for intellectual poverty and an excuse for moral lethargy? Did they use the 1983 code as a springboard for creative new development of canonical jurisprudence? Or did they shrink from the dangers and uncertainties of exploring the new law's potential and prefer the calmer, more passive role of technicians in the service of institutional inertia? I cannot answer these questions; only you can provide my hypothetical historian with the answers.

Let me close with an unconventional suggestion. One characteristic of the canonical system over the past three centuries and more has been that canonists' work has been increasingly restricted to marriage matters. Virtually all other dispute resolution within the Church takes place somewhere other than in the Church's courts—problems are either dealt with through administrative channels, or else they are treated as problems of conscience, or else they find their way into the civil court systems. Perhaps it is time that canonists seriously begin to consider how to put their professional expertise to use in other kinds of conflict resolution situations than those that arise out of Christian marriage.

The immediately obvious riposte to this suggestion, of course, is that there are other ways of dealing with these matters—and besides, don't the civil courts have a monopoly on dealing with such things as contracts, torts, and crimes? While all of this is true, it fails to get to the heart of the suggestion that I want to make.

First I should remind you that historically the business of conflict resolution in Western societies has often been a competitive enterprise—in the middle ages and under the *ancien régime* royal courts vied with manorial courts and municipal courts for much of the same business and all three battled simultaneously with canon law courts for jurisdiction over many of the same parties in many of the same actions. Likewise it is not uncommon in the civil courts of the United States that the same set of facts could give rise to actions in a county court, a state district court, a municipal court, or a federal court.

---

can. 1072: Invalide matrimonium attendant *clerici* in sacris ordinibus constituti.

can. 1559 § 1: Nemo in prima instantia conveniri potest, nisi coram iudice ecclesiastico qui competens sit ob unum ex titulis qui in *can. 1560-1568* determinantur

can. 1087: Invalide matrimonium attendant *qui* in sacris ordinibus *sunt* constituti.

can. 1407 § 1: Nemo in prima instantia conveniri potest, nisi coram iudice ecclesiastico qui competens sit ob unum ex titulis qui in *can. 1408-1414* determinantur.

It is up to the plaintiff and his or her legal advisers to determine where it will be most advantageous to commence an action.

It is certainly not implausible that canonistic tribunals might take a more active role in dealing with conflict resolution processes within the Church. A chronic complaint of judges, lawyers, and litigants in our civil court system is that the courts are overburdened, that judicial process costs too much, that it is too slow, that it takes far too long to get a matter docketed and even longer to get it settled, and that, in short, the justice system is seriously overloaded. It is also commonplace to hear it urged that wherever possible disputes ought to be resolved by some means other than litigation in the civil courts, that greater use needs to be made of arbitration and mediation as alternatives to lawsuits.

Now here, it strikes me, is a place where canon lawyers have a clear opportunity to contribute to society at large, and to the Church in particular, in a worthwhile way. You administer a body of law founded on equitable principles, based upon the Christian ethic, to which most people in our society bear at least nominal allegiance. Collectively you have a vast pool of experience in resolving difficult questions both of fact and of law, mainly in matters dealing with marital relations. Is it unrealistic to suggest that you might prepare yourselves to broaden the operational scope of the Church's tribunal system, to make yourselves available as arbitrators or mediators who will apply the principles of canonical jurisprudence to resolving the conflicts of parties who voluntarily submit their differences to you, as an alternative to civil litigation? I have no reason to believe that a development of this sort would be easy, or that it would be quickly implemented. It would involve some fundamental changes in established habits of thought and action. There is no guarantee that it would be successful; instead there is a significant degree of risk involved. But the challenge is there. It could perhaps be met successfully—but only if you, the practicing canonists who would have to deal with the problem, were able to optimize your competitive position. You would have to make your services preferable to the alternative processes that parties to a dispute now have available.

In order to do this, it seems to me that at least four things would be necessary. First, canonists would have to be willing and able to search for equitable solutions to the problems referred to their tribunals. A narrow legalistic approach simply would not do. Instead, canonists would need to apply guidelines based upon the principles enunciated in the new code[44] and upon Christian ethical ideals in order to find resolutions to problems. Your aim would be to treat the parties fairly, to give each adequate opportunity to be heard, and to achieve an even-handed settlement, rather than simply to award a victory to one side or the other. Second, you would need to develop relatively speedy, inexpensive, cost-effective procedures for dealing with matters referred to you. It is an old aphorism, and a true one, that justice delayed is justice denied. Likewise

[44]A few examples of such general principles of equity in the 1983 code include cc. 35-36, 42-47, 67, 73, 126, 208, 219, 221, 1298, 1313-1315.

16

justice that one party cannot afford is equally denied. Increasing numbers of people in this country and elsewhere find themselves in the unenviable position of being financially unable to seek resolution of their problems through the courts. If canonists can help to alleviate this problem in a significant way, I feel that they not only have an opportunity to apply their professional skills in a socially useful way, but even that they have an obligation in natural justice to do so. Third, in order to achieve the first two objectives, canonists would have to adopt a new intellectual approach to their work, to look upon their job as a ministry, a *diakonia* in the root sense of the term, that aims at providing a specialized but vital service to those members of society who choose to avail themselves of it. Fourth, such a reorientation of institutional practices would require bishops and other church authorities to alter existing patterns of resource allocation within the Church. The costs of embracing such a program would be substantial. It would be difficult to make the process self-financing at the outset, although it might in time become so. I would argue, however, that the social value of a successful program of this type would justify the investment that would be required. Indeed, it would be reasonable to push the argument further, to maintain that the *diakonia* of justice is at the very heart of the Gospel message and thus central to the Church's mission. One might even raise the question of whether the Church has a moral right to abdicate, or to continue to abdicate, its responsibilities in this area any longer.

Lastly let me reiterate the theme that I began with: the implementation of the new Code of Canon Law presents this generation of canonists with a mixed set of opportunities and challenges. You can respond to these opportunities and challenges in many different ways. How you will deal with this situation I cannot now predict: I am only an historian and history and prophecy are two different professions. But there is a finite chance that your generation of canonists, like the generation following the promulgation of the *Liber Extra*, may be able to use the new law as an instrument for types of change that none of us here can at present foresee. The opportunity is yours. The challenge is yours. The decision about how to deal with the situation is also yours. I hope that you will make it wisely.

RIGHTS AND DUTIES OF DIOCESAN BISHOPS

Thomas J. Green

For those working in various diocesan ministries except for tribunal officers, perhaps the most pertinent norms of the revised code are canons 368-572 on the particular church. Those of you who work in chanceries and other non-tribunal ministries will certainly consult Book III on the Church's teaching office and Book IV on its sanctifying mission from time to time. However, more often than not, you will probably be reflecting on the canons on the particular church, interpreting them creatively for bishops and other staff persons and thereby facilitating the Church's ongoing pastoral life.

The focus on the following observations is the office of the diocesan (residential) bishop in light of the significant conciliar and post-conciliar effort to enhance its status. Yet that office can be duly appreciated only if one takes seriously its relationship to the nature and mission of the Church—a key point underlying the 1973 *Directory on the Pastoral Ministry of Bishops*.[1] Accordingly, some brief comments on certain conciliar ecclesiological developments[2] are necessary if one is properly to contextualize the treatment of the office of diocesan bishop in the revised code.

One area of the revised code most notably changed from its 1917 predecessor is the structuring of the particular church. This in turn reflects a shift in focus from the overly institutional ecclesiology of the 1917 code to the more communitarian emphasis of the present law. Instead of focusing primarily on certain individuals exercising power over other individuals, it stresses the common mission of all believers and the special roles of service which some fulfill for others. Only within this broader context can the office of diocesan bishop be properly appreciated.

Two conciliar themes seem particularly relevant to our presentation: the Church as a communion and the principle of subsidiarity. A word or two about each is in order.

The *communio* model seems particularly useful in clarifying recent developments in ecclesiastical organization.[3] The Church is a sign and instrument of the intimate union of God and human persons and of human persons

---

[1]See Sacred Congregation for Bishops, *Directory on the Pastoral Ministry of Bishops* (Ottawa: Canadian Catholic Conference, 1974; cited as *Directory*).

[2]For some perceptive observations on significant conciliar ecclesiological developments affecting legal reform in this area, see W. Aymans, "Ecclesiological Implications of the New Legislation," *Newsletter of the Canon Law Society of Great Britain and Ireland* (June-September 1982) 38-73; J. Komonchak, "A New Law for the People of God: A Theological Evaluation," *CLSA Proceedings* 42(1980) 14-43 (henceforth *PCLSA).*

[3]See *The Jurist* 36 (1976) 1-245 (special *communio* issue).

among themselves. It is a communion of life, love and truth generated by God's redemptive love, rooted in the ministry of Christ and vivified by his Spirit. The notion of communion expresses the union of believers among themselves and with Christ their head. It also clarifies the union of the particular churches among themselves and with the church of Rome. The revised law somewhat transcends the overly centralized perspectives of its 1917 predecessor by highlighting that the particular churches are not field-offices of a giant multi-national corporation, but local realizations of the one Church of Christ (LG 23; CD 11; UR 15; AG 19). Hence, there is a movement towards a renewed view of the universal Church as a communion of communions, each of which is Christ's Church.

Another conciliar theme with notable implications for legal reform is the principle of subsidiarity. It can mean various things; however, here it refers to the post-conciliar movement towards decentralized decisional processes in the Church. The basic orientations of church discipline must be adapted to the diverse peoples and cultures throughout the Church. There are to be more options for decisional initiatives to be taken by the individual particular churches. In other words, canonical pluralism is admissible with theological, liturgical and ascetical pluralism. The implementation of the principle of subsidiarity is meant to strengthen and confirm legislative unity while doing justice to the reasonableness and need of individual institutions to provide for themselves by particular law.[4]

The principle of subsidiarity is reflected in part in the increased decisional freedom of individual diocesan bishops—a key concern of the Code Commission, especially in situations of potential conflict between them and the conference of bishops. This notably enhanced status of the bishop is one of the principle innovations of the revised code.[5]

The 1917 code tended to view the bishop as empowered for his leadership role by delegation of supreme church authority. However, both Vatican II and the revised law see him as sacramentally empowered by episcopal consecration to fulfill the three-fold function (*munus*) of Christ (ruling, teaching and sanctifying) (LG 21; canon 375). In the particular church entrusted to him, the bishop possesses all the ordinary and immediate power he needs to represent Christ, whose vicar he is (LG 27). The authority of the bishop is "proper," i.e., it presumably is operative whenever he must exercise his pastoral responsibilities; it is restricted only when certain limitations are stated in law (canon 381, § 1). Obviously, no particular church is an island unto itself; however, such limitations should seemingly be confined to those issues on which a common legal-pastoral approach is necessary for the unity or welfare of the whole Church or the churches in a given area (CD 8a).

[4]F. Morrisey, "The Importance of Particular Law in the New Code," *PCLSA* 43 (1981) 1-17.

[5]For pertinent reports of the committee on the sacred hierarchy, which formulated the canons on bishops in Book II of the original schema, see *Communicationes* 4 (1972) 40-50; 5 (1973) 216-235 (clerics in particular); 7 (1975) 161-172 (coadjutor and auxiliary bishops). For pertinent reports on the revision of the original schema by a special committee, see *Communicationes* 12 (1980): 275-314; 13 (1981) 140-146.

To a certain extent, the revised code is an episcopal code, since it contains nearly four hundred fifty references to the bishop in one form or another. Yet he is no isolated monarch but rather the leader of a sacramental community in mission (*kerygma, diakonia, koinonia*). He is considered a principle of unity in catalyzing the ministerial resources of the particular church in service to the world. While the 1917 code tended to view him as pursuing the mission of the Church on his own with some trusted advisors, the revised law sees him as fostering various corporate processes whereby different members of the people of God can share actively in the realization of that mission (canon 394). His authority is seen principally in terms of service rather than power. His office is frequently described in terms of his solicitude for persons, be they members of the Catholic community or those not fully in communion with the Church.

Given the vast amount of material on the episcopal office, it is necessary to articulate certain points of reference in dealing with it intelligently, especially given the limitations of this presentation. Since the notion of *authority as service* is a key conciliar theme, which has been reaffirmed in the *Directory on the Pastoral Ministry of Bishops*[6] and again most recently in the apostolic constitution *Sacrae disciplinae leges*,[7] I would like to propose several variations on that theme for your consideration. Perhaps they may assist you in understanding better certain noteworthy aspects of the episcopal office in the revised code. While our primary focus will be the canons of Book II on the particular church, one can properly perceive the full implications of the episcopal office and the various institutes necessary for its exercise only by examining the whole code.[8]

I will discuss six variations on the theme of episcopal authority as service. First, the bishop is to initiate and sustain various collaborative processes in realizing the Church's mission. Second, he is to facilitate the exercise of the gifts of the Spirit within the community. Third, he is to take full advantage of the decisional latitude accorded him in the revised law, while making optimal use of vicars and/or delegates in this enterprise. Fourth, the bishop is to be a key figure in fostering diocesan accountablity in light of the common good of the particular church, for which he is especially responsible. Fifth, he is to foster unity in the diocese, in part by carefully monitoring the exercise of administrative discretion and by seeing to the availability of conflict-resolution mechanisms to preclude pastorally counterproductive tensions from impairing the Church's mission. Finally, he is to encourage various types of ecumenical sharing to the degree that it is commensurate with the degree of unity between ourselves and

[6]See *Directory*, nn.32-38 (Part I, Chapter V: How to Exercise Episcopal Authority).

[7]See John Paul II, apost. const. *Sacrae disciplinae leges*, January 25, 1983 in *Codex Iuris Canonici* (Vatican City: Libreria Editrice Vaticana, 1983), p.xii.

[8]For a brief overview of various aspects of the episcopal office in the revised code, see T. Green, "The Diocesan Bishop in the Revised Code: Some Introductory Reflections," *The Jurist,* 42 (1982) 320-347 (cited as Green, "Diocesan Bishop"). For a more detailed overview of the rights and responsibilities of bishops in the revised code, see T. Green, *A Manual for Bishops: Rights and Responsibilities of Diocesan Bishops in the Revised Code of Canon Law* (Washington, D.C.: USCC, 1983).

other religious traditions. Some of these points are more significant than others, and appropriately more time will be devoted to discussing them.

1. The Bishop as Facilitator of Various Collaborative Processes in Pursuit of the Church's Mission

As regards certain basic ecclesial realities there is a fundamental equality of all believers preceding all types of structural differentiations within the community: baptism, destiny, Lord and mission (LG II placed before LG III). Hence, paternalistic governance patterns reflecting a stratified ecclesiology are inadmissible; church law should articulate interrelationships within the community in such a way as to reflect the values of functional diversity and fundamental equality in realizing the Church's mission.

More specifically, the bishop should initiate and sustain various collaborative processes necessary for the Church's mission (prophetic-priestly-pastoral). Although the Code Commission at times seems to feel that any limitation on the discretion of bishops is unwarranted, a balanced ecclesiology suggests that their pastoral burdens are to be borne in conjunction with the whole community.[9] Accordingly, the bishop should commit himself to making collegial organisms such as presbyteral councils and diocesan pastoral councils genuine vehicles of exchange of insights, articulation of goals and perhaps implementation of priorities.

This prompts some brief comments on consultation in the Church understood here somewhat broadly to refer to different types of sharing in ecclesial decisional processes. The canonical tradition of consultation is not based on an uncritical acceptance of democratic political models. Rather, it is rooted in the nature of the Church as a community of believers sharing in Christ's prophetic office and endowed with various gifts of the Spirit (LG 12;30). Such consultation is related to the exercise of authority in a spirit of genuine service; it is also related to the basic Christian right and duty to express one's opinion on issues affecting the Church (canon 212, § 3). Practically speaking, this means that the bishop has a corresponding responsibility to create a climate facilitating the knowledgeable exercise of that right and the fulfillment of that duty, e.g., by providing appropriate information on issues on which consultation is called for and by conveying a sense of his taking seriously the input of the group/individuals in question in light of their insights and experience.[10] Otherwise, such consultors may function irresponsibly, failing to inform themselves about the issues and/or not honestly and articulately expressing their opinion.

It is a misunderstanding of the consultative process to emphasize unduly the fact that the bishop may act validly and licitly even contrary to the opinion of those individuals/groups enjoying a consultative as distinct from a deliberative vote in policy-making. This would violate the traditional canonical understand-

---

[9]*Directory*, n.95 (principle of responsible cooperation).
[10]Ibid, p.34

21

ing of consultation. Furthermore, canon 127, § 2 cautions him not to act contrary to the opinion of those he consults, unless there is a prevalent reason for doing so. While the law protects the bishop's freedom to act, it also accords a certain presumptive wisdom to those consulted, especially corporate groups genuinely representative of the diversity of the people of God. This in turn highlights the importance of seeing to it that such individuals/groups consulted are truly representative of the various charisms in the particular church in question.

Broad-based episcopal consultation on various aspects of the Church's mission is required by the very complexity of the ecclesial decision-making process, yet at times discussions about that process are too narrowly focused. We may tend to think that real "power" in the Church is limited to the making of a final decision in a given area, e.g., issuing norms on sacramental sharing (canon 844). Or we may think that such "power" is limited to an individual or group's having a deliberative vote in the making of a decision, e.g., diocesan finance council before diocesan property may be alienated (canon 1292, § 1). Regrettably, we have had a tendency to depreciate the significance of the consultive vote ("merely consultative"). Furthermore, the code itself tends to focus on the making of a decision as the key factor to be considered. On the contrary, any decision needs to be situated within the broader context of the process leading up to it and following from it. This seems to involve at least five key stages, which can only be briefly indicated here: (a) creative idea production; (b) factual data-gathering; (c) making of a decision; (d) implementation of the decision; and (e) evaluation of the decision.[11] This insight is especially true when the decision is a complex one, e.g., developing a policy on pre-marital preparation (canons 1063-1064). In fact, the diversity of the elements of the decisional process properly understood may well correspond to the diverse charisms necessary for the proper unfolding of the Church's life.

Frankly, certain aspects of the revised code pose problems for the evolution of healthy consultative relationships, especially if one interprets the law rather narrowly. Canon 135, § 2 precludes a particular legislator, such as a bishop, from delegating his legislative authority unless he is explicitly authorized to do so. This is quite in contrast to his ability to delegate his administrative and judicial authority rather freely as specified in canon 391. Furthermore, there are certain problems as regards the structuring of certain significant consultative bodies, such as presbyteral councils (canons 495-501), diocesan pastoral councils (canons 511-514) and dicesan synods (canons 460-468). Without going into detail on these instututes here,[12] perhaps a couple of general observations might be made. The possible evolution of such institutes in a significant way seems somewhat impaired because the law has not been formulated in as open-ended fashion as desirable. For example, without unduly stressing the value of

---

[11]For a perceptive discussion of the complexities of the decision-making process, see R. Kennedy, "Shared Responsibility in Ecclesial Decision-making," *Studia Canonica* 14 (1980) 5-23.
[12]For a discussion of these issues in a bit more detail, see Green, "Diocesan Bishop," pp.332-339.

deliberative competence, the present law on presbyteral council hardly provides for such an option, contrary to earlier formulations of the text.[13] The present law on the advisability of diocesan pastoral councils somewhat tempers the forcefulness of earlier conciliar and post-conciliar texts regarding the establishment of such councils, which are still facultative.[14] Finally, the force of the obligation to hold a diocesan synod has been somewhat mitigated by way of contrast to the 1917 code and earlier versions of the text.[15]

Since the revised code is not always as satisfactory as it might be, canonists working with bishops need to interpret the law creatively, especially by placing it within the broader theological-pastoral context within which alone it can be properly understood. Above all else, bishops need to be aided to move beyond a narrow legalism that would influence them to consult others only when the law strictly requires it.[16] On the contrary, the bishop's moral responsibility to facilitate broad-based involvement in the decisional process transcends the limited perspectives of the canons, for the law can hardly anticipate all the instances in which consultation is appropriate. This is even more imperative today than in the 1917 code, in light of the various theological-canonical factors significantly reshaping the general context within which the issue of consultation is to be addressed.

In fact, the law itself reflects this broader consultative horizon, for canon 500, § 2 states that the bishop is to consult the presbyteral council in matters of significant pastoral concern ("...negotiis maioris momenti..."), e.g., perhaps in regard to policies on sacramental sharing (canon 844), pre-marriage guidelines (canons 1063-1064), conditions for general absolution (canon 961). This is true, even though no canon expressly requires the bishop to hear the council or obtain its consent in these latter cases. Furthermore, the advisability of broad-based consultation on a regular rather than exceptional basis seems suggested by the broad ecclesial purposes to be served by consultative bodies such as the presbyteral council (canon 495), the diocesan pastoral council (canon 511) and the diocesan synod (canon 460).[17]

2. The Bishop as Facilitator of the Gifts of the Spirit within the Community

Ecclesial structures should facilitate the development and exercise of the gifts of the Spirit throughout the community. The Spirit is the most important source

[13]See canon 500.
[14]See canon 511.
[15]See canon 461, § 1.
[16]For a listing (not exhaustive) of instances when bishops must consult individuals or groups, see T. Green, "Consultation with Individuals or Groups Regarding Episcopal Discretion," in *Code, Community, Ministry*, ed. J. Provost (Washington, D.C.: CLSA, 1983), pp.63-65 (henceforth *CCM*).
[17]Canon 495 speaks of the purpose of the presbyteral council in these terms: "...cuius est Episcopum in regimine diocesis ad normam iuris adiuvare, ut bonum pastorale portionis populi Dei ipsi commissae quam maxime provehatur...." Canon 511 speaks of the purpose of the diocesan pastoral council in these terms: "cuius est sub auctoritate Episcopi ea quae opera pastoralia in diocesi spectant investigare, perpendere atque de eis conclusiones practicas proponere." Canon 460 speaks of the purpose of the diocesan synod in these terms: "...qui in bonum totius communitatis dioecesanae Episcopo dioecesano operam praestant."

of unity and growth in Christ, distributing manifold gifts for the building up of the community. More specifically, the bishop is a key figure in testing and welcoming new manifestations of the Spirit. A key episcopal responsibility is creating a climate in which the diverse gifts of the Spirit can be exercised and in which the fundamental substantive and procedural rights of believers are protected.

Although, unfortunately, there is no explicit affirmation of the basic right of exercising charisms (AA 3), the very incorporation of a series of basic Christian rights into the revised law suggests that this dimension of the status of persons is to be taken very seriously. Despite certain problems in the formulation of these rights, a generally successful effort has been made to fulfill the mandate of the 1967 Synod that the general legal status of laity, clergy and religious is delineated.[18] At times interests of the common good may counsel the restriction of certain rights; however, church authority and more specifically the bishop should strive to prevent unwarranted obstacles to their exercise. The right to use one's charismatic gifts may be supervised but never extinguished by those who preside in the Church.

If one compares the present code with its 1917 predecessor, there are not many more canons which explicitly clarify in detail the various implications of the bishop's role in facilitating the exercise of ecclesial gifts. However, one might point to canon 157, which affirms the fundamental episcopal responsibility to provide for various ecclesiastical offices, especially, but not exclusively, at the diocesan level. This provision of offices function can be interpreted fairly broadly, and de facto it is clearly one of the major administrative responsibilities of bishops. It implies not simply appointing key diocesan/parish leadership personnel, but also supporting them in their ongoing professional and personal development in a changing world and perhaps removing them from office and/or transferring them elsewhere if the ministerial needs of the people of God are not being met. This applies to both clerical and lay officeholders.[19]

What seems particularly noteworthy in this connection is the incorporation in the law of several fundamental rights that are relevant to personnel policy broadly conceived. The issue of rights is complex and all the legal implications of these rights are far from clear.[20] Yet it may be useful to indicate certain rights (and at times duties) that reshape the basic frame of reference within which the issue of the free exercise of ecclesial gifts can profitably be explored in the future.

Among the relevant basic rights of *all believers*, one might note the right (and duty) to participate in the Church's task of evangelization (canon 211), the right

[18]See canons 208-223 on the basic rights and obligations of all believers, canons 224-231 on the basic rights and obligations of the laity and canons 273-289 on the basic rights and obligations of clerics. Also B. Griffin, "A Bill of Rights and Freedoms," in *CCM*, pp.28-31; R. Cunningham, "The Laity in the Revised Code," ibid., pp.33-34; K. Lasch, "The Rights and Obligations of Clerics," ibid., pp.38-46.

[19]*Directory*, n.98 (principle of placing the right people in the right places); n.209b & e.

[20]For a helpful discussion of various dimensions of the issue of rights in the Church, see J. Provost, "Ecclesial Rights," *PCLSA* 44 (1982) 41-62.

to make known to one's pastor one's needs and desires, especially spiritual ones (canon 212, § 2), the right (and duty) to express one's opinion on issues affecting the good of the Church (canon 212, § 3), the rights of free association and assembly (canon 215), the rights to promote the apostolate and to exercise one's own initiative in apostolic work (canon 216), the right to Christian education (canon 217) and the right to academic freedom in research and publication (canon 218).

Certain specific rights of the *laity* might also be noted although, frankly, most of their rights seem to be basically slight modifications of formulations of the rights of all believers. One might note their right and duty to obtain an education appropriate to their ecclesial status, including the possible pursuit of the sacred sciences (canon 229), and their right to an appropriate wage and related benefits if they are engaged permanently or even temporarily in church service (canon 231). At times, the revised code does not speak technically of a "right" but rather of an "eligibility" on the part of the laity, e.g., sharing in the Church's pastoral ministry and in its conciliar life (canon 228) and reception of a mandate to teach the sacred sciences (canon 229, § 3).

Interestingly enough, the revised code states that a basic episcopal responsibility is protecting the exercise of the rights of *priests* and seeing to the fulfillment of their responsibilities (canon 384). To speak more comprehensively of all *clerics*, those rights which seen particularly pertinent in this connection are the right to join with others in the pursuit of goals compatible with the clerical ministry (canon 278), the right to an adequate income in remuneration for fulfilling various ministerial responsibilities and the related right to social assistance to provide for various necessities (canon 281). Furthermore, another relevant canon affirms a basic clerical obligation to continuing education courses and conferences as provided by particular law (canon 279). Such an obligation implies a commensurate institutional responsibility to provide such educational options either within the diocese or elsewhere, depending on the availability of educational resources.

Although this issue of continuing education options is discussed explicity here within the context of clerical rights, such options are applicable as well to laypersons engaged in church service (canon 231). The ongoing spiritual, intellectual and cultural development of priests and other pastoral leaders is clearly a major institutional priority. The complexities of pastoral ministry in a changing world require an enlightened personnel policy respecting individual talents and professional goals and fostering appropriate pastoral adaptation and personal satisfaction.

After the preceding somewhat general observations on personnel policy, perhaps a few specific points might be made before closing this discussion. Especially, but not exclusively, in light of the contemporary crisis of priestly vocations, there is a special diocesan and episcopal responsibility to see to it that all gifts of ecclesial service are duly recognized and fostered, especially those of the *lay members* of the Christian community. Certain significant offices are still restricted to priests;[21] however, numerous offices are not limited to them, whether they are specified in the code[22] or not. A healthy respect for the ecclesial status of the laity implies enabling them to exercise those offices for which they are duly qualified (canon 530, § 2) and to continue to develop their professional skills for ecclesial service.

In this connection one might raise questions about the status of *women* in ministerial positions in our dioceses and parishes. The revised code has eliminated various elements of the sexism characterizing earlier drafts; yet there are still some problem areas, e.g., incapacity for women to be formally installed as lectors or acolytes (canon 230, § 1). However, perhaps the problem often is not precisely a legal barrier but rather our own reluctance to adopt hiring policies enabling women to assume a more equitable place in church life. In any event, such personnel issues need to be examined seriously if we are to be faithful to the Spirit and to fundamental orientations of the law itself, e.g., canon 209 on the basic equality of all believers in terms of their Christian dignity and action in building up the Body of Christ.

In light of the tendency of the revised code to focus largely on priests in its discussion of various clerical ministries, one may raise the question whether more attention needs to be given to the status of *permanent deacons* in our dioceses. There seem to be problems regarding their training, their areas of ministerial involvement and their relationship to priests and lay ministers. It seems imperative to address these issues seriously if the ministerial potential of such clerics is to be duly realized.[23]

Recent developments have made laicization procedures considerably more stringent than in the past.[24] It is uncertain whether such procedures will be mitigated in the foreseeable future. However, a pastoral concern for properly disposed laicized priests and a heightened awareness of the pastoral needs of the people of God suggest taking a serious look at the ministerial options of such clerics, despite restrictions on their eligibility for certain functions.[25] Might not the official openness and spirit of pastoral accommodation manifest in dealings with former Anglican clerics be applicable *mutatis mutandis* to our own resigned clerics?

[21]In the revised Code the following offices are limited to priests: vicar general, episcopal vicar, moderator of the curia, judicial vicar (officialis), assistant judicial vicar (vice-officialis), pastor, parish vicar, rector of a church, chaplain, member of the presbyteral council, and member of the college of consultors—canons 478,§1; 473,§3; 1420,§4; 521,§1; 546; 556; 564; 495,§1; 502,§1.

[22]For various options for lay ministerial service see Cunningham, pp.34-37.

[23]For a discussion of various aspects of the status of permanent deacons in the 1980 schema, the penultimate text in the code revision process, see W. Varvaro, "Proposed Legislation for Permanent Deacons: Developments and Difficulties," *PCLSA* 43 (1981) 238-253.

[24]For two recent discussions of the laicization issue, see M. O'Reilly, "Canonical Procedures for the Laicization of Priests," *PCLSA* 44 (1982) 233-246; E. Kneal, "Laicization: CLSA Survey, 1982," ibid., pp.247-250.

[25]For some useful comments on the possible ecclesial service of laicized priests in light of earlier Holy See norms, see J. Provost, "Dispensed Priests in Ecclesial Ministry: A Canonical Reflection," *Chicago Studies* 14 (1975) 121-138. Though some of the points of the article will have to be rethought in light of the more recent laicization norms, certain points are still relevant, e.g., role of diocesan bishop.

Finally, it might be observed that an integral part of the decision-making process in the Church is the creative ability of its members to envision alternative courses of action.[26] Whenever and by whomever decisions are to be made, be it by bishop or another authority figure, the value of systematically involving creative idea-people cannot be underestimated. Accordingly, the fostering of a diocesan climate conducive to the utilization of the talents of its diverse idea-people is another crucial episcopal responsibility. Likewise, the bishop has the right to expect from such individuals the willing and responsible exercise of their gifts for the service of the particular church. The significant relationship between the bishop and idea-people has been explored most recently at some length in terms of magisterium-theologian interrelationships.[27] However, the principle of such necessary and ongoing interchange within the Church has implications far beyond the realm of bishop-theologian dialogue.

3. The Bishop as One Called to Take Full Advantage of the Decisional Latitude Accorded Him in the Revised Code

As noted earlier, the revised code reflects the beginning of a somewhat historic movement away from highly centralized governmental processes to more decentralized patterns of decision-making. This shift is seen especially in the enhanced pastoral discretion of the diocesan bishop. Canon 381, § 1 indicates that he governs the particular church as a vicar of Christ, not as a vicar of the Roman Pontiff (LG 27). The bishop's authority is ordinary, i.e., flowing from his office; immediate, i.e., directly exercised over those entrusted to his care without an intermediary; and proper, i.e., exercised in his own name. Although in principle he enjoys all the authority necessary for the exercise of his office, he is situated within a hierarchical communion. At times the higher interests of that communion may limit episcopal discretion. Yet the former system of granting faculties to bishops has been replaced by a system of papal reservation, which may restrict the disposition of certain issues to the supreme church authority or to some other supra-episcopal authority, e.g., establishment of or continuance of a system of limited tenure for pastors (canon 522). In short, the relationship between the pope and the bishop has been significantly altered in theory, if not yet in practice. The latter is presumed to have all the authority necessary for his ministry unless the law explicitly provides otherwise. The full implications of this shift can be understood only by a detailed examination of the whole revised code. However, only a few brief observations can be made here.

In practice, the bishop should welcome and follow through on the decisional latitude accorded him in the revised law in various areas formerly within the

---

[26]See Kennedy, pp.10-11.

[27]See L. O'Donovan, ed., *Cooperation between Theologians and the Ecclesiastical Magisterium* (Washington, D.C.: CLSA, 1982). Particularly noteworthy in this connection is "In Service to the Gospel: A Consensus Statement of the Joint Committee" (pp.175-189). For another relevant report which led to the formation of the joint committee which prepared the preceding work, see "Report of the CTSA Committee on Cooperation between Theologians and the Church's Teaching Authority," *The Jurist* 40 (1980) 444-452.

province of the Holy See, e.g., dispensing power in canon 87. He should reflect a healthy autonomy and responsibility in governing the diocese. There is a certain tension in his role: he represents the universal Church within his community, yet he embodies the aspirations and Christian experience of his own community within the *Ecclesia*. While no particular church is an island unto itself, particular churches should undertake creative legal-pastoral initiatives without necessarily waiting for Roman authorization. Such initiatives, however, should be communicated to the other churches so that there may be healthy mutual evaluation of such pastoral ventures and that the positive developments in one church may enrich others.

In this connection it might be noted that what the law does not say is often as important as what it does say. In numerous areas of diocesan and parish organization, the code makes no provisions at all. Hence, there is ample freedom and flexibility[28] in structuring institutional forms appropriate to changing pastoral needs. A noteworthy example of increased episcopal discretion is in the area of parish structural modifications for the spiritual good of persons (canon 515, § 2). The wisdom of the presbyterate especially is to be tapped in this connection, especially through the consultative involvement of the presbyteral council. Yet there should be even broader consultation in this area, especially involving those persons whose spiritual needs are to be met through such structural modifications. There is even greater latitude for creative developments at the supra-parochial level. The traditional deanery structure is not mandatory; rather the basic issue is fostering common pastoral action in a given area, however best this objective might be attained (canon 374, § 2).

The respect for legitimate diversity integral to the principle of subsidiarity is operative not simply in Rome-particular church relationships; it is also a vital legal-pastoral imperative throughout the individual particular church. First and foremost the bishop should freely delegate his authority, especially in the administrative arena. Canons 137 and 391, § 2 are quite open to this possibility, even though certain privileged matters require a special mandate. During the revision process there was a definite tendency to enlarge the number of situations in which such a mandate was required. However, there are generally relatively few constraints on the bishop's administrative discretion by contrast to limitations on the judicial and especially legislative discretion.

Canonists should encourage bishops to take advantage of the legal options provided by vicars or delegates in various aspects of diocesan life, e.g., temporalities, education, liturgy, ecumenism. The scope of episcopal responsibilities in the revised code is awesome; they can probably be implemented responsibly only through judicious delegation of authority with appropriate accountability controls. Delegation without accountability is irresponsible; however, a pater-

---

[28]On the pastoral flexibility characterizing certain aspects of the revised code, see J. Alesandro, "Law and Renewal: A Canon Lawyer's Analysis of the Revised Code," *PCLSA* 44 (1982) 12-13. The whole article extends from page 1 to page 40. It should be noted that it deals with the amended 1980 schema and not the definitive text of the code.

nalistic refusal to delegate violates the gospel call to humble service. In delegating authority the bishop is to give such persons the authority they need to do the job with which they are entrusted while respecting their legitimate competency (*Directory* n.96; n.209c).

In this general context it is appropriate to mention the revised code's enhancing the status of coadjutor and auxiliary bishops. This conciliar concern was explicitated in CD 25-26 and later in ES I, § 13. The revised code reflects the conciliar preoccupation with diocesan unity and the pastoral welfare of the people of God. However, it also indicates that coadjutor and auxiliary bishops are to play a significant diocesan role above and beyond the celebration of the sacrament of confirmation. The coadjutor bishop and an auxiliary with special faculties are to be appointed vicars general and the auxiliary without such faculties is to be appointed at least an episcopal vicar. The former are to be entrusted with a special mandate in preference to anyone else in the diocese (canon 406). Furthermore, the diocesan bishop is to consult the auxiliaries on matters of significant pastoral importance; they are viewed as the privileged counselors of the diocesan bishop in this respect (canon 407). Such consultation is especially crucial in view of precluding conflicts that might jeopardize the unity of diocesan government (*Directory* n.199).

The principle of subsidiarity also implies that the bishop should respect the just initiatives of individuals and groups at the deanery, parish and infra-parish levels. There should be no more insistence on conformity to diocesan policies than is absolutely necessary for ecclesial unity, although the tolerable limits of pastoral diversity are not always easy to determine precisely. Given the practical significance of the parish in the lives of most Catholics, the diocese should support parish level personnel in meeting their own pastoral needs in relating to the world in which they live. It should avoid needlessly draining resources and personnel to serve diocesan objectives, perhaps thereby imparing parish mission effectiveness.[29] This is an especially significant factor to be taken into account in the bishop's determining parish assessments, an option provided for in canon 1263. Here is an area where broader consultation than is specified by the canon might well be called for.[30]

4. The Bishop as a Principal Figure in Fostering Diocesan Accountablity Especially in View of Serving the Common Good of the Particular Church

Vatican II stressed that the exercise of ecclesiastical office was to be viewed in terms of service of the Lord and his believing people. A frequent point of tension throughout church history has been the failure of the Church's public

---

[29]For a consideration of the impact of the revised code on parishes and more specifically on diocese-parish relationships, see J. Provost, "The Impact of the Proposed Book II 'De Populo Dei' on the Local Church," *Studia Canonica* 15 (1981) 371-398, especially pages 372-380.

[30]The bishop must consult the diocesan finance council and the presbyteral council before imposing such a parish assessment. In this general connection, see D. Frugé, "Taxes in the Proposed Law," *PCLSA* 44 (1982) 274-288.

ministers to be held responsible for the exercise of their ministry in a spirit of genuine service—a situation that clearly damages the life of the *communio*.

Accordingly, the bishop should be a key figure in terms of diocesan accountability by his own personal example and by his continuing insistence that persons and institutions serve genuinely gospel priorities. This involves the initiating and sustaining of mechanisms of ongoing assessment of diocesan, deanery and parish enterprises in terms of their fidelity to the Church's mission.

Frankly, there is little explicit reference to the evaluative role of the bishop in the revised code, except somewhat negatively in the provisions for the removal of pastors (canons 1740-1747). However, the interests of the common good of the diocese in a rapidly changing society require constant evaluation of diocesan policies, programs and personnel appointments lest they be ineffective in meeting ecclesial goals and objectives (*Directory* n.93: principle of common good). This requirement of periodic evaluation of diocesan institutes is perhaps one of the least consciously considered aspects of diocesan government either in the 1917 code or in the revised code. Perhaps one might have understood this inadequate approach in the 1917 code when our operative "perfect society" ecclesiology did not easily admit the imperative of regular pastoral change. However, a deeper awareness of the pilgrim character of the Church in Vatican II (LG 9) makes one a bit surprised by the code's failure to provide more systematically for the regular evaluation of our institutions in light of our primary goal of facilitating the growth of persons in Christ. Nevertheless, the absence of explicit mechanisms of evaluation in the code should not prevent sensitive diocesan policymakers from providing for such an objective in light of their specific needs and resources.[31]

The conciliar stress on the pastoral focus of the diocesan curia (CD 27/canon 469) means that the bishop should take the lead in seeing to it that operational priority "should be given to those activities which promote a sense of the Church as a community of faith, hope and love, rather than activities which build up the organization as such. This does not mean slipshod administration. It does mean that efficient administration should be judged in terms of what sense of Church its efficient operations promote."[32]

One might note here the legislator's preoccupation with coordinating diocesan apostolic activities to preclude a counterproductive diffusion of energies and a useless duplication of pastoral efforts. Canon 473 treats this issue in some detail and reflects the tendency of the revised code to specify a given objective while leaving a great deal of latitude for the particular churches to meet it. The code calls for the possible establishment of a new curial figure called a moderator of the curia to supervise diocesan administrative activities; it also suggests the possible formation of an episcopal council composed of the diocesan vicars to

[31]For some insightful reflections on the indispensable importance of evaluation in the decisional process, see Kennedy, pp.15-20.

[32]J. Provost, "Structuring the Church as a Communio," *The Jurist* 36 (1976) 210. The whole article, which is well worth reading, is found on pages 191-245.

foster pastoral activity more efficiently. Perhaps in some of your dioceses these institutes already exist; perhaps in others they are in the process of being formed; perhaps in still others they are deemed inappropriate. What is crucial is that the underlying objectives be addressed by the bishop as creatively as diocesan needs and resources permit (*Directory* n.97: the principle of coordination).

In this context of institutional evaluation, one should note the revised code's continued stress on episcopal visitation (canons 396-398). Though this obligation might be construed in purely *pro forma* terms, it highlights the importance of the bishop's availability to support and encourage priests, other pastoral ministers and local communities.[33] This availability may presuppose some administrative adjustments so as to free him from preoccupation with less significant administrative concerns, e.g., more adequate use of vicars (canons 475-481).

The principle of accountability also highlights the bishop's obligation to view appointment to and continuance in ecclesiastical office more in terms of the pastoral good of the persons to be served than the good of the officeholder, however significant the latter consideration may be. This principle, affirmed in *Maxima cura* in 1910, is no less urgent today when the authority of office is increasingly viewed in less sacral terms as an entity unto itself. Officeholders today are credible to the extent that they attempt to mediate an experience of God and strive to be responsive to those they are called to serve. Such a service orientation is crucial whether one is speaking of the appointment, removal or transfer of a vicar general, officialis, business manager, pastor or associate— all of which fall within the bishop's discretion.

Futhermore, this principle seems to imply that the bishop should foster realistic evaluation procedures to stimulate the ongoing spiritual, intellectual and pastoral development of clergy and other spiritual leaders. Without such procedures, discussions of modified tenure arrangements for pastors do not seem particularly constructive (canon 522). The clarification of minimal standards of ministerial excellence is hardly easy; yet it seems to be an objective worth pursuing.[34] Development of such standards and appropriate procedures should help ministers recognize strengths and weaknesses, achievements and potential and hence facilitate setting workable pastoral goals. The people of God have a right to expect reasonable pastoral service.[35] Hence, a key episcopal priority is enforcing minimal standards of pastoral excellence. Should these not be met, an individual minister should be removed after due process and enabled to function effectively if possible in another capacity. This is true for clerics, religious or laity. Such enforcement options have been facilitated by Vatican II, e.g., CD 31 on removal and transfer of pastors (canons 1740-1752).

---

[33]See *Directory*, nn.166-170.

[34]For some insights that may be helpful in clarifying standards of ministerial excellence, see Lasch; also B. Griffin, "The Pastor's Role and Some Implications for Seminaries," *CCM*, pp.75-80.

[35]Canons 212-213 on the rights of public opinion and access to word and sacrament seem particularly pertinent in this context. See also canon 843,§1 on reception of the sacraments.

5. The Bishop as a Principle of Unity in the Diocese, Especially in Providing for Conflict-Resolution Mechanisms

The Council teaches clearly that the bishop is the key principle of visible unity within the particular church, comparable to the pope for the universal Church (LG 23). In this context one might consider another aspect of episcopal governing responsibilities, i.e., the provision of conflict-resolution mechanisms to preclude intra-ecclesial conflicts from becoming pastorally counterproductive. Perhaps it is not an aspect of the episcopal office to which we normally advert; but it seems rather significant presently, and it will probably be even more important in the future.

It is a regrettable but painful fact of life that conflicts will arise within a pilgrim Church composed of frail, sinful human beings. Some of these conflicts are quite serious and can notably impair the Church's mission. The bishop as the leader of the community of faith can hardly ignore the potentially detrimental effects of such conflicts in view of his responsibility to foster the common good.

In line with our tradition dating back to the apostle Paul, canon 1446, § 1 expresses a strong preference for resolving such conflicts apart from formal judicial or administrative procedures. It states that all believers, but especially bishops, should strive to settle such conflicts peacefully with due regard for the exigencies of justice. While the canon hardly implies that the bishop himself is to be directly involved in the conflict-resolution procedure, it seems to place upon him the primary responsibility for the establishment of appropriate procedures.

Obviously, a major concern of the bishop is providing for a functioning tribunal, especially to expedite nullity petitions in view of fostering peace of conscience and clarity about one's ecclesial status. As the primary judge in the diocese (canon 1419, § 1), the bishop is clearly a key figure in fostering the administration of justice, particularly by providing for an appropriately funded and staffed tribunal. Generally, our bishops have been fairly faithful in this respect during the past decade and a half. The extraordinary number of nullity petitions expedited by our courts testifies to the productive bishop-canonist collaboration in tribunal issues during the 70's. Such collaboration will likely continue in the future as attempts are made to respond to the new demands placed on tribunals by Book VII. Regular tribunal issues are being addressed in other convention presentations; hence, there is no need to pursue them further here.

I would like to focus attention briefly on the issue of the exercise of administrative discretion. This is hardly a new concern, for it was addressed in the famous Due Process procedures adopted over a decade ago. Frankly, however, this has been considerably less of a CLSA priority during the 70's than the refinement of marriage nullity procedures and jurisprudence. Perhaps it is time to turn our attention to this cluster of issues with renewed interest.

With due regard for the pain suffered by our fellow believers experiencing the trauma of divorce, perhaps as much if not greater pain is experienced by those rightly or wrongly feeling aggrieved by administrative action and seemingly having no accessible recourse mechanisms to deal with such conflicts. Probably the largest amount of ecclesial decision-making is administrative in character rather than legislative or judicial. While only a certain percentage of believers are involved in marriage nullity procedures, all believers are affected in one way or another by decisions of church administrators, especially at the diocesan or parish levels. The potential for conflict is extensive in the administrative arena, e.g., the removal or perhaps the failure to remove a pastor, the suppression of a parish, the imposition of a diocesan tax on parishes, the removal of a university professor, etc. Accordingly, we should review existing diocesan conflict-resolution mechanisms to see if changes are in order for them to function more effectively.

The canons on administrative recourse at the end of Book VII (canons 1732-1739) make the bishop the key figure in resolving any controversies surfacing in the diocese as a result of allegedly arbitrary administrative discretion. Canon 1733, § 2 indicates that the conference of bishops may require each bishop to set up an office or board to deal with conflict-resolution issues. Even if the conference does not do this, the bishop may initiate such conflict-resolution mechanisms on his own, and, frankly, we should encourage him to do so. It may simply be a matter of utilizing already existing mediation and arbitration procedures, or it may be expedient to alter them in some respects. In any event, this is a key diocesan administrative priority. Granted, we do not want to encourage unnecessary litigation on the part of our already litigation-prone fellow citizens. However, we need to face the fact of a Code of Canon Law translated and relatively easily available to a larger number of people than ever before in church history. To think that the demands on our ordinary courts and on such administrative offices will be any less pressing in the future than they are now seems rather naive, to say the least.

Perhaps even more important than providing for such conflict-resolution mechanisms is the bishop's setting an example of careful, equitable and just administrative decision-making. I would strongly encourage your rereading the last part of the Due Process Report on the structuring of administrative discretion.[36] Perhaps much of the conflict that is a part of our institutional lives could be avoided if there were serious efforts to eliminate unnecessary discretionary power and monitor the exercise of necessary administrative discretion. For example, the competencies of administrative organs and individual administrators should be clearly delineated. The criteria of administrative decision-making in various areas should be clearly stated, e.g., norms on personnel placement, guidelines on diocesan taxation of parishes. Finally, written findings of fact and reasoned opinions should be issued supporting various administrative decisions whenever they adversely affect believers (e.g., firing of a teacher).

Canonists should inform bishops and other administrators of some significant norms on administrative discretion in Book I. One might specifically note

[36]See NCCB, *On Due Process*, rev. ed. (Washington, D.C.: NCCB, 1972).

canon 50 on the necessity of seeking out pertinent data and consulting those whose rights could be violated before making a decision; canon 51 on issuing an administrative decree in writing with at least a summary exposition for the issuing of a decree; and finally, canon 38 on the validity of decrees, which states that a decree is invalid if it injures the vested right of another or is contrary to the law or an approved custom unless the competent authority adds a clause expressly derogating from the law.

Finally, I would like simply to raise the issue of administrative tribunals. I submit that the dropping of such administrative tribunal options from Book VII was a much more unfortunate development than the reintroduction of the mandatory review of affirmative decisions in marriage nullity cases. This is because the administrative tribunal institute offered a real promise of developing an administrative jurisprudence that would have been a significant contribution to the Church's legal-pastoral life. Although setting up, staffing and implementing the work of such tribunals would have been extremely demanding, our legal-pastoral expertise would have been appropriate for the task, although frankly we probably would have had to reassess our significant investment in marriage nullity procedures. In any event, I propose that we consider seriously the possibility of setting up such tribunals as particular law institutes comparable to our initiative in formulating Due Process procedures and the APN over a decade ago. This system could contribute significantly to the resolution of intra-ecclesial conflicts, especially in those situations where the parties are unwilling to work out their differences amicably, thereby impeding the effectiveness of conciliation and arbitration procedures. The 1967 Synod, in approving principles for the revision of the code, complained about the inadequacy of existing mechanisms for protecting the rights of persons adversely affected by administrative action.[37] Even after the promulgation of Book VII those mechanisms still seem noticeably inadequate; accordingly, there seems to be a responsibility for us canonists to propose viable alternatives to aid our bishops in their task of fostering unity and reconciliation in the diocese.

6. The Bishop as Facilitator of Various Types of Ecumenical Sharing

While the preceding reflections concerned the bishop's fostering of unity within the Catholic community, this last point highlights his analgous responsibilities regarding those who are not fully members of our communion.

Vatican II did much to open the Church to the world and to other religious traditions, especially, but not exclusively, other Christian communions. Church structures should be neither parochial nor sectarian, but rather fully open to implementing various aspects of the ecumenical imperative.

Frankly, ecumenical concerns were not apparently a major Code Commission priority despite the presence of a couple of non-Catholic observers on the special committee that worked on the *Lex fundamentalis*. However, John Paul

[37]See *Communicationes* 1 (1969) 63.

II indicated an ecumenical thrust as one of the principal characteristics of a true and proper ecclesiology in his apostolic constitution *Sacrae disciplinae leges*. What is advisable is collaboration especially between canonists and ecumenical experts in aiding their bishops to take the lead in fostering increased ecumenical sharing of resources, theological-pastoral dialogue, prayer and sacramental life. Obviously, the level of such sharing depends on the measure of unity existing between us and those not fully members of our communion.

Several points in the revised law seem noteworthy in this connection. Canon 383, § 1 reminds bishops that they are to be pastorally concerned about those not fully members of our communion. Canon 755, § 2 calls for bishops to foster the ecumenical movement and to establish practical norms in light of the determinations of supreme church authority. A particularly significant task of bishops and ecumenical officers in the future is leading the way in the effort to come to terms with the implications of the consensus statements emerging from the bilateral and multi-lateral dialogues. Perhaps the focus of ecumenical reflection needs to shift from the halls of academia to the grass-roots level of the pastoral life of the various churches.

An especially significant norm is canon 844 on the sharing of the Eucharist, penance and anointing with other Christians. The canon states general principles of ecumenical polity in our dealings with Eastern and Western Christians, but there is ample latitude for episcopal discretion within the broad framework of Holy See norms. This is especially true if the conference of bishops does not act in this regard. Such a pastoral decision requires broad-based diocesan input; however, the canon makes no explicit provision for episcopal consultation except with hierarchs of the non-Catholic traditions affected by the decision on sacramental sharing. Such consultation with other church leaders is important not only on this issue, but on other sensitive ecumenical issues. In this connection, one might note the significant canon 1128 stressing the importance of providing spiritual assistance to couples and their children in ecumenical marriages. Perhaps in discussing such marriages we are overly preoccupied with canonical issues, such as the *cautiones* and the formalities of granting appropriate dispensations, and we are unduly inattentive to these profound pastoral issues. We canonists should take the lead along with ecumenical and family life experts in aiding our bishops meet these legal-pastoral responsibilities as conscientiously as possible.

Furthermore, we might ask ourselves how effectively we have thus far realized the potential for collaborative action by Christians in various areas. Even prescinding from the institutional stress and strain experienced by all churches today, it seems appropriate that bishops and other church leaders take the initiative in doing together whatever we are not bound to do separately by conscience or religious conviction.

Finally, the bishop might be encouraged to be aware of the need to provide for some type of ecumenical input into regular (diocesan pastoral council) or exceptional (diocesan synod) goal-setting enterprises, lest we legislate without adequate sensitivity to the impact of Catholic policies on members of other communions. Explicit reference is made to such imput only at the diocesan synod (canon 463, § 3); however, the underlying principle, reflecting the experience of Vatican II, seems operative in various synodal or conciliar processes.

Conclusions

The preceding reflections have attempted to highlight certain aspects of the episcopal office in the revised code. Limitations of time precluded discussing any one issue in depth. However, it is hoped that these observations may facilitate your reflecting on your own ministry in our various particular churches. It is also to be hoped that your ongoing service to your bishops will enhance the exercise of their office and enrich the lives of the people of God to whom we minister. Accordingly, the Church will be better equipped to carry out its salvific mission in the world.

SUGGESTED READINGS

1. T. Green. "The Diocesan Bishop in the Revised Code: Some Introductory Reflections." *The Jurist* 42 (1982) 320-347.
2. T. Green. *A Manual for Bishops: Rights and Responsibilities of Diocesan Bishops in the Revised Code of Canon Law.* Washington D.C.: USCC Publications Office, 1983.
3. F. Morrisey. "The Importance of Particular Law in the New Code." *CLSA Proceedings* 41 (1981) 1-17.
4. Sacred Congregation for Bishops. *Directory on the Pastoral Ministry of Bishops.* Ottawa: Canadian Catholic Conference, 1974.
5. *Communicationes* 4 (1972) 40-50; 5 (1973) 216-235; 7 (1975) 161-172 (formulation of original schema on bishops).
6. *Communicationes* 12 (1980) 275-314; 13 (1981) 140-146 (formulation of definitive text on bishops).

INTERNAL GOVERNANCE IN CONSECRATED LIFE

SHARON HOLLAND, IHM

As I reflected on the title of this presentation, it became increasingly clear to me that the topic was much more expansive than the frequently discussed issues of authority and obedience. These questions enter in importantly, but are part of the larger whole.[1]

What then is the governance of which we are speaking? Who are the officials involved? What is it that they do in those roles? Perhaps for just a moment, it may help to look beyond religious government in order to have a broader context.

In his apostolic constitution *Sacrae discipline leges*, Pope John Paul II cited as an essential characteristic of the Church the doctrine by which it is taught that the Church is the people of God, in which hierarchical authority is understood as service. He also spoke of that Church as a communion — one in which all members participate, in their own way, in the three-fold office of Christ: teaching, sanctifying, and governing.

The revised Code of Canon Law speaks of the power of governing in the Church, first of all in Book I, General Norms. This is a change from the previous code in which this material was treated with the clergy and hierarchy in Book II. A broader concept of ecclesiastical office, and the understanding that lay persons can cooperate in the exercise of the power of governing, occasioned this significant shift in the law's structure. When the law later speaks specifically of governance in religious congregations, it makes reference to several of these canons on ecclesiastical governance.

Religious governance, as such, is treated in Chapter V of the law on religious institutes. Its three distinct articles deal with Superiors and Councils, Chapters, and the Administration of Temporal Goods. From this I would like to suggest that in a broad sense, the officials of religious governance include superiors, councilors, capitulars and bursars. While their roles are quite diverse, nevertheless each plays a very distinct and important role in the governing of the institutes — that is, in the ordering of its life in a way which facilitates movement toward the goal for which it exists.

This description of the role of governance is deliberately broad. The Church's law does not really define it, and dictionary definitions are full of words such as sovereignty and control. We have from the gospel, however, from the apostolic constitution just quoted, and from the text of the law on superiors, an imperative that in the Church, authority is understood as service.

---

[1]On that topic, see Richard Hill, S.J. in this volume and Sr. Mary Linscott, "The Service of Religious Authority," *Review for Religious* 42 (1983) 197-217.

In looking at specifically religious governance, rather than following the order in the Code I want to begin with the canons on general chapters because they give us the broadest notion of religious governance, or ordering of the life of the institute. The principles regulating general chapters call forth some of the most basic elements regarding religious government. These are founded upon the teachings of *Perfectae caritatis* (n. 14) and *Ecclesiae Sanctae* (II, 11, 18) which called for more active participation by members in the governance of their institutes.

The general chapter is recognized as having "supreme authority in accordance with constitutions" (c. 631, § 1). What then, has it the authority to do?

No longer are chapters seen as purely legislative and elective, as once may have been the case. There has been significant development since the days when chapters concerned themselves with minute details such as the width of sleeves or cinctures. For many, a radical change was initiated by the call for special renewal chapters, prepared for by wide membership participation.

The canons now charge general chapters with a fundamental responsibility for the fidelity and renewal of the institute. One of its principal functions is described in canon 631, § 1: "to protect the patrimony of the institute mentioned in canon 578, and to foster appropriate renewal in accord with that patrimony." That canon on patrimony refers to the unique founding principles and spiritual heritage of the institute.

Here we have the broadest possible view of the role of religious governance: faithful ordering of the institute's life toward its purpose. The chapter further has the responsibility of electing the supreme moderator, dealing with other matters of great importance, and issuing norms binding on all.

Who are the officials of these governing tasks? The canon notes that the chapter is "to be composed in such a way that it represents the whole institute and becomes a true sign of its unity in charity" (c. 631, § 1). The details of accomplishing this are left to the institute through the constitutions. While not holding an office constituted stably in the usual sense of ecclesiastical office, capitulars of a general chapter surely may be called "officials" of internal governance in a broad sense, during the time that the chapter is in session. They are involved in setting the directions for ordinary governance during the next term of office.

The fact that a chapter is said to be representative clearly does not mean that delegates represent constituencies with vested interests. The chapter ideally is a microcosm of the whole, imaging the institute's unity in charity. It is always the duty of capitulars to seek the common good, the truth, the direction for the congregation, which is faithful to its heritage.

In a 1976 presentation, Cardinal Eduardo Pironio, Prefect of the Sacred Congregation for Religious and Secular Institutes, spoke strongly and broadly of the nature of general chapters in religious congregations. He stated:

> . . . since it is an ecclesial event, the chapter cannot be confined to reviewing specific problems of one congregation only. It must be

essentially an evangelical reflection of the needs and aspirations of the Church at that particular time. It must ask itself, for instance, what evangelization means in the Church today; who are the poor today; what meaning have education, social assistance, human progress, the full liberation of the nations.[2]

As a family meeting, the Cardinal called for the chapter to have an atmosphere of joy and simplicity in charity, of freedom of dialogue, and of great mutual respect in the midst of differences of opinion.[3] Describing chapters as paschal and penitential celebrations which call for conversion, he continues: "Every chapter should leave behind a sense of freshness in the Church, a good measure of Easter optimism."[4] Later the Cardinal notes: "A chapter is measured not by the depth and elegance of its documents, but rather by its capability of transforming the minds and hearts of all."[5]

One of the questions which arises today is the possibility of what is sometimes called a chapter of the whole. The law does not envision this for large, geographically spread institutes, and the practice of the Apostolic See in the approval of constitutions affirms that this is judged to be unwise. Nevertheless, there is no objection to the creative approaches to chapter preparation which have been found by congregations, nor to holding open sessions of chapter which combine the value of broad participation by members of the institute with the value of a smaller deliberative body.

Often, every willing member of a congregation is involved in the reflection and deliberation which prepare proposals to the chapter, and which enable the capitulars better to know the thoughts of other members of the congregation. Those who by office or by election are actually members of the chapter body continue to have a particular responsibility to prepare themselves spiritually, to inform themselves, and to arrange their other obligations in such a way that they can give themselves generously to their duties as capitulars. In a broad use of the term, capitulars are "officials" of governance in an extraordinary and *ad hoc* way, at the time of chapter. Theirs is a role which will have extremely important implications for the congregation, and will give orientation to a new term of ordinary governance.

Those chosen for chapter must invest themselves in spiritual preparation because their decisions will call forth life and conversion in the congregation. They must carefully inform themselves on issues of congregation, Church, and world. They must also prepare themselves for the responsibility stated in the canons on the selection of superiors:

---

[2]*Joyful in Hope* (St. Paul Publications, 1978), p. 125; also in *L'Osservatore Romano* (Eng. Ed.), September 16, 1976.
[3]Ibid, p. 127.
[4]Ibid, p. 120.
[5]Ibid, p. 122.

They are to have nothing but God and the good of the institute before their eyes, and appoint or elect those whom, in the Lord, they know to be worthy and fitting. In elections, besides, they are to avoid directly or indirectly lobbying for votes, either for themselves or for others (c. 626).

As with chapter in general, canonical elections within chapter have become an issue in some congregations. Some wish to have direct vote for the general superior. Again, this clearly is not envisioned by the law for large congregations in which the entire membership does not constitute the chapter. In their role as electors, capitulars play a very decisive role and one with obvious implications for the whole congregation. Once again, congregations are finding a way to honor the essential value of the freedom of delegates in election, and the value of greater consultation with membership prior to elections.

For generations, many congregations feared that any form of consultation regarding persons or qualities needed for offices of governance violated the canonical norm forbidding the procuring of votes for oneself or for another. There has been great interest in recent months as the news media circulated information regarding the little known pre-election procedures used by delegates to the Jesuit General Congregation. Their practice of discreet and positive inquiry regarding persons in order to inform themselves as electors, is precisely a way of fulfilling that equally essential canonical law for elections which was quoted above: "having before their eyes, God and the good of the institute. . . ."

Experimentation with processes of discernment prior to balloting in chapters of election must be looked at closely. A key juridical factor in canonical elections is the requirement of secret ballots—precisely for the purpose of safeguarding the freedom of each elector. While it must be questioned whether a true communal discernment is possible with a relatively large group of delegates in a canonical election, the law clearly does not preclude prayerful processes for discerning qualities and capabilities needed for offices, prior to formal balloting. Many would have strong reservations, however, about actual discussion of persons within the chapter group. The amount of time and prayerful reflection required in order to proceed with elections is once again an argument supportive of the law requiring a capitular body for the election of the highest superior, rather than the use of direct vote by all members throughout the congregation.

From just this much, it is clear that although the general chapter meets for a relatively short time at the close of an administration, its work is critically important in the life and governance of the congregation. While it is an admittedly analogous use of the word, it seems appropriate to call the capitulars, while they are in session, extraordinary officials of governance in a religious congregation.

From this dimension, let us turn now to those whose role is more familiar—those to whom this title "official of governance" properly belongs, because they hold an elective or appointed office as religious superior. Theirs is the role of ordinary administration, which frequently involves the day-to-day implementation of the decisions taken and directions set by the general chapter, as well as involving the personal authority which relates to the religious vow of obedience.

In the general norms for consecrated life, there is one general canon about superiors and chapters (c. 596). It states simply that both superiors and chapters have that authority which is defined in universal law and constitutions. Secondly, it states that in clerical religious institutes of pontifical right, superiors also have the ecclesiastical power of governance for both the external and the internal forum.

The third section of the same canon then refers to that title in Book I of the code called the power of governance, and applies ten of the sixteen canons there to all superiors—clerical or lay. This indicates, then, that all religious superiors are recognized as holding an office which in some way participates in the exercise of the ecclesiastical power of governing. In accordance with canon 129, clerics properly posses this by orders; lay persons are said to "cooperate in the exercise of this power in accord with the norm of law" (c. 129, § 2).

The law, then, applies many of the canons on ecclesiastical governing power to all religious superiors. Some of these are technical; some expand our notion of the role of these "officials" of internal religious governance. For example, canon 131 notes that ordinary power of governance is that which by virtue of the law itself is attached to a given office. Office, according to canon 145 is "any role (*munus*), which by devine or ecclesiastical disposition is established in a stable manner to further a spiritual purpose." Clearly, this includes the role of a religious superior.

The canons on governance continue regarding the use of delegated authority and the loss of ordinary power which follows from leaving the designated office (c. 143). The final canon in this section notes that "in common error, whether factual or legal, and in positive and probable doubt, whether of law or of fact, the Church supplies executive power of governance for both the external and the internal forum" (c. 144).

The example of a few canons illustrates more concretely what this might actually mean. Canon 968, for example, provides for clerical superiors to hear the confessions of their subjects and others living in the house. However, in another place, the canons instruct superiors not to hear the confessions of their subjects unless the latter spontaneously request it (c. 630, § 4). The same canon forbids superiors in any way to induce members to make a manifestation of conscience to them.

The religious ordinary can also give faculties to any priest to hear the confessions of members (c. 969). However, it should also be noted that special faculties are no longer needed for hearing the confessions of religious, and in the new law any priest who enjoys faculties for confessions can hear anyone, anywhere, unless expressly forbidden by the diocesan bishop (c. 967, § 2).

41

Canon 1019 allows for the clerical religious superior to provide the dimissorial letters for members approaching diaconate and priestly ordination.

Canon 1047, § 4 provides for the religious ordinary to grant dispensation from irregularities and impediments to priestly ordination, so long as these are not reserved.

Canon 289 provides for the religious ordinary to give a cleric member the necessary permission to volunteer for military service, or not to use the available civil law exemptions.

Canons 1355 and 1356 provide for an ordinary who has set a juridic trial in motion to remit the ecclesiastical penalty which was imposed.

From these examples, it would appear that with regard to internal government, those areas which are particular to the religious ordinary, and which are of rather practical or regular use, are directly related to the ordination of members by dispensing powers and recommendations for promotion to orders. For practical purposes in the day-to-day exercise of this service of authority, the role is essentially the same for all religious superiors.

In the 1978 document *Mutual Relations* there is a very interesting development of the role of the religious superior. Number 13 of that document gives an expansive expression to the role in terms of each of the three offices of Christ: teaching, sanctifying, and governing. I quote here only the section on governing—keeping in mind the significance of seeing the superior's role as broader:

> c) As to the office of governing, superiors must render the service of ordering the life of the community, of organizing its particular mission and seeing to it that it be efficiently inserted into ecclesial activity under the leadership of the bishops (*MR* 13).

The role of governing, then, is once again described as being in service of the community and its mission in the Church.

The same document, *Mutual Relations,* expresses suscinctly other principles now found in the new law:

> Superiors fulfill their duty of service and leadership within the religious institute in conformity with its distinctive character. Their authority proceeds from the Spirit of the Lord through the sacred hierarchy, which has granted canonical erection to the institute and authentically approved its specific mission (MR 13).

This finds expression in the law at the beginning of can. 618:

> The authority which superiors receive from God through the ministry of the Church is to be exercised by them in a spirit of service.

The canon's statement on the source of authority is traditional doctrinally, but new in its inclusion in the law. The canon synthesizes the doctrine that there is only one authority in the Church—the power of Jesus sent forth in the Spirit. All authority in the Church is a sharing in that one power.

Although theories of how authority is transmitted in the Church continue to be the topic of theological discussion, the canons assume that *Mutual Relations* states more explicitly: the authority of superiors in religious institutes is transmitted by way of ecclesiastical approval of the institute—originally through erection and approbation, and in a continuing way through the approbation of the constitutions which describe the offices of governance. The religious superiors holding those offices share in the authority of Christ—who came to serve: to teach and sanctify and govern.

The authority of the religious superiors' office, then, is that described in universal law and in constitutions. It is real authority in the Church and comes through the Church. Thus it can be said that the act of the chapter which elects the general superior, designates a person to exercise the authority of the office; but the chapter does not confer the authority.

This delicately nuanced but important teaching reflects certain contemporary theories:

    1. That all power in the Church is received through orders and consequently can be exercised only by the ordained—never by laity;

    2. That all power exercised by laity is conferred by baptism;

    3. That power exercised by laity is simply natural.[6]

The same principle has been reiterated in the recent document from SCRIS, "Essential Elements in the Church's Teaching on Religious Life." It states that the particular authority of religious institutes does not derive from the members themselves, but

> . . . is conferred by the Church at the time of establishing each institute and by the approving of its constitutions. It is an authority invested in superiors for the duration of their term of service at general, intermediate or local level. It is to be exercised according to the norms of common and proper law in a spirit of service, reverencing the human person (EE 49).

What then is the role of the religious superior? We have already noted that the directions set by general chapters are implemented throughout an administration by the general superior and those who assist in administration at the general level, and throughout the whole institute. As we have already seen, the first part of canon 618 calls for the spirit of service. We have also noted the obligations of superiors to reverence the members of the institute. Superiors are called upon to be "docile to the will of God" (c. 618).

From such phrases of the law, we may describe the role of religious superiors as unifiers. They are to listen and foster cooperation for the good of the institute and the Church (c. 618); together with members of the institute, they are to build a community of charity (c. 619). They are to promote a spirit

[6]Jean Beyer, "Chiarimenti sul'ufficio dei superiori nell'Istituto religioso," *Vita Consacrata* 17 (1981) 393-402.

which fosters willing obedience and, although superiors retain the authority for decision making, they are advised to work collaboratively with members for the good of the institute (c. 618).

From other phrases of the law we may speak of these officials of governance as persons who foster life, or as persons who foster an atmosphere in the institute which is life-giving. The law speaks of sharing the word and Eucharist, of cultivating virtue and observing the laws and traditions of the particular institute. The religious superior is to be responsive to the particular needs of individuals as they arise (can. 619).

Without detracting from the fact that there is an authority which calls forth a response in obedience, the authority of religious superiors is largely to be used to unify in charity, to foster life, and to advance the mission for which the institute exists. Religious as a whole are called upon to collaborate actively with those in authority at every level to advance these same goals.

Once again, however, the canons which deal specifically with religious superiors do not give the full picture of governance at any level. The traditional requirement that each superior have a council serves a double purpose in governance. First, it provides expanded vision and experience which can and often must be brought to bear on decision making. Secondly, it builds on a protection against abuse or autocratic use of authority. Can. 627 not only provides for the existence of the council to assist the superior in his or her role, but also notes that there are cases in universal law which require the consent or advice of the council for valid action. Proper law may add other such circumstances.

A superior, for example, must have the consent of the council for such matters as valid acts of alienation (c. 638, § 3), for permitting an individual to make the novitiate outside the novitiate house (c. 647, § 2), for erecting, transferring, or suppressing the novitiate house (c. 647, § 1), for allowing a religious in temporary vows to leave (c. 688, § 2), for allowing a religious who has left to reenter (c. 690, § 1), for allowing a transfer to or from another religious institute (c. 684, § 1), or for granting an indult of exclaustration (c. 686, § 1).

In many cases, proper law must determine whether the council's role is one of advice or consent. In a matter such as admission to temporary or to perpetual vows, some congregations require that the council be heard; others require its consent.

Canonists are not always in agreement about just what those terms mean—advice or consent of the council. The canon requiring the use of the council refers to canon 127 as a norm for action.

Canon 127 states that when according to law the advice or consent of a college or group of persons is required, then that college or body must be assembled—unless, in the case of advice only, proper law provides otherwise. For our purposes here, I am going to continue to speak in terms of a "group" of persons, since that would describe the council; "college" more accurately describes a chapter. In cases, then, where the consent of the council is required,

44

the body must be called together and, the canon states, for validity of the act, an absolute majority of those present must give consent. If only advice is required and proper law provides that the group need not be assembled, still the canon requires that the advice of all be sought.

In view of just this much, if there are four councillors who must give consent in a particular case and all four are present, three must agree to the matter—an absolute majority being one more than half. What if only three are present and only two give consent? Is there an absolute majority? It would seen that two of a potential four councillors could assure the superior of a consent upon which to act. The second section of canon 127 speaks of cases where the advice or consent of persons as individuals is required. This does not really refer to councils.

The third section of the canon turns to the responsibility of the councillors. It states: "All whose consent or advice is required are obliged to give their opinions sincerely." It also provides for requirements of secrecy where the matter demands it. Although it is not explicitly related, this last requirement calls to mind the necessity of giving a consultative body enough information to participate intelligently in decision making.

The place where difficulties and differences have arisen is with regard to whether a superior, seeking consent of the council, may break a tie. The canon with which we have just dealt does not refer to this and it is only canon 127 to which the law refers on the use of councils for valid acts by religious superiors. In asking this question, some have turned also to canon 119 which provides for the person presiding to break a tie after two ballots in collegial acts. The problem with this interpretation lies in whether or not the acts of councils are to be seen as collegial acts. I have already indicated that they do not seem to be. A council is—in the kind of situation of which we are speaking—a group of persons, but not a college. We have noted the purpose: a breadth of experience and wisdom and a check on autonomous use of authority.

Since the canon states that the superior, to act validly, must have the consent of the council in certain cases, it would seem that there must be a majority of those who are councillors. The superior has already submitted a vote of sorts, in proposing an action to the council. It is important that there be clear understanding of expectations in proper law, since this may involve very serious matters touching the rights of persons—e.g., admission to or exclusion from vows. If this is left to the advice of the council, there is less problem. Some issues—e.g., a decision to alienate properties—do not always have to be settled on a certain date, and if there is not a majority on something weighty, more information can be sought.

One other factor in the law which seems to argue for considering only the votes of the councillors is that there is one case in which the law explicitly calls for a general council to function collegially (c. 699, § 1). That is in the case of dismissal, and seems to point to an exception in the usual way of functioning as a council.

Now, if we look again at the role of council—as we did at the whole question of governance and of superiors—surely this body is not engaged most of the time in this type of decision. What is the role of these persons? Of course the detail of this varies greatly according to proper law, but councillors are another example of "officials" of internal governance in that more expansive sense. When gathered, certainly councils spend more time in planning, implementing, and evaluating for the good of the province or congregation than they do in specifically giving advice or consent in formal cases requiring it for validity.

As congregations have developed a greater sense of shared responsibility within the governmental groupings, they have often begun to refer to themselves as teams. In fact, this describes well their mode of operation a large part of the time. As this kind of wording entered constitutions, however, problems arose. In giving expression to the role of the council in proper law—precisely as law, and as safeguarding rights and providing balance in the use of authority—more technical language is necessary. It is necessary to recognize the legitimate role of the superior as described in the universal law as holding an office which, in some way, shares in the governing power of the Church. And it must recognize that the advice or consent of that council must be sought in order to have certain acts of the superior stand as valid. Thus, religious are being asked to speak of the superior, with the council, making certain decision called for in the law.

With all of this said, there is no reason why proper law cannot encourage that the councillors be consulted in all important matters, even though their consent is required only in some. Many superiors have experienced the strength of having deliberated with such a body before decision-making, and have seen an improved quality of decisions because of the breadth of experience and information brought to bear on it. Nevertheless, there are times when the superior can and must act more individually. Proper law, while it encourages shared decision making, must not tie the hands of legitimate authority. There are times when decisions must be made quickly; there are also times when a highly confidential and personal matter is involved and the privacy of the individual religious demands that the matter be settled with the superior alone.

By and large, all of this is fairly clear when speaking of major superiors. The burden of explaining the role of a local superior is left largely to proper law. It is clear that the law presumes a level of personal authority between the individual and the major superior—someone who is accessible to the religious. Canon 608 states that a religious community must live in a legitimately constituted house under the authority of a superior designated according to norms of law. The way in which this is fulfilled varies greatly from autonomous monasteries, to large house of religious engaged in apostolic works, to very small residences of religious. Sometimes this role is filled by a resident superior; sometimes it is filled by one superior for more than one small residence; sometimes it is filled by provincial councillors or regional superiors.

46

I believe that at the local level, the notion of superior as unifier is critical. In many congregations there may not be many decisions made at the local level which require the personal authority of the office of superior. The quality of life, however, may argue strongly for a person who serves to unify, to call the religious to reflection on the quality of their life, their prayer and their ministry in light of their congregation's charism, nature, purpose, and constitutions.

Although there is a tendency to think of governance in terms of the two aspects we have already discussed—chapters, and superiors and councils, the section of religious law on governance of institutes includes a third article on temporal goods and their administration (cc. 634-640). Here we find reference to another "official" of internal governance. Canon 636 states:

> In each institute, and in each province ruled by a major superior, there is to be a financial administrator [*oeconomus*], distinct from the major superior, and constituted according to proper law. The financial administrator is to administer the goods under the direction of the respective superior. Even in local communities a financial administrator, distinct from the local superior, is in so far as possible to be constituted.

These persons render accounts of their administration according to proper law. Of course, this office is not new—even if we do not always think of it in terms of internal governance. In looking at other parts of the law, however, we are conscious that the Church is being ever more careful to provide for responsible fiscal management of ecclesiastical goods. With the new law, every parish must have a finance council, as must every diocese.

While the office is not new for religious congregations, the implications of the role have—it would seem—grown, and become more complex in recent years. When we hear the stories of those who guided congregations through founding days, and through the foundering days of crises, fires, and the years of the depression, perhaps it is only the sphere of responsibility and expertise which has changed. Today fiscal officers—treasurers—of provinces and institutes are faced with ever more complex questions of tax exemption, programs of hospitalization, incorporation of apostolates, and processes for the alienation of properties.

This particular office is carried out under the direction of the superior, but it is a role which calls for a particular form of expertise which is of critical importance. Not only are the above areas of financial management important, but the specifically religious dimensions of stewardship, the quasi-corporate witness to poverty called for by the canons, and responsible investment in the face of social issues are serious concerns for the fiscal officer.

With this, we may say that we have spoken of the "officials" of internal governance. This is the aspect of governance most covered by law, but the very title—"officials" of internal governance—recognizes that there is more to the governance in religious institutes than the officials. We know from the Coun-

47

cil, from *Ecclesiae Sanctae*, and from the working principles of the commission preparing this part of the law, that the participation of members in the governing of their institute is considered to be of fundamental importance.

It is beyond the scope of this paper to deal with the forms this can take. The canons are very broad; it is left to proper law to describe other chapters besides the general chapter, and other similar assemblies. Canon 633 speaks of other participatory and consultative bodies only in a general way; the rest is left to proper law—within what has already been reviewed in the canons.

Only one further canon remains to be mentioned at this point. We have spoken broadly and specifically of the officials of internal governance. In the general norms for institutes of consecrated life, canon 586 recognizes the just autonomy of every institute. It states:

§ *1*. A just autonomy of life, especially of governance, is recognized for each institute. This autonomy means that each institute has its own discipline in the Church and can preserve whole and entire the patrimony described in canon 578.

§ 2. Local ordinaries have the responsibility of preserving and safeguarding this autonomy.

When later canons speak of the role of ecclesiastical authority with regard to pontifical and diocesan institutes, this canon on autonomy is referred to explicitly (cc. 593, 594). It is an autonomy which is not really new; it was granted to institutes of simple vows in 1900. However, the understanding of that autonomy has grown greatly over the years. In the descriptions of officials and processes of governance internal to religious institutes, combined with the growth in application of the principle of subsidiarity, it is a notion which has ever greater meaning for religious within the Church, and it must be viewed precisely within the context of Church, through which that power of governance comes.

OFFICIALS OF THE TRIBUNAL: TERMINOLOGY, QUALIFICATION, RESPONSIBILITY

HARMON D. SKILLEN

The subject matter to be dealt with here is the personnel of the tribunal in the revised code, their specific responsibilities and their qualifications for office.

In order to understand clearly the tribunal personnel and their role in court it is necessary to understand how the revised code deals with the matter of processes and compare that with the same subject matter as is found in Book Four of the 1917 code. The old code dealt with the judicial process in three sections: first, judgments; second, causes for beatification and canonization; and third, procedures for specific actions, including the application of penalties. The revised code deals with processes in five sections: first, judgments in general; second, the contentious judgment; third, special processes; fourth, the penal process; and fifth, procedure in administrative recourse and the transfer and removal of pastors. In the revised code the contentious judgment for all practical purposes becomes the exemplar and model for all other forms of judgments. Since the process for the ordinary contentious judgment is the basis for the law of the new code, in dealing with the various officers of the tribunal, their qualifications and their responsibilities, we shall be viewing them principally from the point of view of that process. When the occasion warrants it, however, we shall discuss those responsibilities arising from court functions under various other judicial processes.

With that as background we will now turn to the officers of the court. Here is the plan I shall follow in dealing with this subject. First, I shall describe the nomenclature of the officers, the qualifications for office and the terms of office. Then I shall take each officer of the court and discuss that officer's responsibilities. Finally, I shall try to draw together some of the more significant and important changes that have been enacted in the new law.

THE OFFICERS

Who are the officers of the court and what are their qualifications? First of all, there is the judge. Canon 1419 of the revised code maintains the legal principle that the judge at first instance was the ordinary of the place (*loci ordinarius*: canon 1572, § 1). In the old law, religious superiors were not included in the definition of the term *loci ordinarius* and consequently religious superiors did not possess ordinary judicial power except as extended to them in canons 501, 1579 and 1594. The revised law, however, includes under the name "diocesan bishop" the heads of territorial prelatures, territorial abbeys as well

49

as vicars apostolic and apostolic administrators (canons 381, § 2 and 368 of the revised code). Those persons, therefore, in the revised code possess ordinary judicial power. Canon 1427 of the revised code extends judicial power to the provincial superiors in situations where controversies arise between religious or religious houses of the same institutes for clerical religious of pontifical rite.

Canon 1420 of the revised code binds the bishop to appoint a judicial vicar or an officialis who has ordinary power to judge. As in the old law, the judicial vicar should be distinct from the vicar general unless the smallness of the diocese or the small number of cases to be handled indicate otherwise.

The bishop can also appoint according to that same canon, auxiliary judicial vicars or vice-officiales.

Canon 1421 of the revised code empowers the diocesan bishop also to appoint what are called diocesan judges. The office of synodal and pro-synodal judge and the distinction between those offices are omitted in the revised code.

So, the first officer of the court is the judge, that is the diocesan bishop and then those appointed to that office: the vicar judicial or officialis, the adjutant vicars judicial or vice-officiales, and diocesan judges.

The revised law then lists the qualifications required for the office of judge. The judicial vicar and the auxiliary judicial vicars must be priests of sound reputation, doctors or at least licensed in canon law and thirty years of age (canon 1420, § 4). The new look here is that requirement of at least a license in canon law in order to be an officialis or vice-officialis. The minimal requirement in the old law, as we remember, was simply a thorough knowledge of the law, however obtained.

The qualifications for diocesan judges are that they be of good reputation and hold either a doctorate or a license in canon law. There is no age limit for the diocesan judge.

Canon 1421 states that the diocesan judges should be clerics. However, the episcopal conference can permit lay people to be appointed as judges. From those laity so appointed one lay-person can be assigned to a collegiate judicial bench whenever it is necessary. While consistant with *Causas matrimoniales*, this represents a substantial change from the old code. In the revised code, a lay-woman may be a judge. This is evident from a comparison of the final Latin text of the revised code (*etiam laici iudices constituantur*) and the Latin in previous drafts (*viri laici iudices constituantur*). In the final draft of the revised code, the word "viri" has been dropped.

The new law requires a term of office for the vicar judicial and the auxiliary vicar judicial. They are to be appointed for a definite period of time (*ad definitum tempus*) according to canon 1422. This represents a departure from the 1917 code which stated that the officialis and vice-officialis were removable at the will of the bishop. Similarly, a definite term is to be determined for the diocesan judge.

The next tribunal officer spoken of in the code is the assessor. Canon 1424 of the revised code states: "A single judge can associate with himself two assessors on the occasion of any judicial action." The same canon states the qualifications of the assessor: "They can be either clerics or lay persons of proven life." There is no mention of the need for a canonical degree for an assessor.

Canon 1428 of the revised code establishes the office of the auditor. The canon states: "The judge or the president of a collegiate tribunal can designate an auditor to carry out the instruction of a case." As far as qualifications for the office of auditor the canon says that the auditor is to be selected either from the judges of the tribunal or from among persons approved by the bishop for this office. Section 2 of the canon states: "The bishop can appoint for this office either a cleric or a lay-person who enjoys good morals, prudence and learning."

Here again the absence of the word "viri" in the Latin text of the revised code indicates that the auditor can be either male or female. Nothing is said about the auditor's need for a canonical degree.

The next office dealt with in the new code is the office of *relator* or *ponens*. Canon 1429 says: "The president of a collegiate tribunal must designate one of the judges of the college as *relator* or *ponens*."

Inasmuch as the *ponens* is taken from the collegiate judges, in the cases where the episcopal conference has permitted lay persons to be appointed as judges the *ponens* could be either a man or a woman.

The next officers of the tribunal dealt with in the revised code are the promoter of justice, the defender of the bond and the notary (canons 1430, 1432 and 1437).

The promoter and defender are to be appointed by the bishop and are offices permanently established in the diocese ("constituatur in dioecesi"). These officers may be either clergy or lay persons. They are to be of sound reputation, they must be doctors or at least licensed in canon law, and they must possess prudence and proven zeal for justice (canon 1435).

Two major changes have occured in this revised law. In the 1917 code the defender of the bond and the promoter of justice had to be priests. Now they may be lay persons, male or female. In the old law if they were not doctors of canon law, they had to be at least skilled in that law. Now they must at least have a license in law.

Finally, the duties of the tribunal notary are dealt with in the revised code in canon 1437. The office of notary is established in the revised code in Book Two, canons 482 and 483 in the chapter on the diocesan curia. Canon 470 states that all curial officials are to be nominated by the diocesan bishop. Canon 483 states that besides the chancellor, other notaries may be appointed ("constituatur"), and canon 483 states that the diocesan bishop is the one who can remove the chancellor and other notaries. The notaries must be persons of sound reputation and beyond all suspicion (canon 483, § 2). The law does not make any distinction as to whether notaries, including the chancellor, be clergy or lay. However, it does say that in any case in which the reputation of a priest is at issue, the notary must be a priest. In all other tribunal activities, therefore, the notary could be clergy or lay, male or female.

It should be noted that the offices of court messengers and apparitors are dropped in the revised code.

Besides all these officers of the court, there are other persons intimately connected with the tribunal process. Such persons would be experts, interpreters, procurators and advocates.

The experts are dealt with from canon 1574 to canon 1581 of the revised code. Experts are to be named by the judge. Their qualifications are, obviously, that they possess the skills necessary to enlighten the court adequately on the question at issue.

Canon 1471 of the revised code allows for the use of an interpreter to be selected by the judge. Here again, the qualifications for the interpreter, although not mentioned in the code, are adequate skills for the accomplishment of the task.

Finally, procurators and advocates, although not actually officers of the court but persons who stand in for and advise the petitioner and respondent, are so intimately connected with the tribunal that we shall deal with them as well. The parties to a judicial action have the option of appointing for themselves an advocate and a procurator (canon 1481, § 1). In a penal action the accused has no option. He or she must have an advocate appointed by either the accused or the judge (canon 1481, § 2). The procurator and advocate must be at least eighteen years of age and of good reputation. The advocate must be a Catholic (unless the diocesan bishop permits otherwise), either a doctor in canon law or otherwise skilled in that law, and approved by the bishop (canon 1483). Both these officers enter the tribunal activity by means of an effective mandate which must be deposited at the tribunal (canon 1484, § 1).

Canon 1481, § 3 legislates for an officer called the "defender." The canon states:

> In any contentious action, whenever a minor is involved, or if it is
> an action in which the public good is involved (with the exception
> of marriage cases), the judge may *ex officio* appoint a defender for
> an absent party.

Since this officer is spoken of in the canon dealing with procurators and advocates, the requirements concerning the qualifications of the defender should be the same as those for procurators and advocates.

So much for the names, qualifications and terms of office of the officials and officers of the tribunal. We will now proceed to a consideration of the responsibilities of these individuals.

Canon 1454 of the revised code requires that all who constitute the court or who participate in tribunal activity must swear that they will faithfully and rightly carry out the duties of their office. So the first responsibility of all the members of the tribunal is to conscientiousness and professionalism. That being said we can now study the responsibilities of each of the officers of the tribunal, saving the judge for last, however, because of the extensive nature of his office.

Canon 1428, § 3 of the revised code describes the responsibilities of the auditor. The law demands that the specific functions of the auditor be mandated by the judge. The auditor can be ordered to collect all the proofs in the case and turn them over to the judge. He or she can also decide exactly what proofs should be gathered and how they should be gathered unless the mandate of the judge forbids that.

Canon 1429 states that the *ponens* or *relator* has as his or her responsibility to report on the case and put the sentence of a collegiate tribunal into writing. This represents no change from the 1917 code.

The function of the assessor spoken of in canon 1424 in the revised code, is simply to be a consultor to a single judge.

The responsibility of the notary is rather extensive. According to canon 1437 of the revised code, "A notary should be present at each process to the extent that the acts are considered null if they are not signed by the notary."

"Acts" are defined in the revised code in canon 1472 where it states,

§ 1. The judicial acts, both those which have reference to the merit of the question (that is, the acts of the case) and those which pertain to the manner of proceeding (that is, the acts of the process) must be put into writing.

§ 2. Each page of the acts is to be numbered and accredited by a sign of authenticity (*authenticitatis signo muniantur*).

The requirement of the old code was that each page had to be signed by the actuary and sealed with the seal of the tribunal. The revised code seems to leave the sign of authenticity unspecified. The individual pages of the acts, therefore, can be authenticated either by the signature of the notary or the seal of the tribunal. If the notary does not put his signature at the end of each of the acts, however, the act is null and the sentence, according to canon 1622, § 3 of the revised code is remediably null. It is the responsibility of the notary, therefore, to see to it that all the acts of the case which have been committed to writing are numbered and authenticated and that at least the last page of each of the acts bears the notary's signature.

The responsibilities of the promoter of justice have been reworked. According to the new code, the promoter is to be present for contentious cases, cases in which the public good is at stake, and criminal cases (canon 1430 of the revised code).

53

Provida mater required the promoter of justice to be present when procedural law was to be safeguarded and at marriage cases when the promoter was the one who impugned the marriage (article 16). Unlike *Provida mater*, the revised code does not require that the promoter be present at marriage cases in which he himself has impugned the marriage. Furthermore, in the revised code the diocesan bishop determines whether the public good is at stake, while in *Provida mater* the bishop or collegiate bench makes that determination. Finally, the promoter may present to the judge items on which the parties should be interrogated (canon 1533 of the revised code). If the promoter of justice is present for the examination of the witness, he or she may not directly examine the witness but must propose the questions to be asked to the judge (canon 1561 of the revised code).

Canon 1434 of the revised code contains a new procedure. It states:

> Unless it is otherwise provided for, (1) whenever the law demands that a judge hear one or both of the parties, he must also hear the promoter of justice and the defender of the bond if they are present in the court, (2) as often as, at the instance of the parties, the judge is required to make a determination about anything, the promoter of justice and defender of the bond, when they are present in the court, have the same opportunity to initiate such a request.

An instance in which such an event might occur is contained in canon 1582 of the revised code, where the judge is required to hear from the parties when he feels he needs to go to a certain place or inspect a certain object in order better to obtain information. Canon 1434 of the revised code requires that the promoter and/or the defender also be heard in such an instance.

As with the promoter of justice, the responsibilities of the defender of the bond are generally similar in the revised code to those legislated in the 1917 code. The revised code in canon 1432 describes the establishment and the office of the defender of the bond. It states:

> There is to be established in the diocese a defender of the bond for cases dealing with the nullity of sacred orders or the nullity or dissolution of marriage. The defender of the bond is bound by his or her office to propose and expose all those things which reasonably can be used as arguments against the nullity or the dissolution.

The manner in which this canon is expressed puts the role of the defender of the bond in a decidedly different caste from that established by canon 1968 of th old code. In that canon, no. 3 states that the defender of the bond has as his duty:

> (a) to write animadversions against the nullity of the marriage and to state the proofs of the validity of the marriage: (b) to present everything that he considers useful to uphold the validity of the marriage.

The new law's introduction of the concept of reasonableness to those duties of the defender represent that officer's responsibility to maintain an attitude different from that required in the old code. The old code required that the defender of the bond stand against nullity and for validity, ex officio, and that the defender be utilitarian in his efforts. The new law requires that the defender be a reasonable person in the attempt to uphold the validity of marriage or ordination.

The law in the new code concerning the nullity of the acts in cases where either the promoter or the defender were not cited seems to be less rigid. The acts are null if these officers are not cited unless, even though not cited, they are actually present at the case. But the new law goes farther and says that even if the officers were not cited, the acts are valid if, at least before the sentence, they could have fulfilled their office by inspecting the acts (canon 1433 of the revised code). The old law in canon 1587 required that the acts absolutely be submitted to the defender of the bond afterward when that officer was legitimately cited but not present. The new law appears to offer a rather broad exception which could prevent wholesale nullification of tribunal acts.

Concerning the responsibilities of experts, canon 1574 of the revised code states that experts must be used whenever an investigation and opinion coming from their art or science are required by a prescript of the law or a judge in order to prove anything or to determine the true nature of a matter.

Canon 1471 of the revised code describes the responsibilities of interpreters. They are to be used whenever the person to be questioned does not speak the language of the judge, the petitioner or respondent, or if the person to be questioned is unable to speak or hear.

Canons 1484 and 1485, describing the responsibilities of the procurators and advocate, indicate that those responsibilities are to be contained in the mandate by which they take on their office.

The responsibilities of the judge in the tribunal are overwhelming. Many of those responsibilities remain the same and are expressed in the same way in which they were in the old code and instructions and decrees such as *Provida mater* or the American Procedural Norms. There are some changes and adaptations in the new law, however, which need to be recognized.

The initial responsibility of the judge as described in the new law under the headings of the ordinary contentious case, matrimonial cases and separation of spouses is to see if the matter can be kept from coming to judgment. Early on, therefore, before the judicial contest has begun, the judge acts as a reconciler or arbitrator. Canon 1446 of the revised code states:

> § 1. All the faithful beginning with the bishop are seriously obliged to avoid litigation among the people of God insofar as it is possible and safeguarding justice. They are also obliged to resolve the issue peacefully as soon as possible.

§ 2. The judge at the very threshold of litigation, indeed, at any time, must not fail to exhort and help the parties seek by common counsel an equitable solution to the controversy as often as he sees some good hope of a happy outcome. He must indicate suitable means to accomplish this, even using professional persons to mediate the situation.

Canon 1676 of the revised code advises the judge to act in a similar fashion before beginning a case on the nullity of marriage.

The judge, before he accepts the case and as often as he sees the possibility of a happy outcome, must use pastoral means to encourage the spouses to renew their marriage and restore conjugal life.

In canon 1695 of the revisd code under the heading of cases of separation of spouses we find the following:

The judge, before he accepts the case and as often as he sees the possibility of a happy outcome, must use pastoral means to reconcile the spouses and lead them to restore conjugal life.

These canons represent a significant departure from the instructions of the old law. The old law stated: "It is not as a rule becoming to the dignity of the judge to make such proposals personally; he should rather commit it to some priest, especially to one of the synodal judges" (canon 1925). The new law does not express any incompatibility between the office of judge and reconciler. No longer is it beneath the dignity of the judge to attempt reconciliation. The new legislation requires an attitudinal shift on the part of the judge. Rather than being initially and solely concerned with competency, secrecy, the nullity of acts, weight of proofs, the judge is required now to be initially concerned with keeping cases out of court by bringing about a reconciliation or by preventing people from litigating with one another. The judge must be ready to accomplish this reconciliation at any time before or during the course of the trial.

Once the case has begun it is the ultimate responsibility of the judge to resolve the case by a definitive sentence. In order for him to do that rightly, the sentence must be a valid one. That means obviously that the judge must know the law on procedure in order to avoid issuing a sentence which is null, either irremediably or remediably. This is turn means that the judge must know the new law concerning competence and the competent forum, the number of judges who must sit on a case, the process and the requirements for accepting a petition, the rights and duties of all the officers of the tribunal, the time in which the case must be handled and the various and specific acts that must be accomplished, the procedure for citing the parties and joining of issues, the precepts concerning the abatement of the case. The judge must know the law concerning proofs and consequently, all the law concerning the depositions of parties and the witnesses, the acceptance and use of documents, and experts. The judge must also understand the law concerning the publication of the acts, the closing of the evidenciary phase of the case and the law concerning the discussion of the case. The judge in every instance must understand the new law concerning appeals. It is the judge's responsibility to understand the oral contentious case, the process of matrimonial cases including ordinary matrimonial cases, documentary marriage cases, cases for the separation of spouses, *ratum non consummatum* cases, and favor of the faith petitions. The judge must also know the law concerning cases involving the nullity of sacred orders and the judicial penal process.

It would be impossible to list in detail all the responsibilities of the judge. As I have already said many of these responsibilities are the same as those we have been living with and carrying out for the past 65 years. What follows now, therefore, is a selection of some of the more significant or important changes found in the new law.

One of the responsibilities of the judge is the discernment of competency. As in the 1917 code there is the distinction between absolute and relative incompetence in the new law. The difference between these two, as well as sources from which they arise, are basically the same as they were in the old law. The general principle established in the revised code is that the petitioner follows the forum of the respondent (canon 1407, § 3). In the revised law the legislation that the ordinary has jurisdiction over a subject who is absent is omitted. The legislation concerning competence in marriage cases is not quite the same as that found in the American Procedural Norms or in *Causas matrimoniales*. The following tribunals are now competent for the hearing of marriage cases: first, the tribunal of the place in which the marriage took place; second, the tribunal of the place in which the respondent has a domicile or quasi-domicile; third, the tribunal of the place in which the petitioner has a domicile provided that both of the parties live in the territory of the same episcopal conference and the tribunal of the place of the respondent's domicile agrees after hearing the respondent; or finally, the tribunal of the place in which most of the proofs must be *de facto* collected, provided that the judicial vicar of the respondent's domicile gives consent; and, in this case, the respondent's judicial vicar must previously ask the respondent whether he or she has any exceptions (canon 1673).

The revised code does not contain the provision of *Causas matrimoniales* IV, § 3 which states:

> If there occurs a substantial change in the circumstances, places or persons mentioned in § 1, the instance, before the closing of the case, may be transferred in particular cases from one tribunal to another equally competent one, provided both parties and both tribunals agree.

It is the responsibility of the judge to make the determination as to whether or not his court is competent to accept the case. Consequently, the judge must be aware of all these canons.

Canon 1425 of the revised law establishes the number of judges needed for the various cases. It states in § 1:

> Contrary custom no longer being accepted, a collegiate tribunal of three judges must be used:
>
> 1° in contentious cases concerning (a) the bond of sacred orders, (b) the bond of marriage, with the exception of the documentary cases mentioned in canons 1686 and 1688;
>
> 2° in penal cases (a) concerning delicts which bring with them the penalty of dismissal from the clerical state, (b) the imposing and declaring of excommunication.

According to this canon, therefore, marriage cases must now be judged by a college of three judges. However, § 4 of that same canon states:

> At first instance if a judicial college by chance cannot be established the episcopal conference can permit a bishop to commit cases to a single judge who is a cleric as long as the impossibility exists. This judge must associate with himself an assessor and an auditor insofar as that is possible.

It would seem, then, on the basis of canon 1425 that although a collegiate tribunal is the ordinary method by which a marriage case (among others) must be judged, if the need is present and the episcopal conference allows it, marriage cases can be heard by a single judge at first instance in a given diocese.

Here again it will be the responsibility of the judge to see to it that adequate numbers of judges are assigned to various cases in order to follow the law and avoid remediable nullity.

Canons concerning the acceptance or rejection of a petition in both laws are similar. However, in canon 1505, § 2, 4° of the revised law there is an additional cause presented for the rejection of the petition. That will occur:

> If it is clearly evident from the libellus itself that the petition lacks any foundation, nor will it happen that any foundation will develop as the process moves along.

If the petition is to be accepted, the judge must issue a decree admitting the petition and calling the parties together for the joining of issues (canon 1507 of the revised code). That citation begins the state of prosecution (the *litis instantia*) of the matter (canon 1517 of the revised code).

According to canon 1453 of the revised code:

> The judge and the tribunal are enjoined to take care that all cases are brought to conclusion as soon as possible, justice being preserved, so that at the tribunal of first instance, the cases are not protracted beyond a year and at the tribunal of second instance, beyond six months.

This represents a change from canon 1620 of the old code which allowed two years for a case at first instance and from the American Procedural Norms which required a decision within six months following the acceptance of the petition. The principal thrust of canon 1453 of the revised code, however, is that the case be completed as soon as possible. It will be up to the judge to see to it that the requirements of that precept are met.

Although there has been a general reworking of the section on proofs, the matter dealt with is substantially the same. Canon 1561 of the revised code states that the examination of the witness is to be done by a judge or the judge's delegate or auditor. A notary must assist the one doing the interrogation. It would seem from this legislation that whenever a witness is being examined, two people need to be present. This might require a change in the way some tribunals obtain their testimony.

Canon 1567, § 2 of the revised law admits the use of tape recorders, "as long as the responses are then consigned to paper and signed when that is possible by the deponent." Here it would seem that testimony taken over the telephone and recorded in the hearing of the judge or the judge's delegate or auditor and the notary, would be acceptable testimony.

After the proofs have been assembled, the case moves to the publication of the acts, the conclusion of the case, and the discussion of the case. Canon 1598 of the revised law states:

> When the proofs have been assembled, the judge must permit the parties and their advocates under pain of nullity to inspect at the tribunal any of the acts not yet known to them. Indeed, the judge can even give a copy of the acts to advocates that ask for it. However, in matters of the public good, that judge, in order to avoid extremely grave danger, can determine that some of the acts should not be shown to anyone, realizing however, that the right of defense must always remain intact.

Since canon 1691 of the revised code requires that cases dealing with the nullity of marriage must be handled by the ordinary contentious process, the requirement of canon 1598 allowing the parties to see proofs that have been assembled must be followed in marriage cases. It would seem that in preparing people to present a case to the tribunal, it would be important to advise them that this part of the process must take place. At the same time, it is the responsibility of the judge in the matter to be very sensitive to the possibility of evils which would arise from complying with this law and be careful in his selection of those acts which he feels should not be shown anyone.

Canon 1602, § 1 of the new law states:

> The defenses and the opinions must be written unless the judge sitting for the tribunal, having heard the parties, feels that a debate is adequate.

This canon indicates that even in marriage cases, at the discretion of the judge, the arguments of the advocates and the defender of the bond could be oral rather than written.

Following the arguing of the case and the discussion of the case by a collegiate tribunal, if there is one, the decision is issued. Again, the responsibilities of the judge in the new law are substantially the same as in the old law in the matter of the decision, redress against the sentence, appeal, the closing of the judgment, judicial expenses, and the execution of the sentence.

In the new law there is provision made for what is called the oral contentious process which is an abbreviated or somewhat curtailed process. Judges must familiarize themselves with that process so that they will know when and how to use it.

Canon 1657 of the revised code in dealing with the oral contentious process, indicates that the matter at issue is to be heard by a single judge. The petition when it is presented, besides those things required in the ordinary contentious judgment, must also contain the facts on which the petition is based, the proofs by which the petitioner intends to demonstrate the facts and any documents on which the petition is based (canon 1658).

Upon receipt of the petition, when the other prescriptions of law have been fulfilled, the judge determines the formulation of the doubt and summons the parties to a hearing within 30 days (canon 1661 of the revised code). At that hearing the matter is orally discussed (canon 1619 of the revised law). Immediately following the discussion, the judge then and there pronounces sentence and reads the dispositive section of the sentence before the parties who are present (canon 1668). The appeal process is then available if it is necessary (canon 1670).

The responsibility of the judge also includes understanding the procedures for dealing with all types of matrimonial cases. Some important parts of that process have already been dealt with earlier in this paper. However, there are a few items in the new law which represent changes from the old law and which have not yet been dealt with.

First, canon 1690 of the revised code states that the oral contentious process cannot be used in cases dealing with the nullity of marriage. Canon 1686 and following of the revised law legislate for the documentary marriage case. Here the formalities of the ordinary process are omitted:

> The parties are cited and the intervention of the defender of the
> bond is sought, and a declaration of nullity is granted when there is
> certain proof from a document which is subject to no contradiction
> or exception, that there existed a diriment impediment, that there
> was a lack of legitimate form, or that there was the lack of a valid
> mandate of proxy.

This is the "1990 case" of the old law. The principal change here is that the "lack of form" case is now included among those which must be handled according to this procedure.

The new law also legislates for the instruction of marriage cases dealing with non-consummation. Although only the Apostolic See adjudicates the fact of non-consummation and the dispensation is granted by the Holy Father alone (canon 1698 of the revised law), the diocesan bishop, according to canon 1699 of the revised law, is the one who receives the petition for the dispensation. That bishop according to canon 1700 of the revised law may then commit the instruction of the process either permanently or in particular cases to his own tribunal or to the tribunal of another diocese or to a suitable priest. This represents a change from canon 1963 of the old code indicating that no inferior judge could *institute* proceedings in the case of dispensation from valid unconsummated marriage unless the Holy See had authorized that judge to proceed. Furthermore, canon 1705, § 3 of the revised law states that if the Holy See replies that from the acts offered, there is no proof of non-consummation, a person skilled in canon law can inspect the acts of the process (although not the *votum* of the bishop) at the tribunal hall, to determine whether any serious items can be brought forward in order to propose the petition again.

It is also the responsibility of the judge to understand the law concerning cases for the declaration of nullity of orders which by and large is the same in new law as it was in the old.

Finally, the judge must understand the penal process. Canon 1721 of the revised law states that if the ordinary decrees that a penal judicial process should be undertaken, he must hand the acts of the preliminary investigation to the promoter of justice who then presents the *libellus* of accusation to the judge. In that manner the matter enters the judicial process. Canon 1723 of the revised law requires that the judge invite the accused at the time the accused is cited, to appoint for himself or herself an advocate. This is to be done within a time established by the judge. If, however, the accused does not provide himself or herself with an advocate, the judge himself must name an advocate for the *litis contestatio* for as long a period of time as the accused does not personally appoint an advocate. Canon 1725 of the revised law allows the accused the right in the discussion of the case to speak or write last. This right is not given to the petitioner in the ordinary contentious judgment and represents the opportunity for the accused to develop and present an adequate defense.

Changes Affecting Tribunals

As was stated earlier the responsibilities of the judge are overwhelming. It is for the judge to see to it that justice is served according to the prescriptions of the new law concerning judicial processes. Consequently, a thorough understanding of that law is necessary for any judge. The tribunal of the new code in many ways is similar to the tribunal of the old code. At the same time there are differences which would give the tribunal a new "feel." I would like to conclude this paper by recalling a few of those changes and commenting on them. First, there is the requirement of at least a license in canon law for the vicar judicial, adjutant vicar judicial, the diocesan judge, the promoter of justice, and the defender of the bond. It would seem that when the new law takes effect, any persons who presently fill those offices and who do not have at least a license in law will either have to obtain that degree or cease functioning in that position. This will create difficulties in many tribunals inasmuch as people who have those degrees or are able to obtain them are simply not available to those tribunals.

On the other hand the law provides relief and opportunity by allowing women to act as judges, assessors, auditors, *ponentes*, promoters of justice, defenders of the bond, and notaries. There is relief because a greater number of people will thus be available to serve in understaffed and overloaded tribunals. There is opportunity because women will now be able to participate officially and visibly in the most serious levels of responsibility in tribunal work.

The law requiring the defender of the bond to pursue the validity of marriage and sacred orders reasonably represents a much more pastoral approach to that office. In a similar way the law requiring the judge to try to reconcile the parties coming before the bench makes the law and the institution of the tribunal much more pastoral and evangelical.

The law which requires that parties can review the proofs that have been put forward is going to be difficult to deal with. On the one hand, we are all aware of respondents who have felt unjustly dealt with because they later found out some of the testimony that was given in a case and did not have the opportunity to rebutt it. At the same time we have seen the bitter feelings that arise when parties find out some of the things that have been said and we are well aware of the possibilities of civil litigation as a result of the publication of the testimony. The canonical jurist in each of us will say, "yes the acts should be published" while the judicious pastor in each of us will say, "not on your life"!

It should be the hope of all of us that as we take on the duties and responsibilities of the various offices of the tribunal, we will make the gospel more alive because we know the law and love the Lord.

THE ROLE OF THE CANONIST IN
THE CONTEMPORARY CHURCH

BERTRAM F. GRIFFIN

I am somewhat intimidated by trying to fill the shoes of Robert Kennedy. I remember when he was awarded the Role of Law Award, he quoted from memory large chunks of "A Man for All Seasons." In the parish where I have been a pastor for the past thirteen years, my Baptist and Holiness preacher friends could call me a "back-up" preacher.

I am also intimidated because some of the reflections that I would like to make were dealt with in a far more scholarly way by Thomas Green and by James Coriden in their masterful talks during this convention.

Finally, it was only ten days ago that I was asked to give this presentation. So it is not a scholarly talk. It is more a homily (or as canon 766 would say, a *sermon* for which the power of orders is not required.)

The topic is "The Role of the Canonist in the Contemporary Church." The text that I will be using is *Sacrae disciplinae leges.* I would like to make some reflections on that promulgating document based on my experience over the past year teaching, not in a scholarly way but more in a pastoral way, groups of bishops, of middle management people in the Church, of clergy, sisters, and lay people throughout the United States in various seminars and workshops. *Sacrae disciplinae leges* reminds us that our legal heritage, our legal tradition, does not go back to Justinian. It goes back much further to the Old Testament, to Moses. On Mount Sinai there were two Torahs revealed: the written Torah or the Pentateuch, and the oral Torah which was passed on from Moses to Joshua, to the judges, to the prophets, and to the Great Assembly. This oral law was finally written down after the Hadriatic persecution in about the year 130, and was called the Mishnah.

In the Mishnah, there is a marvelous little tractate called "The Ethics of the Fathers." It is read every year in the synagogue on the six Sabbaths between Passover and Pentecost. In this tractate one of the Mishnahs states that the world was created by ten words, or by ten commandments. You are familiar with them. On Sunday God commanded, "Let there be light." On Monday, "let there be a firmanent." On Tuesday, "let the waters be gathered." Etc. But if you count the commandments by which the world was created, you will discover there were only nine. And so the commentators say that the first and most important commandment which created the world was the implicit one in the first verse, "In the beginning God created heaven and earth." Psalm 33 says, "By the words of His mouth were the heavens created."

Then the Mishnah goes on to say that God's will was revealed on Mount Sinai in ten words, or in ten commandments. If you count them, "Thou shalt not have strange gods before me," "thou shalt not take the name of the Lord thy God in vain," "remember to observe the Sabbath," "honor thy father and thy mother," etc., you will find there are only nine cammandments. And the reason for that, the commentators say, is that the first and most important of the ten commandments is the implicit one that begins the series. "I am the Lord thy God" is the first commandment and is the foundation of all legal tradition—that moment when God reveals himself as personal to "you" (second personal singular), "I am the Lord thy God."

The new Code of Canon Law creates a canonist in ten words. There are ten commandments in the new Code of Canon law requiring the role of canonist for certain church offices.

1. Canon 378, § 1, says the bishops should be either scripture scholars, theologians, or canonists, and have a license or doctorate from a pontifical institute or at least be skilled in one of those disciplines.

2. Canon 478, § 1, says that a vicar general is to be a theologian or canonist with either a license or doctorate or skilled in these disciplines.

3. The same canon says episcopal vicars, that is other local ordinaries, also are to be either theologians or canonists.

4. Canon 1420, § 4, says that judicial vicars and their adjutants are to be licensed or doctors in canon law.

5. Canon 1421 requires judges to be licensed or doctors.

6. Canon 1435 requires the defenders of the bond to be licensed or doctors.

7. The same canon requires that promoters of justice be licensed or doctors.

8. Canon 1483 requires advocates to be doctors or at least skilled in canon law.

9. Canon 253, § 1, says that every seminary faculty needs to have a canon lawyer with a license or a doctorate from a pontifical institute.

If you count these positions there are only nine, and that is because the first and most important one is only implicitly mentioned. That is in canon 19, which states that the authoritative interpreter of the law is assisted by the common and constant opinion of learned canonists. This common and constant opinion of learned canonists is not something that comes suddenly. It is rooted in the social experience of canonists gathering, writing, speaking, studying, and doing that informal interpretation which I believe is our major task during the next years. Common and constant interpretation of learned canonists is based on the more informal interpretation of less learned canonists like myself and others who give our opinions, who assist in the interpretation of the law. It seems to me that this role is now our most important role as canonists.

The first canon law convention I attended was here in San Francisco in 1964, when the "Chicago mafia" took over. Since that time I have seen our role change several times in the course of the past nineteen years. We were very active and at the forefront of *aggiornamento* in America during this period of our Society. We were at the forefront of pastoral renewal. We went through a period of assisting in the drawing up of the schema of the new law and a period of critique of the schemas as they came out. We have now been in a position of teaching the new law during the *vacatio* and will continue that role as well as our role of creatively interpreting and implementing the law.

I think interpretation is even far more important than the sentences we write or the decisions we make. The sentences that we write do not follow the civil law practice of *stare decisis*. Our sentences do not bind other courts. Our jurisprudence only has illuminating value, the value of the wisdom of the interpretation itself which can instruct other canonists. Similarly, any administrative decisions or interpretations that we would make are not binding on others, but have only the value of their wisdom or their illuminating force.

So the theme I would like to develop is based on our experience in interpreting this law and the challenge to create an interpretation for the next generation based on my experience during the past year of teaching the law in a pastoral setting. It has been impressed on me over and over again that our tools, as canonists, are *words*. That is what canon law is all about. And words have a tremendous power. That is why canonists are alternately praised and feared, even hated, in church history. Words can be blessings or can be curses. Words can be used to tame and to domesticate the charisms in the Church. Adam named the animals and, therefore, tamed and domesticated them. Moses wanted to tame the Almighty in the burning bush, so he asked his name. That is why God told him, "My name is Yahweh. I will be who I will be."

So as the canonist names rights and obligations, names institutions, names offices, names relationships and institutes, we are in a sense taming and domesticating the multiplicity of gifts and charisms in the Church. That can be dangerous.

It is also a blessing to name these rights and obligations and offices. The native Americans in the Northwest have a saying that the most important ceremony in life is the naming ceremony of the child because, if the child has no name, then how will it know when God is calling him. It is by naming the rights and obligations, by naming the institutions and relationships that we are freed to be able to carry on the mission and the ministry of the Church.

James Coriden mentioned yesterday that the laws of the Church are laws only in an analogical sense; he drew a parallel between the analogies in our legal system and the civil system. It seems to me we can go even further; all of our words as canonists (when we are at our best) are analogical words. Only when we are in a period of canonical decadence do our words tend to be univocal. Univocal words are competitive, divisive. Analogical words are relational, conversational.

Sacrae disciplinae leges has ten words that have become tremendously powerful words over the past years. They are words that are familiar to all of us, but they are exciting and new words to many, many people in the Church. These ten words I am going to reflect on are: (1) *novitas* or the newness of the law; the threefold *munus* of (2) priest, (3) prophet, and (4) king; the words (5) *rights* and (6) *obligations* and *equality;* the words (7) *Church as people* and (8) *communio;* (9) *ecumenism;* and finally (10) *authority as service.*

I. *NOVITAS*

You have heard ad nauseam the call to have a *novus habitus mentis,* a new habit of mind. The code that we are called to interpret is a *new* Code of Canon Law. *New* because it reflects the renewal program, the *aggiornamento* program, of John XXIII, who called in that famous *aggiornamento* allocution for a synod of Rome, a Second Vatican Council, and a revision of the code. The synod of Rome has mercifully been forgotten. It forbade us to go to the opera, the circus, the beach, the symphony, or the theatre under pain of automatic suspension. I kept a diary and was automatically suspended 53 times in my three years in Rome.

The new Code of Canon Law represents the termination of the literary process of that *aggiornamento* program: the sixteen documents of the Second Vatican Council, the three liturgical books—the Sacramentary, the Lectionary and the Ritual—and then finally the seven books of the revised law. This terminates a period of church history. It is the end of the literary production of the Second Vatican Council, of the *aggiornamento* of John XXIII, and is the beginning of the preparatory phase for Vatican III. John Paul II reminds us in his allocution when he presented the new code to the Church that the canonist is to be an interpreter of this code with a clear understanding of the Second Vatican Council and of the Scriptures. John Paul II draws that famous triangle with which we are all familiar. The Scripture is at the apex. The Scripture is the *lex fundamentalis* of the Church. The Scripture is the *constitution* of the Church. At one corner of the triangle are the documents of Vatican II and at the other corner is the code. The documents of Vatican II represent the conciliar tradition of the Church; the new code represents the canonical tradition of the Church. Therefore to be a canonist, it seems to me, is to be someone familiar with the conciliar tradition and with the sixteen documents of Vatican II, and someone above all familiar with the Word of God, the Torah and the Gospel.

But one of the pains of being a canonist, it seems to me, is that this book is not new. Vatican II, people my age tend to forget, was twenty years ago. There are people being ordained who know nothing except the Second Vatican Church, who do not have any memories of what the Church was like prior to the Second Vatican Council. There has been a lot of excitement in the Church in the past twenty years and a lot of expectations. There has been a lot of rising expectations regarding issues that are not dealt with in the code. The ordination of women, the ordination of married men and women to the priesthood, greater sharing of governmental and pastoral power with the laity, alternatives to the tribunal—all these things have been discussed in the past twenty years and are not reflected in the new law.

Moreover, as canonists, we are disappointed with the absence of administrative tribunals. Decentralization and reform of the Curia is not anywhere near as extensive as many of us would like to see it. And collegiality is not as clearly implemented in the code as many of us wanted. We are teachers, interpreters, and implementers of the code, but I do not think we can ever forget our role as critics, either.

THE THREE-FOLD *MUNERA*

The three-fold *munera* of priest, prophet and king are analogical words. They are, I discovered, exciting new words to many people. Many people in the Church in this country have not realized how powerful these three words are in the Second Vatican Council and in the new Code of Canon Law. These three words speak to Christology on one level, of our understanding of who Jesus is, of who the Messiah is. They speak on a second level of our understanding of ministry. They speak on a profound level of our ecclesiology. This was the new realization of the Second Vatican Council. Thre three-fold *munera* are organizing principles for the documents of the Second Vatican Council, particularly *Lumen gentium, Christus Dominus, Presbyterorum ordinis* and *Apostolicam actuositatem,* and they are organizing principles in the code itself.

Canon 204 reminds us that the Christian faithful are incorporated into Christ by baptism, established as a people, and share in Christ's priestly, prophetic, and royal office. It has been exciting to me to see how people's ears pick up and begin to realize twenty years later the significance of documents that they read twenty years ago and have not returned to since. The Church is a priestly, prophetic, and royal or messianic kingdom. Bishops in canon 375 are described as teachers, priests, and ministers of government. In canon 519 a parish priest is described as carrying out his duties in teaching, sanctifying, and in government. These three-fold munera are analogical terms and have to be understood on the three levels of Christology, ministeriology, and ecclesiology.

Prophetic Office

I would like to deal briefly with the three-fold office of the canonist. First of all, our teaching or *prophetic office* is clear. Canon 19 describes our first and most important duty as assisting in the authentic interpretation of the code. Our code of professional responsibility which we passed yesterday in our business meeting, emphasizes our teaching office, our obligation to educate and advise the members of the Church as to substance and procedures of church law and to correct misinformation. Canon 5 of that code of ethics emphasizes our responsibilities as educators to advise the parties as to their rights and remedies under the law, to advise the ordinary on canonical matters, to educate and supervise canon law practitioners who are not professionally trained, to advise practical ministers on the rights of persons and church administration, and finally, to raise the consciousness of people in possible areas of injustice and inequitable practice.

It is essential that the canonist have deeply ingrained a "new habit of mind," that we be both educators and critics. The Scripture says if we have the key of knowledge, we must open the door for others and enter in ourselves. We have an obligation for continuing education not only in law and jurisprudence, but, as our code of ethics states, we are to deepen our appreciation of the real mysteries. Compassion without competence is a cruel hoax. We are to have substantive background of Sacred Scripture, and ecclesiology, and church history. John Paul's triangle of Scripture, Vatican II, and the code seems to me to be the challenge for every canonist. *Sacrae disciplinae leges* implies that our legal tradition goes far beyond Justinian. It goes back to the Old Testament. I am wondering if the Church would have been different had canon lawyers studied the Torah, the Mishnah, the Tosefta, and the Talmuds, as well as we discussed and studied the Constitutions, Institutes, Pandects, and the Novellae of Justinian.

We do have some special education problems. John XXIII mentioned that the gospel is unchanging, but is contained in a changeable envelope. Those of us who have been popularizers, preachers, educators realize the danger inherent in teaching truth in language people do not understand. We could even produce heresy in people's minds by explaining the truth in outmoded language. The word "annulment" is one example. Our canonical annulment does not have civil implications. By our canonical annulment we are not saying that marriage is a nothing. We are, in fact, ordered by the new code to place in our sentences a *monitum* (canon 1689) regarding the obligations arising from the previous marriage toward the spouse and toward the children. People from a previous marriage, even a null one, must have permission of the bishop to remarry if there are outstanding obligations to that previous union. The children are not illegitimate. The life together is not erased and forgotten. The civil contract is not touched. It is not null and it is not void except in certain jurisdictions where there is a noncordat. Out West forty per cent of our cases are between two non-Catholics, and well over fifty to sixty per cent of our respondents are non-Catholics. When we say that we have granted an annulment from the marriage, we are creating a tremendous piece of misinformation in their minds. The study that we have voted for this year on "languaging" annulments is pastorally important.

My concern about the words we use has led me to an unpopular opinion. It seems to me that defect of form cases need to be handled now by the special documentary process rather than by the administrative process of *Provida Mater.* The reason is that it seems to me no longer tenable to hold that a marriage outside the Church lacks any *species matrimonii.* This is contrary to the ecumenical thrust of the Second Vatican Council, contrary to the sense that a marriage outside the Church founds ethical and, of course, legal obligations. And finally, if it is possible now for some Catholics to marry validly outside the Church if by a formal act they have rejected Catholicism, then we have to raise the question of the presumption in favor of marriage, even in those situations. It seems to me, for these and for other reasons, the Church is asking us to adjudicate marriages outside of the Catholic Church as putative marriages which need to be proven null and which need to be presumed valid until proven null. I realize, however, that this is a very unpopular opinion because of the amount of paper work it is going to involve.

There are a lot of other examples where our law has only analogical relationship to civil law terms. Our concept of a juridic person is far different from the civil law concept of a corporation. Our concept of the ownership of church property is far different.

Sanctifying Office

Without appearing maudlin or overly pious, I would like to talk about the *sanctifying office* of the canonist. Here, too, the priesthood is a very analogical term from the Second Vatican Council. The document *Lumen gentium,* no. 10, reminds us that the word "priesthood" has three different levels of meaning: the one *priesthood* of Christ, the common *priesthood* of all the faithful, and the ministerial *priesthood.* The common priesthood and the ministerial priesthood are essentially different, not only in degree, and are ordered to one another such that the ministerial priesthood is to equip the saints for their ministry. In an earlier age priesthood was thought of as a univocal word. Martin Luther in his *Babylonian Captivity* said that all the laity are priests, and the ordained have no other powers than that which the laity have by baptism. For Martin Luther the lay priesthood was a univocal term. The Tridentine church, at least in the popular mind, reacted against that by talking about the priesthood of the ordained and refusing to use the expression "lay priesthood."

You will notice in the Second Vatican Council and in the code the relationship is not between the lay priesthood and the ordained priesthood, but between the common priesthood of all of us and, within that, the ministerial priesthood. In times of anger such as the time of the Reformation, univocal language divided us. In this ecumenical Second Vatican Council, analogous language is tending to unite us.

On the other hand, many of us have noticed in the past years a blurring of the distinction, at least on a practical level, between the ministerial priesthood and the common priesthood. Although there are debates among ecclesiologists and theologians as to the "essential difference," it is clear as canonists that there is a very distinct juridic difference. The office of pastor is an analogical term. It includes the pope, the bishop, and the parish priest, and in the code is restricted to the ministerial priesthood.

Canon 210 reminds all of us of our obligation to live a holy life, and canon 214, of our right to follow our own spirituality. What is the spirituality of the church lawyer? Our code of ethics talks about the ethical component. James Coriden, in his masterful article on interpretation, discusses the virtues of prudence, equity, epikeia, and oikonomia. Rule number 3 on the principles of reform of law from the 1967 Synod of Bishops mentions the virtues of justice, charity, temperence, humanity, and moderation. Our code of ethics says a church lawyer is a person fully committed to Christ and His Church, open to the Holy Spirit, seeking to grow in Christian virtue, marked by a zeal for justice, by integrity in the pursuit of justice, foreswearing self-interest and egotistical ambition, a person of compassion, emotional balance, and sound judgment.

The spirituality of the code is a liturgical piety, as we used to say. But it is a deeper liturgical piety even than that of Abbot Marmion and Louis Bouyer, the heroes of my seminary training. The liturgical-piety proposed by the code is a profoundly ecclesial piety. If you look at the seven definitions of the sacraments in the new code, you will see that they are based on, and quote specifically from, number 11 of *Lumen gentium.*

The Church in canon 834 fulfills its office of sanctifying especially in the sacred liturgy, the exercise of the priestly office of Christ. Liturgical actions are not private actions, but celebrations of the Church itself. The code quotes that audacious language of the Second Vatican Council, "The Church is a sacrament itself, a holy people."

When I was young, we were told in the seminary to imitate what you hand on. It seems therefore that the ecclesial and liturgical piety of the code must be essential to a canonist. Canon 731 of the 1917 code merely referred to the sacraments as means of sanctification and salvation. Canon 840 of our code describes them as actions of Christ and the Church. They express and strengthen faith. They provide worship of God, sanctification of the human person, and strengthen, establish, and manifest ecclesial communion.

In the 1917 code baptism was described as the gate of the sacraments. The new code, in canon 849, describes the effects of the sacrament of baptism as regenerating us as sons and daughters of God, configuring us to Christ, and incorporating us into the Church. The ecclesial dimension of confirmation is clear in canon 879, where the baptized continue our journey of Christian initiation and are bound more perfectly to the Church. The Eucharist in canon 897 is the sacrament by which the Church constantly lives and grows. The Eucharistic Sacrifice signifies and reflects the unity of the people of God and builds the Body of Christ. The Eucharistic celebration in canon 899 is an action of Christ and the Church. In the Eucharistic Assembly the people of God or the Church is convoked.

The canon on penance defines the sacrament of penance as reconciling, not only forgiving our sins, but reconciling us with the Church, wounded by sin (canon 595). Anointing of the sick is defined as a sacrament in which the Church commends the dangerously ill to the suffering and glorified Lord (canon 998). The sacrament of orders is defined as a sacrament whereby the ordained shepherd the people of God (canon 100).

The ecclesial dimension of marriage is mentioned in several places. Canon 226, § 1, states that lay persons who live in the married state are bound by a special duty to work for the up-building of the people of God through their marriage and their family. Canon 1063, § 3, states that the fruitful liturgical celebration of marriage should clarify to the spouses that they share in that mystery of unity and faithful love that exists between Christ and the Church.

All of the above references to the ecclesial dimension of the sacraments are quotations from *Lumen gentium,* no. 11 on the "sacred nature and organic structure of the priestly community."

Besides the liturgical piety, which is profoundly ecclesial in the new code, there is another aspect of canonical spirituality. Canon 839 says the Church carries out the office of sanctification in other ways than by liturgical action: by prayer, by penance, and by works of charity, which help to root and strengthen the kingdom of God in souls—quoting, I would suspect, from Matthew, chapter 6, on prayer, fasting, and alms. The Jewish word for alms is *Tzedakah,* which means justice. It seems therefore to me that the two-fold dimension of the canonist's spirituality includes that ecclesial, sacramental, liturgical piety of the code, but also love, or works of love, which is also justice. In the "Ethics of the Father," in the Mishnah, Simon the Just, one of the last surviving members of the Great Assembly says, "The world is founded on three things: on the Torah, on Liturgy, and on the practice of Covenant love, the practice of charity."

This emphasis on charity, justice and peace in the new code reflects the teachings of the Second Vatican Council. The Second Vatican Council reminds us that the purpose of the Church is the kingdom, and it quotes from the preface of Christ the King where the kingdom is described as a kingdom of justice, of compassion, and of peace. The Second Vatican Council reminds us of the six rules for charity:

1. We must see in our neighbor the image of God and Christ the Lord to whom is really offered all that is given to the needy. When I was an assistant, I lived with a priest who really believed that the next poor person at the front door might well be Christ. He used to give the poor people food, money, his own clothing, his own shoes, my clothing, my shoes.

2. The Second Vatican Council reminds us further that the giver of charity is to respect the liberty and the dignity of the person helped.

3. Purity of intention requires the absence of self-seeking; the demands of justice must first be satisfied.

4. That which is due in justice is not to be offered as a gift.

5. The cause of evils, not merely the symptoms, must be eradicated.

6. The beneficiary is to be free from dependence.

Canon Law, although not as profoundly as one would like, reflects this teaching of the Second Vatican Council. Canon 222 describes the ubiquitous obligation of the members of the Church to support the Church for purposes of divine worship, decent support of ministry, and works of the apostolate and charity. Pope John Paul II added to canon 222 two additional obligations. All the Christian faithful are obliged to promote social justice, and to assist the poor from their own resources as the Lord commands.

Clerics in canon 282 are required to cultivate a simple life style and to donate our superfluous money for the good of the Church and for works of charity. The parish priest, in canon 529, is to have a special concern for the poor, the afflicted, the lonely, the exiled. Canon 676 says that lay religious institutes of consecrated life fulfill their pastoral office in the Church by the spiritual and corporal works of mercy.

The code goes beyond the mere giving of charity. It talks about social justice and the social order. Canon 225 states that the laity are obliged to transform the social order in the spirit of the gospel. Canon 298, § 1, says that associations of the Christian faithful have seven purposes, among which are the works of charity, the exercise of the apostolate, and animating the social order with a Christian spirit. Canon 327 says the laity are to value such organizations, especially those which intend to animate the social order with a Christian spirit. The clergy are to foster, in canon 287, that peace and harmony based on justice. Pastors, in canon 528, § 1, have among our prophetic obligations to encourage programs by which the spirit of the gospel with special reference to social justice is promoted. Canon 747, § 2, says the Church vindicates the right to preach moral principles of the social order and the fundamental rights of the human person. Canon 768, § 2, says that preachers are to teach the dignity and freedom of the human person, the social obligations of the human person, and the ordering of the social order according to God's plan.

Canonists must have not only a liturgical and ecclesial piety, but a commitment to justice, to compassion, and to peace. This is not only a commitment to justice in our own learned society and in our Church, but in the social order. In this day and age, we have many examples of learned societies committed to peace: Physicians and Nurses for Social Responsibility, Educators for Social Responsibility, Psychotherapists, Architects and Planners for Social Responsibility, performing artists for nuclear responsibility, poets for peace, lawyers against nuclear arms. It is time for us to have a group called "church lawyers for social responsibility"?

Royal Office

In the "Ethics of the Fathers" Rabbi Simeon, the son of Gamliel—the great grandson of Gamaliel, mentioned in Acts—says the world is founded on three things: on judgment, on truth, and on peace. I'm going to be very brief about *the royal office* of the canonist. However, I would like to mention that our role extends far beyond the area of serving in courts and serving as administrators. We are interpreters of administrative law, of government in the Church, and one of the important elements in our interpretation in the next few years is our emphasis on consultation as the preferred manner of church government. We have a danger in this country, as Thomas Green pointed out, of using analogies from business, or of using civic and political models in describing church government. We have experimented with boards and with parliaments. We have talked about veto power and decision by majority vote. We have learned parliamentary process and Robert's Rules of Order. It seems to me that the consultative process described in the code brings us to a sense of consensus in the Church. We are people of consensus and consultation. This cannot be merely *pro forma*. People have the right to be heard in the Church. People have a right to information. Charisms in the Church need to be brought to the public order by the consultative process. The issue of consultation is extremely important, not only in chanceries, but even on the levels of school boards and parish councils; it is the canonist's obligation to teach and to implement the whole sense and theory of the consultative process.

It is also important for us to deal with the extension of participation in church government. There are two revolutionary canons in the new code which need interpretation. Canon 274 does say that only the ordained clergy are eligible for offices requiring the power of orders. But canon 129 says that the Christian laity may cooperate in the exercise of the power of government. The meaning of that canon and its extension in the years to come will be important. Canon 150 says that only ordained priests are eligible for offices involving the full care of souls and the exercise of priestly order. But canon 517, § 2, says that deacons and lay persons can participate in the exercise of pastoral care. The implementation of those two canons needs to be extended and taught by canon lawyers.

RIGHTS AND OBLIGATIONS

Rights and *obligations* are again words that are part of our tool box. Alexander Hamilton said that "the sacred rights of mankind are not to be rummaged from old parchments or musty records. They are written by the hands of divinity itself, and can never be erased or obscured by mortal power." Robert E. Lee said that "duty is the sublimest word in our language. Do your duty in all things. You cannot do more; you should never do less."

Rights and duties can be powerful words. But in teaching canon law I have heard many people, particularly in lay groups, after I described the rights and duties of the laity in the code, say "that is not true." "People are not dealt with as equals in the Church." It is important, I think, as canonists in the years to come, to fill out these empty words by making them true. We have in our founding documents of the United States the famous statement: "All men are created equal, and are endowed by their Creator with certain inalienable rights." When that was written, it really meant all men, not women. It meant Anglo-Saxon, not native American or Black. It meant Anglo-Saxon Protestants, not Catholic, immigrant, or Jew. It meant aristocrat, not poor and the propertyless. It has taken us 200 years to fill out the empty words of that founding statement, "All men are created equal," and it still has not been fleshed out completely in our country. And so the eighteen rights and freedoms, the "Bill of Rights," mentioned in our new code are words that have to be filled out by canonists. They are criteria for decision-making. You have to be sure that there are conditions, real conditions for the exercise of these rights. These are tasks to be achieved by the canon lawyer.

THE CHURCH AS PEOPLE OF GOD AND *COMMUNIO*

Richard McBriden, a major speaker of one of our previous conventions, reminded us that the role of law in the Church is to reflect our ecclesiology and to provide an instrument for mission. The two words from *Sacrae disciplinae leges,* "people of God" and *"communio,"* reflect the over-arching ecclesiology of the Second Vatican Council.

"Church" in *Lumen gentium* is an analogical concept.

The Church of Christ is described in canon 204, § 1: "The Christian faithful are . . . incorporated in Christ through baptism . . . and constituted as the People of God." Canon 96 states, "By baptism one is incorporated into the Church of Christ and is constituted a person in it with duties and rights which are proper to Christians." Canon 204, § 2, goes on to say that this Church subsists in the Catholic Church. This universal Catholic Church is the first meaning of the word "church."

Canons 368 and 369 describe the particular church and especially the diocese as a portion of the people of God entrusted for pastoral care to a bishop with his presbyters gathered in the Holy Spirit through the gospel and the Eucharist in which the one, holy and Catholic and apostolic Church of Christ is truly operative. The particular church is in a sense conceptually prior to the universal Church. The universal Church is a *communio* of churches.

Finally, canon 515 describes the "parish church" as a stable community of the faithful in a particular church entrusted to a parish priest for pastoral care under the authority of the bishop.

These definitions are a far cry from the pre-Vatican II ecclesiology which at least on the popular level thought of the Catholic Church merely as the universal church; the diocese and parish were basically territorial divisions.

This sacramental view of churches is balanced by the concept of *communio* in the new code. Ecclesial communion is also an analogical term and is threefold.

Canon 205 defines full communion as the bond of profession of faith, communion in the sacraments and communion in ecclesiastical governance. Canon 209, § 1, states the fundamental obligation of all the Christian faithful always to maintain communion with the Church. Canon 392, § 1, states a fundamental obligation of the diocesan bishop to protect the unity of the universal Church. Canon 529, § 2, reminds the parish priest to see that members of his congregation have a concern for parochial communion as well as a sense of membership in the particular church and the universal Church. Canon 840 states that sacraments as actions of Christ and the Church establish, strengthen, and manifest ecclesial *communion.*

Besides ecclesial communion among the baptized, hierarchic communion among the bishops is also defined in the code. For example, canon 336 describes the college of bishops with the Supreme Pontiff at the head and whose members are bishops by virtue not only of sacramental consecration, but also by their hierarchic *communion* with head and other members.

Finally, canon 206 describes catechumens as not incorporated into the Church and therefore not yet in full communion, but still having a special union with the Church. They are incorporated into the Church *in voto* as it were and are united to the Church by their lives of faith, hope and charity.

For the canonist, then, our church order is both sacramental (based on the indelible sacraments of initiation and orders) and communal (based on the commitment of faith and the bond of love). Although we recognize competing ecclesiologies on both the academic and operative levels, we have the task as canonists of teaching and implementing this Vatican II ecclesiology as reflected in our canon law.

First, our church order is clearly an episcopal church order. The new Code of Canon Law does not define a congregational church order. Our churches have a covenant relationship with one another; but they have far more than a *mere* covenant relationship, or *communio* of faith. *Communio* is important, but it is founded on a sacramental relationship based on initiation on the one hand and ministerial priesthood on the other.

Second, the covenant relationship, the *communio,* is itself a "novitas" of the Second Vatican Council referred to in *Sacrae disciplinae leges.* The implications of *communio* need to be spelled out in our church government, and in our relations with churches not in full communion with the Catholic Church and which have a stronger emphasis on congregational forms of church government.

As canonists, therefore, we must be people who appreciate the sacramental foundation of our church order, its episcopal structure and the importance of *communio* as the fundamental obligation, both of the faithful and the hierarchy.

The importance of ecumenism for the canonist cannot be measured merely by the number of canons in which ecumenism is mentioned. Canon 755 describes the responsibility of the episcopal college, the Apostolic See, the episcopal conference and bishops themselves for Catholic participation in the ecumenical movement. Canon 383 describes the particular obligation of the diocesan bishop. Canon 844 is the famous canon on reception of the sacraments of penance, Communion and anointing of the sick by Catholics in non-Catholic churches, and by non-Catholics in the Catholic Church. Canons 1124 through 1129 are the law on mixed marriages. In canon 463 ministers, or members of non-Catholic church communities, may be invited to participate in Catholic synods and in canon 874, § 2, non-Catholics may be chosen as baptismal witnesses.

The commitment to ecumenism is mentioned in *Sacrae disciplinae leges* as essential to the *novitas* of Vatican II, and, therefore, to the new habit of mind of the modern canonist.

Our two patron saints, Raymond of Peñafort and Thomas More, did not live in ecumenical ages but in their own way, and according to their own lights, they were ecumenists. They shared a wider vision and interest than mere Catholic canon law.

Raymond of Peñafort, as we were reminded by Professor Brundage, collected the *Liber Extra* of Gregory IX and is known for his major contribution to the Corpus. He also is known for his *summa* or moral theology for confessors. But he is not known as well for his interest in the new science of Aristotle and the studies of the Moslem scholars. Raymond of Peñafort inaugurated a school of Arabic studies and persuaded Thomas Aquinas to write the *Summa Contra Gentiles.*

Thomas More lived during the Lutheran Reformation. He died thirty years before the conclusion of Trent. He was an expert canon lawyer as well as a civil lawyer. He was lay chancellor for two and a half years, and during that time gave four thousand decisions. When he resigned, there was no backlog in the chancery court. But he was also more than a canonist. The world was awash at that time with the religious reform of Luther and Calvin, and the new humanism of Erasmus. Thomas More was a deep friend of Erasmus and the humanists. So, it seems to me that our concern for *communio* in the Church involves also an obligation to be concerned about ecumensim.

AUTHORITY AS SERVICE

I would like to end with a final word about authority as service. Service, too, is an analogical word in Vatican II and the code. Christ is the servant, the *Ebed Adonai,* the suffering servant. The Church itself is a serving Church or minister or deacon. The authority of the Church is described in *Sacrae disciplinae leges* as service. When speaking around the country, someone always raises his hand at the end of the talk and says, "But why is this concept considered new? Haven't we always taught that authority is service?" How quickly we forget! How quickly we forget the critique of triumphalism, clericalism and ambition at the time of Vatican II. How quickly have we forgotten the legalistic burdens that manual moral theology and canon law placed on people. How quickly we have forgotten the abuses of authority in a Church run by personal whim, suspension by screaming at people, etc.

To repeat the challenge of Professor Brundage, the canonist has to make real the words "authority is service." We have to implement canon 1733 on conciliation and arbitration. We have to write a commentary on the thorny areas of administrative recourse. I am in favor of that study which we approved regarding national and regional administrative tribunals. Perhaps we even ought to investigate the possibility of chancery courts. Perhaps Professor Brundage, as Dr. Coriden suggested, is a bit romantic in suggesting that we can have parallel court systems. Nevertheless, we are going to have to develop some kind of administrative jurisprudence. When Paul in I Corinthians says: "Is there not a wise man among you, no one that shall be able to judge between the brothers? The brother goes to law with brother, and that before the unbeliever." I suspect that Paul had in mind decisions based on the jurisprudence of the Torah and the Mishnah.

IN CONCLUSION

The canonist is a servant of the Church. Our pastoral frustration is essential to being a good canonist. I think it was the frustration of canonists that brought about the American Procedural Norms. It was the frustration of canonists that brought about our reflection on the informal or internal forum solution. It is the frustration of people today in the Church that is going to bring about better personnel policies and administrative procedures. I am constantly reminded again and again in talking throughout the United States of the anger and the pain of women regarding issues of canon law. In fact I often have to tell people that I did not write this book, I am only explaining it.

This suffering or pain of the canonist, this frustration of the canonist, is important for our continuing creative evaluation and interpretation of the code. We are going to have to enter coalitions not only with academic societies, but with all the other pastoral organizations that are on the cutting edge of renewal in the Church today: people in the RCIA, liturgists, vocation directors, personnel directors, the planners, and ecclesiologists.

The final virtue of the canonist, it seems to me, is humility. Canon law is nothing more than words. It is nothing more than a reflection of ecclesiology and a tool or instrument for mission. It is the art of naming rights and obligations, relations and institutions, offices and procedures. Canon law is not God. We are annually haunted by the Lectionary in this Society. Every year when we meet, we are asked to read from Romans and from Luke.

Romans in the first three chapters reminds us that the Gentiles lacked the Torah, but nevertheless are condemned for failing to find God because the Torah is also written in nature. The Jews had the Torah, but failed to return to God, whose will is known in the Torah. And so the true Torah is the Torah of faith. The true Torah is faith in God, the God of both Jews and Gentiles. Our justice comes from faith, not from law.

On Thursday of this week we are reminded in chapter eleven of Luke's Gospel, "Oh you [canon] lawyers, you load upon men burdens that are unendurable, burdens that you yourselves do not move a finger to lift. Oh you [canon] lawyers, you have taken away the key of knowledge. You have not gone in yourselves and have prevented others going in who want to."

Our challenge is to be creative interpreters and implementers of the law. We cannot leave the law as merely empty and sterile words. The code is a book of words that have to be filled in. We have to flesh out these words by deeds of covenant love, as Simon the Just suggests—or by justice, truth, and peace, as Simon the son of Gamaliel teaches. Our role as a canonist is to be a teacher and interpreter of the words of this code.

The words of the code cannot remain merely empty words. The canonist should never hear that melancholy reflection at the end of Umberto Eco's marvelous book, *The Name of the Rose:* "Stat rosa pristina nomine; nomina nuda tenemus." "The original rose is what the name *rose* refers to—but all we have are empty names." The Church is named in our code; let no one accuse us of teaching empty names.

LAWS AND NON-LAWS

JAMES A. CORIDEN

Pope Paul VI on more than one occasion[1] asked of canonists a *novus habitus mentis* with regard to the revised code and its application in the Church. It is important to reflect on the meaning of that expression which has by now become almost a slogan. It means more than a changed attitude (e.g., positive rather than negative, diaconal rather than triumphalist) or a different point of view (like the different visions of the city of San Francisco from the Bay Bridge and from the Golden Gate). A *habitus mentis* is a basic mindset, the cluster of in-grained dispositions and acquired skills which guide persons in their life or work, like a doctor's medical knowledge and professional experience which combine in the healing art, or an experienced architect's sense of balance and design and use of materials. A *habitus mentis* is the kind of radical orientation that conditions a person's whole approach to and accomplishment of a task.

What did Pope Paul mean by *novus*, a different mindset? He gave many indications in his several addresses on canonical issues.[2] And his stimulating words have led to a veritable flood of canonical writing, especialy in the last decade, on the nature of canon law.[3] These several studies on the distinctive character

---

[1]E.g., on November 20, 1965 (*AAS* 57 [1965] 988), and on December 14, 1973 (*AAS* 66 [1974] 10).

[2]Confer F. Morrisey, "The Spirit of Canon Law and the Teachings of Pope Paul VI," *Origins* 8(1978)34-40, and J. Beyer, "Significato e funzione del diritto canonico. Il Pensiero de Paulo VI," *Vita Consecrata* 12(1982)421-427. See also F.X. Urrutia, "De Natura Legis Ecclesiasticae," *Monitor Ecclesiasticus* 100(1975)401-402.

[3]F.X. Urrutia, "De Natura Legis Ecclesiasticae," *Monitor Ecclesiasticus* 100(1975)400-419; G. Ghirlanda, "Il diritto civile 'analogatum princeps' del diritto canonico?" *Rassegna de Teologia* 16(1975)588-594; F. Retamal, "Derecho y pastoral en la Iglesia," *Ius Canonicum* 15/2(1975)43-78; J. Passicos, "Quel droit pour quelle église; quelques questions fondametales pour un nouveau temps de réformes," *Année Canonique* 21(1977)19-37; K. Mörsdorf, "Kanonische Recht als theologische Disziplin," *Archiv für katholisches Kirchenrecht* 145(1976)45-58; K. Demmer, "Ius Ecclesiae—Ius Gratiae; Animadversiones ad Relationem inter Ius Canonicum et Ethos Christianum," *Periodica* 66(1977)5-46; the following papers from the International Congress held at the Gregorian University in February, 1977, which appeared in *Periodica* 66(1977): F. Coccopalmerio, "De conceptu et natura iuris Ecclesiae animadversiones quaedam," 447-474; A. de la Hera, "Liquet Ius Canonicum esse Ius Sacrum prorsus distinctum a iure civile," 475-497; H. Müller, "De analogia Verbum Incarnatum inter et Ecclesiam (L.G. 8)," 500-512; L. Vela, "De conceptu specifico legis ecclesiasticae," 521-533; G. Fransen, "De analogia legis apud canonistas," 535-547; W. Bertrams, "De natura iuris Ecclesiae proprii notanda," 567-582; P. Bonnet, "Eucharistia et Ius," 583-616; G. Ghirlanda, "De caritate ut elemento iuridico fundamentali constitutivo iuris ecclesialis," 621-655; R. Sobański, "De theologicis et sociologicis praemissis theoriae iuris ecclesialis elaborandae," 657-681; F. Vera Urbano, "De natura iuris canonici," 683-704; see also E. Corecco, "Ordinatio Rationis ou Ordinatio Fidei," *Communio* 6(1977)1-22; V. de Paolis, "Ius: notio univoca an analoga?" *Periodica* 69(1980)127-161; P. Garin, "Hacia una teologia del derecho canonico," *Estudios Ecclesiasticos*(1981)1433-1450; R. Kenyon, "A Concept of Ecclesial Law," *Studia Canonica* 15(1981)399-417; P. Huizing, "Reflections on the System of Canon Law," *The Jurist* 42(1982)239-276.

of law in the Church were not the result of a massive identity crisis among canonists, nor were they attempts to influence the revision of the code. They were in response to the challenge of Paul VI which is epitomized in his call for a new mindset.

The pope himself gave at least a partial description of the *novus habitus* in two passages which are frequently cited in the various writings of the canonists:

> The council...has plumbed the depths of the doctrine of the Church and has thrown into sharp relief the mystical aspect which is proper to it; therefore it has obliged the canonist to search more profoundly in Sacred Scripture and in theology for the bases of his (her) own teaching.[4]

He went on to contrast this theological quest with the secular bases, Roman law in particular, upon which canonists have long been accustomed to rest their reasoning. It is in the mysterious constitution of the Church itself that the pope asked canonists to look for the why and the how ("il perché e il come") of the ancient and renewed canonical discipline.

Later, in even stronger language, the pope spoke of the need to ground canon law in the theology of the Church, especially viewed as communion and as sacrament.

> Canon law after the Council cannot fail to be ever more closely related to theology and the other sacred sciences, because it too is a sacred science; certainly it is not that "practical art," as some people would wish, whose task would only be to clothe in juridical formulas the theological and pastoral conclusions pertinent to it.[5]

He went on to conclude:

> To limit the law of the Church to a rigid order of injunctions would be to do violence to the Spirit who leads us towards perfect love in the unity of the Church. Your first concern, therefore, shall not be to establish a juridical order modelled purely on civil law, but to plumb the depths of the work of the Spirit which must be expressed in the law of the Church.[6]

One of the characteristics, therefore, of our *novus habitus mentis* is that we are to scrutinize the nature and mission of the Church for the contours and direction of our discipline, rather than looking to parallel places in civil systems, whether ancient or modern. This attempt on the part of Pope Paul VI to return or redirect canonical thinking from civil sources to ecclesiological ones led into the great debate about the nature of church law which has caused the spilling of so much ink in the past decade. The literature makes fascinating reading for canonical theorists, and it leads me to posit three propositions:

[4]January 20, 1970 (*AAS* 62[1970]108-109; *The Pope Speaks* 15[1970]72).
[5]September 17, 1973 (*The Pope Speaks* 18[1973]276).
[6]September 17, 1973 (*Communicationes* 5[1973]131; *The Pope Speaks* 18[1973]283).

1. concerning the nature of law in the Church: it is so distinctive as to be law only in an analogical sense;

2. the structures and terminilogy which the 1983 code gives to the various forms of rules for church discipline do not reflect the analogy, instead they retain a purely secular or civil cast;

3. about the jurisdiction of the teaching function in the Church: the distinction between teaching and governing needs reassertion.

I. THE NATURE OF LAW IN THE CHURCH

The relationship between law in the context of Church and law in the context of civil society is not univocal but analogical.[7] Univocity means that the term has the same meaning in both settings; analogy means that the meaning of the word is partially the same and partially different. Civil society provides the primary analogate of a legal system, and when transferred to the ecclesial context it takes on a meaning that is more unlike than like civil law, a major dissimilitude. The meaning of law and legislation, while somewhat the same, is so diverse in the setting of the Church that the analogy is strained and stretched quite thin.

What is the import of this rather philosophical observation? Does this theoretical claim about legal terminology really make any difference? Before going on to consider the arguments in support of the assertion, it might help to reflect on the negative results of using legal terminology inappropriately in the Church. Such expressions as "canon law," "legislative authority," "decree," "juridical order," and the like are used commonly and casually for rules and rule-making in our Church. If these descriptive terms are not accurate, that is, if the realities to which they point are actually quite different from what the words imply, then they not only convey a false impression but they can lead to a serious distortion in the identity of the community and the way it functions. Those who engage in the Church's "legal activity" can misperceive what they are about, and those within and outside the Church can receive a wrong impression about the nature of this community of faith and the quality of the relationships within it.

"Law" is a serious and heavy concept in our culture. Michael Himes spoke to the CLSA convention last year about the attitudes, sometimes paradoxical, which North Americans have toward the law.[8] The word evokes the grave categories of obligation and punishment. "Legislation" is what happens in Congress or in state or provincial legislatures. "Decrees," on the other hand, call to mind emperors and kings; we associate decrees with Caesar Augustus. Language is a critical matter; the labels and terms we employ have profound and pervasive effects, far deeper than their ephemeral and fleeting impressions.

[7]Virtually all of the authors cited in footnote 3 above are in basic agreement with this conclusion; it is only fair to add that they approach the question from very different directions and variously qualify their agreement.

[8]M. Himes, "Reflections on American Attitude Toward Law," *CLSA Proceedings* 44(1982)63-92.

The Roman Catholic Church has been faulted, from within and without, for its exaggerated use of judicial structures and titles since well before the Reformation. It was a calculated symbolic gesture on Martin Luther's part to consign the *Corpus Iuris Canonici* to the bonfire as a part of his protest.[9] Catherine of Siena voiced similar criticisms to the Avignon popes in the late fourteenth century.[10] The retention of procedures and nomenclature derived directly from civil law sources continues to be an ecumenical obstacle today. Even more unfortunate is the ministerial and pastoral confusion engendered by the use of legal labels, as, for example, in marriage as a *contract*, penance as a *judicial act*, the cardinals as a *senate*, the Mass offering as a *stipend*, or the *precept* to receive Holy Communion.[11]

So much for the negative fall-out, the mistaken impressions. Now to the argument. Canon law is law only by analogy; it is far more unlike civil law than it resembles it.[12] It is easy to state the similarities: both Church and state are visible, human societies with the need for orderly procedures and recognized structures. It can be summarized this way: *ubi societas, ibi ius;*[13] wherever people are thrust together there are relationships involving rights and obligations. These are basic and undeniable facts. But the arguments for the *major dissimilitudo* of rules in the Church, which lead to the conclusion that these rules are laws by analogy only, fall into several categories.

a. The Church is a radically different kind of community than the state. Theologically the Church is a mystery, "a reality imbued with the hidden presence of God";[14] it is the temple of the Holy Spirit, resplendent with the gifts of the Spirit; it is the sacrament of Christ, the visible and effective sign of His saving work in the world; it is a communion, a unique relationship with God and among its members based on faith in a revealed God. In sum, the Church is a society *sui generis*, unique, *toto caelo* different from the state— different in origins, different in history, different in identity and inner dynamic, and different in destiny.

[9]J. Pelikan, *Spirit Versus Structure: Luther and the Institutions of the Church* (New York: Harper & Row, 1968), pp. 1, 20-24.

[10]For an overview see K.A. Fink, "The Curia at Avignon," in *History of the Church, Vol. IV: From the High Middle Ages to the Eve of the Reformation* (New York: Seabury, 1980), pp. 333-344.

[11]The Church's judicial apparatus is another anachronism with questionable pastoral implications; it is used almost exclusively for the determination of the nullity of marriages. Even though our "marriage tribunals" employ procedures which resemble courts of law, they are really pastoral instruments for the reconciliation to the Church of those who have experienced more than one marital relationship. Both the procedures and the nomenclature used actually impede the attainment of the pastoral purpose.

[12]Pope Paul VI declared on two occasions, "...liquet ius canonicum esse ius sacrum prorsus distinctum a iure civili." December 13, 1972 (*AAS* 64[1972]781) and January 22, 1973 (*AAS* 65[1973]96). And on January 28, 1971 the same pope stated that the power of jurisdiction in the church is "solo analogicamente simile a quelle di origine umana" (*AAS* 63[1971]138).

[13]Urrutia, "De Natura Legis Ecclesiasticae," pp. 404ss; de Paolis, "Ius: Notio univoca," pp. 146-171.

[14]R. McBrien, "A Theologian Looks at the Role of Law in the Church Today," *CLSA Proceedings* 43(1981)23.

b. Rules or obligatory norms have a different purpose in the Church. In addition to the basic need for peace and order and the safeguarding of personal rights (which are purposes of any legal order), the Church's regulations have a transcendant purpose which must never be lost sight of: the spiritual good of its members, their ultimate salvation, their communion with or reconciliation to God. The Church's discipline must be concerned with virtue and not simply external behavior for it is an instrument of salvation in service to the Holy Spirit.[15] *Salus animarum suprema lex* cannot be said of civil law; the law of the state aims at justice, but the Church's rules must strive on toward love.

c. The sources of authority are different in the Church. The political theories which attempt to explain the origins of civil authority include the natural rights of the citizens, some kind of social contract, and the divine right of kings. In the Church all power is dependent on the faith of the community. Our faith sees authority derived from the power of the Risen Christ and authenticated by the claims of apostolic succession (or at least a substantial continuity) and by the guidance of the Holy Spirit. The believing community was convinced from its earliest years of being actively directed by the Spirit of Christ.[16]

d. Canon law is a different discipline from civil law. Canon law is a theological discipline rather than a juridical one. The order and discipline of the Church is derived, shaped and directed by the truths of revelation and their theological interpretation. It has an entirely different warrant and basis from any civil or secular legal system, whether Roman, Germanic, modern European or Anglo-American. Canonists use theological starting points and reasoning—revelation, tradition, church teaching, theology—rather than legal philosophy or jurisprudence. Ours is a theological discipline. Canonists are engaged in a specialization within ministry, not within the practice of law.

e. The Church is a voluntary association, and the modern secular state is not. Sociologically ecclesial communities are described as among those "bodies of people who have voluntarily organized themselves in pursuit of particular goals."[17] The internal regulations of a voluntary association are vastly different from those of a sovereign state simply because a person is joined to or separated from the group by an act of the will. People must be free to enter the Church (coerced faith is not salvific), and they are free to walk away from it. (*Extra ecclesiam nulla salus* has a highly qualified meaning in our tradition.) The mitigating effect this has on the obligatory force of the Church's rules is obvious, both in theory and in practice.

f. Church law has a different kind of effectiveness, a different level of reality. Civil law violations, whether defiant or negligent, have real and telling ef-

[15]Fransen, "De anologia legis apud canonistas," pp. 541-542. Note the citations from Joannes Andreae about the purpose of canon law being "quaedam coelestis amicitia."

[16]Recall the "Council of Jerusalem" described in Acts 15, and the language of its resolution: "It is the decision of the Holy Spirit, and ours too,..." (Acts 15:28).

[17]P. Berger and R. Neuhaus, *To Empower People* (Washington: Amer. Enter. Inst., 1977), p. 34. Confer D. Robertson, ed., *Voluntary Association: A Study of Groups in Free Societies* (Richmond: John Knox, 1966).

fects. This applies not only to criminal violations, which can result in fines or imprisonment, but also to the disregard of tax laws, contractual language, the formalities of wills and trusts, or even bankruptcy laws—any of these can have drastic, verifiable effects on the transfer of property, personal freedom or employment. In the Church, however, the violation of rules whose observance is termed "necessary for validity" (our most serious category) has a much more ambiguous result. For example:

—alienation of church property without the required permission[18]—the contract is honored, the money spent, the building built and used;

—a marriage entered into with an undetected diriment impediment, i.e., a putative marriage,[19]—the relationship endures and is fruitful, it is grace-filled and even a sign of Christ's love for His Church;

—a pastor appointed by a bishop before he takes possession of the see or by an administrator before the see is vacant for a year[20]—the pastor functions effectively, carries out the teaching, sacramental and pastoral ministries without any hindrance or lack of results;

—a novitiate spent in a house not designated for that purpose or which lasts less than a full year; the subsequent temporary profession is invalid[21]—the person is consecrated to God, lives a life of prayerful witness and mission as a member of the institute;

—a Eucharist celebrated with proper matter and form but, on account of the physical or moral impossibility of their participation, without an ordained priest or bishop[22]—Christ is present, His death and resurrection is commemorated, grace is given, the communion of the faithful is built up.

The radical purpose of each one of these serious religious acts is accomplished in spite of the fact that they all could be judged to be canonically invalid. It illustrates the point that canon laws have a different kind of effectiveness from civil laws, a different level of reality.

The reason it is necessary to point out that church rules are laws only analogously is that our Church has so closely compared its disciplinary system to civil systems, imitated them, borrowed from them, and, as a result, has a church order characterized by an exaggerated juridicism. It has too little in common with an ecclesial communion and too much in common with secular states. Robert Bellarmine wrote that the Church resembled the Republic of Venice externally, and canonists have crafted a legal system which proves his point.[23]

[18]Cc. 1291-1292.
[19]Cc. 1061, § 3 and 1073.
[20]Cc. 382 and 525.
[21]Cc. 647-648 and 656.
[22]Cc. 924 and 900.
[23]Other Christian churches have adopted somewhat less law-like language for their rule books, eg., *The Doctrines and Disciplines of the Methodist Church, The Book of Order of the United Presbyterian Church, The Constitutions and Canons of the Protestant Episcopal Church, The Constitutions and By-Laws of the Lutheran Church in America* (same title for the United Church of Christ), and *A Baptist Manual of Polity and Practice* (which is a privately authored and descriptive publication rather than an official one).

The causes of this "civilization" of the canonical tradition are mostly historical coincidences. The law of the Roman Empire and that of the Germanic tribes influenced the Church strongly in its formative years and early centuries of existence; many direct borrowings are with us still.[24] Later, in the Gregorian Reform, the struggle was with the encroaching secular forces, and one of the battlegrounds was legal.[25] The rediscovery and study of Roman law in the twelfth century proceeded *pari passu* with the development and refinement of canon law.[26] The Church's system had to be technically suited to the elaborate negotiations over benefices and tithes, exemptions and privileges, even finances and armies, because these issues were thrust upon the bishops and popes of the time. Church bureaucracies operated in parallel and interacted with those of the monarchies of Europe.[27] Then, when under attack by the secularizing forces of the Enlightenment, the Church elaborated the theory of the *societas perfecta*, the autonomous society which has all the juridic resources to meet its own needs and pursue its own ends.[28] This vision of the Church reinforced the conscious comparability between ecclesial and civil legal structures.

The concatentation of these largely coincidental historical phases left the Church with a very highly juridicized structure and disciplinary language much of which was developed in deliberate imitation of the civilists. The Church's resort to a codified system of law at the beginning of this century was admittedly an admiring imitation of the system of juridical abstraction which ruled France, Switzerland, Germany and Italy at the time.[29] And even now in the 1983 revision the same tendancy is evident. In the discussion of the *Lex Ecclesiae Fundamentalis* in the *coetus* of the Commission comparisons were made to the Magna Carta and to the constitutions of the United States and of Australia.[30] The tripartite division of the *potestas regiminis* into legislative, executive and judicial authorities is in conscious imitation of the separation of powers language used by modern secular governments.

The renewed ecclesiology of the Second Vatican Council has enabled us to see clearly the excessive incursions of the civilists.[31] The Council's teaching on the nature and mission of the Church permits us to detect the distortions which have resulted from over-juridicizing the relationships within the Church. It is incumbent upon today's canonists to carry on the renewing work of the Council; we must describe and treat those relationships appropriately, and not allow the subtle influence of the new code's secular legal language to lull us into an

[24]E.g., titles like *pontifex* and *diocese*, parishes described as *benefices*, the *incardination* process for *clerics*.

[25]E.g., the extravagant claims in the *Dictatus Papae* (a. 1075) of Gregory VII, for example, that the pope could depose emperors.

[26]A. Van Hove, *Prolegomena* (Mechlin.: Desclee, 1945) pp. 235-242, 461-466, 523-528.

[27]E.g., confer J. Brundage, "Canon Law as an Instrument for Ecclesial Renewal: An Historic Perspective," in this volume. He notes that the post-Tridentine Roman Curia was modelled on contemporary European monarchical bureaucracies.

[28]A. Ottaviani, *Institutiones Iuris Publici Ecclesiastici*, vol. I, (Vatican, 1947), pp. 33-389.

[29]S. Kuttner, "The Code of Canon Law in Historical Perspective," *The Jurist* 28(1968)139-140.

[30]*Communicationes* 3(1971)59-60.

[31]Confer P. Huizing, "Reflections on the System of Canon Law," *The Jurist* 42(1982)239-276.

insensitivity about ecclesial realities. We must think through and assert the churchly differences in norms and rules.[32]

II. Structures and Terminology

At the level of practice the renewed code provides a new set of general norms for ecclesiastical laws and similar rules and commands.[33] They can be outlined as follows:

A. Laws and their equivalents:
  1. laws (cc. 7-22)
    —obligatory norms of action
    —given by a person or group possessing legislative authority (c. 135, § 1)
    —for a community capable of receiving laws
  2. customs (cc. 23-28)
    —have the force of law when approved by a legislator
    —by a community capable of receiving laws
  3. general decrees (cc. 29-30)
    —equivalent to laws
    —given by a legislator or by one having executive authority who has been deputed by a legislator
    —for a community competent to receive laws
B. Subordinate and subsidiary norms:
  1. general executory decrees (cc. 31-33)
    —to determine ways in which laws are to be observed or to urge their observance
    —given by a legislator or by one who has executive authority
    —for those who are obliged by the laws
    —issued in directories or as norms for implementation, etc.
  2. instructions (c. 34)
    —to clarify the law and to spell out the ways it is to be observed
    —given by those who have executive authority
    —for the use of and obliging those charged with carrying out the law
C. Administrative acts (cc. 35-93):
    —issued by those having executive authority (except for privileges, which derive from legislative authority)
    —for individuals or communities
    —not to be extended beyond the expressed cases
  1. decrees (cc. 48-58)
    —decisions or provisions made according to law for particular cases
  2. precepts (c. 49)

---

[32]Along the way we might give some attention to our own titles. For example, our society would be more appropriately named the *Catholic Canonical Society of America*, we should describe ourselves as *canonists*, students of *church order*, or engaged in *church administration*, and *The Jurist* should change its name to *The Canonist!*

[33]Cc. 7-95.

86

—decrees which order a person or persons to do or refrain from doing something, especially to observe the law

—oblige only those for whom they are given and in the matter stated, and oblige them everywhere

3. rescripts (cc. 59-75)

—concessions of privileges, dispensations or other favors in response to requests

4. privileges (cc. 76-84)

—favors granted to physical or juridical persons

5. dispensations (cc. 85-93)

—relaxations of the law in particular cases

D. Statutes (c. 94)

—regulations which define the purpose, constitution, governance and operation of aggregates of persons or things; they oblige only members; are treated like laws if issued in virtue of legislative authority

E. Rules of order (c. 95)

—rules for assemblies which define the constitution, leadership and procedures for the gathering; oblige those taking part

F. Constitutions or fundamental codes, other codes (c. 587)

—norms enacted by general or provincial chapters (cc. 631-32) have the effect of laws for the members of religious institutes, and, in the case of clerical institutes of pontifical right can result from legislative authority (c. 596, § 2).

This skeletal summary and overview reveals a set of norms which are probably functional and, beyond that, rather unremarkable.[34] They would have been as well suited to the governance of the Republic of Venice in the sixteenth century as they are for church order in the twentieth. They have no distinctively ecclesial character.

Although this system of legal norms was elaborated carefully, it does not appear to be entirely coherent. There seem to be some distinctions without differences. For example, is there any real difference between laws and general decrees? If there is not, then the non-delegability of legislative authority (c. 135, § 2) is meaningless.[35] However, the minor inconsistencies are not radical, and the norms are usable.

The fact that the *labels*, the legal terms, are borrowed from various civil traditions is a very important reality. I would argue against their use in practice.

[34]For helpful commentaries see G. Michiels, *Normae Generales Iuris Canonici*, vols. I & II (Paris: Desclee, 1949); F. Urrutia, *De Normis Generalibus* (Rome: Gregorian Univ., 1983); L. Orsy on Laws and Customs and J. Risk on Decrees, Instructions and Administrative Acts in the forthcoming *CLSA Commentary* on the 1983 Code.

[35]Another example: it appears mildly anamolous to describe the dispensing power as an exercise of executive authority (c. 85) and to link the granting of privileges to the possession of legislative authority (c. 76).

Instead we ought to use disciplinary language that is either congenial to the nature of the Church and drawn from its own traditions, or that is at least neutral and non-alienating. For example, instead of "laws" or "general decrees," we can use "canons," "regulations," "rules," "norms," "guidelines" or "directions." For "individual decrees" or "precepts" we use letters of appointment, approvals, grants or admonitions. "Statutes" in the code's sense are usually called constitutions and by-laws; "rules of order" is a good rendering of *ordines*. Religious communities possess an abundance of creative imagination with which to devise their own disciplinary nomenclature in place of "fundamental codes" and "other codes."

The terminology we employ for our Church's discipline, though very important, is secondary to results. What matters most is the outcome. In the apostolic constitution (another label in need of revision!) of promulgation John Paul II describes the purpose of the code:

> ...the purpose of the code is not to substitute for faith, grace, charisms and especially charity in the life of the Church or of the Christian faithful. On the contrary its purpose is to create an order in the ecclesial society so that, while giving priority to love, grace and charisms, at the same time their ordered development is facilitated in the life of the ecclesial society as well as in the lives of those who belong to it.[36]

The same test of purpose can be given to particular norms. Do they contribute to the quality of Christian life in the community? Do they facilitate and make effective the mission and witness of the believing community? Are the rules accepted and followed by the people, and do they move them in the right direction?[37]

The making of the rules is key to their effectiveness. That is, in contemplating the prospect of particular legislation the process followed in arriving at and drawing attention to the norms is critical for their wisdom, suitability and acceptance. The better the participation in the rule-making process, the more likely the positive reception and effectiveness of the rules. The principle of consulting the presbyters and people is far more than a pragmatic strategy, it is a theological imperative. It is based on the implications of membership in the Church and the active sharing of all members in its mission. The principle was articulated by St. Cyprian who said that he would do nothing without consulting both presbyters and people;[38] it is embodied in the medieval canonical rule: *quod omnes tangit, ab omnibus approbari debet*.[39] Recent writings have detailed the

[36]*Sacrae disciplinae leges,* p. xi of the 1983 *Codex Iuris Canonici.*

[37]Only then are they serviceable laws in the sense used by L. Orsy, "The Interpretation of Laws: New Variations on an Old Theme," *The Art of Interpretation* (Washington: CLSA, 1982), p. 49.

[38]"...nihil sine consilio vestro et sine consensu plebis mea privatim sententia gerere," Epist. 14, 4.

[39]G. Post, "A Romano-Canonical Maxim, Quod Omnes Tangit, in Bracton and in Early Parliaments," *Studies in Medieval Legal Thought* (Princeton, 1964), pp. 163-240; Y. Congar, "Quod omnes tangit, ab omnibus tractari et approbari debet," *Revue historique de droit français et étranger* 36(1958)210-259.

elements of effective consultation and suggested sound procedures for this vital part of the rule-making process.[40]

III. JURIDICIZATION OF THE TEACHING FUNCTION

There is need to keep clear the distinction between teaching and governing. (This is a corollary by way of a *scholion* rather than a logical consequence or application of the foregoing propositions.) There has been a marked tendency in our Church for the last century and a half to juridicize the teaching function, in effect, to impose truth by command.[41] This alarming trend is continued and intensified in the 1983 Code of Canon Law. There is real danger in this development, not only for the teacher or preacher who happens to be in the wrong place at the wrong time, but for the entire ecclesial community and its ongoing quest for truth.

One of the places where this disciplinary "thought control" impacts is the area of theological reflection. Since the time of St. Anselm theological investigation has been described as *fides quaerens intellectum*, but it now stands in peril of becoming *fides ecclesiastica quaerens justificationem*.[42] Theological repression, that is, the extrinsic monitoring and control of teaching and research in theology, has a chilling effect on investigation, dialogue and progress for these in the discipline, but it also, in the long term, has a stultifying and paralyzing effect on the entire community.

This repression can result from various causes, but it stems in part from a confusion of functions or an incursion of pastoral authority into the teaching process. It has become an accepted practice to impose teaching by dint of authority without regard to the truth claim of the teaching itself. This distortion finds theoretical justification in *Lumen gentium*,[43] one of the unfortunate

---

[40]E.g., R. Kennedy, "Shared Responsibility in Ecclesial Decision-Making," *Studia Canonica* 14(1980)320-347; "Canonical Consultation" in the study "Canonical Reflections on Priestly Life and Ministry," in *American Ecclesiastical Review* 166(1972)368-370, and in *Catholic Mind* 70(1972)46-48; see also J. Provost, "The Working Together of Consultative Bodies—Great Expectations," *The Jurist* 40(1980)257-281.

[41]For some milestones along this road confer: Pius IX, letter *Tuas libenter*, December 21, 1863; Response of the Pontifical Biblical Commission, July 27, 1906; Decree of Holy Office, *Lamentabili*, July 3, 1907; Pius X, encyclical *Pascendi*, September 8, 1907; Pius X, motu proprio *Praestantia Scripturae*, November 18, 1907; Pius XII, encyclical *Humani generis*, August 12, 1950.

[42]For example, the disciplinary defense of the male, celibate structure of ordained ministry forecloses a free and objective reflection on the history of ministry and open speculation on a ministry truly adapted to the needs of the contemporary church.

[43]Confer J. O'Boyle, "The Rights and Responsibilities of Bishops: A Theological Perspective," in *Cooperation Between Theologians and the Ecclesiastical Magisterium*, ed. O'Donovan (Washington: CLSA, 1982), pp. 1-30; M. Seckler, "Die Theologie als kirchliche Wissenschaft nach Pius XII und Paul VI," *Theologische Quartalschrift* 149(1969)209-234; Y. Congar, "Bref historique des formes du 'magistére' et de ses relations avec les docteurs," *Revue des sciences phil. et théol.* 60(1976)99-112.

and compromised passages among the Council's teaching.[44] The theory is now reflected in the discipline of the 1983 code:

> c. 752 calls for *obsequium religiosum intellectus et voluntatis* to be given to the teachings which are enunciated by the authority of the pope or college of bishops even though they are not definitive (i.e., not final or infallible), and the faithful are to avoid those teachings which disagree with them;

> c. 753 declares that the faithful are to adhere *religioso animi obsequio* to the teaching authority of their individual bishops (a considerable extension of c. 1326 of the 1917 code);

> c. 754 says that all faithful are to obey the constitutions and decrees which are issued by church authorities to propose teachings or to proscribe erroneous opinions;

> c. 1371 allows for the just punishment (undetermined) of one who persistently rejects the non-definitive, non-infallible teachings spoken of in c. 752.

Note the mixing of the teaching and ruling authorities: c. 754 calls on the faithful to *obey decrees about teaching* (as c. 1324 of the 1917 code did, but there only regarding decrees of the Holy See); c. 1371 is found among the delicts against church *authority* (rather than among delicts against *religion*, where the punishments of apostates, heretics and schismatics are dealt with). The language of all these canons relates only to the teaching authority and its manner of exercise (e.g., definitive or not), but not to the relation of the truth taught to revelation or tradition. The 1917 code was more careful about "theological notes," e.g., cc. 1323 and 2317; likewise, c. 750 of the revised code is much more theologically judicious.[45]

Other manifestations of this juridical control of the teaching function in the revised code include:

> cc. 803-806 on the authorization and control of grade and high schools (down to the hiring and firing of religion teachers);

> cc. 808, 810, 812 on the authorization and control of colleges and universities, especially the mandate for teachers of theology;

> cc. 816-818 on the authorization and control of pontifical faculties and their monopoly over academic degrees with canonical effects;

> cc. 823-832 on the prior censorship of books;

[44] "In matters of faith and morals, the bishops speak in the name of Christ and the faithful are to accept their teaching and adhere to it with a religious assent of soul."

[45] "All that is contained in the written word of God or in tradition, that is, in the one deposit of faith entrusted to the Church and also proposed as divinely revealed either by the solemn magisterium of the Church or by its ordinary and universal magisterium, must be believed with divine and catholic faith; it is manifested for the common adherence of the Christian faithful under the leadership of the sacred magisterium; therefore, all are bound to avoid any doctrines whatever which are contrary to these truths." (Derived from c. 3 of *Dei Filius* of the First Vatican Council.)

c. 833, §§ 6 and 7 on prior profession of faith for seminary professors and university instructors in disciplines concerned with faith and morals.

The Church must be concerned with sound doctrine and authentic teaching; it always has been. The question is, how is that concern best manifested, how is it most effectively carried out? The answer is probably not by more laws, tighter controls by pastoral leaders over schools, teachers and teaching materials. The answer probably is: by attention to good teaching—by doing it, by insisting on others doing it, and by commending those who do it well—and by challenging poor, shallow or unfounded teaching with reasoned, persuasive presentations of authentic teaching.

One of the Bay Area's fine theologians, Massey Shepherd, once wrote that the Church has little to fear from heretics. They are simply misguided or wrongheaded individuals. But the Church must attend to "heresiarchs," i.e., those who command others to follow them in error, who impose it on others.[46] Disciplinary enforcement, by and large, should be reserved for heresiarchs. To recall the title of this essay, teaching is definitely not law, and, for the most part the quality, accuracy and effectiveness of teaching are not assured by legal strictures. "The truth cannot impose itself except by virtue of its own truth, . . ."[47]

> I charge you to preach the word, to stay with the task whether convenient or inconvenient—correcting, reproving, appealing—constantly teaching and never losing patience. . . . be steady and self-assured. . . perform your work as an evangelist, fulfill your ministry.
>
> (II Tim 4, 2 and 5)

[46]"The Rights of the Baptized," in *The Case for Freedom: Human Rights in the Church*, ed. J. Coriden (Washington: Corpus, 1969), pp. 41-42.
[47]Con. Vat. II, Declaration on Religious Freedom, 1.

COLLABORATION: KEY CONCEPT FOR
RELIGIOUS AND BISHOPS IN THE DIOCESE

M. Thaddea Kelly, PBVM

Before entering into the main part of our topic for this morning, namely collaboration, it is important in my thinking to review the place of religious in the Church according to the documents of the Second Vatican Council.

After looking at the place of religious in the Church, I consider it essential to discuss the charism or special call of religious. Again, our source for this includes Vatican II documents as well as various subsequent publications from the Holy See.

From here, we shall move to the place of religious in the local church, reflecting on their labors, their gifts, their contributions, their zeal all of which help to make up the warp and woof of the pattern of ecclesial life on the local level. If truly motivated by the inspiration of the Holy Spirit, these can be a source of dynamism making the local church a truly vibrant reality.

Moving from the place of religious in the local church, we want to study the genuine relationship which should exist between religious and their respective bishops. It is in this area that we must look not only at the relationship, but also at the active cooperation between religious and bishops, so necessary to fulfill the purpose for which the Church was established, that is communion and mission. How will the gospel be preached unless there is collaboration among those in leadership positions?

In this section also the obligations of religious and of bishops must be addressed if the goal to which we are being called is to be reached, genuine collaboration. And that same spirit of collaboration should extend from religious in positions of leadership and bishops in charge of a diocese to their companions and fellow-workers.

As we progress through this discussion I shall mention concrete examples—a few real life situations culled from my experience of these past years.

The question of how we work towards mutual cooperation, trust and confidence looms largely before us. Are there methods of working together that will assist us—religious and bishops—in advancing towards a real and practical spirit of collaboration? I think there are.

You will doubtless notice that there is much repetition not only in documents of Vatican II but also in many other post-conciliar publications.

The members of the Vatican Council in their Constitution on the Church, *Lumen gentium*, placed religious in the heart of the Church, stressing the point that religious receive the gift of their vocation from God so that by their lives they may promote the salvific mission of the Church.

From the point of view of the divine and hierarchial structure of the Church, the religious state is not an intermediate one between the clerical and lay states. Rather, the faithful of Christ are called by God from both these states of life so that they may enjoy this particular gift in the life of the Church and thus each in his or her own way can forward the saving mission of the Church (*L.G.*, n. 43).

We might cite sections from many other documents both from the Council itself and from publications issued after it. It is sufficient to note that these quotations strengthen the importance of religious as those totally consecrated to spread the gospel, to contribute to the task entrusted by Christ to his Church. However, at the risk of being repetitious, I quote here from the words of Pope John Paul II in his address to the religious women of the diocese of Bergamo:

Who does not know what and how great a contribution sisters make in pastoral activity and in modern ecclesial animation? If the fields of the apostolate have rightly been opened to more sensitive and generous lay people, how much vaster is the sphere in which these sisters of ours are called to operate! The charism of their special religious vocation, the consequent bond of the vows they pronounce, the innate spirit of understanding and the other gifts of their femininity, act in them jointly, causing a powerful thrust which can reach, and does in fact, reach all sectors in which the Church is responsibly engaged (quoted from *Consecrated Life*, 7: 1, p. 22).

Again and again we find in church documents special care and concern for the protection of the charism belonging to each institute. What is the charism if it is not the particular gift or grace given to a founder of foundress to be used not by that person alone, but to be shared by his or her followers and to be used in response to the needs of the time, to be shared with others for the sake of the Kingdom! In addition, the charism should be the source of a dynamic life of the congregation for the Church. Canon 574, § 2 of the revised code tells us:

Certain Christian faithful are specially called to this state by God so that they may enjoy a *special gift* in the life of the Church and contribute to its salvific mission according to the purpose and spirit of the Institute.

Canon 578 reads:

The mind of the founders and their plans, ratified by competent ecclesiastical authority, about the nature, goal, spirit and character of the Institute and its wholesome traditions, all of which constitute the patrimony of the institute itself, should be observed faithfully by all.

Perfectae caritatis emphasizes the place of religious in the Church according to their respective characteristics. These are the varied expression of the special gift or charism given by the Holy Spirit to the founder or foundress (*PC*, 2 c).

Continuing our reflection on these charisms and traditions and realizing clearly that they are from the Holy Spirit for the entire Church, we move to a consideration of the place and use of a given charism in a particular part of the world and try to see its contribution to the global Church. While today religious are endeavoring to participate generously and whole-heartedly in the local Church—they have done this for generations—it must always be borne in mind that the local church should reflect the universal Church. It is a microcosm of the entire Church. In this respect, we can say that the charism and place of religious in the local church take on a communitarian aspect.

In a selection from *Consecrated Life* we read:

> However, one thing is certain: a charism is of its very nature a gift of the Spirit to the entire Church, and if the local Church to which it was given wants to be really the "Church of God," it must endeavor to ensure that this gift does not remain confined within the limits of the local Church. . . .
>
> Institutes should be imbued with a real communitarian spirit, which should be marked by the characteristic indicated by the Council: "It must embrace not only the local church, but the universal Church also" (*MR* 23, c). (Quoted from *Consecrated Life*, 7:1, p. 60.)

The pastoral zeal of the Church will touch the hearts of all if there is a sharing of the charisms and gifts by the institutes themselves. In a sense, our global world is becoming a small village and we religious must keep before us the concept that "no man is an island." We must share our gifts, our talents, our charisms and even our limitations in our ministry on the local level for the good of the entire Church. Only in this way will Christ's command be fullfilled, "Go, therefore, and make disciples of all nations. . ." (Matt: 28:18). Pope John Paul II when addressing the superiors general in 1978 said,

> By your vocation, you are for the universal Church; by your mission you are in a definite local church. Your vocation for the universal Church, then, is exercised within the structures of the local church. You must make every effort to carry out your vocation in the individual local churches, so as to contribute to their spiritual development, in order to be their special strength. Union with the universal Church through the local church: this is your way (John Paul II to Superiors General, November 24, 1978; quoted from *The Contemplative Dimension of Religious Life*, p. 44).

Moving into the practical application of our discussion and at the same time keeping before us the place of religious in the heart of the Church, we turn to the document, *Directives for the Mutual Relations Between Bishops and Religious in the Church*, commonly referred to as *Mutual Relations*. This publication is the result of a joint plenaria held by the Congregation of Bishops and the Sacred Congregation for Religious and Secular Institutes. It was initiated in 1975, but the document went back and forth between the two congregations for study and revision until its completion in 1978.

The special role of each member of the Body of Christ is clearly delineated almost from the very first pages of *Mutual Relations*. We read:

All members - pastors, laymen, and religious each in his own manner, participate in the sacramental nature of the Church. Likewise, each one, according to his or her proper role, must be a sign and instrument both of union with God and of the salvation of the world. All, in fact, have this twofold aspect of their calling: (a) to holiness: "all in the Church, whether they belong to the hierarchy or are cared for by it, are called to holiness" (*LG* 39); (b) to the apostolate: "the entire Church is driven by the Holy Spirit to do her part for the full realization of the plan of God" (*MR*, n. 4).

After a description of the function of the bishops in union with the Roman Pontiff this same document clarifies the obligations of the hierarchy regarding religious life. Here we find that repetition, so obvious both in Vatican II documents and in subsequent publications. Reference is made to the oft-quoted and singularly beautiful statement in *Lumen gentium:*

By the charity to which they lead, the evangelical counsels join their followers to the Church and her mystery in a special way (n. 44).

At this point it will be good for us to look at canon 204, § 1 of the new code where we find the following:

The Christian faithful are those who inasmuch as they have been incorporated in Christ through baptism, have been established as the people of God. For this reason, since they have become in their own manner, sharers in Christ's priestly, prophetic, and royal office, they are called in accord with the condition proper to each one of them to exercise the mission which God has entrusted to the Church to fulfill in the world.

This sharing in the mission of the Church is based upon important concepts enunciated in *Lumen gentium* which gives to all members of the Church consequent upon their baptism a share in the threefold office of Christ and of the Church,—priestly, prophetic and kingly. Each member shares in that office according to his or her particular role in the Church (*L.G.* 31-36). How much of a responsibility does this place upon those who have been called by God to consecrate their entire persons to a special service in the Church!

The importance of unity among bishops is mentioned in *Mutual Relations* in regulating the practice of the evangelical counsels, in authentically approving rules presented to them, as well as other specific duties. While those other duties are specified, it is even more important to point out the consequences resulting from them. Chief among these, so it seems to me, is the following:

All pastors, mindful of the apostolic admonition never to be "a dictator over any group that is put in (their) charge, but to be an example that the whole flock can follow" (1 Pet 5:3), will rightly be aware of the primacy of life in the Spirit. This demands that they be at the same time *leaders* and *members*; truly, *fathers*, but also *brothers; teachers* of the faith, but especially *fellow-disciples of Christ;* those indeed, responsible for the perfection of the faithful, but also true witnesses of their personal sanctification (*MR*, 9d).

All of the foregoing assist us in looking at religious life within the ecclesial communion and we see as well the responsibility shared by all the members of the Church to appreciate and protect the unique characteristics of each religious institute. We understand also the obligation of each baptized person to fulfill his or her unique role in the threefold office of the Church. The religious and the laity together have the responsibility to cooperate with the members of the hierarchy.

Mutual Relations offers us a crystal-clear description of the outstanding mark of religious authority, namely, service. Religious superiors in their position of authority share in the triple office of Christ and the Church, namely teaching, sanctifying and governing. These responsibilities must be carried out in union with the bishops if they are to be authentic means within a religious congregation and within the Church of fulfilling Christ's command to preach the gospel. Conclusions listed in *Mutual Relations* give us, religious and bishops alike, much food for thought and prayerful reflection.

Rather than continue with a lengthy, detailed resumé of the document to which we have been referring, I consider it sufficient here to quote from the introduction to the publication itself, in which the purpose of the paper is stated:

> The matter treated is circumscribed by well-defined limits. . . . The direct subject of discussion are the relations which *should exist* between the local ordinary, on the one hand, and religious institutes and societies of common life on the other (*MR*, Intro., III).

For me, collaboration as a key concept for religious and bishops is summed up in these words:

> In each diocese the bishop should strive to understand what the Spirit wants to manifest, even through his flock and especially through the individuals and religious families present in the diocese. That is why it is necessary for him to cultivate sincere and familiar relations with superiors, in order the better to fulfill his ministry of shepherd towards men and women religious. In fact, it is his specific office to defend consecrated life, to foster and animate the fidelity and authenticity of religious and to help them become part of the communion and of the evangelizing action of his Church, according to their distinctive nature (*MR*, n. 52).

To try to attain an understanding of that degree of collaboration mandated by *Mutual Relations* and by the revised code we will profit by discussing some of the everyday situations common in many parts of the world. Both negative and positive aspects of these situations will prove helpful to us. We must remember that the situations of misunderstanding, the problems of a very human dimension do not come from ill will. Rather such situations only prove that the Church is very human even though it has a divine founder. The sources for these are not given since I have culled them from my own experience, from conversations with major superiors of men and of women and also from some bishops in various parts of the United States.

For the sake of clarity I shall number these cases/situations.

1. Canon 609, § 1 of the revised code states:

> Houses of a religious institute are erected by the competent authority according to the constitutions, with previous consent of the diocesan bishop.

It has happened that because of internal congregational problems, groups of religious have been allowed to separate from the larger congregation and, until 1979, were allowed to retain their vows provided a bishop would accept them in his diocese. Unfortunately, perhaps because of insufficient knowledge, sometimes these religious have considered themselves independent of the bishop and have purchased property, opened a house and only then informed the bishop of the diocese.

A situation such as this does not promote collaboration between religious and the bishop of a diocese.

2. In contrast to the above case, I have heard very positive comments from bishops in different parts of the United States. Among these comments, I mention the following:

> a. Excellent collaboration/cooperation is found when the bishop spends an entire day meeting with major superiors to discuss mutual plans for the respective congregational ministries and the plans for the good of the diocese. Included among topics touched upon at some of these gatherings have been schools—diocesan, parish, and congregational; the importance of the religious presence presence in the schools; methods of reaching out to various nationalities and ethnic groups; participation of religious in parish ministry in the diocese; encouragement given to religious congregations regarding training for positions of administration and leadership.

> b. Religious congregations should be familiar with diocesan operations, not only ministerial needs but also financial needs. Collaboration is needed in every area of diocesan life.

> c. On the other side of the coin, however, it must be acknowledged that fears arise on the part of the hierarchy when one after another religious congregation withdraws members from parish schools. The question tormenting both pastors and bishops is, "What have we done wrong?"

For most of us religious it is not a question of having done wrong, but it is a question of lack of personnel for the schools. Perhaps, in many situations of this nature, if the religious superiors had contacted the pastor and the bishop early on, a better understanding would have resulted both for the members of the community and for the diocesan personnel.

The above case is clearly referred to in *Mutual Relations* where we read in paragraph n. 38:

Major superiors will take great care not only to have a knowledge of the talents and possibilities of their religious but also of the apostolic needs of the dioceses where their institute is called to work. Wherefore it is desirable that a concrete and global dialogue be carried on between the bishop and the superiors of the various institutes present in the diocese, so that, especially in view of certain precarious situations and the persistent vocational crisis, religious personnel can be more evenly and fruitfully distributed.

3. Enclosed monastic communities also have something to offer us for our consideration. Recently, the abbess of a monastery shared the following thoughts with me. This abbess sees enclosed monastic communities holding a vital place, not only in the universal Church but also in the local church. As a result of her conviction of the necessary role these religious hold in the Church, she stresses the assistance needed from the local church and also indicates some problems possible within the enclosure.

Sister stated clearly that those elected to govern must be psychologically strong; otherwise, they could easily fail to recognize problems which could be a cause of harm to members of the community. Sister also recommends regular visitation by vicars so that the nuns will have an appreciation of the interest the vicars have for them and will share their confidence with them. It is the bishop personally or his vicar who should carefully attend to the needs of the enclosed religious. Above all, sister emphasizes the necessity of a monastery having a much deeper relationship with the diocese than just a superficial one.

In my opinion, the message of this abbess puts into concrete reality the words found in the document published by the Sacred Congregation for Religious and Secular Institutes in 1980. I quote:

> Their contemplative life (contemplative institutes) then, is their primary and fundamental apostolate, because it is their typical and characterisic way in God's special design to be Church, to live in the Church, and to achieve communion with the Church and to carry out a mission in the Church. In this perspective which fully respects the primary apostolic purpose of the cloistered life, in which contemplative religious give themselves to God alone (cf. *PC*, n. 7) they offer assistance—without prejudice to enclosure and the laws that govern it—to persons in the world and share with them their prayer and spiritual life in fidelity to the spirit and traditions of their Institute (cf. *MR* n. 25) (*The Contemplative Dimension of Religious Life,* SCRIS, Vatican City, 1980).

Much more time might easily be spent in presenting examples for a continued discussion between bishops and major superiors but I am certain that were we to share our experiences we would find not only many similar situations, but we would also search together for solutions. At this moment I prefer that we turn our focus on the future with a great sense of optimism and trust.

All of us are keenly aware of the recent letter from our Holy Father to the bishops of the United States and of the document from the Sacred Congregation for Religious and Secular Institutes, *Guidelines for the Essential Elements of Religious Life.* At the first announcement of these publications and at the news of the appointment of a commission of bishops to study the causes for the decline of religious vocations, many religious began to experience fear and anxiety. I feel that even now some may still have these feelings, but I think that the positive atmosphere in which the work has been started will help to allay fear and anxiety. This positive atmosphere indeed, will possibly be at the heart of genuine collaboration and cooperation for future relations between religious and bishops in a diocese.

I consider some of the words of Archbishop John R. Quinn in the recent address he delivered to the members of the National Assembly of the Leadership Conference of Women Religious a fitting close to this morning's session and an appropriate doorway to the future of religious life both on the local level and on the universal level.

Archbishop Quinn said,

> For over the past twenty years as you moved through this period of experimentation, your partners in dialogue have been the members of your own congregation and other congregations. Now what the Holy See is asking for is an extension of this dialogue to a larger group, to the bishops and to the Church as a whole. For there is much incomprehension here, either about what the religious have accomplished or why they have gone in the directions they have chosen, as well as some confusion about what the Church has been asking of religious since the Council. Through the bishops, the religious orders can engage all of the Church in this renewal of religious life: those whom they serve, those with whom they serve and the bishops in union with the Pope whose ministry is to confirm and validate this service (August 16, 1983).

Certainly clear communication and dialogue should lead to genuine collaboration and cooperation!

THE PRELIMINARY EXPERIENCE OF
MANDATORY REVIEW IN DIOCESAN TRIBUNALS

Daniel J. Murray

The purpose of this paper is to discuss the various models proposed by tribunals in the United States for the processing of the mandatory review and/or appeal in accordance with the requirements of the revised Code of Canon Law[1] which will become effective on November 27, 1983.

There have been several seminars in past annual conventions of the Canon Law Society of America dealing with the topic of the mandatory appeal.[2] Each of these dealt with the theoretical question of *what if?* or *what should we do if?* But in less than two months we will have to have in actual operation a system of appellate courts ready to handle thousands of affirmative decisions which must be reviewed in accordance with the law (canon 1682). We will no longer be able to request from the National Conference of Catholic Bishops a dispensation from this mandatory appeal.[3]

Most dioceses and archdioceses have formed a plan for the processing of cases in mandatory review. We will outline some of these plans and the proposals for implementing them, and then give the participants in this seminar an opportunity to discuss these proposals so that we might work together to function with the mandatory review and/or appeal of every affirmative decision.

SURVEY OF METROPOLITAN TRIBUNALS

On July 29, 1983 I wrote to the officials of every metropolitan tribunal in the United States asking that he answer four questions. These questions were:

1. Please describe the manner in which your metropolitan tribunal and/or tribunals of the dioceses in the province will handle the mandatory review of cases which have received an affirmative decision in first instance.

---

[1] *Codex Iuris Canonici*, auctoritate Ioannis Pauli PP. II promulgatus (Vatican City: Libreria Editrice Vaticana, 1983).

[2] See, for example, Dennis J. Burns, "Procedure in Second Instance Courts," *C.L.S.A. Proceedings* 39 (1977) 112-130; Edward J. Dillon, *"De Processibus:* An Analysis of Some Key Provisions," *C.L.S.A. Proceedings* 42 (1980) 161-170; Edward M. Egan, "Appeal in marriage Nullity Cases: Two Centuries of Experiment and Reform," *C.L.S.A. Proceedings* 43 (1981) 132-144; Kenneth J. Ruzick, "Competence, Nullity of the Acts, and the Appellate Process: A Look at the Procedural Law of the New Code," *C.L.S.A. Proceedings* 44 (1982) 105-120.

[3] See "Provisional Norms for Marriage Annulment Cases in United States," *Canon Law Digest* 7: 950-966; particularly Norm 23, part II, page 964.

2. Have you applied for and/or received permission to set up an interdiocesan tribunal for second instance cases? (If so, please send me copies of the documentation, if at all possible.)

3. Do you have any creative suggestions or proposals which I could share with the participants of the seminar? (If so, please give details.)

4. Do you anticipate any serious problems or delays in the handling of cases because of the mandatory review? (Please explain.)

I received responses from all 31 metropolitan tribunals,[4] and have compiled several hundred pages of raw data from these responses. The balance of this paper will consist of summarizing the responses, and reflecting on them. Let me hasten to point out that many responses indicated that no definitive plans have been formulated. I am sure that some here present are still in the process of formulating plans for the mandatory appeal.

There are three basic models which are envisioned for the handling of the mandatory review. These are (1) the traditional metropolitan system, (2) the interdiocesan tribunal, and (3) the interprovincial tribunal. In the first model, the traditional metropolitan system, all suffragan tribunals of the province appeal to the metropolitan tribunal, and the metropolitan tribunal appeals to its own fixed court of appeals. In the second and third models, the interdiocesan and interprovincial tribunals, an independent tribunal is established with the permission of the Holy See,[5] and all first instance tribunals of the one province or of the several provinces (including the metropolitan tribunal) appeal to this independent tribunal in second instance.

Four provinces have chosen to retain the traditional system, at least for the present: Kansas City, Los Angeles, Miami, and Philadelphia. As this system is already embodied in the Code of Canon Law (canon 1438), no permission of the Holy See is required. Hence, these appelate courts are already functioning to some extent. All suffragan tribunals will appeal to the metropolitan tribunal, and the metropolitan tribunal will appeal to its fixed appellate court: Los Angeles appeals to Orange, Miami appeals to Pittsburgh, and Philadelphia appeals to Baltimore. As of the date of the survey, Kansas City had not yet designated its appelate tribunal. There are several advantages to this traditional system, but we will save the examination until we have mentioned the other models.

The second model is the interdiocesan tribunal. This is the system most commonly selected by American tribunals. Twenty provinces have applied for or soon will apply for permission of the Holy See for the establishment of an interdiocesan tribunal with competence to handle marriage nullity cases in second instance, for all tribunals of the province: Atlanta, Baltimore, Boston, Denver, Detroit, Dubuque, Hartford, Indianapolis, Louisville, Milwaukee, Newark,

---

[4]See Appendix A for a list of the 31 archdioceses of the Latin Rite in the United States.

[5]The "Norms for Interdiocesan or Regional or Interregional Tribunals," issued by the Apostolic Signatura on December 28, 1970, are reported in *Canon Law Digest* 7: 920-926. These norms form the basis for the establishment of interdiocesan and interprovincial tribunals in the United States.

Oklahoma City, Omaha, St. Louis, St. Paul and Minneapolis, San Antonio, San Francisco, and Santa Fe.

The third model is the interprovincial tribunal. Seven provinces have requested permission for such a system, forming a total of three interprovincial tribunals: the provinces of Anchorage, Portland, and Seattle will form one interprovincial tribunal; the provinces of Cincinnati and Washington will pair together; and the provinces of Mobile and New Orleans will form the third interprovincial tribunal.

A great deal of study has gone into the decision by each province to choose the system which the ordinaries and tribunal officials hope will work best for them. Whether one system is objectively better than the other is beside the point. All three models are provided for in the law, and each has its own advantages and disadvantages.

Advantages and Disadvantages

One of the most difficult tasks in this survey was to gain some sort of perspective on what is being done throughout the entire United States. What may work in a province with dozens of degreed canonists will not work in a province which must operate with a very limited staff of trained personnel and perhaps a large corps of helpful, but non-degreed, volunteers. With this disclaimer in mind, let us examine the relative advantages and disadvantages of the three models as reported by those responding to the survey.

The four provinces which have chosen the traditional model of the metropolitan system believe that they can readily handle the review cases in this manner. Their judges, defenders of the bond, and other officers have been or will be appointed prior to the implementation of the provision of the revised code requiring at least a licentiate in canon law for these officers, and hence will be "grandfathered" (or grandparented?) in for some years before their term expires. This gives these tribunals some breathing space to send people for canonical training or await an indult or permission for some equivalency clause for non-degreed personnel. Of course, this system places most of the burden on the metropolitan tribunal itself and, if the metropolitan tribunal has a large number of first instance decisions to be reviewed, this places a great burden on its own appellate tribunal. Obviously, some streamlined system of reviewing cases is envisioned. We will look at this streamlining in a later part of this seminar. One special advantage of the traditional model is that these provinces can readily request permission to form an interdiocesan tribunal should the need arise. I do not know how readily an already established interdiocesan tribunal could transfer back to the traditional model. Finally, and I think this is one of the most important advantages of the traditional model, there is the matter of what to do when the first instance tribunal gives a negative decision and the case is appealed to second instance. The law (canon 1683) permits the appelate tribunal to admit a new ground and try the case as at first instance. If this new trial results in an affirmative decision, the appellate tribunal (say, the metropolitan tribunal if the case had originally been given a negative decision by a suffragan tribunal) would then send the case to its own appellate court for the mandatory review and/or appeal. Thus two concordant decisions could be rendered, despite the original negative decision. In the case of the interdiocesan tribunal, there would be no ordinary appellate court other than the Sacred Roman Rota, although a request could be made for a designated court of third instance (or more precisely, second instance).

The reason I mention this latter advantage is the possibility of a situation whereby a new pharoah (officialis or judge) who knows not Joseph (the adopted gentleperson's agreement) could cause some problems by rendering numerous negative decisions which must be appealed to the interdiocesan court of second instance for which there is no real provision for further appeal except to the Rota. Of course, the appellate court could remand the case back to the first instance tribunal for a new trial on the new ground, but that would not solve the problem if another negative decision were rendered. While I do not envision this happening in this best of all possible worlds, it could happen a few years down the line.

Perhaps I have seemed too biased toward the traditional model. If so, it is because in the province of Los Angeles we have chosen that model as the most practical for ourselves, at least at this time. All the tribunals of the province have too few degreed personnel and there is little likelihood that we will have a significant increase in the number of these trained canonists in the foreseeable future, given the other needs in our dioceses. Orange, of which I am the vice-officialis, is the appellate tribunal for Los Angeles. We do not anticipate any serious difficulty in continuing to handle their cases on appeal or mandatory review. Perhaps I will feel differently by the next annual convention.

The majority of provinces in the United States have elected to request permission to establish an interdiocesan tribunal system in accordance with the provisions of the 1970 norms issued by the Apostolic Signatura. There are advantages and disadvantages to this model. I have already mentioned what I consider to be one disadvantage, namely the problem of handling a negative decision which should be reversed. I suppose the most appealing (please pardon the pun) advantage of this model is that of the "in house" review. The advantage of the interdiocesan tribunal is that personnel of the same diocese can be appointed to two different tribunals, one the diocesan tribunal and the other the interdiocesan tribunal. A case need never leave the physical office of one tribunal because it would be tried in first instance by duly appointed officers of the diocesan tribunal and then to be sent across the hall to be reviewed by the duly appointed officers of the interdiocesan tribunal. As long as the same individuals do not handle the case on both levels there would be no problem. Many provinces are planning to handle all mandatory review cases by the "in-house" method. Of course, there is also (for lack of a better term) the "out-house" method. This latter method would usually be reserved for those cases which have actually been appealed by a person, whether the respondent or the defender of the bond. In such cases, the moderator or officialis of the interdiocesan tribunal would send the case to another tribunal for review by officers of the interdiocesan tribunal. Some provinces have a fixed pairing of tribunals for this purpose.

Although I do see some advantage to having an "in-house" review (savings in postage, transmission of acts, time involved, etc.), I honestly do not see that it meets the requirement of the law. For example, one metropolitan tribunal which has selected the traditional model (Miami) originally petitioned the Signatura for permission to establish its own court of second intance so that a second turnus would review cases given an affirmative decision. This permission was denied by the Apostolic Signatura. The *Canon Law Digest*[6] records another example in which Dubuque requested permission for a second tunus of its own tribunal to review a second instance decision by its tribunal (on appeal from Omaha). The Signatura denied the permission and remanded the case to the Tribunal of the Archdiocese of St. Paul and Minneapolis for third instance. There have been other such cases, but I know of no other case in which any tribunal, other than the Rota, may assign a new turnus of its own tribunal for another instance. Of course, theoretically at least, these officers are not acting in the same tribunal; they just happen to be sitting in the same building.

A possible disadvantage of the interdiocesan tribual model is the situation in which a given diocese does not have sufficient personnel to provide a full turnus for two separate instances (at least one judge and a defender of the bond in first instance, and then three judges and a defender of the bond in the mandatory review). Where such a problem is anticipated, the cases are forwarded to the moderator of the interdiocesan tribunal for processing by whatever turnus is available—which defeats the advantage of an "in-house" review. Provinces with several small dioceses that have limited staff may end up doing as much work as the traditional metropolitan model.

It is interesting to note at this point that almost no one indicated that this mandatory review would entail lengthy delays in the processing of marriage cases. Some expect delays of a few weeks or even two or three months, but this is not serious in light of the dire predictions that were made some years ago when it became apparent that the American Procedural Norms would not be renewed and every affirmative decision would require a review. I am happy to see that most of us have accepted the inevitable and have developed a system with which we can still handle our cases with justice and equity, unencumbered by years of delay because of useless and needless procedures. As many officiales stated in their replies, we will do the best we can with what we have.

The interprovincial tribunal is little more than an interdiocesan tribunal, with the exception that it handles cases for more than one province. In the three interprovincial tribunals established in the United States, the operation seems to be similar to that planned for the interdiocesan tribunals. Particularly for Region XII, encompassing the vast territory of the provinces of Anchorage,

---

[6]*C.L.D.* 7: 933-935.

Portland, and Seattle, this model was chosen because of the shortage of personnel in an individual province.

Several people were kind enough to send me copies of the documentation requesting the establishment of the interdiocesan tribunal and the response from the Apostolic Delegation and the Apostolic Signatura. I do not know whether any province has completed all paperwork required for the establishment of their interdiocesan tribunal, but many provinces have experienced some difficulty in obtaining final approval. There seems to be little or no difficulty in obtaining the initial *nihil obstat* from the Signatura, but then they request that a decree of erection be drawn up in Latin. This decree must follow a set of guidelines given by the Signatura. I was quite edified by the apparent number of still-living Latin scholars who could draw up these decrees. One province debated about whether a verb should be in the imperfect passive subjunctive or the present passive subjunctive. As I do not know the difference, I could not tell from reading the decree which side had won this debate.

The decree of erection must address the following points:

1. The name by which this new tribunal shall be known (sounds like something out of the Rite of Baptism!);

2. The competence of this tribunal is limited to second instance marriage cases only, safeguarding the right of appeal directly to the Rota;

3. A list of the first instance tribunals which will appeal their cases to this interdiocesan (interprovincial) tribunal;

4. The name of the moderator of the tribunal (usually the metropolitan in the case of interdiocesan, or one of the metropolitans in the case of interprovincial tribunals);

5. The seat where this tribunal will be located (again, usually the metropolitan see);

6. An indication of how the expenses of this tribunal will be met (usually by proportion among dioceses);

7. The officers of the tribunal will be elected by vote of the bishops of the dioceses participating;

8. The date on which this new tribunal will begin its operation (this would also be the effective date for the termination of previous arrangements for appellate courts).

The decree is then signed by each participating bishop.

Several provinces have then been requested to send a list of all officers of the interdiocesan tribunal, giving canonical degrees and a *curriculum vitae* of each officer. In some lists, all officers have the requisite licentiate degree in canon law so there will probably be no difficulty. However, some lists include individuals who do not have the licentiate in canon law. It will be interesting to see whether some kind of dispensation is forthcoming. This will be a good topic for the discussion portion of this seminar. Several officiales responded by saying that they were still "negotiating" with the Signatura over certain points, and these matters will also be very worthwhile sharing for our mutual benefit.

CREATIVE IDEAS

An unnamed individual once said that God inflicted the Church with canonists so that she would never be without persecution. But sometimes we canonists come up with some great ideas that facilitate the doing of justice and equity for our people and that is what we are about today. American ingenuity has been at work in the halls of the tribunals! Let us take some time to examine these ideas.

First of all, many tribunals are making a distinction between the mandatory review of an affirmative decision (canon 1682) and the actual appeal by a person. This appeal might be by the respondent or the defender of the bond, assuming that the first instance decision is in the affirmative. The case which is given an affirmative decision against which no one lodges an appeal will receive a review by the second instance defender of the bond and probably a speedy confirmation by the three judges. In many provinces, this confirmation will be done by a second "in-house" turnus operating as officers of the interdiocesan tribunal. However, should an actual appeal be lodged, then most provinces would require that officers sitting in a location other than that which rendered the first instance decision be called upon to review the sentence. If the appeal seems to have no solid basis, the defender of the bond in second instance could state that he or she has no objections to a confirmation of the decision and the three judges could simply ratify the affirmative sentence. This might be done especially when the appeal by a respondent appears to be merely vindictive. If, on the other hand, the appellate court sees merit in the appeal, they could order a new examination of the case in second instance. At least for now, most provinces are expecting few actual appeals and expect that most (perhaps the vast majority) cases will receive the simple "in-house" review, and that the "out-house" review will be reserved for the exceptional cases. We shall see.

The Province of Chicago has established an independent Court of Appeals, with a full-time judicial vicar (Bill Schumacher), a full-time notary-secretary, and a separate office and budget. In their interdiocesan tribunal of second instance, all reviews and appeals will be heard in Chicago in the halls of the Appellate Court. Judges from the various dioceses of the province will be assigned to consider cases by means of a fixed schedule. The judges will travel to Chicago and remain there for 1½ to 2 days to decide the 60 or so cases for that week. The sentence will already have been reviewed by an "in-house" defender of the bond in second instance, and his or her observations will be forwarded to the Appellate Court, together with the sentence and any other required acts. The judicial vicar of the Appellate Court will then make photocopies and send one set to each judge for review prior to the meeting of the judges (about 3 weeks in advance). This system sounds good on paper but could get quite burdensome for judges who must travel a long distance. The consideration of sixty (or so) cases at one time would boggle the mind of most mortal canonists.

Regarding the question of what will actually be subject to review, a number of proposals have been offered. Some want to see a rather strict interpretation of canon 1683 and therefore require that the entire *acta* be reviewed in every case. However, most provinces seem to have worked out some sort of "gentleperson's" agreement whereby only the sentence is reviewed. If the sentence contains all the information desired by the appellate tribunal, this should be sufficient for the review.

Some appellate tribunals will require changes in the writing of sentences by first instance tribunals. For example, some indication must be made as to the basis for competence in first instance. This will be especially true now that we have new rules for competence based on the domicile of the petitioner. The sentence should state the basis for competence and, if required, whether the proper permission was given by the officialis of the tribunal of the respondent's domicile. The sentence should indicate in what manner the respondent was cited, whether he responded and whether he manifested any intention to appeal an affirmative decision. Did the respondent's officialis "hear" him or her before giving the required permission? Did the respondent receive a copy of the petition? Did the respondent receive a copy of the sentence? Was the respondent notified of the first instance decision and given an opportunity to lodge an appeal within fifteen days? Exactly what should be in each sentence will be a matter for common agreement among the officers of the tribunals involved.

Of course, when an actual appeal is lodged by a person, it may well be necessary for someone in the appellate tribunal to review the entire *acta* to determine whether there is basis for the appeal. If a rather perfunctory sentence is produced in the first instance, it may be next to impossible to determine from that whether the proofs and indications contained in the *acta* are sufficient to enable the court to reach moral certitude. The difficulties anticipated with the confidentiality problematic may make it imperative to have ready access to the *acta* in contested cases. It is in just such contested cases that the respondent is likely to be cognizant of his or her every right, pointing to each and every canon and portion of a canon (in the readily available English translations, of course) which he or she believes will vindicate his or her rights. Such cases will cause canonists to be creative indeed! While we may have all manner of "gentleperson's" agreements worked out, they will be put to a real test by the vindictive respondent who threatens, and sometimes carries through with this threat, to appeal the case "all the way to the Pope." I am sure that other tribunals have shared the Orange experience of having some sacred tribunal in Rome request the complete *acta* of a case to determine whether an angry respondent has substantial basis for the complaint against our jurisprudence or procedures or very persons.

One area of creativity is in word processing. A few relatively wealthy tribunals have agreed to transmit sentences and even *acta* by means of interconnected word processors. Unless I misread their statements, it seems that the sentence will be constructed from various programmed options in the computer, then transmitted to the appellate tribunal via phone hook-up, and reviewed by someone (the key punch operator?) who will then punch a few buttons giving the decree of confirmation. Of course, in actuality, this will be done properly but it does lend itself to all manner of imagined results.

Those who use word processors will have standardized protocol numbers which can be inserted in any branch office, then filed by computer in the central data bank or wherever these things will be stored. In that way, no matter where the officers are actually sitting, their actions will be recorded in the seat of the interdiocesan or metropolitan tribunal. This will facilitate preparation of the annual report and keep bookkeeping simple. Many provinces have an agreed upon *taxa* which will be added to every nullity case to pay for the appellate court operations. An ideal use for the word processor is the sending of letters. Form letters may be individually prepared to suit the case and save a great deal of typing. Letters to the petitioner and respondnent, appointment of officers, decrees and notifications may all be programmed for ready transmittal from any branch office of the appropriate tribunal, whether diocesan or appellate. I think we are just beginning to see how such machines can be used to aid in our work.

Several provinces have prepared rather complicated forms for the appellate court. They have several form letters—notification of parties and advocates, letter remitting case for review, letter acknowledging that case has been received, letters to judges and defenders, citation for hearing of review, notification of decision, etc. In addition to all these letters, these appellate tribunals have a myriad of procedural forms—acceptance of case, constitution of the tribunal, substitution of officers, *litis contestatio,* observations of the defender of the bond, and a lengthy decree of confirmation that reads like a judicial sentence—a new outline of the facts, new citation of the law, marshalling of cogent arguments for the nullity of the marriage on the grounds alleged, etc. While some of these letters and forms may be necessary in particular circumstances, I think a much more streamlined approach is realistic and legally acceptable. I now present a sample form which I hope will contribute to our discussion.

The sample form (see Appendix B) could serve as a one-page record for the processing of the mandatory review. I suggest that this form, or something similar, be printed on a triplicate NCR form (no carbon required). The last copy would be retained in the *acta* of the first instance tribunal. The other two copies would be attached to a copy of the sentence (and other *acta* as required), in a manner similar to that presently employed in requesting the dispensation from appeal through the offices of the National Conference of Catholic Bishops. Following the review by the appellate tribunal, one completed copy of the form would be returned to the court of first instance. The original would be retained in the archives of the appellate tribunal. The copy of the sentence could be destroyed, with provision that ready access could be made to the sentence and *acta* kept in the archives of the first instance tribunal. This procedure provides for a true review and, I believe, meets the requirements of the law but limits paperwork to minimum, thus saving many trees in this beautiful northwest portion of our country—otherwise destined for papermills to create the reams of paper which would be needed otherwise.

Let us look at the sample form. At the top of the page we put the name of the arch/diocese which heard the case in first instance, followed by the names of the case (last names of parties) and the first instance protocol number. The appellate tribunal will probably assign its own protocol number. The first portion of the form states that the case is being transmitted *ex officio* to the appellate tribunal for review of the first instance affirmative decision. It is signed and dated by the officialis (or his delegate) of the first instance tribunal.

Once the form and attachments have been received by the appellate tribunal, the officialis or other designated officer who has proper mandate will appoint the turnus for review and request the defender of the bond to make recommendations regarding the immediate confirmation or admission to a new examination. To facilitate the defender's task, there is provision for one of two options: (1) I have no objections to the ratification of the affirmative decision given in first instance; or (2) I request that the court of second instance admit this case to a new examination. In most cases the judges will probably accept the recommendations of the defender of the bond and immediately ratify the affirmative decision. The decree of confirmation also provides for a relatively simple handling of the notification of parties and of the churches of baptisms and marriage.

Some courts may decide that a more detailed exposition of law and reasons should be contained in the decree of confirmation. It is simple enough to refer to the law as already cited in the first instance sentence and state general reasons, e.g., the proofs and indications in the sentence have established solid basis for moral certitude, the good of the parties demands a prompt decision by the appellate tribunal, justice and equity have been served, and so forth. Again, each appellate tribunal may arrange its own form based on the agreement of the officers. I sincerely hope this streamlined approached will work out in practice.

I am grateful to Father William Schumacher, Judicial Vicar of the Interdiocesan Tribunal of Second Instance for the Province of Chicago for sharing the wealth of material he and the other officials of the Chicago province have compiled and concocted. They have revised forms and form letters, have established an entirely independent court of appeals with its own office in Chicago, and have even installed a WATS line (800) for calls from anywhere in Illinois. I wish I had their budget to work with, but we can all take advantage of the work they have done in the preparation of their interdiocesan tribunal. Many people sent me reams of paper with minutes of meetings, copies of proposals and counterproposals, and all sorts of creative ideas. While I cannot acknowledge each by name, I do want the record to show that I am grateful for your kindness and willingness to share ideas. One thing that does stand out in much of the material I have received is the constant effort to reinvent the wheel. Many people have spent many hours, each in his or her own province, doing exactly what someone else is doing in another province. Today offers a good opportunity to learn from one another.

APPENDIX A

ARCHDIOCESES IN THE UNITED STATES—APPELLATE COURT SYSTEM

Anchorage	Interprovincial Tribunal (with Seattle & Portland)
Atlanta	(still pending)
Baltimore	Interdiocesan Tribunal (entire province)
Boston	Interdiocesan Tribunal (entire province)
Chicago	Interdiocesan Tribunal (entire province)
Cincinnati	Interprovincial Tribunal (with Washington, DC)
Denver	Interdiocesan Tribunal (entire province)
Detroit	Interdiocesan Tribunal (entire province)
Dubuque	Interdiocesan Tribunal (entire province)
Hartford	Interdiocesan Tribunal (entire province)
Indianapolis	Interdiocesan Tribunal (entire province)
Kansas City, KS	Metropolitan system (Kansas City to ??)
Los Angeles	Metropolitan system (Los Angeles to Orange)
Louisville	Interdiocesan Tribunal (entire province)
Miami	Metropolitan system (Miami to Pittsburgh)
Milwaukee	Interdiocesan Tribunal (entire province)
Mobile	Interprovincial Tribunal (with New Orleans)
Newark	Interdiocesan Tribunal (entire province)
New Orleans	Interprovincial (with Mobile Province)
New York	Interdiocesan Tribunal (entire province & Military)
Oklahoma City	Interdiocesan Tribunal (entire province)
Omaha	Interdiocesan Tribunal (entire province)
Philadelphia	Metropolitan system (Philadelphia to Baltimore)
Portland, OR	Interprovincial Tribunal (with Seattle & Anchorage)
St. Louis	Interdiocesan Tribunal (entire province)
St. Paul and Minneapolis	Interdiocesan Tribunal (entire province)
San Antonio	Interdiocesan Tribunal (entire province)
San Francisco	Interdiocesan Tribunal (entire province)
Santa Fe	Interdiocesan Tribunal (entire province)
Seattle	Interprovincial Tribunal (with Anchorage & Portland)
Washington, DC	Interprovincial Tribunal (with Cincinnati)

Data based on survey of all metropolitan tribunals in the United States, September 1983

APPENDIX B

APPELLATE TRIBUNAL   ARCH/DIOCESE OF _____
PROTOCOL NUMBER _____   CASE NAME_____
_____   PROTOCOL NUMBER _____

EX OFFICIO TRANSMITTAL OF CASE

The Tribunal of the above-named diocese has rendered an affirmative decision in the first instance in the above-named case for nullity of marriage. The Defender of the Bond in first instance has offered no objections to this affirmative decision. The Tribunal of first instance hereby encloses the attached sentence in this case for mandatory review by the court of second instance.

Date _____   _____
                                           Officialis or delegate

APPOINTMENT OF TURNUS IN SECOND INSTANCE

Since there has come to us the mandatory review (canon 1682) of the affirmative decision given in first instance, we hereby appoint the following

as Presiding Judge_____
as Associate Judge_____
as Associate Judge_____
as Defender of the Bond _____
as Notary_____

and other officers at the discretion of the Court, granting them all necessary and useful faculties in accordance with canon law. We request the Defender of the Bond to review the sentence (and other acts or documents as required) of this case and make a recommendation regarding the ratification of the affirmative decision.

Date _____   _____
                                                Officialis or delegate by special mandate

OBSERVATIONS OF THE DEFENDER OF THE BOND

As defender of the Bond in second instance, I have reviewed the affirmative decision and the sentence of this case and have no objections to the procedures and formalities used to instruct the case, and make the following observations:

_____I have no objection to the ratification of the affirmative decision given in first instance.

_____I request that the court of second instance admit this case to a new examination.

Date _____   _____

DECREE OF CONFIRMATION

The court of second instance must answer the following doubt: WHETHER THE AFFIRMATIVE DECISION OF FIRST INSTANCE SHALL BE CONFIRMED?

We, the undersigned judges of the Tribunal of second instance, having invoked the Divine Name, having considered the law and the facts in this case, have answered the proposed doubt as follows: IN THE AFFIRMATIVE, that is to say, the Tribunal of second instance ratifies and confirms the affirmative decision given in first instance on the same grounds.

We order the court of first instance to maintain the acts of this case in the diocesan archives, to notify the parties, and to send the proper notification to the churches of marriage and baptism of the parties.

Date _____   _____
                                                Presiding Judge
Place
Seal   _____
                                                Associate Judge

_____   _____
Notary   Associate Judge

OFFICES OF THE DIOCESAN CURIA
INTERRELATIONSHIPS AND CREATIVE POSSIBILITIES

CHARLES TORPEY

With the new institute of moderator of the curia given us in canon 473, §
2 of the revised Code of Canon Law, we are presented an occasion for reviewing some structures and assumptions of diocesan-level administration in the
Catholic Church. Our topic will be covered in four parts in order to provide
a broad context for critiquing and adapting present local church administration. Clearly, reorganization and adaptation of diocesan administration depends
on the size of church to be administered. But there are other factors that may
influence the personnel and effectiveness of church administration.

The four parts of our presentation will be: (1) canonical perspective of the
vicars and fiscal officer; (2) context of diocesan administration; (3) tasks and
skills for administration; and (4) possibilities for organization. Our purpose will
be to provide some basic data about the canonical questions, the context of
administration, and developmental directions for individuals and the institution.

CANONICAL PERSPECTIVE

The revised law addresses the topic of general governance in canons 129-144.
We will review some of the basic canons by way of introduction. Ordinary power
of governance, as in the old law, is joined to an office by law, whereas delegated
power is that which is granted to a person (canon 131). Ordinary power of governance can be either proper or vicarious (canon 131). Ordinaries and the ordinary
of place are the diocesan bishop, others who have been placed over a particular
church, and the vicars general and episcopal (canon 134). When the law speaks
of the diocesan bishop in the context of executive power it refers only to the
diocesan bishop and not to the vicar general or episcopal vicar, unless they have
received a special mandate.

The power of governance is distinguished into three areas: legislative, judicial,
and executive (*exsecutivam,* canon 135). A person exercises executive power over
his subjects, even if they are outside his territory, under certain conditions, according to canon 136. Executive or administrative power can be delegated for
all cases or for individual cases (canon 137), and both ordinary and delegated
executive power is to be broadly interpreted (canon 138) if it is delegated for
all cases (*ad universitatem casuum*). Furthermore, anyone who is delegated some
power is understood to have been granted those powers without which that same
delegated power cannot be exercised, according to canon 138.

Ordinary power ceases by the loss of the office to which it is connected (canon
143). In factual or legal common error and in positive and probable doubt of
law or of fact, the Church supplies, both for the internal and external forum,
the executive power of governance (*potestatem regiminis exsecutivam,* canon

144). The same norm applies to the faculties spoken of in 883, 966, and 1111 (confirmation, penance, and marriage).

Administration of the local church is given in section II, part II, of Book II of the revised law. A diocesan bishop in his own diocese possesses all the ordinary, proper and immediate power required for the exercise of his office except for those cases reserved to the Supreme Pontiff or other supreme authority (canon 381). He is to rule his own local church with legislative, judicial and executive power in accord with the norm of law (canon 391), and he may exercise this executive power himself or through vicars general and episcopal.

The diocesan curia, constituted by those persons and institutes who perform some of the work for the diocesan bishop in the governance (*regimine*) of the diocese, in directing pastoral activity, in caring for the administration (*administratione*) of the diocese, and in exercising judicial power, is the subject of chapter II of this section. Canons 469 to 494 cover most of the material on the curial personnel, especially vicars, the moderator of the curia, and the finance officer. These offices are appointed by the diocesan bishop. The legislative power pertains to the bishop alone (canon 391, § 2), but the judicial power he exercises himself or through the judicial vicar. For the cases and persons pertaining to judicial power, the code refers us to Book VII (472). Our topic will not deal with the legislative and judicial parts of governance of a diocese, but it might be kept in mind that the vicar general, who should be established in every diocese, assists in the governance (*regimine*) of the whole diocese (canon 475) and not merely the *exsecutiva*.

All matters which pertain to the administration of the whole diocese should be ordered and coordinated for the good of that protion of the people of God entrusted to the diocesan bishop, according to canon 473. This is one of the more important canons on the topic, since it mentions the vicars, the moderator of the curia, episcopal vicars, and the episcopal council. All of these institutes serve this primary goal, coordinating pastoral action and administrative matters of the local church (canons 469 and 473). Even though it is the responsibility of the diocesan bishop to take care of all that pertains to the administration of the diocese, the law clearly presumes that vicars general and episcopal will be appointed to assist in that. It is for the bishop himself to coordinate the pastoral activity of those vicars (473, § 2).

There exists no strong presumption that the diocese will need or have a moderator of the curia. If it is expedient, a moderator can be named (canon 473, § 2). He must be a priest, and he should be a vicar general or one of the vicars general. The function of the moderator is to coordinate, under the authority of the bishop, those matters that pertain to administrative matters. In addition, he is to see to it that others in the curia fulfill the office entrusted to them. This latter task of the moderator is a clear and significant innovation regarding vicars, since it introduces very clearly some other lines of accountability and responsibility. It may become the responsibility of the moderator to hand on, or even to establish criteria and occasions for the accountability of other vicars, delegated administrators, and others in administration of a diocese. This may introduce into diocesan administration some complications—more lines of communication and expectation—or more clarity—more explicit expectations and accountability. Along with the increased diversity of both local church pastoral activity and the models of church operative in dioceses, this mention of accountability may bring more attention to the area of clarifying functions and responsibilities.[1]

It makes eminently good sense that the law strongly suggests that the moderator of the curia by named a vicar general (473, § 3), or at least one of them. It would not be wise to have someone coordinating key administrators of executive power without the coordinator having the full executive power of the ordinary. Finally, the bishop may establish the vicars general and episcopal as a specific group for promoting better pastoral activity, which group is called an episcopal council. Diocesan administration and coordination may best be served if other vicars are an integral part of that council, however.

Canon 474 requires that the juridic acts of the curia must be signed by the ordinary from whom they originate; they must also be signed by the chancellor or notary who must inform the moderator of those acts. This may or may not affect administrative functioning in a curia, depending on the number and type of juridic acts generated by the curia, and the administrative arrangement with the curia. Most simply, it might be taken care of by having the moderator be appointed chancellor—and we are right back to square one with the chancellor doing administration! Since validity is involved, creative attention should be given this canon.

The vicar general, of course, in the revised law as well as in the 1917 code, is meant to be the main adminisrative connection in the local church between the diocesan bishop and others in administration and pastoral activity of the local church. He is to assist the bishop in the entire governance of the diocese (*universae diocesis regimine* in canon 475). Keep in mind that *regiminis* includes *exsecutivam* and judicial and legislative, according to canon 135. Does this mean that the vicar general also has some new role in governance in coordinating the tribunal and some legislative functions? Possibly the code's vision of diocesan coordination has shifted slightly to include the tribunal more closely in the curia than some dioceses are used to. At this point it may be too early to judge, partly since the law is not consistent in using *regiminis, exsecutivam* and *administratione* in this chapter of the code. Also, canon 1420 seems to maintain the same identity between the bishop and the vicar judicial, thus indicating no intention of changing the relationship of the vicar judicial to other diocesan vicars.

The general rule for vicars general is that only one is appointed for a diocese, unless the size of the diocese or some other pastoral reason indicates otherwise. The vicars general or episcopal cannot be the same as the canon penitentiary, nor related to the bishop up to the fourth degree.

[1] Also see Robert G. Howes, "Moderator of the Curia: New Boy in Town," *The Jurist* 42 (1982) 517-524.

Episcopal vicars, according to canon 476, can be appointed to take care of matters, with the full authority of the bishop, for a determined part of the diocese, or certain types of matters, or for a determined rite or for a certain group of persons; and they exercise the same authority in law as the vicar general does.

Chancellors and notaries are treated in canons 482 to 491, and their function is to insure the authenticity and preservation of curial acts. Vice-chancellors can also be appointed, if required. Canons 487 and 488 presume that the moderator and the chancellor are two different people. Others can be appointed notaries, however, according to canon 483, so there does not seem to be any reason why the moderator could not be appointed a notary.

The finance council and the fiscal officer (*oeconomus*) are covered in canons 492, 493 and 494. The bishop is to name a fiscal officer who is truly skilled in financial matters and absolutely distinguished for honesty. The fiscal officer is appointed for a five year term, may be re-appointed for other five year terms, and may not be removed except for a serious reason. The fiscal officer can only be appointed after the bishop consults the finance council and the college of consultors (494, §§ 1 and 2).

The role of the fiscal officer is to administer the goods of the diocese under the authority of the bishop in accord with a budget determined by the finance council. From the income of the diocese, the fiscal officer is to meet the expenses which the bishop and others legitimately authorized by him decide. Finally, at the end of the year the fiscal officer must give to the finance council a report of receipts and expenses.

The fiscal officer has responsibilities listed in Book V, *The Temporal Goods of the Church*, beginning with canon 1254. Canon 1278 says that the bishop can assign to the fiscal officer of the diocese those duties outlined in canons 1276 and 1279. It is the responsibility of the ordinary to supervise carefully administration of goods which belong to the public juridic persons subject to him. Canon 1279 says that the administration of the goods of a public juridic person which does not have its own administrator can be taken care of by the ordinary appointing suitable persons as administrators, and they may be re-appointed. Thus, the fiscal officer may have to take care not only of matters dealing with diocesan finances but also the finances of other public juridic persons in the diocese.

Delegation

Before leaving this thumbnail sketch of offices that we will later deal with, let us attend to the rules of delegation. Delegation, spoken of in canons 131 and 132, is that power granted to a person but not by means of an office. Habitual faculties (canon 132) are likewise governed by the prescriptions for delegated power. According to canon 137, ordinary executive power can be delegated both for a single act and for all cases, unless the law provides otherwise. § 3 adds that executive power delegated by someone having ordinary power delegated for all cases can be subdelegated only for individual cases. Canon 140, § 3 states that executive power delegated to several persons is presumed to have been delegated to them *in solidum*. This means that the delegation has been given to the group as a group.

While there is certainly a distinction between ordinary and delegated power, we need not let that difference in canon law obstruct the fashioning of administrative channels by relegating delegated power and vicars with delegated power to secondary position. There may well be dioceses whose administrative tasks are very numerous and very substantial. It may not be reasonable to expect a vicar general to be the head of each one of the main clusters of administrative tasks. Worse, it may be confusing to have a lot of vicars general who in effect are a vicar for a specific area of administration. We need not shy away from appointing administrators for a specific administrative arena simply because they would have delegated rather than ordinary power as a vicar general would.

The qualifications of an administrator other than the ones mentioned in the law probably come under the provisions of Title IX—Ecclesiastical Offices, Provisions of Ecclesiastical Offices, Free Conferral of Ecclesiastical Offices; these are covered in canons 145-157. That last canon states that it is within the competence of the diocesan bishop to provide for ecclesiastical offices in his own particular church by free conferral. Presumably, therefor, the bishop is free to provide both for those ecclesiastical offices mentioned in the law as well as ecclesiastical offices which are required for the effective administration of the particular church. Qualifications for ecclesiastical offices are rather basic, namely, the person must be in communion with the Church as well as qualified, that is, with those qualifications required by the task.

Organization of administration of a diocese including the episcopal vicars, the vicars general, administrators, the staff, the regional administrators, and the lower groups might take advantage of the organization experiences of other dioceses.[2] Some distinctions are worthwhile keeping in mind. For example, there is the distinction of policy formation and policy implementation; policy implementation is a special responsibility of those with skills and responsibilities for various effects to take place. There is the distinction between line and staff, in which line provides direct services and staff refers to the supporting functions required for the line to create the effect. Another important component to keep in mind is the span of control that a particular administrator (vicar) can reasonably take care of. If personnel needs and development are to be attended to, the administration cannot be organized so that the administrator personally cannot attend to the personnel associated with him. The point seems to be, of course, that there is an almost unlimited variety of combinations of vicars general and episcopal vicars in service to the diocesan and parish churches if we value adequately specific authority in the Church.

[2] See James Provost, "Diocesan Administration," *The Jurist* 41 (1981) 88.

116

Some specific requirements for vicars general and episcopal are delineated in canon 478. They must (1) be priests, (2) be at least 30 years of age, (3) have a doctorate or licentiate in canon law or theology, or at least by truly an expert in these disciplines, and (4) be commendable or highly recommended for soundness of doctrine, integrity, prudence, and experience in taking care of things. Before dealing with the role of vicars, both general and episcopal, we turn to another aspect of administration.

II. Context of Diocesan Administration

The interrelationship of the roles of vicars, moderator, fiscal offices, and those who have administrative functions below those offices presupposes some purpose; the flow of the administrative activity, the effective completion of tasks, presupposes some operative set of goals and a vision. The specific tasks and area to be taken care of by a particular department will be established and have their priority in accord with some part of the vision to be implemented. Some vision of the Church will be operative and will serve to coordinate and focus the energy of these personnel around a particular aspect of incarnating the Church. Part of the vision is already given to us in the teaching of the Church, in the revised code, as well as in other sources that define the Church in our day.

But an important part of any vision of the Church derives from local conditions in each church. This quite variable component of the local church's vision strongly influences the presence of the universal Church in a particular place and time, but it also substantially determines the form and effectiveness of the ministry for the church there. Each local church is determined by the local particular limitations, gifts and history, resources and needs of its own people in this place. These limits, gifts and unique characteristics substantially affect how and which ministry a particular church engages in. The ministries and resources will in turn shape the structure and relationships of those who coordinate those ministries. It is not difficult to perceive the priorities and basic vision, to some extent, in the organization of a diocese.

One recent archdiocesan organization plan called for 65 different services to be administered and grouped into 5 different major departments. Another archdiocese has eight department heads taking care of and coordinating about 25 major ministry areas. Structures provide some idea of the vision of Church, but not perfectly, and we should not expect them to. Structures and organization are meant to be vehicles for bringing the energy of a vision to a set of tasks. The more clear the vision—and therefore, the more the local vision explicitly incorporates the limits, gifts and history of the specific diocese—the more effective will be the ministry for that vision.

The most desirable manner of discovering the vision of a local church and those who exercise administrative functions within that church would be a planning and visionary process. There is a National Pastoral Planning Conference

117

whose work assists dioceses in this regard.[3] Whatever the process used to discern the operative vision, it must then be articulated; after the vision has been articulated the further steps of setting goals, assessing resources, organizing personnel and implementing the plan can be determined. But we must first discern the operative vision of Church that moves the administration.

Once the vision is discerned for the local church, some goals are made known, and some basic structure is delineated, comes the step of separating tasks, and then combining them in the most effective way. For our purposes today, we can presuppose the basic structure of bishop, vicars and staff, as well as some basic goals of coordination. After the tasks are clearly described comes the need for a job description, a role description of the personnel who will implement or coordinate the fulfillment of the various tasks.[4] The tasks and job description require some skills on the part of the personnel involved. But even before we get to skills there is the question of leadership style.

Leadership styles run the gamut from autocrat, to clarifier and supporter, to charismatic leader, servant and synergist.[5] We are all aware of different leadership styles, both within the Church, in government, and in business. The significance of leadership style for our topic of vicars lies in this: the implementation of vision of Church will be much more efficient in the local church if the leadership style of the ordinary, the vicars, and others who exercise administrative responsibility are somewhat similar. That is to say, an independent person whose leadership style is one of facilitating and creatively producing will function much better if those around him are similar in their leadership and followship styles. By contrast, an independent person may not function well at all in a situation that includes a lot of dictators or a person who is quite prophetic and a synergistic in his vision.

Not only are there leadership styles, but there are correlative followship styles; the followship style of a person on one end of the continuum will not work well with a leader who is on the other end of the continuum. On the next page are listed some leadership and followship styles.

[3]For more detailed information contact the National Pastoral Planning Conference, 11 Loyola Place, Oakland, New Jersey 07436, in care of Rev. William C. Harms, Chairperson until March of 1984.

[4]For background and perspective in church administration, I am indebted to Robert Kennedy and his course in Administration at Catholic University of America, September to December, 1977.

[5]Brian Hall and Helen Thompson, *Leadership Through Values* (New York: Paulist Press, 1980), p. 64. But see also Chapter 3, pp. 59-84, and 104-108.

LEADERSHIP STYLE*	CHARACTER	FOLLOWSHIP STYLES
1. Tyrant/Dictator	Alienated Person	Oppressed, Totally Dependent
2. Father/Mother, Benevolent Dictator	Preservative Person	Servant, Blindly Obedient
3. Bureaucrat, Benevolent, Maternalistic/ Paternalistic	Organization Person	Delegated Servant, Loyally Devoted to the Institution
4. Clarifier, Supporter Listener	Communal Person	Role Confusion, Clarifier, Supporter, Listener
5. Charismatic Leader, Facilitator, Producer/Creator	Independent Person	Intermediate Peer, Participation
6. Collegial, Leader/ Servant, Inter- dependent Adminis- trator	Creative Person	Collegial Participation
7. Liberator, Syner- gist, Global Net- work of Persons	Prophet Person	Peer, Visionary

*Hall and Thompson, pp. 64, 101, 108-109.

It would seem helpful for anyone involved in diocesan administration to make some preliminary assessment of the leadership styles that will be or are influencing the local church ministry, as well as assessing the followship style which might enable or limit the effective completion of that mission. As one can imagine, the leadership style tends to appreciate and foster the correlative followship style; but conversely, if the leadership style and followship style are widely separated of people in the same organization, confusion, frustration and stress are likely to result.[6]

Those dioceses considering reorganizing or adapting to the revised law might save themselves some trouble by asking what is the leadership style of those who are directly affected, or what is the expectation for the relative leadership and followship styles in the local church at the present time. The point is, if the vicars are to implement the vision of the local church (and the ordinary), it would be helpful to have some similarity between both the operative vision and the leadership styles of the bishop, vicars and staff.

III. Tasks and Skills for Administration

In this section we will deal with the specific tasks for administration in the diocese, combinations of those tasks, skills, conversions, major department

[6]For direction, discovery and assistance with this material, I am indebted to Mr. Lawyer, Henneberry Hill Consultants, Pompey, New York, and his Life Planning Workshop.

heads (vicars), and consultative bodies. First, to the administrative tasks. What are the current administrative tasks that go on (or need to go on) in the diocese? This will vary, of course, from diocese to diocese, more than you might imagine. By listing the current activities that go on, we can begin to deal with combining them under department heads as well as adding others to the particular group of activities.

In making up your list of diocesan administrative activities, it is important to list every type, whether it has to do with educational services, chancery, special apostolates, peace and justice, the handicapped, pro-life, Catholic men and women's organizations, campus ministry, liturgy, family ministry, chaplaincies, etc.. List *all* of those that are currently operating.

Having listed all the tasks of the diocesan level, the next question is: what is the best possible combination of these tasks and services for which a vicar could be appointed? Also figure out a name for that group and what type of vicar would be best. The criteria that you use for grouping these tasks is entirely up to you and your vision of the Church (or your vision that you see at work in the diocese). One basic principle of management and efficiency, of course, is to group like tasks together to avoid unnecessarily complicating the tasks and the communication needed between the personnel who do them.

As we approach the question of the role description and qualifications of the vicar who will coordinate a particular department, we meet the question of skills. What are the skills that each department head will need? A skill is defined as the internalized ability to actualize a value in our behavior. For each value that we hold there are skills that can be identified with incorporating that value into our behavior. We will consider skills under four basic categories.[7]

The first of these categories is instrumental skills. Instrumental skills are oriented towards the completion of manual tasks which involve a development of eye-motor coordination and some mechanical ability. Instrumental skills are very basic to any type of administration and to most types of productivity. An instrumental skill is a blend of intelligence and manual dexterity which enables us to be competent for dealing with ideas, the immediate environment, and for producing something within that context.

The second type are interpersonal skills, or human relations skills. They enable us to establish social relationships and to intensify and improve our basic social relationships. These interpersonal skills enable us to act with some generosity and understanding towards others; this flows from a knowledge of oneself, and the ability to objectify one's own feelings so that cooperation, rather than isolation, is enhanced. Not everyone who is good at instrumental skills automatically has all the gifts and development for interpersonal skills and vice-versa.

The third set, imaginal skills, include skills which enable us to envision possibilities by creating alternatives for the way things are. An imaginal skill is a blend of internal fantasy and feeling that enables us to externalize our ideas

7Hall and Thompson, pp. 29 ff.

120

in an effective and practical manner. An imaginal skill enables us to see and make sense out of increased amounts of data, to learn from direct experience, and to act on complex alternatives creatively.

A fourth set of skills are related to the management of institutions. They involve the integration and use of instrumental, interpersonal and imaginal skills. They are called system skills. A system skill is a blend of imagination, sensitivity and competence which enables a person to envision the parts of a system as they relate to the whole system. It is an ability to design change so as to enhance the growth of the individuals, the persons, and the parts of the organization at the same time. System skills require a breadth of experience and competence so that integration of many skills and gifts can be accomplished in a variety of situations.

Even with this brief outline of basic skill groups, it is possible to describe the skills that a particular vicar or a department head might need for the effective and efficient ministry that he will be directing or coordinating. It seems rather obvious that the vicar for personnel services will require a different set of skills (and level of developement?) from that of the administrative or financial or educational department, or the community and social services vicar. Given the leadership style of the ordinary and the vicars general, it remains for us to match up the primary set of skills needed for a particular vicar in our local church.[8]

The next questions are: are there personnel available who have the appropriate skills? Are there resources available for obtaining and sharpening the relevant skills? And is the local church willing to utilize resources for the skill development of those who will be in administration? It can happen that administrators who are responsible for assigning personnel to administrative tasks confuse one type of skill with another, and with unhappy results. We should not presume that persons with good instrumental skills, able to handle physical/mechanical tasks well, are equally competent for another skill such as interpersonal or imaginal skills. Another example is that of a large institution (such as the Church) in which people confuse the requirement for systems skills with competency in interpersonal skills. Perhaps the many cases of reported burnout in the Church and ministry result from the expectation that one's previous skills are adequate for a new task or for every task that he or she is involved in. It is not uncommon, either, for a particular mentality to pervade a local church so that consciously or unconsciously the leaders deny the need for any type of human skill development in the light of the "grace of office." Skill development will certainly not eliminate original sin nor solve all the problems of administration, but it might allow us to prevent and sort out some of the problems that arise from local church administration.

There are other values, of course, that the local church requires in administrators; some of these are directly connected with the gospel and the incarnation of the Kingdom of God in our world. They are directly connected

[8]See also James J. Gill, "Educating for Leadership," *Human Development* 4 (1983) 7-15.

with faith and ministry, but this is not the time to enter into a full elaboration of qualities of the perfect Christian administrator. It is, however, worthwhile to point to the connections between visions and skills and administration and some basic Christian conversions.

For example, the development of interpersonal skills is directly connected with the Christian conversion to unconditional self-acceptance of oneself and others. One's willingness and ability to listen to and to disclose oneself to another requires acceptance of one's own strengths as well as one's brokenness and vulnerability. Imaginal skills require some conversion to valuing a new order and another beauty in the world, as well as the commitment to unselfish giving and working for that vision. Imaginal skills have to do with a selfless looking beyond the present to the realization of all sorts of potential. These skills require a level of trust, both personal and communal, to take the risks and to do the work. Systems skills require a conversion to community and institution that accepts the incompleteness and brokenness of the whole group. This conversion requires some identification with institutions as life-giving and necessary. Systems skills require a high level of integration and acceptance of the breadth and struggle of both individuals and institutions.

No doubt the Church cannot expect all administrators to be fully skilled or highly developed in every possible human level and Christian value. But the local church can do much to enable both the institution and each individual involved by encouraging the development of various skills, by establishing resources available for that development, and by seeking people with skills for the appropriate tasks and roles. It is a bit naive to believe that the Church has no need to work toward growth and conversion on the part of those who care for the Church. At the same time, it is inimical to the Christian spirit to believe that any number of personal skills can replace the life-giving Spirit as the primary maker-of-Church.

Finally, the revised law requires consultation by the ordinary with various groups which may affect how the administration is organized. To the extent vicars and finance officers are affected by this consultation, and dependent on the style of leadership and communication that obtains in a given locale, it is important to attend to the relationships between consultative bodies and administrators.

The first group of consultative bodies are the pastoral council and the diocesan synod. These two groups are not mandated definitively by the revised law, and they suggest a different, broader, and relative type of consultative process. These groups will more reflect the data-gathering and listening style of leadership and will be more highly determined by the personal style and perspective of the leadership of the local church than will the required consultation.

The required consultation we wish to keep in mind considers seven institutes: the college of consultors, the finance council, the presbyteral council, the deans, pastors, religious superiors and superiors of lay religious institutes. The main canons on consultation for these bodies are ten, and listed in corresponding order to the consultative bodies mentioned above: 494, 1227, 1292, 1293, 515, and 1263 for consultors, finance council, and presbyteral council; 524, 547, 520, and 567 for the deans, pastors, religious superiors, and superiors of lay religious institutes. Of these 10, only canons 1277 and 1292 require that the ordinary obtain the consent of both bodies, the finance council and the consultors.

As we strive to implement both the revised law and realize the vision of Church given in the Second Vatican Council, we might do well to review critically our attitude toward consultation in the Church, both with an eye to simplifying consultative procedures, and with a sharpened ear for better listening to what the churches are saying.

IV. Possible Organization

We have considered the essential canons, the basic administrative tasks, leadership/followship styles, types of skills, and required consultation that pertain to the vicars, moderator, fiscal officer and other administrators of the local church. We have not exhaustively delineated every detail of local church administration, but rather gathered the essential ingredients from various fields of church administration to provide a more complete and realistic grasp of the issues involved. The assignment, skills, and relationships of curial offices remain complicated and relative. Since they will vary from local church to local church, the following become more and more individualized for each church.

We begin with the moderator of the curia. Clearly the moderator should be granted the full authority of governance of a vicar general and should probably be the vicar general (therefore, also, a priest, 30 years of age, with at least a license in canon law or theology, of sound doctrine, probity of character, prudent and competent for good management, according to canon 478). There may be instances in which the moderator would not be the vicar general—a business manager, vicar for administration, etc.—but the revised law says he should be a priest (canon 473). Other considerations might influence the name or function of this role depending on the local church.

Closely connected with the moderator are the other main vicars. First, considering the scope of administration required, we need to determine the number of main vicars that would best serve for this particular administration. With an approximate number of main vicars in mind, which should be episcopal vicars and which should be vicars general? Could some be administrators who are delegated, rather than vicars? From the point of view of skills, we need to consider the requirements for the area of activity (schools, communication, social services, finances) as well as the persons or groups with whom this vicar will interact immediately (vicar general, administrative core, bishop's staff, etc.), and occasionally (presbyteral council, finance council, pastoral council, school boards, etc.).

The fiscal officer need only be competent in economic matters and of outstanding honesty of character, and appointed for a 5 year term but renewable for additional 5-year terms indefinitely (canon 494). The possibilities for the person and role of the institute are quite extensive. This person could be male or female, bookkeeper, priest or lay person, part-time or full-time, very much or very little involved in diocesan pastoral activity, in charge of property or only finances, or any type of vicar, it appears. In the appointment to this office we have a grand opportunity to combine the vision and requirement of the revised law with the unique administrative requirements of each local church. Not only should we attend to the vision of Church regarding consultation and expertise outside the Church, but we also should attend to simplification and non-multiplication of offices for the sake of offices. One diocesan situation comes readily to mind in which the vicar general is for all practical purposes the fiscal officer, and this may work well for that church. Another diocese may require very little financial administration and staff, so that the appointment of a fiscal officer need not require the addition of more people.

Perhaps more crucial in the appointment of a fiscal officer is the interrelationship of this person to the finance council and the diocesan agencies that send and receive money from him or her. The other requirement that might fit well with this institute is that of civil law expertise, thus enabling the person to combine the financial and legal expertise for contracts, administration for public juridic persons, and other legal matters that might affect the financial condition of the local church.

The assignment of other vicars (including the vicar general, if not already appointed), might be considered in the light of how many vicars, how the administrative work is divided up, and whether they should be delegated administrators rather than vicars, and, of course, most importantly, how this vicar will best serve the area of ministry that is being administered. In light of the administrative tasks, the leadership style, and the personnel available how would you arrange and assign personnel for the vicars of your local church? Since episcopal vicars have to be priests (canon 478), it might be more clear in the minds of the administrators who are more or less equal that they not be called episcopal vicars. Indeed, perhaps we need a different title for administrators that would be clear for everyone to understand immediately; "Secretary for something" is a common one, but perhaps gets too long: "Secretary for social concerns with special emphasis on peace and the handicapped." "Delegate" might be confused with the franchised participant at national conventions. Whatever name emerges for the several administrators (in dioceses that have more than one) we must be aware that the names and titles can be quite powerful in determining and expressing the relative importance of an administrator and the ministry served by that administrator.

Besides the chancellors and other notaries, who can be appointed easily for the convenience of the vicariate or the person they serve, it might be helpful to consider the vicars forane, or deans. Since canon 524 specifies that the dean must be consulted in the appointment of someone to take care of a parish, some new relationship might be called for between personnel boards, vicars and parish ministers. Perhaps a thorough review of personnel policies, evaluation, training and coordination would be appropriate in light of this new canon. Or this may be a canon which simply is no help in our present American church, and it may fall into a mere formality, and later into total neglect. However, in light of the many dire warnings about the shortage of priests in the United States in the very near future, this may be the time to activate some regional awareness, training and responsibility for neighboring parishes. Undoubtedly the personnel question will more and more look to what is the best combination of priests and other ministers, rather than what priest goes where. How would this new requirement for consulting the dean before appointing a parish administrator affect your own diocese's personnel policy and functioning?

The revised law presents us with a minimal outline for administering in and for the local church, the diocese. The task remaining for the local churches is to assess and serve the ministry needs of that church, then to critique, adapt, and utilize the institutes of the revised law to serve the Kingdon of God alive in our midst.

THE CANONIST: OBSTRUCTIONIST OR ENABLER
FOR WOMEN IN THE CHURCH

I. JUDITH BARNHISER

In the past ten years the Committee on Women has researched various issues regarding the status of women in the Church. It has contributed to seminars, research projects and resolutions in a continuous effort to eradicate the injustices affecting women's status in the Church.

In these ten years, the committee has gone through many changes in membership, leadership and tasks. While at times these changes resulted in a struggle as to focus and direction the committee has remained true to its original mandate: to continue the study of the status of women and to address itself to the achievement of an equality for women in the Church's law.

During the past two years, the Committee has endeavored to support the Canon Law Society's educational thrust. The Committee has focused on producing an educational package which covers the wide spectrum of issues regarding the status of women in the Church. Three sections of the seven part package are now ready to present to you and the Society's membership. In the Learning Handout that has been provided for this workshop are three sections. The first is an analysis of a survey of the female membership of the Society. The second section is the basis for this seminar and will be explained in a moment. The third section is a survey of the ecclesiastical offices, functions and ministries open to women in the revised code. It is the committee's intention, upon the Board of Governors' approval, to complete the four remaining parts of the educational package which include preparation of a study guide for affirmative action, stories of women canonists, a speakers bureau, and models for workshops for educating persons on the rights of women in the context of social justice.

The second section of the Learning Handout is the basis for this seminar. In this section, the committee designed models for workshops and seminars on issues regarding women in the Church vis-à-vis the revised code. We believe that in the process of our educating ourselves in the new code and before educating others we have to deal with our own concepts, knowledge and attitudes toward women in the Church. To that end, we have to address the basic question of whether we as canonists are enablers or obstructionists.

II. CECELIA BENNETT

My portion of the presentation will be patterned on the workshop model in the Learning Handout. The Learning Handout addresses four groups: women; professional church ministers; diocesan chancery and parish personnel; and laity.[1] The process for this workshop will be designed following the model for group three, professional church ministers.[2] The flow of this workshop follows the same outline for workshops in the Learning Handout. This includes an Introduction, Historical Overview, Practical Methods for Responding, and Ways of Futurizing.

The Introduction to the models includes a statement of purpose and a statement of the objectives for the workshop. Judy has discussed our purpose. The objective of this workshop is first of all to provide an experience of what it means to be a woman in today's Church; second, to explore immediate possibilities for women in light of the revised code; third, to improve the status of women in the Church; fourth, to look beyond the immediate to the future. The style of the workshop will include input and process. Part of this process will be an evaluation of the revised code as it affects women. The framework for doing this will be that suggested in the educational packet. This brief historical overview will be followed by some practical methods for resolving the issues. This is the process portion of the workshop.

Approaching the topic from the historical perspective I raise two questions. How do changes in the revised code affect women? How does the current praxis of the Church affect women?

My response to the first question is that the revised code recognizes some of the progress that has been made concerning the status of women in the Church during the last two decades. It incorporates the work of the council and the praxis of the Church in most areas. For example the canons on the special ministers of baptism and Eucharist.[3]

I believe the revised code clarifies some of the issues for future discussion. One of these issues centers around the question of status in the Church. Is gender the status determinant or is it baptism? The article cited in the bibliography in the Learning Handout by Katherine Meagher, "The Challenge, A Common Status for Men and Women" in *Studia Canonica* addresses the question in detail and is one of the best discussions on the topic that I have seen.[4]

The issue of orders and jurisdiction is raised several times in the revised code. For women the capacity to fill administrative office in the Church is an issue to be studied in light of the canons in the revised code that have opened ecclesiastical offices and ministries which require jurisdiction to women. These include the office of collegiate judge, the delegate of marriage, and lay preaching.[5] Questions are raised in the area of women participating in cultic functions, for example women being excluded from the permanent ministries of

---

[1]See the Learning Handout prepared for this seminar for a detailed explanation of these populations, p. 16. [Page numbers refer to original Handout—Ed.]

[2]In the Handout a general framework is provided for the workshop followed by specific outlines for each section and each target group; cf. pp. 16-17.

[3]Canons 861, 910.

[4]See the Selected Bibliography in the Learning Handout, p. 25.

[5]Canons 1421, 1112, 766.

acolyte and lector when these are open to lay men.[6] In addition the exclusion of women from orders will keep this an open question in the minds and hearts of many.[7]

The revised code does indeed open several ecclesiastical offices and ministries to women. The third section of the learning handout has a detailed discussion of these canons.[8] I will briefly review some of them for you now. From my reading to the text I have divided the canons into three group.[9] The first are those offices or ministries that are open to women, as well as men, because they are qualified. Some of these qualifications will include experience, training and education. The offices include: chancellor and notary, the function of advocate, the offices of defender of the bond, promoter of justice, collegiate judge, business manager. Canon 473 on the moderator of the curia is an interesting one in that it states that the moderator "ought to be a priest" leaving the question of the possibility of appointing a women to this office.[10]

Women may also participate on pastoral and financial councils on both the diocesan and parish levels. Women may participate in various degrees at synods and councils.[11] In accord with the statutes of a conference of bishops women may hold offices within a conference, one of these possibly being that of general secretary. And finally from this group of canons women may serve as censors and at pontifical missions.

The second set of canons opens to women ministries and offices based on one's obligation to spread the gospel flowing from baptism and confirmation.[12] These are the offices of catechist and missionary, the obligation and right to study and teach the sacred sciences, and preaching (with restrictions).

The third group of canons opens ecclesiastical offices and ministries to women based on pastoral necessity, again raising the issue of women partici-

---

[6]Canon 230. It is of special concern that this canon is placed in the section of the code entitled "The Obligations and Rights of the Lay Christian Faithful." I propose that this further highlights the issue of gender as a status determinant for women and further points out the Holy See's reluctance to include women in cultic functions as baptized persons in the Church.

[7]Canon 1024.

[8]Learning Handout pp. 28-36. If canons are cited in the Learning Handout they will not be cited again in the text.

[9]These three groups have been divided based on reasons for fulfilling an ecclesiastical office or ministry. These are my divisions based on my reading of the text. The three divisions include: the persons being admitted because they are qualified, the persons having an obligation to fill an office because of baptism and confirmation, or there is a need for the person to fill the office based on a pastoral necessity, usually a lack of clergy.

[10]Learning Handout, pp. 21-22 and 29-30.

[11]Canon 346 provides for superiors of clerical religious orders to be called to the synod of bishops, but does not have a similar provision for non-clerical religious orders, thereby, excluding women as participants. Canon 443 provides for the participation of major superiors of both clerical and non-clerical religious orders at particular councils and canon 463 provides for the representation of women religious and lay women at diocesan synods.

[12]See canon 759, and Learning Handout, p. 31.

pating in cultic functions. These ministries and offices include the temporary ministry of lector and the special ministers of Eucharist, baptism and the blessed sacrament. I believe a case can be made for girls and women being altar servers based on canon 930 which provides for "a properly instructed lay person" helping a blind priest celebrate the Eucharist and canon 906 which states that a priest should not celebrate the Eucharist without at least one member of the Christian faithful present.[13]

Out of pastoral necessity and with the approval of the conference of bishops and the permission of the diocesan bishop, women may be the official delegated witness for marriage. The language in canon 528 is stronger. As a result of a "dearth of clergy" women may be assigned the care of a parish. And finally, women may administer certain sacramentals.

Canon 1024 is the canon in the revised code which restricts orders to baptized males. Canon 1035 requires the ministries of lector and acylote before ordination to the diaconate.

Other gender related issues in the revised code of special interest relate to domicile and rites. Gender is no longer a status determinant for either. The place of marriage is now that of the bride or the groom. The canon on abduction as an impediment to marriage was retained for cultural reasons. The difference in the age of marriage for boys and girls has also been maintained.[14]

In response to the second question, "How does the current praxis of the Church affect women?" it is difficult to generalize. The revised code will provide some new opportunities for women in the Church; however, each place is different and will respond accordingly. In those areas where, for example, bishops have written pastoral letters,[15] established commissions to study the status of women, or have approved affirmative action plans for women, the code will more than likely be used as a means to further improve the status of women and to increase opportunities for women to serve the Church in that area. In other places the revised code will not be implemented, and worse might be used to limit the role of women in a given area.

The canons on rights of the Christian faithful in the revised code have specific implications for praxis.[16] The first is canon 212 concerning the freedom of the Christian faithful to reveal their needs, especially spiritual ones, and the right and duty to make known their opinions. This canon coupled with canon 215 on the freedom to found and run associations and canon 216 on the right to promote and support apostolic activity, raise serious concerns about the conflict between praxis and theory following the recent statement of John Paul II on withdrawing support of groups which advocate the ordination of women.[17]

[13]Learning Handout, p. 36.
[14]Learning Handout, p. 35-36.
[15]See the Selected Bibliography in the Learning Handout for a partial list of these pastoral letters, pp. 25-26.
[16]Learning Handout, pp. 21, 33-34.
[17]"The Bishop: Sign of Compassion, Sign of Fidelity," *Origins* 13/14, p. 239.

Canon 219 on freely choosing a state of life is another canon that raises questions between praxis and theory. Canon 229 concerning the right to study the sacred sciences and the capacity to teach the sacred sciences raises questions of praxis especially in light of the current seminary study and Bishop Marshall's letter.[18]

And finally canon 231 states the obligation to be properly formed for the ecclesiastial work and office one fills and the right to a just remuneration for this work. This canon has special implications for women employed by the Church. The results of our survey clearly show this is the case, especially for women religious who responded to the survey, the majority of whom earn between $4,000 and $9,000 a year.[19] The survey also showed that very few degreed women canonist have positions of managerial or line authority in the Church.[20]

As we can see the praxis does and will vary. Some areas are looking at women as chancellors, as judges; others will not. When I travel and speak on the topic of women and talk about the revised code and the increased opportunities for women, inevitably women say, "How is that going to help me when I ask in my parish to read and the pastor says only men read?" As canonists we have our work cut out for us.

You were told that this workshop would give you an experience of what it means to be a women in today's church. In order to help do that I would like to share with you for a few minutes my story, my experience as a woman and a canonist in today's church. After working for five years in a tribunal in the south the bishop of the diocese sent me to Catholic University for the Master's in Church Administration. Upon completion of the degree I was to work for the diocese for at least another three years. When I returned the former officialis after two weeks terminated me. His reasons centered around my now being a woman professional. The theory of my going to school was easier to accept than the reality. I was told it was better for me to leave and accept the "gift" of my education than to have both of us placed in an impossible situation. I returned to Catholic University and earned my J.C.L. What I then found was the experience that if I wanted to use the degree I needed to hunt around for a job situation that I felt might accept me as a women and that would also provide some degree of opportunity to use the degree. If I found such a position the next step was their acceptance of me. As a woman canonist I am only able to partially use my degree. I could be a defender with an indult, never a judge or officialis. In chancery work the options I found were even more limited. As a result, I chose not to begin the long job search and instead went into educational administration.

Another experience I have had as a women working for the Church is that on one hand I have felt, and in fact have been, the token woman, taken out for

---

[18]Bishops Marshall's letter, dated August 6, 1983, reported in October 21, 1983, *NCR*.
[19]Learning Handout, p. 7.
[20]Learning Handout, p. 3.

"show and tell." Then on the other hand, I was not invited to participate in certain meetings or events, or I was not consulted on something because I was a woman.

These are just a few of my experiences. For some of you they will be all too familiar, others will have other stories. They are shared in the hope of giving you a greater appreciation for the dynamics of the dilemma facing us as canonists today.

Now I will give you an opportunity to respond. I would like you to spend a few minutes writing on two questions. What is your personal response to the issues? What can you do as an individual? Your reflection is just for yourself, it is not to be shared.

We will now move on to the third part of the presentation: "Practical Methods for Responding." You were promised process during this workshop and this is it. I want you to break up into groups of six persons each. As a group I want you to discuss the four questions on the newsprint. Choose one person from the group to act as a recorder and in twenty minutes we will come back together to report. Move quickly through the questions so that you do not spend all the time on only one or two questions. (1) How can the revised code be seen as a beginning-challenge to improve the status of women in the Church? (2) In what ways is the canonist an obstructionist of women in the Church? (3) How can you as a canonist be an initiator of affirmative action, an enabler of women in the Church? (4) What specifically can you do?

Reports from small groups

In reply to questions one, the following responses were given:
> we need to help people give up bad theory and chauvinism; must continue process, keep moving forward; issues of orders and administration are not separate, issues need to be defined, e.g. clerical-non-clerical presupposition, clerical canonists are not in line positions: problem is not just confined to women canonists; need to look at future and Vatican III; need to look at as a challenge and not to undo what is already being done, responsibility to use revised code in a constructive way; need to work on the fundamental rights of all people, use canonical due process to handle all disputes; look at the code as it exists, as the beginning of an affirmative action program in each diocese.

In reply to question two, the following responses were given:
> the obstructionist puts bad law over reality; tension between women religious and lay women in the area of salary has negative effects; Vatican II opened windows, but there are still screens: the canonist is identified with the screens; because canonists are seen as enforcers of law they are often mistakenly looked at as obstructionists.

In reply to question three, the following responses were given:

the enabler needs to concentrate on rights of persons, needs to intensify affirmative action; canonist has an opportunity on a daily basis to implement code; implementation of revised code will bring about pain if it changes the current reality in the negative, canonist's role is to help avoid this; canonist needs to help structure affirmative action, Seattle personnel policy is an acceptable model; facilitate educational workshops; need to look at what we can do when due process will no longer work; need to be aware of the educational needs of women and discover, implement ways of involving women in education; need to recognize politics involved in the issues, recognize problems women face in society; need to discourage recourse of disputes to higher level, if can be done at lower level; canonists need to help change limited access to education for women; need to work on personnel issues to enable women to fill offices; complain louder, work harder; quality of education needs to be strengthened, stress adult education first; facilitate dialogue session to familiarize women with law regarding themselves; should be a radical, but speak like a conservative; question: who speaks for Rome? Rome sends mixed messages; then there is the question of the official church and non-official church work of women and the major influence of women in the Church; need to encourage persons to take offices open to them and to look at new offices in order to open more offices to women; canonists need to be creative interperters, not merely implementers of law.

III. HARMON SKILLEN

My purpose here is to wrap up this seminar and give us some direction for the future. I would like to talk about the future by starting with the past. I want to say a few words about why I am a member of this committee, and that has a lot to do with my past. You see, I was born and raised right here in this city. I was one of five children and a member of a strong Catholic family. But like a lot of families, Catholic families, of that time I was raised with a strong dose of Catholic Calvinism and a lot of that came out in attitudes toward sex and sexuality—negative attitudes. At the same time, I had three sisters, so there were also a lot of healthy things going on in my childhood with regard to the relationships between men and women. Then, at age thirteen, I left the family and went to the seminary. And that was a disaster, because it was a totally male society and aggressively sexist. What I really needed at that time of my life was to continue to grow up in a family situation, but that did not happen. The decision to enter the seminary was my own, but the institution's approach to relationships with females was disastrous.

As a matter of fact, it was not until about two years after my ordination that I began to realize that I could feel comfortable around women. It was then that

I began to realize that a grave injustice had been done to me by the institution and I realized that I was angry. I accept the responsibility for my own maturation process. Perhaps I did not take hold as I should have, but the institution did not help. I was taught that women were to be avoided and dealt with from the position of suspicion. When I started to become aware of what had been going on I was angry.

That anger became the source of energy for me, energy that I wanted to use to undo this terrible injustice of sexism that had touched my life and created such fear and anxiety for me. And then several years ago, I had the opportunity to participate in a workshop put on by Joan Ohannesan. It was an outstanding workshop and really opened my eyes to the problem of sexism that exists not only in our Church, but also in our society. So, my participation in this committee is generated from a desire to undo all this injustice of sexism.

In this seminar today we have given you a tool to do the same thing—to go out and undo the injustice of sexism. I think, though, that there are a lot of women out there who should be involved in this fight, but who are not. I think they are not because they won't take a look around and recognize or admit the problem. I believe the reason why they won't is because deep down they know there is a lot of anger within themselves, and if they start to deal with the problem of sexism and how it has affected them personally, that anger will surface. The anger is so strong, that it scares them—they are afraid they won't be able to handle it. But I think we need to help people, especially women, see the problem, recognize the anger, and channel the energy produced by the anger to fight against the injustice of sexism.

Anger is a good and healthy emotion and I think we can use it to deal with the problem of sexism. We have to be aggressive in fighting, too. By that I mean we have to actively look for opportunities to speak out about sexism, opportunities to discover and reveal the problem, opportunities to move women into the mainstream of church life and administration.

So the future would involve this: recognize the problem, do not hide from it or avoid it or ignore it. And then be aggressive about doing something to remove it. So let us go out there and have at it. Thank you all for being here today.

LEARNING HANDOUT
COMMITTEE ON WOMEN IN THE CHURCH

The following material was prepared as a "learning handout" for the seminar conducted by the Committee on Women in the Church and is reproduced here for the convenience of C.L.S.A. members. The Handout has three parts:

Part I. Analysis of the Survey of the Female Membership of the CLSA, 1982-1983

Part II. Proposed Models for Workshops/Seminars on Issues Regarding Women in the Church vis-à-vis the Revised Code of Canon Law

Part III. Survey of Ecclesiastical Offices, Functions and Ministries Open to Women in the Revised Code.

PART I. ANALYSIS OF THE SURVEY OF THE FEMALE MEMBERSHIP OF THE CLSA 1982-1983

I. *History and Purpose of the Survey*

The genesis of this project was part of the committee's planning since the national convention in Chicago, October of 1981. The committee strove to create plans to be part of the CLSA's priority for education regarding the revised code and canonical issues.

Through its subsequent meetings and correspondence in 1982, the committee proposed for the BOG's consideration an educational package which focused on the issues regarding women in the Church vis-à-vis the revised code and the CLSA's priority for education. The first part of this package was to be the survey of the CLSA's female membership. Once authorized by the BOG to prepare its educational package, the committee completed the first part, the survey. By the national convention in Hartford in 1982, the committee had completed its survey.

The purpose of the survey was not just to compile statistics. Its purpose was four fold:

1. to present objective information and data on the female CLSA membership including the various attitudes toward the Society, what it has to offer for women, and what the women can contribute;

2. to form the basis for women canonists telling their stories and a composite profile of the woman canonist;

3. to provide a base for future agendas for committee work and support the interests of women in the Society;

4. to continue the role of the committee to raise the consciences of the total CLSA membership on the status of women in the Church and its attitude toward its own female membership.

II. *Statistical and Attitudinal Analysis*

A. Population Studied

143 surveys were sent to the CLSA female membership in the summer of 1982, from the mailing list provided by the Office of the Executive Coordinator. 70 surveys were returned.

Question areas included: (1) personal information: name, address, phone, title/position, age, status, institutional affiliation; (2) educational background: degrees earned, institutions attended, canonical seminars/institutes attended, interest in earning a canonical degree; (3) employment history: present position/description, status or canonical appointment, if any, salary rate; (4) CLSA participation: type of membership, meetings attended, personal resources, areas of expertise, thesis/dissertation topics, publications, workshops given, courses taught, perception of personal role in the Society and future contribution; (5) what CLSA resources can be offered: topics/issues, CLSA's contribution to women canonists or practitioners of the law; to women in the Church, meetings with other women in the Society; personal feelings about being a CLSA member.

Of those responding, 53 had BA/BS degrees; 8 with J.C.B.; 37 with MA/MS; 9 with M.Ch.A.; 12 with J.C.L.; 1 with M. Div.; 6 with Ph.D.; 1 with S.T.D.; and 9 with J.C.D.

B. Statistical/Attitudinal Analysis

Because of the length of this section, the complete breakdown of data and information is contained at the end of this report (cf. Appendix to Part I). [Due to length of material, not reproduced here but available on request from C.L.S.A. Executive Coordinator—Ed.]

III. *Observations*

After reviewing the compilation of the surveys as well as the individual responses, the committee discussed the results at length. The following represents the committee's observations. In the continuing efforts to dialogue on the issues affecting women in the Church and the Society, we urge all of you to share your own observations with us and each other. (Note: the individual responses are available through the chairperson of this committee.)

A. Of the women religious degreed canonists, very few have positions of managerial authority, i.e., line positions with the responsibility of final decision making. While two persons have the title/position of director, one is executive secretary, and one is a chancellor, the clear majority are assistants, defenders of the bond, and notaries. These women represent a median age of 40; the highest grouping is in the salary range of $4,000-14,000. The clear majority are active in the Society and represent a wide range of interests and expertise other than religious law. Some feel that their expertise in these fields is not being tapped by the Society. Those responding are split as to the degree of comfortableness in the Society.

B. The women religious non-degreed canonists reflect an educated body with 18 having masters degrees. While they have attended seminars and institutes dealing primarily with tribunal issues, they represent a far more significant number with lesser positions of managerial authority. Of all the groups studied, they feel the most comfortable in the Society.

C. Three laywomen degreed canonists responded. They represent the youngest age group and are in a larger salary range. Like their religious degreed counterpart, they do not have managerial positions with final decision making authority. Their titles include: vice-chancellor, pastoral minister and administrative assistant, and part time advocate. Two feel uncomfortable in the Society and one feels comfortable.

135

D. The clear majority of canonical degreed and non-degreed religious women are working in tribunals.

E. The laywomen non-degreed canonists are 17. Their ministry is more in the realm of advocacy in the tribunal system. They represent an older age group and feel comfortable in the Society.

F. The survey results destroy the myth that if a woman is a degreed canonist or practitioner in canon law, that woman is a religious and no laywoman is competent to be a canonist.

G. The survey results destroy another myth or presumption that women (especially laywomen) are only secretaries in tribunals.

H. The survey results indicate that the majority of women responding to the questionnaire are either canonists or degreed in other fields which mitigates another myth that female members of the Society tend to be uneducated or lacking canonical credentials.

I. Women are interested in earning a canonical degree—an interest that should be pursued by the Society, dioceses, and canon law schools.

J. It is estimated that in 1972, there were five female members in the Society. The total membership presently is 143, a substantial increase.

IV. *Recommendations*

After studying and discussing the results of the Survey, the committee makes the following recomendations to the Board of Governors and general membership of the CLSA.

A. The Survey indicates that a number of female members are still uncomfortable with the convention liturgies. Even though there were efforts to have the Society endorse a resolution at the 1978 national convention (St. Louis) to use Canon Four for the liturgy to avoid the use of exclusive or sexist language (cf. 1978 *Proceedings,* pp. 156-157), that resolution was tabled. There has been no obvious, serious attempt to eradicate this problem to involve more women in the liturgy.

Therefore, it is recommended that this issue be addressed effectively, lest the sensitivity, credibility, and the authenticity of the CLSA be questioned. We further recommend that the BOG make a special effort to bring this to the attention of the liturgy planners and get more women involved in the liturgy planning.

B. A continued effort needs to be made in addressing women's issues vis-à-vis major presentations at the national convention. There has not been a major presentation on women's issues given since the 1975 national convention (San Diego).

Therefore, it is recommended that the R & D committee collaborate with/consult the Committee on Women in the Church in the planning for each national convention for a suggested list of topics and speakers on issues regarding women, with the hope that in the near future the theme of the convention be on the role of women in the Church. (Note: we realize that any committee/CLSA member can make suggestions to the R & D committee, but a concerted effort and definite relationship should be made between this committee and R & D on those issues affecting women.)

Secondly, one of the sections of this committee's proposed educational package was to produce a Speakers Bureau. We recommend that the BOG support/mandate the committee to accomplish this task by the 1984 national convention.

C. It is recommended that this committee support and provide our services in providing information and data to the women's caucus group.

D. There seems to be some confusion as to women applying for membership and the question of being degreed or sponsored.

Therefore, it is recommended that the BOG direct the Membership and Nominations Committee to clarify the criteria for sponsorship and that it be equitable and non-sexist.

E. The Survey results show that the female membership want an active role in the work of the Society and be involved in areas other than religious law.

Therefore, it is recommended that the BOG continue to consider qualified women to be members of various committees, especially Standing Committees; General Convention Chairperson; Press Officer; for substantive participation in the CLSA's on-going educational work.

It is further recommended that the female membership be encouraged to seek and accept membership on CLSA committees and positions on the BOG.

F. The survey results show that women active in canonical ministry need to be integrated into managerial/line positions in the institutional Church. Not only do the statistics show that this has not been achieved, but the responses in the latter half of the survey show that some women seek it.

Therefore, it is recommended that the BOG, working with this committee, provide a consultant upon request from those persons looking for ways to integrate women into the institutional, managerial, political life of the Church.

PART II: PROPOSED MODELS FOR WORKSHOPS/SEMINARS ON
ISSUES REGARDING WOMEN IN THE CHURCH VIS-À-VIS THE REVISED CODE OF CANON LAW

I. *Purpose of the Models*

The purpose of the models includes several aims which will take on a specific focus for each of the target groups. The following is a general statement of purpose of the models.

A. To focus on the issues regarding women in the Church vis-à-vis the revised Code of Canon Law.

B. To inform canonists and other interested persons on the topic of women in the Church as related to the revised Code of Canon Law.

C. To stimulate a conversion within/among the participants.

D. To provide an experience which fosters dialogue among individuals and groups.

II. *Populations to be Addressed*

A. Group One: Women

This population group includes women religious and lay women. The package is designed to be used with a variety of audiences within this population group. For example: women religious; lay women; professional church women: lay and religious; mixed groups of women religious and lay women from all professional and vocational areas.

B. Group Two: Professional Church Ministers

This population group includes bishops, priests, deacons, religious and lay ministers, as well as those in formation for professional church ministry (i.e., seminarians, diaconal candidates, theology students). The package is designed to be used with a variety of audiences within this population group. For example: bishops, various clergy groups; candidates for ministry; mixed groups of pastoral ministers: lay and ordained.

C. Group Three: Diocesan, Chancery and Parish Personnel and Councils

This population includes diocesan officials and department personnel, parish personnel and councils on both levels. The package is designed to be used with a variety of audiences within this population group. For example, chancery department heads, vicars, diocesan pastoral councils, presbyteral councils, personnel boards, episcopal councils, parish councils.

D. Group Four: Laity

This population group includes laity in general and lay organizations. The package is designed to be used with a variety of audiences within this population group. For example: parish groups such as general congregations, adult education groups; lay interest groups; marriage and family life groups; youth and young adult groups; lay associations.

III. General Model for Workshop/Seminar

A. *General Overview*

Workshops for all four groups are designed to contain the following elements.

1. Introduction
   a. a statement of the issue as it relates to the specific audience to be addressed.
   b. Objectives for the workshop. (This may be done by sharing with the participants the agenda or outline for the workshop.)

The statement of the issue and objectives of the workshop arise from the purpose of the models as described in the preceeding section.

2. Historical overview
   a. Women in Scripture, tradition, law, Vatican II, revised code, current praxis.
   b. Women as members of people of God, members of Christian faithful, what are women's rights in the Church, how are they protected, current status.

3. Practical methods for responding/resolving the issues/questions raised
   a. Personal reflection.
   b. Revised code as a beginning and a challenge.
   c. Initiator of affirmative action.
   d. Action plan.

4. Ways of futurizing or moving beyond the immediate.
   a. What is our vision for the future?
   b. How do we build our vision for the future?

B. *Specific Outline*

The following is a detailed breakdown of the workshop by sections. Where appropriate suggestions are made for group process and or discussion as well as references to specific population groups.

1. Introduction
   a. Statement of the Issues(s)
   The issues at hand include: How is the status of women in the Church affected by the revised Code of Canon Law? What has been the historical development of women's status in the Church? What is the future of women in the Church? Is there a gender gap in the Church? If so, what does this mean? What are the feelings associated with the gap? What are its legal implications? How can it be healed?
   b. Objectives for the workshops.
      1. To focus on the issues.
      2. To give information on the revised Code of Canon Law vis-à-vis the status of women in the Church.
      3. To give historical genesis of the current status of women in the Church and its legal effect on women.
      4. To share some practical ways of responding to, resolving the issue(s) and questions raised.
      5. To move beyond the immediate to the future in our thinking.

2. Historical overview
   a. What is the history of women in the Church that brings us to where we are today?
      1. What are those images of women in Scripture and tradition that affected the role of women in canon law and the status of women in the Church?
      2. What has been the history of women in canon law?
      3. What does Vatican II have to say about women?
      4. How do the changes in the revised code affect women in the Church?
      5. How does the current praxis of the Church affect women?
   b. What issues are raised by these historical observations?
      1. Is there a gender gap in the Church? If so, what does this mean? What are the feelings associated with the gap? What are its legal implications?
      2. Who or what decided what the status quo would be?
      3. What do the 1917 code, Vatican II and the revised code say to women in the Church?
      4. What does the "new way of thinking" in the revised code mean to women as members of the people of God, as members of the Christian faithful in full communion?
      5. What do the new canons on rights have to say to the issues of women in the Church?
      6. What ministries and offices are open to women in the revised code?
      7. Does the revised code go far enough?

Under the section of historical overview an outline has been prepared (see the audio-visual section of this package). This may be used also as a handout, as an overhead, or put on newsprint. It is a quick overview of the topic and can be done in an hour if there is no discussion or process.

For Group I some ways of engendering discussion include:
   1. Ask women to share their relationship with the institution. For relig-

ious, areas of concern might be their formation and ministries; for lay women areas of concern might be marriage, the role of single or divorced women in the Church, lay women in ministry.

2. What was your recollection of Vatican II; how did it affect your life as women in the Church?
3. Did you ever want to be an altar server? Did you ever want to be a priest?
4. What are the difficulties that you face in your ministry as a woman in the Church?
5. Use prayer and meditation to celebrate the giftedness of women and to lift up in prayer the pain of coming to the altar with empty hands.

For Group II some ways of engendering discussion include:

1. Use word association; i.e., give them ten words for women and have them write down what comes to mind (cf. attached suggestion list in audio-visual section).
2. Use a script and have the participants imagine: you are a woman in the Church . . . you are applying for a job. . . . Another way to do this is to role play various negative and positive situations centered around women in the Church.
3. Ask them to share their experiences of the gender gap.
4. Ask questions of the group in general following the input in b.1.

For Group III some ways of engendering discussion include:

1. Ask questions: Do you see sexism; is it there; is there really a gender gap in the Church?
2. Chart the personnel history of your parish or diocese with respect to hiring women. What boards do women serve on; what ministries are they active in?
3. Discuss the demographic study of the committee with this group.

For group IV some ways of engendering discussion include:

1. What did it mean to be a Christian prior to and after Vatican II?
2. Ask them to share their experience of the gender gap in the Church.
3. Ask question of the group in general following the input in b.1.

3. Practical methods for responding/resolving the issue(s)

1. What is your personal response to the issues? What can you do as an individual?
2. How can the revised code be seen as a beginning and a challenge to improve the status of women in the Church?
3. How can you as a group (or individuals) be initiators of affirmative action?
4. What is your action plan?

For all groups time to reflect personally or to write on the first point can be taken. This information can then be shared in small groups or with the larger group.

Groups I and II might want to develop an action plan on how they would move the issues of women in the Church in their local area. This could be done in small groups us-

140

ing brainstorming, newsprint, reporting back to the larger group, prioritizing items, beginning to work on them.

Groups II and III might want to develop principles for affirmative action in a diocese or parish. They might want to go about finding a way to assess the status of women in their diocese or parish. They might want to develop an action plan as suggested for Group I. These groups might also want to reflect on how they can improve the life of women already in church work. This group might want to in some way commit itself to assuring that the minimum is done.

    4. Ways of futurizing or moving beyond the immediate

        a. What is our vision for the future?

        b. How do we build our vision for the future?

           1. What are the issues for the future?

           2. What future do we want for our daughters; granddaughters; neices?

C. *Suggested Audio-Visuals*

Here are some ideas for inclusion on transparencies, chart forms, newsprint, etc., for use with the historical overview section.

    1. Women in:
        Scripture
        Tradition
        Law
        Vatican II
        Revised Code
        Future

    2. Scripture:
        O.T. and N.T.
        Eve
        Property
        Roman Law
        Jesus—Individual Dignity

    3. Early Church:
        Culture
        Office as Service
        Widows and Deaconesses
        Council of Laodicea (343 A.D.)

    4. Early Church Theologians and Fathers
        Two Choices
        Wife/Mother
        Consecrated Virgin

    5. Theology and Law—Middle Ages
        Gratian
          Subjects
        Aquinas
          Image
        Carry over to 1917 Code

6. 1917 Code
    Status by
       Inclusion; Exclusion
    Sex—Status Determinant
    Orders
    Subjects
    Roles
    Capacity

7. Law: Reasonable Norm of Action
    Good of Community
    Equity
  Law: Follows Theology/Praxis

8. Vatican II: Council and Women
    Non-Discrimination (GS 29)
    Symbols: Eve-Bride-Mother
    New Relationship pattern (GS 9)
    Theology of Laity (GS 30)
    Marriage and Family (GS 48)
    Religious Life
    Women and the New Creation (GS 20)

9. People of God
  Should lead to a common status for women and men
  Juridicial Application
    Revised Code
       Rights
       Ministry
    Ten Principles of Revision
       #3 Foster Pastoral Care
       #s 6-7 Rights: Defined; Protected

10. New Canons
  All Christian Faithful
       204 People of God
       205 Full Communion: Profession of Faith; Sacraments; Government
       208 Rebirth in Christ
          Equality: Digity; Activity
          Proper Condition and Function
  Rights and Duties of all Christian Faithful (importance to women in particular)
       211 Spread the divine plan of salvation
       212 Make known needs/opinions
       215 Associations/Assembly
       216 Support Apostolic Activity
       217 Christian education
       218 Freedom of inquiry and expression
       219 Free from coercion choosing state of life
       220 Good name/reputation-privacy
       221 Vindicate rights/judged with equity according to law
  Rights and Duties of Lay Persons
       225 Lay person: baptism, confirmation, specific work

226 Married lay persons

227 Civil liberties

228 Hold ecclesiastical office — Be experts and counselors

229 Acquire Christian knowledge: study; teach: sacred sciences

230 Laymen: acolyte; lector

All laity: temporary lector and other related offices

231 Formation and Remuneration

Offices and Ministry Open to Women

To qualified persons:

483 Chancelor

483 Notary

1483 Advocate

1435 Defender of the Bond/Promoter

1428 Consultors, Assessors, Auditors

1421 Collegiate Judge

494 Business Manager

473 Moderator

492, 494, 511-514, 536, 537, 443, 463, 451, 830

Pastoral and Financial Councils; Synods and Councils; Episcopal Conferences; Censor

363 Pontifical Mission

1279-1280 Administrators of ecclesiastical goods, councils

Obligation

785 Catechists

229 Teach Sacred Sciences

784 Missionaries

766 Preach with restrictions

Pastoral Necessity

910 Lectors; Altar Server (906, 930)

910 Special Minister of Eucharist/Blessed Sacrament (943)

861 Special Minister of Baptism

1112 Delegated to witness marriages

528 Care of Parish

1168 Administer certain Sacramentals

Women Excluded

1024 Orders

1035 Lector and Acolyte

Other offices: Episcopal Vicars; Single Judge; Judicial Vicars

Other Changes/Comments from 1917 Code

Residence

Rites

Abduction

Confession

Age of marriage

11. Future

Affirmative Action

Education

Theological investigation

Bishops: acolyte and lectors; Diaconate
Status of women common with men in the Church
What is ministry/Who are the ministers

D. *Suggested Group Activities*

1. Word Association Game

In addition to Group II this word association game would also be appropriate for groups I and III. Pencils and paper will be needed for this exercise. Game A or B or both may be done. Ask the participants to be still and reflect for a few moments silently on the women they have known in their lives, in their childhood, their youth, their early adulthood, women they presently know. . . . Then instruct the participants to write down the first feeling, name, or other word that they associate with the word that is read to them. Depending on the group you will want to assure the participants before you start this exercise that this information is not to be shared.

Game A	*Game B*
Eve	Mother
Catholic Woman	Virgin
Mother Teresa	Weak
Woman Priest	Strong
Teresa of Avila	Temptress
Mary Magdaline	Handmaid
Parish Housekeeper	Docile
ERA	Uppity
Theresa Kane	Emotional
Blessed Mother	Nurturing

After the exercise the facilitator might then want to reflect on his/her own personal experience with the exercise and the insights he or she gained from the exercise. Suggested reading before facilitating this exercise in Joan Ohanneson's book, *Woman Survivor in the Church.*

2. Imagine . . .

This exercise is designed for Group II and could also be used with Group III.

Imagine you are a woman in the Church. You have just received your J.C.L. and you are applying for a diocesan tribunal position. You are told you will be appointed a notary, but you will not be appointed a judge or defender. The other members of the court are not ready for a woman in those offices. However you will be able to do the work and that is after all the important thing.

Imagine: You and your husband and children have moved across the country. Your previous parish was an active Vatican II community where you were a lector and Eucharistic minister. In the small country town where you have moved theirs is the only one Catholic church. You inquire about the liturgical program and ask to be a lector and Eucharistic minister. You are told only the men in the parish lector and when necessary act as Eucharistic ministers. However there is a ladies society and they take care of the sacristy and clean the church; you would be most welcome to join.

Imagine: You are the parish DRE and the only woman on the pastoral team. A new pastor has just been appointed and he notifies you that your position is being terminated at the end of the month and will be filled by the two permanent deacons in the parish on a part time basis. Your contract with the previous pastor and the parish council was for two years. You attempt contract negotiation, but the pastor has made it clear to members of the parish council that he wants an all clerical team. There is no other means of recourse set up in the diocese for discussion of the issue.

Imagine: You are the first woman graduate of the local seminary with a M.Div. You have just been offered the position of parish administrator in a rural parish where there are no priests.

Imagine: You are a woman religious in the process of leaving your community but wish to remain in your teaching position at the Catholic college where you teach theology. Your religious community has endorsed your request; however, the local bishop has requested that you resign.

Imagine: You are a woman canonist and are job hunting. A nearby diocese has heard that you are looking for a job in the chancery as an administrator or would be interested in tribunal work. They contact you because they have an affirmative action plan for hiring women.

The above situations may also be role played. With a little imagination others may be created by yourself.

SELECTED BIBLIOGRAPHY

"Consensus Statement from the Symposium on 'Women in Church Law.' " *Proceedings of Thirty Eighth Annual Convention CLSA*. The Canon Law Society of America, 1976, pp. 183-193.

Coriden, James A., ed. *Sexism and Church Law: Equal Rights and Affirmative Action*. New York: Paulist Press, 1977.

Meagher, Katherine. "The Challenge, A Common Status for Men and Women." *Studia Canonica* 13 (1979) 363-401.

Ohanneson, Joan. *Woman Survivor in the Church*. Minneapolis, Minn.: Winston Press, 1980.

Osiek, Carolyn. "The Church Fathers and the Ministry of Women." *Women Priests: A Catholic Commentary on the Vatican Declaration,* eds: Leonard and Arlene Swidler. New York: Paulist Press, 1977, pp. 75-80.

Raming, Ida. "From the Freedom of the Gospel to the Petrified 'Men's Church': The Rise and Development of Male Domination in the Church." *Women in a Men's Church. Concilium* 134 (1980), pp. 3-13.

Range, Joan. "Legal Exclusion of Women from Church Office." *The Jurist* 34 (1974) 112-127.

Ruther, Rosemary Radford, ed. *Religion and Sexism*. New York: Simon and Schuster, 1974.

Tavard, George H. *Woman in Christian Tradition*. Notre Dame, Ind.: University of Notre Dame, 1973.

Vasquez, Lucy. "The Postion of Women According to the Code." *The Jurist* 34 (1974) 128-142.

Pastoral Letters on Women:

Balke, Victor H., and Lucker, Raymond A. "Male and Female God Created Them." Bishops of Crookston and New Ulm, Minnesota: 1981.

Borders, William D. "Women in the Church: Reflections on Women in the Mission and Ministry of the Church." Archbishop of Baltimore: August 1977.

Buswell, Charles A. "Ecclesial Affirmative Action: A Matter of Simple Justice." Bishop of Pueblo, Colorado: December 1975.

Clark, Matthew H. "The Fire in the Thornbush." Bishop of Rochester: April 1982.

Cummins, John S. "Women in Ministry." Bishop of Oakland: August 1981.

Dingman, Maurice J. "Women and the Church." Bishop of Des Moines: April 1976.

Dozier, Carrol T. "Women Intrepid and Loving." Bishop of Memphis: January 1975.

Gerety, Peter L. "Women in the Church." Archbishop of Newark: 1981.

Hunthausen, Raymond G. "Pastoral Statement on Women." Archbishop of Seattle: 1980.

Maher, Leo T. "Women in the World." Bishop of San Diego: August 1974.

The Roman Catholic Bishops of Minnesota (John D. Roach, Archbishop of St. Paul and Minneapolis; Paul E. Anderson, Bishop of Duluth; Victor H. Balke, Bishop of Crookston; Raymond A. Lucker, Bishop of New Ulm; George H. Speltz, Bishop of St. Cloud; Loras J. Watters, Bishop of Winona; John F. Kinney, Auxiliary Bishop of St. Paul and Minneapolis). "Women: Pastoral Reflections." St. Paul: March 1976.

PART III. SURVEY OF THOSE ECCLESIASTICAL OFFICES, FUNCTIONS, AND MINISTRIES IN THE REVISED CODE OF CANON LAW WHICH ARE OPEN TO WOMEN

The following is a survey of those ecclesiastical offices, functions and ministries in the revised Code of Canon Law which are open to women. As this survey will show, the revised code begins to recognize some of the progress that has been made during the last two decades in the area of women's participation in the Church. In the revised code this progress is reflected in the fact that the offices of chancellor, collegiate judge, defender of the bond and financial officer are all now open to women.

As was expected, the ordained ministries are all closed to women and as a result a substantial number of offices, functions and ministries are still closed to women; for example, the offices of episcopal vicar and judicial vicar; the non-ordained ministries of acolyte and lector are still closed to women while open to lay men.

From the above and the following, the reader will be able to observe that for the most part women have achieved parity with lay men in the revised code; but because women are not numbered among the clergy or ordained, they still, in general, do not enjoy parity with men in the Church. This, therefore, is an issue of concern that will be before us for a long while. Having said that, we will now get on to the business at hand and look at those offices, functions and ministries in the revised code which are open to women, with the hope that a future detailed study of these canons and the offices they represent will help facilitate the increased participation of women in these areas.

First, we begin with General Norms. Canon 129 states that the power of governance or jurisdiction ". . . can be possessed by those who have received a sacred order . . ." The canon then goes on to read: "Christian faithful lay persons can share in the exercise of this power according to the norms of law." Women as lay persons are able to exercise this power, making the way for women to be appointed to ecclesiastical office. As defined in canon 145, an ecclesiastical office is "any function constituted in a stable manner by divine or ecclesiastical law to be exercised for a spiritual end."

Turning to Book II, the People of God, we encounter the first offices that will be open to women. Canon 253, for instance, establishes the qualifications for persons who teach the philosophical, theological and juridical disciplines in a seminary. There is no restriction by virtue of sex mentioned in this canon. Consequently, those offices would be open to women.

Canon 228 opens ecclesiastical offices to women and specifically mentions the roles of expert or advisor:

§ 1. Lay persons who are found to be suitable are capable of assuming from their sacred pastors, those ecclesiastical offices and duties which they are able to exercise in accord with the prescriptions of law.

§ 2. Lay persons who excel in the necessary knowledge, prudence and uprightness are capable of being of assistance to pastors of the Church in the role of expert or advisors. They can do so even in councils in accord with the norm of law.

Canon 229, § 2 establishes the right of women to pursue the sacred sciences. Section three of the same canon further reads: "If they [lay persons] meet the conditions required by law lay persons likewise become capable of receiving from legitimate ecclesiastical authority a mission to teach the sacred sciences."

Canon 230 treats the ministries and offices of lector and acolyte. These ministries can be invested only in males. Section two of canon 230 provides for a temporary deputation for the office of lector and then mentions other related liturgical offices, all of which are open to women. "Lay persons can fulfill the office of lector during liturgical actions by means of a temporary deputation. All lay persons likewise have the faculty to fulfill in accord with the norm of law the office of commentator, the office of cantor, or other offices."

Section three expands on these liturgical offices:

When necessity of the Church warrants it, and when ministers are lacking, lay persons even if they are not lectors or acolytes, can also supply for some of their offices, namely to exercise the ministry of the word, to preside over liturgical prayer, to confer baptism and to distribute Holy Communion in accord with the prescriptions of law.

Canons 362 and 363 and following leave open the office of "Legate of the Roman Pontiff" to women and men.

Canon 443 lists those who are to be called to a particular council. Section four of that canon reads: "Priests as well as other members of the Christian faithful can also be called to particular councils; if they are, however, they enjoy but a consultative vote."

Canon 451 refers to the episcopal conference and the preparation of a conference's statutes, leaving to the judgment of the conference provisions for "a general secretary of the conference, and also other offices and commissions, which in the judgment of the conference will more efficaciously help them fulfill their purpose." This canon leaves open to the episcopal conference the possibility of developing an organizational structure which would allow for the appointment of women to these offices and commissions.

Canon 463 which lists those who are to be called to the diocesan synod states in § 1, 5º:

> Lay Christians, even members of institutes of consecrated life, are to be selected by the pastoral council in a manner and number to be determined by the diocesan bishop, or, where such a council does not exist, other members of the Christian faithful are to be appointed in a manner determined by the bishop.

Although the canon does not speak of numbers it certainly requires the presence of lay people at the diocesan synod. Consequently, women may be among those who are appointed to that synod.

Canon 369 defines the diocesan curia as follows: "The diocesan curia consists of those institutions and persons which furnish assistance to the bishop in the governance of the entire diocese, that is in directing pastoral activity in providing for the administration of the diocese and in exercising judicial power." As a result of that definition it may well be that many women in a given diocese would be members of the diocesan curia.

Canon 482 states that in every diocese a chancellor is to be established. Section two of that canon makes provision for a vice chancellor and section three automatically calls them notaries or secretaries of the curia. Canon 483, § 1 calls for the appointment of other notaries other than the chancellor. Canon 483, § 2 establishes the qualifications of the chancellor and notaries.

> The chancellor and the notaries ought to be of good character and above reproach; however, a priest ought to be the notary in cases in which the reputation of a priest can be called into question.

There is no mandatory restriction of these offices to clerics, and consequently these offices may be filled by women.

Canon 492 mandates the establishment of a "finance council." The canon states:

> § 1. In each diocese a finance council is to be constituted by the bishop over which he himself or his delegate is to preside and which is to be composed of at least three members of the Christian faithful, truly skilled in economic affairs as well as in civil law and of outstanding integrity . . .
>
> § 3. Those persons are excluded from the finance council who are related to the bishop up to the fourth degree of consanguinity or affinity.

Therefore, the canon leaves open to women membership on the finance council.

Canon 494 § 1 mandates the appointment of a finance officer and does not restrict that office to males. Section two establishes a five year term for that office and sections three and four give a job description for the new office.

Canon 512, § 1 discusses the makeup of the diocesan pastoral council in which women are included.

> The pastoral council shall consist of Christian faithful who are in full communion with the Catholic Church, clerics, members of institutes of consecrated life, and lay persons especially, who are to be designated in a manner to be determined by the diocesan bishop.

148

Canon 517 leaves open to women the care of a parish. The canon reads:

§ 2. If the diocesan bishop should decide that due to a dearth of priests, a participation in the exercise of the pastoral care of a parish is to be entrusted to some person who is not a priest or to a community of such persons, he should appoint some priest, endowed with the power of a parish priest to moderate the parish's pastoral care.

Canon 536 discusses the establishment of pastoral councils in each parish.

§ 1. After the diocesan bishop has listened to the council of priests and if he should judge it opportune, a pastoral council should be established in each parish. The parish priest presides over it and through it the Christian faithful along with those who share in the pastoral care of the parish in virtue of their office, furnish assistance in fostering pastoral activity.

2. This pastoral council possesses a consultative vote only and is ruled by norms issued by the diocesan bishop.

There is no restriction here concerning the participation of women on the pastoral council.

Canon 537 legislates for the financial affairs council in the parish. Here again, women are not restricted from being members of such a council.

Canon 776 calls for pastors to employ the services of "members of the lay Christian faithful, catechists above others" for the catechetical formation of adults, youths and children.

Canon 784 defines the concept of missionaries and includes women among their number. "Missionaries are those persons who are sent to fulfill missionary work by competent ecclesiastical authority."

Canon 785, § 1 discusses the role of missionary catechists:

Catechists should be employed in accomplishing missionary work. Catechists are those lay Christian faithful who have been duly instructed, who stand out by reason of their Christian manner of life, and who devote themselves to propounding the gospel teaching and to arranging liturgical functions and works of charity under the moderation of a missionary.

The last canon in Book II which we will look at is canon 830. This canon concerns itself with the office of censor and leaves that office open to women.

The conference of bishops can compile a list of censors known for their knowledge, correct doctrine and prudence who could be of assistance to the diocesan curias or it can establish a commission of censors which the local ordinaries can consult . . .

In Book III on the Church's Teaching Office, canon 759 states the general principle:

Lay members of the Christian faithful in virtue of their baptism and confirmation are witnesses to the gospel message by word and by example of Christian life. They can also be called upon to cooperate with the bishop and priest in the exercise of the ministry of the word.

Then in canon 766, the following principle is established:

Lay persons can be allowed to preach in a church or oratory. This can be allowed in accord with the prescriptions of the conference of bishops if in certain circumstances necessity requires it or in particular cases if utility urges it, with due regard for canon 767, § 1.

Canon 767 then treats of the homily and states that the homily is a part of the liturgy reserved to a priest or deacon. It cannot be omitted without serious reason. Putting these two canons together, one could imagine a scenario in which the homily was omitted from the Sunday Eucharistic liturgy, for instance, and a woman would preach at that liturgy.

Book IV on the Church's Office to Sanctify contains several canons which open areas of sacramental ministry to women.

Canon 861 speaks of the minister of baptism. In section two of that canon we find the following:

> If the ordinary minister is absent or impeded, a catechist or some other person deputed by the local ordinary for this office, licitly confers baptism. But in a case of necessity, any person whatsoever, who is motivated by the necessary intention, licitly confers baptism.

According to this canon, therefore, women may be deputed by the local ordinary for the office of minister of baptism.

Likewise, in canon 910, § 2 women may also be deputed special minsters of Communion: "The special minister of communion is an acolyte or other faithful deputed in accord with canon 230, § 3."

Canon 943 lists those who can act as the minister of the exposition of the Blessed Sacrament.

> In special circumstances the minister of exposition and reposition only, but without benediction, is an acolyte, a special minster of Holy Communion or another person deputed by the local ordinary, the prescriptions of that ordinary being observed.

Women, therefore, are included in this ministry.

Canon 112, § 1 provides for the delegation of lay persons to assist at marriages.

> The diocesan bishop can delegate lay persons to assist at the celebrations of marriage whenever priests or deacons are lacking. He can do so after a previous favorable vote by the conference of bishops, and after he has obtained this faculty from the Holy See.

In Book V on the Temporal Goods of the Church, we find a series of canons on administrators of ecclesiastical goods, offices which may be filled by women.

> Canon 1279, § 1. The person who immediately governs the persons to whom ecclesiastical goods belong is responsible for the administration of the same goods . . . § 2. When the goods of a public juridic person do not have administrators assigned for them by law . . . the ordinary to whom such a person is subject should appoint suitable individuals to act as their administrators for a period of three years.

> Canon 1280. Each juridic persons should have its own financial council or at least two advisors who, according to its statutes, assist the administrator in carrying out his or her office.

In Book VII on Procedures the following offices are all open to women: collegiate judge, asessors, auditors, promoters of justice, defenders of the bond, proxy, and advocate.

> Canon 1421, § 2. the conference of bishops can permit that lay men or lay women also be appointed judge. When necessity warrants it, one of them can be employed to establish a collegiate tribunal. § 3. The judges should

150

be of unimpaired reputation and possess doctorates, or at least licentiates, in canon law.

Canon 1424. For any trial a single judge can take for himself as consultors, two assessors, clerics or lay persons of upright life.

Canon 1428, § 2. The bishop can approve for the office of auditor, clerics and lay persons who possess good character, prudence and learning.

Canon 1435. It is the task of the diocesan bishop to name the promoter of justice and the defender of the bond. They are to be clerics or lay persons of unimpaired reputation who hold doctorates or licentiates in canon law and who are proven in prudence and in zeal for justice.

Canon 1483. The proxy and the advocate must be at least eighteen years of age and of good reputation. The advocate must furthermore be a Catholic unless the diocesan bishop permits otherwise, must have a doctorate in canon law or be otherwise truly expert, and must be approved by the same bishop.

Over and above the canons that deal with ecclesiastical offices and ministries there are several other canons which will affect women in broader areas of church life. This is by no means an exhaustive treatment of the subject matter and does not include any canons from the canons on institutes of consecrated life.

The first of those which affect women is canon 208:

In virtue of their rebirth in Christ, there exists among all the Christian faithful a true equality with regard to the dignity and activity by which each cooperates according to his or her own proper condition and function for the building up of the body of Christ.

This is obviously a basic and fundamental statement of the equality of all Christians.

Canon 210 states:

All the Christian faithful according to their own proper condition have the obligation and the right to work for spreading the divine plan of salvation ever [sic] increasingly to all people in every era and in every land.

Again the operative word here is "all."

Canon 212, §§ 2 and 3, identify rights which sometimes women feel they are not able to exercise:

§ 2. The Christian faithful are at liberty to reveal openly to the pastors of the Church their needs, especially spiritual ones and their desires.

§ 3. By reason of the knowledge, confidence and outstanding ability which they may enjoy, they have the right and, indeed, sometimes the duty to express their opinions to the sacred pastors on things which concern the good of the Church. Respecting the integrity of faith and morals and taking into consideration the common good and the dignity of persons, they have the right to make these things known to the Christian faithful.

Women also enjoy the right which is expressed in canon 215:

The Christian faithful are at liberty freely to found and to run associations for charitable and religious purposes or for promoting the vocation of Christians in the world. They are at liberty to hold meetings for the purpose of pursuing these purposes in common.

Canon 216 states:

> Since they participate in the mission of the Church, each of the faithful has the right to promote or support apostolic activity even with their own initiative, each one according to his or her own state and proper condition. However, no project may claim the name "Catholic" unless it has obtained the consent of the competent ecclesiastical authority.

Again, the canon expresses a universal right and thus includes women.

Canon 218 states:

> Those who apply themselves to the sacred sciences, enjoy a lawful freedom of inquiry and of expressing their minds prudently about those matters in which they enjoy competence, reserving a proper submission to the magisterium of the Church.

Canon 219 indicates that all Christian faithful enjoy the right to choose freely their state in life.

> All the Christian faithful enjoy the right to be immune from any coercion whatsoever in choosing a state of life.

This certainly is a controverted canon for those women who feel called to the ordained ministry or for those who feel the current law is merely a disciplinary one.

Canon 221 states:

> § 1. It is within the competence of the Christian faithful to vindicate the rights which they ligitimately enjoy in the Church and to defend them in the competent ecclesiastical forum according to the norms of law.

> § 2. It is also a right for the Christian faithful, that if they are called to judgment by competent authority, they be judged according to the prescriptions of law applied with equity.

It would be difficult for women in the Church to say that their rights are not protected in the general and fundamental norms expressed in these canons. However, much needs to be done so that women and the church pastoral leadership are made aware of the fundamental rights which women enjoy in virtue of these enactments.

In the revised law, there are several other canons which affect women. Some of these represent changes from the law as expressed in the *Codex Iuris Canonici* of 1917.

Canon 97 enacts the distinction between a major and a minor person. It states:

> § 1. A person who has completed the 18th year of age is considered to be a "major"; below this age is "minor."

> § 2. A minor, before the completion of the 7th year, is said to be an "infant," and is held to be *non sui compos*—incompetent; with the completion of the 7th year, a person is presumed to have achieved the use of reason.

The interesting thing about this canon is that it avoids any mention of the concept of puberty, the establishment of the age at which that condition is achieved and the distinction between the male and female achievement of the condition.

Canon 101 deals with the place of origin of a child. It states:

> § 1. The place of origin of a child or of a convert ("neophyte"), is that in which the parents had a domicile or in its absence a quasi-domicile, at the time when the child was born; or if the parents did not have the same domicile or quasi-domicile, that of the mother.

§ 2. In the case of a child of *vagi*, the place of origin is the very same place of birth. In the case of an abandoned child it is that in which the child was found.

This canon also is different from the norms established in the 1917 code. In the 1917 code the origin depended upon the domicile or the quasi-domicile of the father rather than the parents.

Canon 104 establishes the principles for the domicile of spouses. It states:

Spouses have a "common" domicile or a quasi-domicile; by reason of a legitimate separation or some other just cause, either may have a proper domicile or quasi-domicile.

This canon is substantially different from the concept of the domicile of spouses as expressed in the 1917 code. There the domicile of the wife depended upon the domicile of the husband. Furthermore, in the old code there was no such thing as the establishment of separate domicile by some "just cause."

In Book II, the People of God, canon 83 describes the responsibility of a diocesan bishop.

§ 1. A diocesan bishop should show in the exercise of his pastoral office that he is concerned with all the Christian faithful who are committed to his care. Such concern should be shown without regard to anyone's age, condition, or nationality; and it should be shown both to those who live within his territory and to those who are staying in it but for a time.

This canon is interesting when viewed in light of the canons from the fundamental law of the Church establishing the competency of all the Christian faithful to vindicate their rights.

Turning to Book IV, the Church's Office to Sanctify, we will look briefly at several canons.

Canon 906 states that "A priest may not celebrate the Eucharistic Sacrifice without the participation of at least one of the faithful, unless there is a good and reasonable cause for doing so." Canon 930, § 2 provides for "a properly instructed lay person" to help a blind priest celebrate the Eucharist. No restriction is placed on women serving this role. From both of these canons a case could be made for girls and women serving as altar servers.

Canon 1070 states that "Marriages should be celebrated in the parish where either of the contractants has a domicile, quasi-domicile, or month long residence." This changes the stated preference in canon 1097, § 2 of the 1917 code that the marriage be celebrated before the pastor of the bride-to-be, and does away with the preference of the rite of the groom for marriages between Catholics of different rites.

DECEIT/ERROR OF PERSON AS A *CAPUT NULLITATIS*

J. James Cuneo

Since 1960 a good number of articles have been written on the topic of error and deceit as grounds for nullity of marriage[1]. In particular they deal with the concept of deceit as a grounds of nullity distinct from already existing canons on error. The revised Code of Canon Law has indeed added a specific canon isolating the nullifying effect of deceit. The purpose of this seminar is to discuss the meaning of this new canon and to see what we can learn about its practical use in tribunals. It is my intention to summarize some of the points which are gathered from the above articles. I am also aware that recently Philip Sumner,[2] Ellsworth Kneal[3] and Geoff Robinson[4] have presented papers in anticipation of the new canon. This seminar paper does not pretend to add to the excellent research and synthesis accomplished by them.

In this seminar presentation we can first examine the general disposition of the canons on error and deceit in the 1917 code and the revised code. Next we shall look at some theoretical points which seem interesting from the background of this topic. Finally we discuss some points of jurisprudence.

I. General Concepts in the Code of 1917 and Revised Code

Both error and deceit are treated in the 1917 code. The revised code differs by adding deceit as grounds for nullity of marriage. In Book I on general norms,

[1]Franescus Bersini, "De interpretatione evolutiva erroris qualitatis reduntantis in errorem personae," *Monitor Ecclesiasticus* 106(1981) 88-100; Andrea Bride, "De errore in contractu matrimoniali: An opportunum sit novum inducere impedimentum," *Apollinaris* 39(1966) 258-272; Jose F. Castano, " 'Il dolus' vizio del consenso matrimoniale commentario al Can. 300 dello schema," *Apollinaris* 55(1982) 655-676; P. Ciprotti, *Annali di dottrina e giurisprudenza canonica,* Vol. II, *Il dolo nel consenso matrimoniale* (Vatican City: Editrice Vaticana, 1972); Pio Fedele, "Il dolo nel matrimonio canonico: Ius vetus et ius condendum," *Ephemerides iuris canonici* 24(1968) 1-67; Benito Gangoiti, "Dolus vel melius error constituitne titulum sive causam nullitatis matrimonii," *Angelicum* 50(1973) 376-430; Jose Maria Gonzales Del Valle, "Ignorancia, error y dolo al elegir conyuge y al celebrar matrimonio," *Ius canonicum* 21(1981) 145-165; Antonio Mostaza Rodriquez, " 'De errore redundante' in doctrina et iurisprudentia canonici," *Periodica* 65(1976) 385-444; Angela Maria Punzi Nicolo, "Problematica attuale dell'errore e del dolo nel matrimonio," *Ephemerides iuris canonici* 37(1981) 135-164; Luigi Notaro, "Il problema dell'errore circa qualitatem: Guirisprudenza innovativa," *Monitor Ecclesiasticus* 106(1981) 101-110; Jose Maria Serrano, "El dolo en el consentimiento matrimonial," *Revista espanola de Derecho Canonico* 29(1978) 175-185; Antonius Stankiewicz, *De iurisprudentia recentiore circa simulationem et errorem* (Rome: Pontificia Universita Gregoiana, 1981); Alexander Szentirmai, "De constituendo vel non 'impedimeto deceptionis' in iure matrimoniali canonico," *Revista espanola de Derecho Canonico* 16(1961) 91-102.

[2]Philip Sumner, " 'Dolus' as a Grounds for Nullity of Marriage," *Studia canonica* 14(1980) 171-194.

[3]Ellsworth Kneal, et. al, "A Proposed *In Iure* Section for the New Statute of Fraud," *The Jurist* 42(1982) 215-222.

[4]Geoff Robinson, "Background to the Question of the Invalidating Effect of Deceit on Mar-

in both the 1917 code (canon 103, §2) and revised code (canon 125, § 2) the general rule is stated about the effect of deceit on the validity of a juridical act: acts placed out of grave fear or deceit are *valid* unless elsewhere the law advises otherwise; however, the act can be rescinded by a judge. The revised code does allow elsewhere for exception to this rule when it comes to marriage consent. The old code did not make this exception for marriage entered under deceit, although it did make the exception for the case of force and fear.

Canon 1098 of the revised code reads: "A person contracts marriage invalidly who is deceived by fraud perpetrated to obtain consent concerning some quality of the other party which by nature can seriously disrupt the *consortium* of conjugal life."[5] An initial and general explanation of the purpose of the new canon is given in the report of the Commission for the Revision of the Code:

> There was long discussion whether to introduce a defect of consent rising from deceit. Finally with unanimous consent the committee concluded that defect of consent derived from deceit should be admitted in the new law. Nevertheless serious conditions would be established, namely: that the fraud by perpetrated to obtain matrimonial consent, that the deceit involve a quality of the other party and indeed by such a quality of the spouse which would be destined to disturb gravely the *consortium* of conjugal life. . . . Among the consultors there was some dispute concerning the motive of nullity of matrimony contracted out of deceit. Some said it is to be attributed to the injustice of deceit and others to the weakening of the freedom of consent caused by deceit[6].

In a later report of the commission the relationship between deceit and error is discussed and debated. Some felt that a canon on error of quality could be added to the preceding canon dealing with error of person, without specifying deceit as a condition for the nullifying effect of the error of quality. Some felt that it was sufficient to say that error of quality invalidates consent provided the quality by its nature gravely disturbs the *consortium vitae conjugalis* and provided the error of quality gives cause for the contract. It could be asked what difference does it make if the error of quality is induced by deceit or is simple error. Would not the error itself invalidate the consent? Others held strongly that only *error dolosus* (i.e., error induced by deceit) could have an invalidating effect when dealing with error of quality rather than error of person. In the case of deceit there would be no real joining of wills in consent while in the case of simple error (i.e., erroneous judgment about a quality which has not been induced by deceit) there really is a joining of the wills in consent. Still

riage," a paper privately distributed at St. Paul's University, Ottawa and whose previous publication details are not known to this author.

[5] Translation by author: "Qui matrimonium init deceptus dolo ad obtinendum consensum patrato, circa aliquam alterius partis qualitatem, quae suapte natura consortium vitae coniugalis graviter perturbare potest, invalide contrahit."

[6] Pontifical Commission for the Revision of the Code, "Acta Commissionis," *Communicationes* 3(1971) 76-77. Translation by author.

others worried that if a simple error of quality were considered invalidating whether deceit was involved or not then too many cases of error could raise doubts about valid marriage. At the end of this long discussion the commission finally decided to present a separate canon on deceit[7].

From this report we can see some of the confusion built into the background of the new canon as well as the unfolding of legislative progression which makes the canon significant. Canon 1098 on deceit must be viewed in context with the preceding canon 1097 on error and the old code (c. 1083) which dealt with error of person.

Therefore we must compare the disposition of the two codes not just on deceit but also on error. The disposition of the new code on deceit is significant in light of the expanded possibility of error of quality to nullify the matrimonial consent.

In Book I on general norms, the old code (canon 104) states the general principle: "Error renders an act invalid if it concerns something which constitutes the substance of the act or which becomes a condition *sine qua non;* but in contracts error can give rise to a rescinding action according to the norm of law." Canon 126 of the revised code states the same general principle.

With regard to an exception for the marriage contract, however, the 1917 code (canon 1083) states: (1) error of the person renders the marriage invalid; (2) error of a quality of the person, even if it gives cause for the contract, invalidates marriage *only if* the error of quality redounds to error of the person, or if a free person marries a slave believing the slave to be free. Except for error of slavery the old code does not recognize error of quality as invalidating unless the quality is equivalent to the identity of the person. The nullifying factor or error of quality was quite limited and did not bring relief to many cases where persons entered marriage only to discover a serious quality making life unbearable and which would have disuaded the party from marriage if known before.

Now canon 1097 of the revised code reads: "§1. Error of the person renders matrimony invalid. §2. Error in the quality of the person, even if it gives cause for the contract, does not render matrimony invalid unless this quality is directly and principally intended."[8] This represents an extension of the invalidating effect of error of quality. To be nullifying the error of quality need no longer be proven to be the equivalent to error in the identity of the person. In fact this canon permits the contract of matrimony to be treated somewhat according to the general norm for any juridical act (canon 126), namely that error invalidates if it concerns something of substance to the contract or is equivalent to a condition *sine qua non.* The code of 1917 did not recognize at all that sim-

[7]Ibid. 9(1977) 371-373.

[8]Canon 1097: " §1. Error in persona invalidum reddit matrimonium. §2. Error qualitatis personae, etsi det causam contractui, matrimonium irritum non reddit, *nisi* qualitas directe et principaliter intenditur" (emphasis added).

ple error of quality could be considered affecting the substance of the contract and therefore its validity. We notice here that error of quality affects the substance and therefore the validity of the matrimonial contract because of the direct intention of the party contracting marriage in error of this kind. In some way the quality, about which there is error, was directly and principally intended in the act of consent along with the intention for marriage itself. The quality need no longer be equivalent to the identity of the other spouse, but the quality must be directly and principally intended.

The revised code further extends the nullifying effect of error of quality in the next canon (1098) on deceit. But here again the extention has been made carefully. In canon 1098 error of quality invalidates, but under two conditions. The conditions are different from the preceding canon. Error of quality here invalidates *if* there has been deceit perpetrated to obtain matrimonial consent and *if* the quality erroneously judged is serious enough to disrupt conjugal life. In this case it is not necessary that the erring party principally and directly intend the quality which was misjudged. The nullifying effect on the error of quality is derived from the deceit perpetrated by the other party and from the seriousness of the quality involved in relation to this *consortium vitae*. Here the consent of the deceived party is invalid not because a certain quality was intended by the deceived party, but because the error was induced by the fraud of the other party and the quality is seriously and naturally disruptive.

It seems that the revised code has made a very subtle, careful, studied and almost reluctant extension of the nullifying effect of error of quality. Both the canon on error and the canon on deceit make it clear that in different ways error of quality invalidates, but only if it can be shown to affect the substance or heart of the act of the will for marriage and the object of the contract. The painfulness of this legislative progression is perhaps better understood by looking at some points taken from traditional canonical doctrine.

II. Some Theoretical Points on Deceit and Error

A. Traditional Difficulties Against Recognition of Nullifying Effect

1. The first and perhaps primary difficulty arises from our understanding of the act of consent according to the theories of rational psychology—scholastic philosophy. Rational psychology did not consider that deceit or error of quality could substantially affect the act of the will. Deceit and/or error of quality did not make the matrimonial consent involuntary.

Matrimonial consent is an act of the will whose object is marriage, the exchange of conjugal rights and obligations between two persons. An accidental quality of a person is not the object of the act of the will for marriage and error about that quality does not make the consent involuntary. Consider that Susan contracts marriage with John. John is a convicted criminal which is only accidental to his identity as partner to Susan. If Susan wants and chooses matrimony with John, what effect does this accidental quality or circumstance have on Susan's will for marriage? Rational psychology makes a distinction between the primary, direct goal of the will, which is marriage, and secondary motives or reasons which may be involved at the time of choosing marriage. Circumstances and qualities of the partner may affect motives or reasons for marrying *(causam dans contractui),* but in themselves they do not change freedom of the will acting toward its primary object, marriage. If Susan contracted marriage with John, she has marriage with John whether he happens to be a convict or not.

Let us consider futher that Susan enters marriage *not knowing* that John is a convicted criminal. Afterwards she says she would not have married him if she had judged him differently before. Did the error of quality affect Susan's will for marriage? Again traditional arguments seem to have said "no." The object of the will is marriage. Susan intends marriage. The quality of John as convict is not part of the substance of the contract, nor does the error about this quality render the act of the will involuntary. How Susan would have acted differently had she known the truth is considered merely hypothetical. In fact she willed marriage and that is what she got.

Let us take this sad case one step further. If Susan's error about John's criminal nature was caused by some deceit or lying on John's part or by his family, traditional rational psychology and canonical doctrine would still have difficulty recognizing that deceit removes freedom of the will for marriage. Marriage consent is an act of the will. Deceit is a machination or cheating for the purpose of causing erroneous judgment of the intellect in the other person. Deceit affects the intellect, not the will. If the intellect is deceived about an accidental quality, the freedom of the will is left intact consenting to its primary object which is marriage. (And so we see both in the old code and in the revised code, according to general norms, acts placed under force and fear or deceit are valid unless the law states otherwise.)

Following principles of rational psychology it was the long-standing tradition of canon law not to recognize error of quality or deceit as affecting the substance of the contract of marriage or impeding freedom of the act of the will.[9] Gratian had explained that not every error excludes consent. Error is either of person or of fortune or of condition or of quality. The error is of person when one who is thought to be Virgil is in fact Plato. It (the error) is of fortune when one who is thought to be rich is instead poor; of condition when one who is thought to be free is a slave; of quality when one who is thought to be good is bad. Error of person and of condition invalidate consent. Error of fortune and quality do not exclude consent. Sanchez states that not every error makes an act involuntary, but only an error which concerns a quality *per se* necessary for the essence of the contract. Henry Pihring held that qualities come under

---

[9]For especially helpful summaries of the historical development of canonical doctrine, see articles by Andrew Bride (*supra,* n. 1) and Geoff Robinson (*supra,* n. 4) For treatment of rational psychology, see articles by Fedele and Gangoiti (*supra,* n. 1).

the heading of motives or extrinsic final causes for marriage. Reiffenstuel explained that error of quality does not touch the subsance of the contract. According to Schmaltzgrueber, in error of quality the consent to marriage is real and actual; the dissent is only hypothetical. Etc., *et alibi aliorum.* . . .

2. In addition to canonical-philosophical difficulties against the nullifying effect of error and deceit, there secondly were theological arguments. Deceit can be either bad or good. *Dolus malus* is defined from Labeon in Roman law as any cunning, trick or machination used to circumvent, trip or cheat another. *Dolus malus* is intent to harm another or break the law. But some deceit was understood as good (*dolus bonus*), tricking someone into something good, as when St. Paul writes, "Since I am cunning, I took you by deceit" (2 Cor. 12:16). Deceit leading to spiritual good is not *dolus malus.* Since matrimony is a spiritual good and sacrament, being tricked into it was perceived as *dolus bonus.* It was not harmful. If, however, a person in fact felt injured by the deceit, nothing could be done since marriage as a sacrament is indissoluble. Whereas other contracts made under deceit, although valid, could be rescinded, the marriage contract cannot be rescinded because of the theological doctrine of its sacramentality and indissolubility.

3. The final major difficulty about error or quality and deceit was political-legislative. Canonical tradition believes the authority of the Church could legislate error of quality and deceit as impediments to valid consent. The legislative authority of the Church has not done so lest there be doubts and litigations about too many marriages when errors are discovered by the parties. This was the reasoning given by Cardinal Gasparri when he explained that the Code of Canon Law did not legislate deceit as an impediment for marriage consent whereas some civil codes at that time had done so.[10]

Other difficulties, which we could call political or legislative, also have appeared throughout the writings. Here are some examples. (a) Error of quality and deceit are more difficult to establish in a court since their juridical relevance to the essential substance of marriage and object of marriage consent is vague and subjective. (b) If deceit were recognized as an impediment it would encourage persons to be imprudent when considering marriage. After all, it is only natural for a person to accentuate good qualities and try to control bad qualities. If the other party later claims to have been deceived, would there really have been fraud by one party or merely imprudence and carelessness on the part of the other party? (c) Some of the types of cases of deceit offered as examples of possible impediment to consent were similar to those cases given by Luther as grounds for dissolving marriage, such as error about virginity, free status, health of body, nobility[11].

[10]Petrus Cardinal Gasparri, *Tractatus canonicus de matrimonio* (Vatican City: Typis Polyglottis Vaticanis, 1932), Vol. II, p. 21: "Etiam Ecclesia de rigore iuris potuisset lege poitive constituere dolum alterius partis irritare matrimonium non quidem pro parte decepta tantum, sed pro utraque parte; sed hoc impedimentum non tulit, imo expresse declaravit matrimonium in casu valere, ut constat ex dictis, ne innumera coniugia evaderent dubia et litibus exposita."

[11]Cf. Alexander Szentirmai (*supra,* n. 1).

B. Development of Argument in Favor of Deceit and Error of Quality as Nullifying Matrimonial Consent

At the risk of oversimplifying perhaps it could be said that the various arguments now offered on behalf of the juridical relevance of deceit and error of quality may be summarized as a reversal of the above arguments against.

1. Political-legislative arguments. Since the Church has the power to make deceit and error of quality impediments to consent, it should do so. For example, the Church has given separate legislation recognizing force and fear as an impediment to the matrimonial contract, even though the general law does not do so. The 1917 code also specifically recognized that deceit invalidates a vote given in an election (canon 169), an act of resignation from office (canon 185), entrance into a religious novitiate (canon 542), and the act of profession of religious vows (canon 572). We notice in these cases deceit actually invalidates the acts involved and does not merely make them subject to a rescinding order as understood in the general norms (canon 103).

Therefore in the consultation period prior to Vatican Council II, bishops, jurists, faculties of canon law variously suggested the introduction of specific revisions in order to have recognition of the nullifying effect of deceit and certain error of quality.

2. Theological arguments. The proposals for these revisions were most probably based on pastoral experience and insights into the relevance of injury to the spiritual good of matrimony. Most persons perceive deceit as injury and injury looks for justice and relief. To consider deceit into matrimony as *dolus bonus* has become inconsistent with more personalistic understanding of the sacraments and the status of people in the Church. In the medieval period the sacredness of the matrimonial state was quite institutional. The perception of an individual person's injury being tricked into marriage seemed irrelevant next to the institutional spiritual goodness of the state of marriage. Contemporary theology and philosophy of personhood, sacraments and religious freedom cannot separate individual rights and injuries when evaluating the goodness of one's state. Being tricked into matrimony cannot be considered good deceit. Injury must have pastoral theological relevance to the contract of marriage.

3. Arguments from traditional doctrines of rational psychology. Although sensitivity to injury and desire to give canonical relief seems to have been the chief motivation for early suggestions of revision, it is my opinion that the revised code does not accept injury as the primary cause of the invalidating effect of error of quality or of deceit. It seems quite clear that the new canons do not permit a declaration of nullity based simply on the fact that one party feels *injured* by either a mistake made about the partner's qualities or by being tricked. It seems that the canons fall back upon traditional rational psychology. Error of quality and deceit invalidate the consent only insofar as these affect the substance of the contract and the act of the will. It is not the injury itself or perception of harm which invalidates, but the defectiveness of the consent caused by the error and deceit.

As we have seen the history of juridical doctrine found error of quality to be accidental to the matrimonial contract, not affecting the substance of it. Likewise deceiving a person was not viewed as removing the freedom of his or her act of consent. But more recent arguments try to show the opposite.

(a) Error of quality is compared with error of condition of slavery. In the old code the condition of slavery was still mentioned as such a serious detriment to the fulfillment of the marriage contract that error about this condition invalidated consent. It is argued that there are other qualities of persons equally or moreso detrimental to fulfillment of the marriage contract and equally touching the ability of the parties to achieve the substance of the contract.

(b) Error of quality affects the substance of the contract in the sense that certain qualities assume the importance of a condition *sine qua non* in the contract. Consent is an act of the will for marriage. This act of the will, however, presupposes certain practical judgments of the intellect, not only that marriage in itself is good and therefore to be willed, but also a practical judgment that certain means to fulfill marriage are good and necessary and present with this person. It is reasoned that error of certain qualities is equivalent to error regarding essential means or conditions for obtaining marriage. Therefore the error of these qualities does affect the act of the will choosing its primary object.

(c) With regard to deceit an analogy is made with force and fear as an impediment to consent. Force and fear can invalidate not only because it is unjust but also because it takes away the freedom of the act of the will. It can be argued that deceit is equally unjust, and in fact persons may feel themselves even more harmed when they have found themselves tricked into marriage than if they had been forced into it. Besides the injurty of deceit, however, deceit affects the act of the will. Force and fear act directly on the will, but deceit coerces the will indirectly through error, through the intellect which has been induced into a mistaken judgment which moves the will to choose marriage.

(d) Regarding deceit as an impediment we also find another argument which is taken from the definition of marriage in *Gaudium et spes.* Marriage is the mutual giving of self to each other. Deceit acts as an impediment to the *traditio et acceptatio* of self. It impedes the act of self-bestowal of both the deceitful party and the deceived party. *Consortium vitae,* essential object of the contract, is not really established by the consent of parties acting out of deceit.[12]

III. JURISPRUDENTIAL CONSIDERATIONS

At this point you will probably feel deceived. After all the rambling on the theoretical significance of the revised canons, I must announce that literature seems to leave jurisprudential considerations to the future. For the sake of some discussion, however, we make these general observations.

---

[12]Philip Sumner, " 'Dolus' as Grounds for Nullity," pp. 179-180, 183-191.

A. Canon 1097: Simple Error of Person and of Quality

1. According to canon 1097, § 1, error of *person* renders matrimony *invalid*. This is the same disposition as in the 1917 code and refers to the situation of basic mistaken identity of the physical person of the intended spouse. The old code had further stated that error of quality which redounds to error of person also invalidates. The new code does not specify this type of error. Recent jurisprudence had come to equate certain qualities of a person as so identified with the person of the intended spouse that the error of quality was equivalent to error of person. The jurisprudence had gradually expanded the number of qualities which could apply to the canon of the old code. Arguments showed that the intention of one party for a certain type of person for spouse equivalently made that person's identity mistaken because of the error of the quality. The jurisprudence had to argue that the quality had to equal identity of the person. This developed jurisprudence helped the legislative process toward the second paragraph of this revised canon.

2. According to canon 1097, § 2, error of quality does *not invalidate* even if it gave cause for the contract *unless* the quality was directly and principally intended.

(a) Therefore in jurisprudence, first of all, we would note that it need not be proven that the error of quality was equivalent to error of person, but it must be proven that the quality was principally and directly intended by the person in error.

(c) The error of quality, *even if it gave cause for the contract* does not invalidate.... Error of quality does not affect consent simply because it gave rise to the contract or motivated the person to consent to marriage. If Susan does not know that John is a criminal and discovers it after the wedding and then states that she would never have married him had she known, in this case the mistaken judgment may have motivated consent or caused it but does not in itself invalidate the act of the will to marry John.

(d) *Unless the quality is principally and directly intended...*, then error of quality invalidates. What would we look for to determine that a quality had been directly and principally intended? Must the judge be morally certain that Susan had explicitly intended beforehand that she would not marry John if he were a convict or that she intended to marry only a person who was not a convict?

If we compare this canon with the canon 126 in general norms, perhaps we can draw some insights. The general norm states that acts are invalid when placed as a result of error which concerns the substance of the act or which amounts to a condition *sine qua non*. Therefore can we treat principal and direct intention as including a condition, at least implicit, placed on the consent? In this case must we then prove that Susan entered marriage in error about John's criminal status and that she had implicitly conditioned the contract on his not being a convict? Or would it also be permitted to consider or presume that certain qualities by their nature would have to be included in the substance of the matrimonial contract and therefore included in the principal and direct intention for marriage? In an article by Benito Gangoiti, he lists certain defects in a partner which by their nature would be excluded from the intention of the will for matrimony.[13] Can the judge presume that there are certain qualities which enter the substance of the act of consent or amount to conditions *sine qua non* or would naturally be intended by the party entering marriage?

The Code Commission avoided casuistry in these canons by not providing a list of the qualities that could be involved with invalidating effects of error. These who desired to expand the impediment of error, however, did envision these qualities as physical attributes such as health or sickness, moral attributes such as freedom from crime or previous marital or extra-marital relationships, social attributes such as wealth or nobility or educational status, juridical attributes such as freedom from legal obligations, etc.[14] We could also suggest here that recent jurisprudence developed for cases of error of quality redounding to error of person were dealing with the types of qualities that would be pertinent to the application of this revised canon. In effect that recent jurisprudence had extended error of person beyond error of physical identity and touched the wider area of psychological or moral identity of the person because of their qualities.[15]

In our tribunals we shall be looking for these types of qualities, but we will also need to prove that the quality was principally and directly intended. The existence of the quality is not sufficient; otherwise there would be a situation of nullifying any marriage where one party discovers later some quality that is not likeable in the other person. For example, John married Susan and learns she is sterile. He petitions nullity on the grounds of error of quality principally and directly intended at time of consent. Witnesses report, however, that before

---

[13]Benito Gangoiti, "Dolus vel melius error," pp. 404-406 lists the following defects: (1) sterility and impotence, (2) homosexuality, (3) "hiposexualismus" rendering sexual life almost impossible anatomically or functionally, (4) sadism—even in the wide sense of rendering matrimonial life a burdensome cohabitation, (5) nymphomania or hypersexuality, (6) debility of mind or will, (7) contagious diseases, (8) any sickness which renders matrimonial life impossible, (9) having children from a previous union, (10) intention to desert spouse after so much time elapses, (11) criminal record or living under a penalty which affects married life economically or in terms of personal good name, (12) extravagance ("prodigalitas insanabilis"), (13) pathological toxicomania, (14) deficiencies of person or object in essential constitutive elements or properties for marriage. We keep in mind reading this list that Gangoiti understands that when the will consents to matrimony it follows not only a speculative judgment of the intellect that marriage is good but also a practical judgment that the essential means necessary for marriage are present with this spouse. Thus the act of the will intends marriage and the essential means to fulfill this marriage.

[14]Geoff Robinson, "Background," pp. 18-19.

[15]Cf. Antonius Stankiewicz, "De iurisprudentia recentiore" (*supra*, n. 1), pp. 49-56. Stankiewicz gives several citations to Rotal decisions involving such qualities as state of pregnancy of the woman, state of virginity, ability to generate children, sexual maturity, illegitimate paternity, doctoral degree, civil status, military rank, civil bond, origin from a determined family tree, citizenship, effeminate nature, vice of transexualism.

marriage John frequently said that having children would not be important to him. In fact, his mother heard John say, "I would be happier without children." In this case have we proven that the error of sterility involved a quality directly and principally intended by John in contracting marriage?

Let us compare that with another possible example. Again poor Susan married John only to discover soon after that he has that criminal record and must go to prison. She claims nullity on the basis of error of quality. Her older sister testifies that Susan always said she wanted a family man for a husband, a quiet man of good character who would always be around and help with the children and home and be a good influence. She was always afraid to marry someone like our father who was a problem, always in trouble and we suffered a lot with him. In this case would the quality of John be principally and directly intended by Susan?

Proof of this direct and principal intention shall be important in the jurisprudence of this revised canon on error. Therefore it seems essential that the court carefully investigate the various component parts of the person's judgments and intentions leading to marital consent, attitudes previously expressed *tempore non suspecto,* and the spontaneous reactions and effects of discovery of error after consent. The confessions of parties, statements of witnesses concerning existence of quality, error of judgment, motives, intentions, conditions, circumstances are important for the evidentiary process.

(e) Finally, not to be overlooked, is the necessity of proving that the alleged problematic quality did exist at the time of consent. Susan claims that she discovered John is a criminal and convict. Evidence shows that he was never arrested or indicted for anything before the marriage, but he committed a crime at some point before the wedding, a surprise, first offense. Or suppose witnesses say John was simply a restless man and soon after their marriage moved to Arizona to think out his decision to marry and he intended to return to Susan. When he came back four months later Susan had met another man and would not take John back and is now saying that John must be some kind of convict to be running away like that. The existence of both the error and quality is doubtful.

B. Deceit

Canon 1098 reads: "The person who enters marriage deceived by fraud, perpetuated to obtain consent, regarding some quality of the other party which, by its very nature, could seriously disrupt the partnership of conjugal life, contracts invalidly."

1. The chief jurisprudential advantage of this new canon is the possibility of extending error of quality as an impediment for the act of consent. With this canon the error of quality invalidates not because of the antecedent intention or condition for the quality by the erring party, but because the error was imposed by the fraudulent party. The induced error limited the freedom of the

act of the will of the party in error, even if the quality involved was not principally or directly intended. Here the instruction of the case shifts from the intention of the deceived party to the intention of the deceiving party and the effect that has on the possibility of *consortium vitae.*

2. The court must first establish that there was deceit.[16] There must be proof that a deliberate cunning trick was pulled off to make the party misjudge a quality of the person: lying, concealment, falsifying documents, etc. We notice the following points about proof of deceit.

(a) The deceit can be perpetrated by the other spouse or by a third party. John's mother told Susan that John was not a convict, that he was a good boy never in trouble. The mother hoped to push Susan into marriage with John thinking that Susan's love could change his life around.

(b) The deceit must be proven to have been perpetrated for the purpose of obtaining consent: "I knew she would not marry me if she knew the truth. I had to make her want to marry me." Now what would happen if John entered marriage with Susan for the purpose of tricking the parole officers that he was a changed man? Susan later finds out his motive and says that is deceitful. In this case the deceit was not perpetrated to obtain marriage consent, rather the marriage consent was exchanged to get the parole officers off his back.

(c) It must be proven tht the deceit was perpetrated prior to the consent. John promised to raise the children Catholic. Then after marriage he changed his mind because of pressure from his strongly anti-Catholic mother. The change of mind is not deceit perpetrated before the wedding, although the spouse may feel deceived. If it could be proven that the promise was simulated before marriage, then perhaps there is deceit. Unfulfilled hopes or promises do not constitute deceit.

(d) It must be proven that the deceit, that is, the cunning trick, did work, that error was in fact effected at the time of consent. If Susan finds out the truth before the wedding, the trick failed, deceit is not effective and Susan is not deceived in entering marriage. If she has discovered the truth in the last moments before the ceremony and is afraid to call it all off, but goes through with it on condition that John change his life afterwards, and then he does not change, *then* perhaps we have a case of conditioned consent rather than deceit. Or if Susan, upon learning the truth at the last moment, enters the consent to avoid embarrassment but intending to leave John soon afterwards, then there is a case of simulated consent by Susan; but the attempt of John to deceive did not work. It would not be a case of deceit.

3. The court must establish that the quality of the other party is of its nature able to disrupt the consortium of conjugal life. There are several points to notice here.

[16]Geoff Robinson, "Background," pp. 17-18; Lawrence Wrenn, *Annulments*, 4th Edition (Washington: Canon Law Society of America, 1983), pp. 78-80; J. Edward Hudson, *Documentation II on Marriage Nullity Cases* (Ottawa: Saint Paul University Faculty of Canon Law, 1979), pp. 45-76.

(a) The canon does not list the possible qualities that could be pertinent here. The commission devised a general formula which would limit the impediment of deceit to cases of grave error of quality. The canon defines that gravity of the error according to the potential of the quality seriously to disrupt the consortium of conjugal life. For the most part it seems that tribunals will be dealing with the same types of qualities that would be involved also in the previous canon on error of quality when the quality was principally and directly intended, precisely because such qualities would substantially affect the object of matrimonial consent.[17]

(b) Secondly, we can repeat here that the seriousness of the quality does not stem from the intention of the deceived party but from the existence of a quality which itself by nature can disrupt the communion of life. The tribunals will be measuring the effect of the quality on married life.

(c) It would seem that this canon on deceit could come to apply to certain cases involving the discovery of a psychological disorder in the other party, homosexuality, for example. It may be possible for the tribunal to establish several grounds for nullity. It could be a case of psychological incapacity to fulfill essential obligations of marriage, using canon 1095; or it could be a case of deceit if the quality was concealed fraudulently. If it is clear that deceit was involved and that the homosexuality was by nature able to disrupt communion of life, then this canon 1098 could govern the instruction and arguments for the case. Psychological evaluation of the capacity for marriage is not necessary. If the circumstances of the case involve availability of extensive counseling reports from previous therapy, then it may be more appropriate to establish the grounds of psychological incapacity for marital consent rather then deceit.

4. Is this canon on deceit retroactive? Does deceit invalidate consent only if the marriage shall have taken place after November 27, 1983, the effective date of the revised code? Or can the canon be applied to matrimonial consent exchanged in the past? If deceit is considered a new impediment whose force is derived only from positive ecclesiastical law, such as the impediment of lack of canonical form, then it is not clear that this canon applies to any earlier marriage and it looks to the future. If the canon on deceit is considered a written expression of natural law defined through previously developed ecclesiastical jurisprudence, then this would apply to any act of consent. Date of marriage would not be pertinent.

I personally opt for the second interpretation. It seems that the Code Commission issued the revision based more on the philosophical arguments than on the political argument of the Church's authority to establish the impediment. The commission has clearly related the nullifying effect of deceit upon the effect of deceit upon the act of the will and the substantial object of the contract. Date of marriage would not change that.

---

[17]Cf. *supra*, nn. 13, 14.

LIGAMEN AND MULTIPLE SUCCESIVE MARRIAGES: THE STATE OF THE QUESTION

Anthony C. Diacetis

My understanding of a workshop at these conventions is that we all are here to work, both presentors and participants. My purpose, therefore, is not to present a quasi-scholarly position paper or to write an article for the *Proceedings*. My intention is rather to spark a discussion, a long overdue discussion, hopefully a heated discussion on a controversial topic, the impediment of *Ligamen*.

The question of where and how to begin when confronted with multiple successive marriages among non-Catholics (remember, Roman Catholics are bound by canonical form) was addressed by Frank Morrisey and Bert Griffen at the Canadian National Convention in 1979 and the Northwestern Regional Canon Law Convention in 1981. I want to bring this question to a national discussion of the Canon Law Society of America.

A more accurate description of my role here today would be that of facilitator. I want to facilitate an open discussion among us canonists, tribunal personnel, who must face this question each day. My suspicion is that we are split right down the middle in this question.

To begin the discussion I want to simply lay out (1) the two different approaches; (2) those canons pertinent to the issue; and (3) some key concepts. In particular I want you all to consider seriously what Bert Griffen refers to as the difference between "external or juridic validity" and "internal validity."

After presenting the above mentioned items I will open the floor and podium for what I know will be a lively and heated discussion.

Two Different Approaches: Time vs. Presumption

Where there are multiple successive marriages,

1. one view holds for the examination of the validity of a first union, usually through the formal procedure, and if found invalid, similar formal examinations of each of the successive unions in turn;

2. a second view holds that the presumptive validity of the first union holds and renders all subsequent unions invalid, even if the first union is later found to have been invalid. The subsequent unions will not have been validated by a new act of consent. They are all therefore held to be certainly invalid, without the need for formal investigations of each individual union.

1917 Code	1983 Code
c. 1990. If an impediment of disparity of cult, orders, solemn vow of chastity, *valid marriage bond* . . . rendered a marriage invalid, and the existence of the impediment can be proved from a certain and authentic document which cannot be contradicted or objected to, and there is the same certainty that no dispensation from these impediments was granted, the above mentioned formalities of a trial need not be observed. After consultation with the defender of the bond and the summoning of the parties, the ordinary may declare the nullity of the marriage.	**c. 1686.** When a petition has been received in accord with c. 1677, the judicial vicar or a judge designated by him, omitting the formalities of the ordinary process, but having cited the parties and with the intervention of the defender of the bond, can declare the nullity of a marriage by a sentence, if from documentation which is subject to no contradiction or exception there is certain proof of *the existence of a diriment impediment* or a defect of legitimate form, provided that it is clear with equal certitude that a dispensation was not granted. . . .
c. 1014. Marriage enjoys the favor of the law. Wherefore, in case of doubt, the marriage is to be considered valid until the contrary is proven.	**c. 1060.** Marriage enjoys the favor of the law; consequently the validity of a doubtful marriage is to be upheld until the contrary is proven.
c. 1069. § 1. A person who is bound by a previous marriage bond, though it be not a consummated marriage, cannot validly contract another marriage. The exception as to the Privilege of the Faith remains. § 2. Though the first marriage be for any reason invalid or dissolved, it is not lawful to contract another marriage before there is legal and sure proof of the invalidity or the dissolution of the first marriage.	**c. 1085.** § 1. A person who is held to the bond of a prior marriage, even if it has not been consummated, invalidly attempts marriage. § 2. Even if the prior marriage is invalid or dissolved for any reason whatsoever, it is not on that account permitted to contract another before the nullity or the dissolution of the prior marriage has been legitimately and certainly established.
c. 1135. § 1. If the impediment is *public*, the consent must be renewed by both parties in the form prescribed by law.	**c. 1156.** § 1. To convalidate a marriage which is invalid due to a diriment impediment, it is required that the impediment cease or that it be

§ 2. If the impediment is *occult* and known to both parties, it suffices that the consent be renewed privately and secretly by both parties.

dispensed and that at least the party who is aware of the impediment renew consent.

c. 1158. § 1. If the impediment is a *public* one, the consent is to be renewed by both parties according to the canonical form, with due regard for the prescription of can. 1127, § 3.

c. 1099. § 2. Non-Catholics, whether baptized or unbaptized, who have never become converts to the Catholic Church, are never bound to observe the Catholic form of marriage if they marry among themselves.

c. 1117. With due regard for the prescriptions of c. 1127, § 2, the form stated above is to be observed whenever at least one of the contractants was baptized in the Catholic Church or was received into it and has not left it by a formal act.

c. 1827. He who has a presumption of law in his favor is freed from the burden of proof, which is thus shifted to his opponent; if the latter cannot prove that the presumption failed in the case, the judge must render sentence in favor of the one on whose side the presumption stands.

c. 1585. A person who has a legal presumption in his or her favor, is freed from the burden of proof which then devolves upon the adversary.

The above translation of the 1917 Code of Canon Law is taken from *A Practical Commentary on the Code of Canon Law*, Stanislaus Woywod and Callistus Smith, Vol. I & II (New York City: Joseph F. Wagner, Inc., 1952). The above translation of the 1983 Code of Canon Law is taken from a preliminary draft translation of the 1983 *Codex Iuris Canonici* prepared under the auspices of the Canon Law Society of America, and submitted for approval to the National Conference of Catholic Bishops.

KEY CONCEPTS

Ligamen is a diriment impediment by the natural and positive divine law.

All persons, whether baptized Roman Catholic, baptized non-Catholics, or non-baptized, are subject to the law regarding this impediment.

The impediment of previous bond is also an eccesiastical impediment founded on the presumptively valid marriage.

169

External or *juridic validity* is founded on the fact of the celebration of a marriage in accordance with those solemnities required for valid recognition in the juridic order and without clear and definite impediments.

Internal validity or the divine law validity is founded on the internal consensual level of discretion, knowledge, intent and capacity.

Positive and insoluble doubt of the validity of the first marriage refers to the external or public validity of the first marriage with regard to the solemnities required and/or the existence of any impediments.

Who can attack the validity of the first marriage? (c. 1971)

a. The promoter of justice in cases where impediments are public of their very nature;

b. only the parties have the right to allege nullity due to internal invalidity.

BACK TO THE QUESTION

In which order should each marriage be investigated?

a. Chronological order?

—To begin with the first marriage means that the formal annulment process would be necessary for each marriage.

—To begin with the last marriage means that the later marriages could be adjudicated according to c. 1990 because of *ligamen*.

b. Do it all at the same time in the same sentence, *because* it is the public or external validity of the first marriage which founds the impediment of *ligamen*?

These notions and questions are founded in two works done by Rev. Francis Morrisey and Rev. Bertram Griffin.

Morrisey, *The Impediment of Ligamen and Multiple Marriages*, a paper presented at the fourteenth annual meeting of the Canadian Canon Law Society, Quebec City, October 23-25, 1979 and later published in *The Jurist*.

Griffin, *The Samaritan Woman and the Matrimonial Tribunal*, an address given at the Northwest Regional Canon Law Convention, April 1981, at Portland Oregon, and later published in *Marriage Studies*, Vol. II, T. Doyle, ed.

CONFIDENTIALITY IN TRIBUNALS

Edward J. Dillon

The question of divulgence of information acquired by the tribunal in investigating a marriage arises at a number of points in the formal process. The underlying concern is always the right of defence. As a concept, that applies not just to the notion that the respondent has a right of defending against allegations made by the petitioner but applies to the petitioner's right to pursue the claim made in the petition, the respondent's right either to oppose or support the claim made in that petition, and the defender of the bond's right to oppose the claim. Sequentially, the first point at which this issue arises is at the very beginning of the process.

The revised code states that by the decree which admits the petition, the judge must call or cite the other party for the *contestatio litis*.[1] That decree of citation must be communicated to the respondent as soon as possible[2] and if it is not done the process is null.[3] Furthermore, the petition must be made available to the other party, either by being attached to the citation or by communication after the other party's judicial deposition.[4]

The general principle is that the respondent must have access to the information necessary to present an adequate defence. But immediately, it is possible to see that while this is a general principle, it is not an absolute one, nor is access to information so essential a right that any restriction would irreparably damage the right of defence. The judge has the discretionary power[5] to withhold the information contained in the petition until after judicial deposition by the respondent. Consequently the specific allegations made by the petitioner are not necessarily known to the respondent at the time of the *contestatio litis*. Obviously, the law demand that this be done only for grave cause. But the absence of that information is not seen as essentially destroying the right of defence, at least at this stage of the process, so that it can be omitted without the entire process being invalid. Thus, an exception to complete divulgence has already been established.

The next point of the process at which a person other than an official of the

---

[1] Canon 1507, §1: "In decreto, quo actoris libellus admittitur, debet iudex vel praeses ceteras partes in iudicium vocare seu citare ad litem contestandam,..." All citations of canons will be from the revised code of 1983 unless otherwise indicated. Citation of canons from the code of 1917 will be indicated by the letters O.C.

[2] Canon 1508, §1: "Decretum citationis in iudicium debet statim parti conventae notificari,..."

[3] Canon 1511: "Si citatio non fuerit legitime notificata, nulla sunt acta processus, salvo praescripto canon 1507, §3."

[4] Canon 1508, §2: "Citationi libellus litis introductorius adiungatur, nisi iudex propter graves causas censeat libellum significandum non esse parti, antequam haec deposuerit in iudicium."

[5] The only restriction is that he exercise it for a grave cause, and he is the only one who determines whether such a cause exists and in what it consists. See canon 1508, §2.

court has access to the information gathered is treated in canon 1678. This states that the representatives[6] of the parties have a right to be present at the examination of the parties, the witnesses and the experts.[7] It does not give the parties any rights both because this paragraph of the canon does not mention the parties and also because it specifically exempts the situation mentioned in canon 1559. This latter canon says that the parties have no right to be present unless, if the case involves the private good, the judge admits them.[8] A marriage case always involves the public good, and the parties are never to be admitted to the examination of the opponent, the witnesses or the experts.[9] Furthermore, the judge may also decide that because of the nature of the matter or of the person involved, the deposition is to proceed in secret, excluding even the advocates and procurators of the parties.[10] In addition to this, the second part of canon 1678 specifically excludes the parties from attending such sessions.

Before the witnesses are examined, the judge is to communicate their names to the parties.[11] However, if in the prudent estimation of the judge this cannot be done without grave difficulty at this point, it may be done later, but before the publication of the testimony.[12] This is another dimension of the right of defence. As a requirement, it is established so that the parties will have an opportunity to object to a witness and lodge a petition that a perticular witness, or witnesses, be excluded.[13]

Canon 1554 of the revised code is almost identical in tone and wording to canon 1763 of the 1917 code.[14] Article 123 of *Provida Mater* is even closer to the revised code in wording.[15] Following up on that was article 130 which pro-

[6] The word used is *patronis* which implies a function broader than that of advocate or procurator considered singly.

[7] Canon 1678, §1: "Defensori vinculi, partium patronis et, si in iudicio sit, etiam promotori iustitiae ius est: 1. examini partium, testium et peritorum adesse, salvo praescripto canon 1559; 2. acta iudicialia, etsi nondum publicata, inviscere et documenta a partibus producta recognoscere."

[8] Canon 1559: "Examini testium partes assistere nequeunt, nisi iudex, praesertim cum res est de bono privato, eas admittendas censuerit. Assistere tamen possunt earum advocati vel procuratores, nisi iudex propter rerum et personarum adiuncta censuerit secreto esse procedundum."

[9] Canon 1678, §2: "Examini, de quo in §1, n. 1, partes assistere nequeunt."

[10] See above.

[11] Canon 1554: "Antequam testes examinentur, eorum nomina cum partibus communicentur; quod si id, prudenti iudicis existimatione, fieri sine gravi difficultate nequeat, saltem ante testimoniorum publicationem fiat."

[12] Ibid.

[13] Canon 1555: "Firmo praescripto canon 1550, pars petere potest ut testis excludatur, si iusta exclusionis causa demonstretur ante testis excussionem."

[14] O.C. canon 1763: "Partes debent sibi invicem nota facere testium nomina antequam eorum examen inchoetur, aut, si id, prudenti iudicis existimatione, fieri sine gravi difficultate nequeat, saltem ante testificationum publicationem."

[15] S. Congregatio de Disciplina Sacramentorum, *Instructio servanda a tribunalibus diocesanis in pertractandis causis de nullitate matimoniorum,* August 15, 1936: *Acta Apostolicae Sedis* 28(1936) 313-361, commonly cited as *Provida Mater.*

Article 126, §1: "Testium nomina parti, cuius interest, a tribunali tempestive nota fieri debent, ut ipsa exceptionem, si velit, testis reprobatioriam opponere possit."

vided that if necessity demanded it[16] the judge or auditor could bind the advocates and even the procurators[17] under an oath of secrecy.[18] Further, the judge could even go so far as to permit a witness to testify on condition that his name would not be revealed to either or both parties.[19] In the ordinary course of events, the actual testimony would later be divulged to the parties at the time of publication. However, the basic principle here established is that if essential testimony is obtained or induced under a condition or promise of confidentiality, this condition or promise must be honored assiduously from that point on. So far, this addresses only the identity of the witness. But that is an important issue in and of itself since, in the revised code, the identity would ordinarily be disclosed.

As a further consideration on this point, it is worth noting that if the judge had cause to doubt the sincerity of an oath of secrecy taken by an advocate or procurator he would treat them in the same way as he would treat the party, namely he would not reveal the identity of the witness.[20] This particular provision was not articulated in the law itself, but was a sufficiently probable interpretation that it could be followed.[21]

The services of experts, court appinted or nominated by the parties and approved by the court, may be used whenever the judge determines that their skill or knowledge is required to prove something or to determine the true nature of a thing.[22] These experts are to have access to the acts of the case, to documents and whatever else is necessary to permit them to carry out their function correctly and faithfully.[23] Their work may be viewed from two perspectives: (i) their evaluation is for the purpose of proving something, or (ii) their evaluation is

---

[16]For example, to avoid serious dissension or to insure that the witnesses not be exposed or subjected to some grave danger or serious inconvenience.

[17]The inclusion of the procurator is significant. Ordinarily a proxy could not withhold information from the principal.

[18]Article 130, §1: "Potest semper instuctor, si id exigat necessitas impediendi ne gravia dissidia, neve testes gravi alicui periculo obiiciantur, procuratores et advocatos iureiurando adstringere de secreto servando." For a further expanation of this, see William J. Doheny, *Canonical Procedure in Matrimonial Cases* (Milwaukee: Bruce, 1938), pp. 244-246.

[19]Article 130, §2: "Si testis suam fecerit depositionem ea lege, ne suum nomen manifestetur alterutri parti vel neutri, et instructor censuerit hanc legem esse gravi ratione innixam, illi fas est delegare duas aut tres personas, quarum causa nihil intersit, omni exceptione maiores, et parti vel partibus quantum fieri potest, non suspectas, quibus significetur testis nomen ut inquirant an ipse fidem mereatur."

[20]Actual violation of the oath would be sufficient cause to impose a fine or other penalty, even deprivation of office. See O.C. canon 1625, §3.

[21]See Felix M. Cappello, "Quaestio Canonica," *Periodica* 19(1930) 71-73.

[22]Canon 1574: "Peritorum opera utendum est quoties ex iuris vet iudicis praescripto eorum examen et votum, praeceptis artis vel scientiae innixum, requiruntur ad factum aliquod comprobandum vel ad veram alicuius rei naturam dignoscendam."

[23]Canon 1577, §2: "Perito remittenda sunt acta causae aliaque documenta et subsidia quibus egere potest ad suum munus rite et fideliter exsequendum."

Canon 1581: §1: "Partes possunt peritos privatos, a iudice probandos, designare."

"Hi, si iudex admittat, possunt acta causae, quatenus opus sit, inspicere, peritiae exsecutioni interesse; semper autem possunt suam relationem exhibere."

for the purpose of assisting the judge in arriving at a conclusion as to the true nature of the matter before the court. If the evaluation is for the purpose of proving something it is no different from any other proof. On the other hand, since the judge is not obliged to use the services of a *peritus*[24] but may do so where he finds it useful or necessary to assist him in sifting through the facts, the report of the *peritus* may well be viewed in the same way as the report of an assessor, in this case an assessor who is an expert in a particular field, and consequently available to no one but the judge.

The issue of confidentiality has arisen most urgently in connection with the requirement that the acts be published.[25] Since the promulgation of the American Procedural Norms, it seems to have become a general practice among American tribunals to deny to both parties access to the testimony of the witnesses. The reason for this is that tribunals which lack the power of subpoena would be unable, or at least find it very difficult, to obtain testimony in most cases unless they assure witnesses that their repsonses are held in confidence. Such a practice is justifiable both for practical considerations and as a matter of law. But it is important, as a setting for considering the revised code, to understand that ecclesiastical law has always taken the position that the parties should have access to the acts unless, in a particular case, such access is to be restricted or denied. The principle is openness, the exception is secrecy. This may be seen clearly in the A.P.N., in which norm 18 states "when, after consultation with the advocate and the Defender, the Judge has decided that all necessary and available evidence has been obtained, the principals will be permitted to read the Acts unless, in the opinion of the Judge, there is a danger of violation of the rights of privacy. The Judge will consider the requests by the principals for further instruction before bringing the case to a conclusion." So the revised code does not articulate a new concept in law, nor is it re-establishing an old concept, long unused and only now being revived, even though the reality of practice might seem to be that secrecy is the norm and openness the exception. In short, in practice, what has developed is that the current rule has become the exception, and the exception has become the rule.

Canon 1598 stipulates that once the proofs are gathered, the judge is to permit the parties and their advocates, under pain of nullity, to inspect the acts which have been kept secret from them up to that point. The advocate may ever request a copy of the acts. This right of access, however, is not entirely unrestricted. In the first place, the inspection permitted to the parties and the advocates is restricted in such a way that they must go to the office of the tribunal to view the acts. In the second place, the canon provides that in cases which pertain to the public good,[26] the judge may decide that in order to avoid the

---

[24]Canon 1680: "In causis de impotentia vel de consensus defectu propter mentis morbum iudex unius periti vel plurium opera utatur, nisi ex adiunctis inuitilis evidenter appareat; in ceteris causis servetur praescriptum canon 1574." See footnote 22 above.

[25]See C.L.S.A. *Proceedings* 42(1980) 164.

[26]Marriage cases pertain to the public good as distinct from the purely private good of individuals.

most grave danger, a particular part of the acts is to be shown to no one, insuring always that the integrity of the right of defence is maintained.[27]

This particular canon is very similar to two canons of the 1917 code. According to canon 1858 of that code, before the pleading and sentence in a case, all proofs which still remained secret had to be published.[28] Publication involved granting to the parties and their advocates permission to inspect the acts of the process.[29] These provisions were further clarified by article 175 of *Provida Mater,* which specified that the presiding judge, by decree, was to grant to the parties and their advocates the authority to examine the testimony and all the other proofs contained in the acts which had been kept secret up to that time, and also permission to request a copy of the acts.[30] It was out of this background that canon 1598 of the revised code came. A review of the commentators on those canons of the 1917 code and the articles of *Provida Mater* provides insight for understanding the concept of publication and its relationship to the right of defence as found in the revised code.

Oddly enough, a number of authors did little more than simply state the canons of the 1917 code or the provisions of *Provida Mater,* with little or no commentary.[31] Those who comment on them in any way are agreed that the essential consideration is the right of defence. The information supporting or contradicting the petition must be available to the parties so that they may put forward in the pleading stage an adequate representation of their contentions. Wernz-Vidal explain, for example, that the proofs cannot be impugned unless they are known.[32] Augustine sees it as giving the parties an opportunity to defend their positions.[33] Others merely speak of it as being necessary for the right of defence.[34] Most seem to be agreed that publication is necessary for validity,

[27]Canon 1598, §1: "Acquisitis probationibus, iudex decreto partibus et earum advocatis permittere debet, sub poena nullitatis, ut acta nondum eis nota apud tribunalis cancellariam inspiciant; quin etiam advocatis id petentibus dari potest actorum exemplar; in causis vero ad bonum publicum spectantibus iudex ad gravissima pericula evitanda aliquod actum nemini manifestandum esse decernere potest, cauto tamen ut ius defensionis semper integrum maneat."

[28]O.C. canon 1858: "Ante causae discussionem et sententiam omnes probationes quae sunt in actis et quae adhuc secretae permanserunt, sunt publicandae."

[29]O.C. canon 1859: "Concessa partibus eorumque advocatis facultate acta processualia inspiciendi petendique eorum exemplar, intelligitur facta publicatio processus."

[30]Article 175, §1: "Perpensis a defensore vinculi, a iudice instructore et a praeside probationibus hinc inde adductis, facienda est actorum omnium communicatio inter partes." §2: "Haec facultas communicationis fit decreto praesidis, quo partibus eorumque advocatis ipse concedit potestatem inspiciendi testificatione ceterasque omnes probationes quae in actis reperiuntur, quaeque secreta permanserant, et petendi actorum exemplar."

[31]Examples are: Doheny, *Canonical Procedure;* Archibald Bottoms, *The Discretionary Authority of the Ecclesiastical Judge in Matrimonial Trials of the First Instance,* Canon Law Studies no. 349(Washington: Catholic University of America, 1955), p. 145; Dominicus Prummer, *Manuale Iuris Canonici* (Friburgi, 1933), p. 605.

[32]Wernz-Vidal, *De processibus,* n. 476.

[33]Charles Augustine, *A Commentary on the New Code of Canon Law* (New York, 1918), VII: 301.

[34]See, for example, Petrus Cardinal Gasparri, *Tractatus Canonicus de Matrimonio* (Romae, 1932), II: 304; A. Veermersch-I. Creusen, *Epitome Iuris Canonici* (Romae, 1949), III: 107; Fernando Della

although the opinion is not unanimous. Augustine, on the other hand, states that publication is not required for the validity of the trial.[35] Certainly, in the legislation prior to the 1917 code it was not a requirement for validity and, no doubt, that influenced the post-code writers.[36] But the intent of the 1917 code seems to be that it is required for validity.[37]

Most authors take for granted that publication will be made and a number go so far as to state unequivocally that it is required for validity,[38] and that its omission would cause nullity in the process, albeit remediable nullity.[39] Wernz-Vidal even go so far as to say that since it is of the substance of the process, the *tempus utile* for submitting additional proofs or pleadings does not begin to run until after all proofs are divulged.[40] The general view of publication, therefore, seems to have been that it was an essential and substantial part of the process and that it was required so as to maintain the integrity of the the right to defence. Substantial omission would, as a consequence, impair seriously a person's right of defence and would nullify the proceeding.

It is important to understand this issue as it emerged in the post-code commentaries because it is so similar to the legislation of the 1983 code. When they see restrictions or limitations, we can at least consider their applicability today.

In spite of the paramount importance of the right of defence, it was always to be balanced against the welfare of the Church, the public good, and even against the welfare of the individual in situations where full publication might impair justice. The rule, therefore, was that publication be effected but always with the possibility of an exception based upon the particular circumstances of the case. Vermeersch-Cruesen assert that publication could be omitted if it would be seriously detrimental.[41] Cappello strongly espoused that position. In

---

Rocca-John Fitzgerald, *Canonical Procedure* (Milwaukee, 1961), p. 266; Mateo Conte a Coronata, *De processibus,* p. 294.

[35]Augustine, VII:301.

[36]See Rotal decision January 28, 1918: *A.A.S.* 11(1918) 24; see also Francis Wanenmacher, *Canonical Evidence in Marriage Cases,* Canon Law Studies no. 9 (Washington: Catholic University of America, 1920), p. 386.

[37]See Wanenmacher, pp. 386-387. He is hesitant to declare publication absolutely necessary for validity. However, he approaches it this way: "The publication of the acts is in justice due to the parties, but it does not clearly appear whether its omission vitiates the proceedings and the sentence.... The Code seems to indicate that making an adversary acquainted with the other's proofs is so necessary that its omission vitiates the proceedings."

[38]For example, see Della Rocca-Fitzgerald, p. 266; Wernz-Vidal, n. 476.

[39]See M. Cardinal Lega-Victorio Barocetti, *Commentarius in Judicia Ecclesiastica* (Romae, 1939), II, tit. xii.

[40]Wernz-Vidal, n. 477. This is similar to the position taken by Franciscus Roberti in *De processibus,* vol. II (Romae, 1941). He points out that publication is a necessary corollary to the fact that testimony is taken in secret (n. 350). Without this publication the case may not be concluded and, if it is concluded, is null (n. 435).

[41]Vermeersch-Creusen, III: 107. Della Rocca-Fitzgerald speak of the exceptional cases where publication is not permitted. However, this has little bearing here since they are referring to non-consummation cases and the code of 1917 did not permit publication in such cases. See O.C. canon 1985.

responding to a question about publication, he stated that the parties not only may petition for a copy of the acts but have a true right to this so that the ordinary or the judge cannot per se deny the petition for a copy of the acts. To avoid difficulties with witnesses, the judge could bind all concerned under an oath of secrecy according to the provision of O.C. canon 1623, §3. However, if the party threatened to make the acts known and the ordinary or the judge prudently feared damage from their divulgences and also feared that the party would not be faithful to an oath of secrecy, the ordinary or judge was not bound to grant the petition for a copy of the acts.[42]

In the revised code there is no question about whether or not publication is necessary for validity. Canon 1898 clearly states that the proofs are to be made available for inspection under pain of nullity. The remainder of the canon is in line with the history and understanding of prior legislation, and must be understood in accordance with that legislation. Such an approach is entirely in accord with standard approaches to interpreting ecclesiastical law.

Accepting, then, the position that ecclesiastical law gives the parties and their advocates a right to inspect the proofs which have been gathered and even goes as far as to give the advocates a right to petition for a copy of the acts, the question must be asked: Are these absolute rights or are there circumstances in which either or both may be restricted or even denied completely without, thereby, invalidating the process?

Considering first the right of the advocate to inspect or obtain a copy of the acts, the only conclusion available is that it is not an absolute right but rather is subject to restrictions. In accordance with previous legislation, the judge could bind the advocate under an oath of secrecy not to reveal to the party either the content of the testimony or even the name(s) of the witness(es). Such an action would be justifiable only in the case where the judge has alrady made a determination, in accordance with the remainder of canon 1598, that this information is to be withheld from the party. As Doheny explains: "It is the natural tendency of an attorney or advocate to keep his client perfectly informed."[43] Where the transmission of such information from advocate to party would effectively negate the value the judge is trying to preserve by means of withholding information from the party, he would be justified in binding the advocate by such an oath of secrecy. Further action in this regard would be in accord with the principles enunciated above pertaining to the divulgence of identity of witnesses.

Turning now to the right of the party to inspect the acts, canon 1598 establishes a restriction in regard to place. The party is given the right of inspecting the acts, but only in the chancery of the tribunal. Not only is the judge under no obligation to permit this inspection elsewhere, but it would seem he is not free to do so. The second restriction evident in the wording of the canon is that

---

[42]Capello, pp. 72-73.
[43]Doheny, p. 254.

the party does not have a right even to petition for a copy of the acts, much less a right to obtain a copy of them. The first phrase of the canon speaks only of inspection when it includes both the party and the advocate. The second phase which speaks of a right to petition for a copy of the acts, mentions only the advocate and is entirely silent about the party. It is reasonable to conclude that the legislator did not intend to give the party a right to petition for a copy of the acts.

Marriage cases always involve the public good,[44] so the latter portion of the canon is applicable to them. The judge can determine, therefore, that any particular act is not to be made available to anyone. This means that the judge may exclude any or all items in the acts by this decision, but it also means a decision is to be made in regard to each individual item of proof. Further, from the actual wording of the canon, it is clear that the intent of the law is for the judge to have this exclusionary power not only in regard to the parties but also in regard to the advocates. It goes without saying that what he could exclude from the party he could also exclude from the procurator since the latter, as a proxy, is canonically identical to the party.

This type of action may be taken only to avoid the gravest danger. The judge is the one who makes the decision as to whether this very grave danger is present and whether the only means of avoiding it is to restrict the right of access in whole or in part. In making that decision, he may be guided by the provisions of *Provida Mater* and the commentaries thereon.[45] Consequently, the judge can take into account such individual and particular considerations as avoiding family dissensions, or the possibility that a witness might be subjected to harrassment or law suits, or he may take into account more general considerations such as the lessening of likelihood that testimony will be available in future cases if anything is done to erode the trust people in general have that information communicated to the Church or to an official of the Church will be held in confidence. Again, the rule is that the party and the advocate have the right of free access to the proofs gathered but this is not an unrestricted right. A decision must be made in each individual case—and within the individual case, about each individual item of proof. But in fact, that is not significantly different from what the present law requires.

At the conclusion of the case in first instance, a sentence must be rendered which articulates the decision of the judge about the controversy before him. Generally speaking, most tribunals have modelled their sentences on those given by the S.R. Rota so that the sentence contains a rather extensive review of the testimony introduced.

---

[44]Canon 1691.

[45]*Provida Mater* is not abrogated in whole by the revised code. Canon 20 of that code states the principle that prior legislation is abrogated or derogated only if such is expressly established or if it is directly contrary to later legislation. Further, canon 21 states that if there is any doubt, the revocation of the prior legislation is not to be presumed but, insofar as possible, the two are to be reconciled.

Canon 1614 of the revised code says that the sentence has no force until it is published.[46] Canon 1615 then defines publication as being effected either by giving a copy of the sentence to the parties or their procurators, or by transmitting a copy of it to them by the public postal service or in another safe way.[47] Again, the right of defence is the main consideration. A party who feels aggrieved by the decision rendered has the option of filing a complaint of nullity[48] if there is a ground of such nullity present,[49] or of interposing an appeal against the decision to a higher court.[50] Ordinarily, therefore, the sentence in its entirety is to be communicated to the parties.

The code makes provision for the situation where the sentence is not communicated. Obviously, the proceeding in first instance is concluded so it cannot become invalid. However, the period within which appeal may be lodged does not begin to run until publication is effected.[51] From the wording of canon 1682, §1, it would seem that the parties have the option, even though not the strict right, of presenting their observations on the sentence for consideration by the appellate court in its decision on whether to confirm the first instance decision or to remand it for trial in the ordinary process at the second instance. That would, of course, presume an awareness by the parties of the reasons on which the first instance decision was based. But the reasons do not necessarily have to include a detailed recounting of the various proofs. Also, this may not be a major concern in a marriage case since it is required that there be a review by a court of appeal.[52] In fact, at the appellate level, the approach is the same whether the case comes to the court as a matter of procedural requirement or

[46]Canon 1614: "Sententia quam primum publicetur, indicatis modis quibus impugnari potest; neque ante publicationem vim ullam habet, etiamsi dispositiva pars, iudice permittente, partibus significata sit."

[47]Canon 1615: "Publicatio seu intimatio sententiae fieri potest vel tradendo exemplar sententiae partibus aut earum procuratoribus, vel eisdem transmittendo idem exemplar ad normam canon 1509." Canon 1509 orders communication of decrees, citations, sentences and the like by the public postal service or in another "most" safe way.

[48]Canon 1621: "Querela nullitatis, de qua in canon 1620, proponi potest per modum exceptionis in perpetuum, per modum vero actionis coram iudice qui sententiam tulit intra decem annos a die publicationis sententiae." Canon 1623: "Querela nullitatis in casibus, de quibus in canon 1622, proponi potest intra tres menses a notitia publicationis sententiae."

[49]Canon 1620 lists the various grounds on which a sentence might be irremediably null. The most critical of these from the points of view of the subject here under consideration is n. 7: "ius defensionis alterutri parti denegatum fuit;..." Canon 1622 lists the grounds on which a sentence might be remediably null.

[50]Canon 1628: "Pars quae aliqua sententia se gravatam putat, itemque promotor iustitiae et defensor vinculi in causis in quibus eorum praesentia requiritur, ius habent a sententia appealandi ad iudicem superiorem, salvo praescripto canon 1629."

[51]Canon 1634, §2: "Quod si pars exemplar impugnatae sententiae intra utile tempus a tribunali a quo obtinere nequeat, interim termini non decurrunt,..."

[52]Canon 1682, §1: "Sententia, quae matrimonii nullitatem primum declaraverit, una cum appellationibus, si quae sint, et ceteris iudicii actis, intra viginti dies a sententiae publicatione ad tribunal appellationis ex officio transmittatur."

whether there is also an appeal by one or other of the parties.[53] In a marriage case, action upon a party's appeal would not be distinct or different from action taken upon routine review.

There are two issues to be considered in arriving at a conclusion.

1. Information the sentence should contain

It would seem that the sentence might consist in the required recital of identifying facts and of the procedural acts which occurred, coupled with a very brief dispositive part.[54] The dispositive part of the sentence is the portion which renders decision on the controversy. It is, therefore, a statement of the conclusion arrived at by the judge. The revised code states that this must be preceded by the reasons on which it is based.[55] That portion can be very brief and consist in nothing more than a statement of the various conclusions arrived at by the judge from the proofs offered, without giving any extensive detail as to what individual witnesses might have said.

2. How the sentence is to be communicated

It would seem to be a matter for the discretion of the judge as to whether he orders publication by means of handing a copy of the sentence to the parties or whether he orders that it be done by transmitting a copy to them. The 1917 code offered three alternatives:

a. Summon the parties to the tribunal to hear the sentence read by the judge;

b. Notify the parties that the sentence is at the tribunal and that they have the right to read it and to petition for a copy of it; and

c. Send a copy of the sentence to the parties by the public mails.[56]

In fact, most tribunals seem to have opted for the second alternative. Since the judge has an alternative according to canon 1614 of the revised code, he would be justified in determining that publication is to be by means of handing the parties a copy of the sentence. This would, of course, require that they be summoned to the tribunal to receive the copy. It would seem advisable to indicate to them, in the same notice, the actual decision rendered.

---

[53]Canon 1682, §3: "Si sententia pro matrimonii nullitate prolata sit in primo iudicii gradu, tribunal appellationis, perpensis animadversionibus defensoris vinculi et, si quae sint, etiam partium, suo decreto vel decisionem continenter confirmet vel ad ordinariorum examen novi gradus causam admittat."

[54]Canon 1612 lists the identifying facts which must be included and the other formalities to be observed.

[55]Canon 1612, §3: "Hisce subsequatur pars dispositiva sententiae, praemissis rationibus quibus innititur."

[56]O.C. canon 1877: "Publicatio sententiae fieri potest tribus modis, vel citando partes ad audiendam sententiae lectionem sollemniter factam a iudice pro tribunali sedente; vel partibus denuntiando sententiam esse penes cancellariam tribunalis, unique facultatem ipsis fieri eandem legendi et eiusdem exemplar petendi; vel tandem, ubi usus viget, sententiae exemplar transmittend ad partes per publicos tabellarios ad normam canon 1719."

Canon 1634, §2, ordains that the *tempus utile* within which appeal must be lodged does not begin to run until the party receives a copy of the sentence. It could be argued that the failure of the party to obey the summons of the tribunal to appear and receive a copy of the sentence would be an equivalent forfeiting of the right of appeal. Further, the case will receive the same kind of review at appellate level whether the party appeals or not. Consequently, a decision by the judge to hand the sentence to the party rather than mail it would not, no matter how the circumstances might transpire, be a violation of any strict right.

Canon 1481, §1 of the revised code gives the judge power to appoint a procurator, even for an unwilling party. If such an action is taken in a particular case, the sentence may be communicated to the procurator and such communication is sufficient to bring the sentence into force as envisioned in can. 1614.

There is, of course, always the possibility that the party or parties will appear at the tribunal to receive a copy of the sentence. It would seem advisable, therefore, to insure that the decision is written in such a way that it does not violate any of the concerns regarding communication of the proofs which might previously have arisen in the particular case. If it is necessary to send further information to the appellate court, this may be accomplished either by sending a photo-copy of the entire acts, or some kind of summary of the testimony, much like an assessor's report, as an addendum to but not part of the sentence.

RIGHTS AND DUTIES OF PASTORS

Thomas G. Doran

The very first document promulgated by the Second Vatican Council—*Sacrosanctum Concilium*—spoke a bit about the organization of the Church: "But because it is impossible for the bishop always and everywhere to preside over the whole flock in his church, he cannot do other than establish lesser groupings of the faithful. Among these, parishes set up locally under a pastor who takes the place of the bishop are the most important: for in a certain way they represent that visible Church as it is established throughout the world" (*Sacrosanctum Concilium*, n. 42).

The revised code's treatment of "Parishes, Pastors and Parochial Vicars" (Chapter VI, of Title III, of Section II, of Part II, of Book II, *De Populo Dei*) in its very first canon (1983 CIC, c. 515, § 1) fleshes out this new vision of parishes. The 1917 code described parishes as "the distinct territorial parts" into which "the territory of every diocese" is to be divided (1917 CIC, c. 216, § 3). As a matter of fact we were wont to consider the parish primarily as a territory, not materially different from a civil township or county.

Instead, the council bids us consider the parish as a "kind of a cell" of the diocese (*Apostolicam actuositatem*, no. 10). Now, says the revised code, "A parish is a definite community of the Christian faithful established on a stable basis within a particular church; the pastoral care of the parish is entrusted to a pastor as its own shepherd under the authority of the diocesan bishop" (1983 CIC, c. 515, § 1). This Christian community is entrusted to a pastor who shares in the power of the bishop but is not the vicar of the bishop, any more than the bishop, under the ecclesiology of the Second Vatican Council, is the vicar of the pope. The pastor is here empowered by law; therefore he has proper power in his own name, under the leadership of the diocesan bishop because of the hierarchical character of the people of God. This clearly follows the teaching of *Christus Dominus*, which states: "Pastors, however, cooperate with the bishop in a very special way, for as shepherds in their own right they are entrusted with the care of souls in a certain part of the diocese under the bishop's authority" (*Christus Dominus*, no. 30).

How is the community of the faithful determined? The normal criterion is territory: "As a general rule a parish is to be territorial—that is, it embraces all the Christian faithful within a certain territory . . ." (1983 CIC, c. 518); still, the emphasis is not placed on this criterion but on the community. The criterion could be a different one: "[W]henever it is judged useful, however, personal parishes are to be established based upon rite, language, the nationality of the Christian faithful within some territory or even upon some other determining factor" (1983 CIC, c. 518). This reflects the teaching of *Orientalium Ecclesiarum* that ". . . attention should everywhere be given to the preservation and growth of each individual Church. For this purpose,

182

parishes and a special hierarchy should be established for each where the spiritual good of the faithful so demands" (*Orientalium Ecclesiarum*, no. 4) and of *Christus Dominus* that "where there are faithful of a different rite, the diocesan bishop should provide for the spiritual needs either through priests or parishes of that rite . . ." (*Christus Dominus*, no. 23) and "Provision should be made for the faithful of different language groups, either through priests or parishes of the same language" (ibid.). Thus the community could be a personal parish not linked to a territory, but assembled around the pastor for any other reason like language or rite; for example, a university parish is a personal parish for all those people who are made into a community by reason of their linkage to a university of studies.

Just as the parish is a somewhat different institution in the revised code from what it was in the first one, so the pastor in the 1983 code has an appearance different from the one we could perhaps have drawn from the former code, and which we did carry into practice, in some instances perhaps too long and too well. The parish priest, the pastor, in the 1917 code was supposed to be an administrator primarily and principally. He would see to it that everything would run smoothly within the parish: he built the church; he built the school; he saw to it that the school ran well, that collections were made, that services were rendered properly, professionally, punctually. In sum, the pastor was an adept manager.

This managerial model is not that of the revised code. The emphasis there is put on the three-fold mission of the pastor: the teaching mission, the sanctifying mission, the governing or ruling or moderating mission: "The pastor is the proper shepherd of the parish entrusted to him, exercising pastoral care in the community entrusted to him under the authority of the diocesan bishop in whose ministry of Christ he has been called to share; in accord with the norm of law he carries out for his community the duties of teaching, sanctifying and governing, with the cooperation of other presbyters or deacons and the assistance of lay members of the Christian faithful" (1983 CIC, c. 519). "In exercising this care of souls, pastors and their assistants should so fulfill their duty of teaching, sanctifying, and governing that the individual parishioners and the parish communities will really feel that they are members of the diocese and of the universal Church" (*Christus Dominus*, no. 30).

These duties of the pastor are then spelled out in canons 528 and 529, where the more important aspects of the three-fold *munus* are catalogued.

The *teaching mission* in spelled out in canon 528, § 1:

> The pastor is obliged to see to it that the word of God in its entirety is announced to those living in the parish; for this reason he is to see to it that the Christian faithful are instructed in the truths of the faith, especially through the homily which is to be given on Sundays and holy days of obligation and through the catechetical formation which he is to give; he is to foster works by which the spirit of the gospel, including issues involving social justice, is promoted;

he is to take special care for the Catholic education of children and of young adults; he is to make every effort with the aid of the Christian faithful, to bring the gospel message also to those who have ceased practicing their religion or who do not profess the true faith.

Notice in this canon that the pastor has to "announce" the word of God to his flock and to *all* living in his parish. He has to *teach* the faith, not just preach it. So he has to see to it that the truths of the faith are "taught thoroughly" (*edoceatur*). *Christus Dominus* no. 30 puts it succinctly:

In the exercise of their teaching office it is the duty of pastors to preach God's word to all the Christian people so that, rooted in faith, hope, and charity they may grow in Christ, and that the Christian community may bear witness to that charity which the Lord commended. Pastors should bring the faithful to a full knowledge of the mystery of salvation through a catechetical instruction which is adapted to each one's age. In imparting this instruction, they should seek not only the assistance of religious but also the cooperation of the laity, and should establish the Confraternity of Christian Doctrine.

Mention of the homily in c. 528, § 1 seems to subsume as an obligation of the pastor the implementation of all those things which are said in cc. 762-772, Chapter I of Title I of Book III on "Preaching the Word of God." For example, "It is the duty of the pastor or the rector of a church to see to it" that all of the prescriptions on the homily at Mass are carried out (1983 CIC, c. 767, § 4).

It is well for us as canonists, in explaining such points as this, to be mindful of the fact that for the greater part of the adult population of a given parish the homily is normally the only means of permanent, continuing, ongoing education for our people. They do not have, or do not take the time, to read; they do not have the taste, sometimes they lack the capability, to undertake programs involving classes or special studies, or do specialized reading in books on religious subjects. They do not have time for meetings or classes. Many of them do not belong to the parish societies or church associations, no matter what we do. So they really do not get any education, even any training, in their religion. Not only are they thus disadvantaged, but media dogmatism on religious subjects leaves them helpless. The homily is really the one means left for permanent formation, but this puts a terrible burden on pastors and on all parish priests to give well-prepared homilies with content that teaches the people something. Not only that, but the place and time for the homily must be defended against all, or at least most, of those intrusions that attempt to displace it in favor of a host of good causes, some of them promoted by very high ecclesiastical authority. I am sure I tell you nothing you do not already know when I point out that so many Sundays are taken up with other needs to communicate extra-parochial needs to the people that the time left for the homily is severely attentuated or even preempted. Nor should the homily be the simple pious exhortation Sunday after Sunday, as happened far too often in days of yore and is still, sad to say, an art form in not a few places.

Unlike the 1917 code, the pastor does not have the sole responsibility for the homily personally. In that law, it was said that the pastor had personally to preach the homily at the most heavily attended Masses. That answered to the needs of the old-style rural parish where there were two Masses, the low Mass at the crack of dawn, and the high Mass later in the day. The pastor was to preach at one of those two Masses, the one attended by most of the people. Today at every Mass where the faithful take part, whenever that is, we ought to have a homily, regardless of who celebrates the Mass. It is still, note, the responsibility of the pastor to see to it that this is done, and done properly (1983 CIC, c. 767, §§ 2, 4).

Likewise, the canons on "Catechetical Instruction," the second chapter of that Title in Book III, state several obligations of the pastor with regard to catechesis. Among other things found there, we read: "There is a proper and serious duty, especially on the part of pastors of souls, to provide for the catechesis of the Christian people so that the faith of the faithful becomes living, explicit and productive through formation in doctrine and the experience of Christian living" (1983 CIC, c. 773) and: "In virtue of his office the pastor is bound to provide for the catechetical formation of adults, young people, and children, to which end he is to employ the services of the clerics attached to the parish, members of institutes of consecrated life and of societies of apostolic life, with due regard for the character of each institute, and lay members of the Christian faithful, above all catechists . . ." (1983 CIC, c. 776). Canon 777 specifies that the pastor, under the bishop's guidance, is to make particular provision for suitable catechesis for the reception of the sacraments, children's first reception of penance, the Eucharist and confirmation, children's formation after first Communion, the mentally and physically handicapped, and young adults.

Obviously the pastor is to be as much a coordinator of catechetical activity in his parish as he is to be the teacher or catechist, for he himself could not do all of it alone physically. But it is the pastor's responsibility to see that this is properly done. In this regard, the pastor should be mindful of the need to use "the various means which are available . . . to proclaim Christian teaching" which, besides the principal ones of preaching and catechetical formation, include teaching in schools, conferences, "meetings of every type" and "public declarations by legitimate authority . . ., by the press, and by the other instruments of social communication" (1983 CIC, c. 761).

Canon 528, § 1 also notes the pastor's obligation, using the assistance of the Christian faithful, to bring the gospel message to two groups of people very difficult for him to reach: "those who have ceased practicing their religion or who do not profess the true faith." How the pastor is to reach those who are negligent in their duty is not said, perhaps because it is so difficult given the erratic life-styles that people have today, with strange living schedules and work commitments and other social obligations. Nor is it said how the pastor is to reach those who do not profess the true faith. Surely they are in a certain sense his responsibility, but how is he to reach them, care for their souls, without resorting to a proselytism that would be out of place? It is the clear teaching of *Christus Dominus*, though, that ". . . the care of souls should always be infused with a missionary spirit so that it reaches out in the proper manner to everyone living within the parish boundaries. If the pastor cannot contact certain groups of people, he should seek the help of others, including laymen, who can assist him in the apostolate" (*Christus Dominus*, no. 30).

The pastor's *sanctifying mission* is dealt with in the second section of c. 528: "The pastor is to see to it that the Most Holy Eucharist is the center of the parish assembly of the faithful . . ." (1983 CIC, c. 528, § 2). The council taught:

> In discharging their duty to sanctify their people, pastors should arrange for the celebration of the Eucharistic Sacrifice to be the center and culmination of the whole life of the Church. They should labor to see that the faithful are nourished with spiritual food through the devout and frequent reception of the sacraments and through intelligent and active participation in the liturgy. Pastors should also be mindful of how much the sacrament of penance contributes to developing the Christian life and, therefore, should make themselves available to hear the confessions of the faithful (*Christus Dominus*, no. 30).

The law attempts something new when it enjoins the devout celebration of the sacraments, particularly penance and the Eucharist, and prayer in the family. It used to be the old Catholic practice that the Catholic family would get together and pray the Rosary, read the Scriptures, or perform other family devotions and prayers. Now this is disappearing if not already gone. How can a pastor lead his families back to this kind of prayer, some kind of common prayer? Certainly it would have to be brief prayer, or it cannot be sold. But perhaps the revised code is not resorting to hopeless idealism in making this a part of its norms. For unless children see their parents praying, they will not pray. If they do receive this example, perhaps the whole Christian family will take new inspiration from this. Perhaps one should seek to have families do this once a week, and in that way gradually reintroduce the spirit of family prayer. Note that the pastor, under the authority of the diocesan bishop, is the "supervisor" of the sacred liturgy. It is up to him to see that the liturgy is not eroded by abuse.

Canon 529 deals with the pastor's *mission* as *ruler* of this Christian community. The pastoral spirit that animates these canons seems very evident here: "In order to fulfill his office in earnest [diligently] the pastor should strive [to take pains] to come to know the faithful who have been entrusted to his care." *Christus Dominus* has it:

> In fulfilling the office of shepherd, pastors should first take pains

to know their own flock. Since they are the servants of all the sheep, they should foster growth in Christian living among the individual faithful and also in families, in associations especially dedicated to the apostolate, and in the whole parish community. Therefore, they should visit homes and schools to the extent that their pastoral work demands. They should pay special attention to adolescents and youth, devote themselves with a paternal love to the poor and the sick, and have a particular concern for workingmen. Finally, they should encourage the faithful to assist in the works of the apostolate (*Christus Dominus*, no. 30).

How is he to do that? By meeting them, by visiting them, sharing in their cares, their suffering, their sorrows especially. This canon is almost too beautifully worded. We are tempted perhaps to say that it says too much. Yet there is no doubt that if every pastor, and every parochial vicar, would attempt completely to fulfill it, first in spirit, and then to the letter as much as circumstances of time and place and human fraility would allow, much of the alienation so frequently spoken of today would become quickly a memory, would cease being a concern. "In exercising this care of souls, pastors and their assistants should so fulfill their duty of teaching, sanctifying and governing that the individual parishioners and the parish communities will really feel that they are members of the diocese and of the universal Church" (*Christus Dominus*, no. 30). Everyone has problems. For the most part, our faithful people suffer. They should have a spiritual friend in their pastor. Some will perhaps eschew the term "Father," but there is nothing wrong with being a father in that sense. To the extent that the pastor shares his people's problems as much as they confide them to him, to the extent that they make their problems known to him—if to that extent he is available, then they have evidence of his support. It is not always necessary that our people immediately have advice. Sometimes it is enough just to be there.

A part, and not the happiest—or it should not be the happiest—of the pastor's duty is to correct the faithful when they err. The especial objects of his charity are the sick, particularly the dying. His special efforts must be to seek out the poor, the afflicted, the lonely, those exiled, the sorely tried. "Among this group are very many migrants, exiles and refugees, seamen, airplane personnel, gypsies, and others of this kind. Suitable pastoral methods should also be developed to sustain the spiritual life of those who journey to other lands for a time for the sake of recreation" (*Christus Dominus*, no. 18). Of all the challenges that confront the pastor today, none can be more vexing than efforts to assist those married in Christ to live out their vocational commitment. Today marriage means wedding. And weddings last at most a day. Marriage in Christ is a vocation, a life-calling from God, of which the wedding is the inauguration. Except the parties grow in their response to God's calling, it will die within them.

The second paragraph of canon 529 seems especially important, and it is good that it is part of the law of the Church, having to do with the pastor's office, mission, as "ruler" in the Christian community. He simply cannot do all these things of and by himself alone. It is part of his "ruling" office to "acknowledge and promote the proper role which the lay members of the Christian faithful have in the Church's mission. . . ." As the council noted: "Bishops, pastors of parishes, and other priests of both branches of the clergy should keep in mind that the right and duty to exercise the apostolate is common to all the faithful, both clergy and laity, and that the laity also have their own proper roles in building up the Church. For this reason they should work fraternally with the laity in and for the Church and take special care of the lay persons engaged in apostolic works" (*Apostolicam actuositatem*, no. 25). "Offering an obvious example of the apostolate on the community level is the parish, inasmuch as it brings together the many human differences found within its boundaries and draws them into the universality of the Church. The laity should accustom themselves to working in the parish in close union with their priests, bringing to the church community their own and the world's problems as well as questions concerning human salvation, all of which should be examined and resolved by common deliberation. As far as possible, the laity ought to collaborate energetically in every apostolic and missionary undertaking sponsored by their local parish" (*Apostolicam actuositatem*, no. 10). "Let them be Apostles both in their family communities and in their parishes and dioceses . . ." (ibid., n. 18). "They should be so involved in the local community of the parish that they will acquire a consciousness of being living and active members of the people of God" (ibid., 30).

Further, he is to cooperate with the bishop and with his fellow priests. "All priests are sent forth as co-workers in the same undertaking, whether they are engaged in a parochial or supraparochial ministry, whether they devote their efforts to scientific research or teaching, whether by manual labor they share in the lot of the workers themselves—if there seems to be need for this and competent authority approves—or whether they fulfill any other apostolic tasks or labors related to the apostolate. All indeed are united in the single goal of building up Christ's Body, a work requiring manifold roles and new adjustments, especially nowadays" (*Presbyterorum ordinis*, n. 8). There is too much individualism in our modern life, at least in our technocratic society. This has in the past crept into the Church, and will creep back in the future, unless we have so cultivated the community spirit, our sharing, our communion through our parish community in our particular church as part of the universal Church. As the same document notes, "This union of priests with their bishops is all the more necessary today since in our present age for various reasons apostolic activities are required not only to take on many forms but to extend beyond the boundaries of one parish or diocese. Hence no priest can in isolation or singlehandedly accomplish his mission in a satisfactory way. He can do so only by joining forces with other priests under the direction of church authorities" (ibid, no. 7). "Since the people of God lives in communities, especially in dioceses and parishes, and becomes visible in them in a certain way, it also devolves on these to witness Christ before the nations" (*Ad gentes*, n. 37).

Canon 530 spells out some functions "especially entrusted to the pastor"; in the 1917 code these were functions reserved to the pastor to the exclusion of others (1917 CIC, c. 462). These are:

1) administration of baptism
2) administration of confirmation in danger of death
3) administration of (a) Viaticum, (b) anointing of the sick, and (c) apostolic blessing
4) (a) assisting at marriages and (b) imparting the nuptial blessing;
5) performing funerals
6) (a) blessing the baptismal font in paschal time, (b) leading processions outside church, and (c) imparting solemn blessings outside church
7) more solemn celebration of the Eucharist on Sundays and feasts of precept.

These categories of functions ought to be presided over by the pastor. However, they are not, in the strict sense, "reserved" to him. The intent of the law seems to be that all other things being equal, the pastor ought to perform these functions when, as and if it is possible for him to do so. Nothing prevents him, however, from allowing someone else to do them in his stead.

In the *Relatio* of 1981 it was proposed that this canon read: "Functions especially entrusted to the pastor, so that he is bound to celebrate them personally or through another suitable priest, and before all others the parochial vicars, are the following." The reason for the proposed change was "so that the relationship between the pastor and his vicars be clearer." The Commission replied: "The proposed addition does not seem necessary. For the canon says: 'functions . . . entrusted'; it does not say 'reserved'."

The pastor "represents the parish in all juridic affairs in accord with the norm of law" (1983 CIC, c. 532), the norms of law being, in this case, cc. 114 and 118, among others. He is bound to administer the goods of the parish in accord with the norms of Book V, and particularly those in cc. 1281-1288. The point that other canonists have made in other contexts could well be made here. We are accustomed to downplay the laws of the Church dealing with the administration of property, thinking that if we follow the civil law, all the important things will be done. After all, the civil law is the one that can get us in trouble. But we perhaps would do well to begin now to consider carefully whether we administer church property as if it were the property of a Church. Or do we handle business affairs pretty much according to the commandments of colleges of business administration? Particularly in a time when the Church does not blush to call governments and business corporations to accountability for the manner and motives of their management of monies, we should be sedulously careful that we administer the property given to the Church for such ends as are embraced by the norm of c. 1254, § 1. Do we in fact regard the principal goals of church goods as being those set down in the second paragraph of that canon?

Pastors, as well as bishops, should be aware of what constitutes ordinary administration, of what constitutes extraordinary administration, and should observe those limits when contemplating the expenditure of monies or alienation of properties (1983 CIC, c. 1281), conscious that they act in the name of the Church and at no time in their own interest or to their own advantage (1983 CIC, c. 1282), that they carefully keep separate and to all intents and purposes distinct their own properties and those of the Church, carefully inventoried and appraised (1983 CIC, c. 1283). Canon 1284 is an adequate fiscal examination of conscience for any church administrator at any level. The consideration regarding acts of charity on behalf of the parish might be attended to (c. 1285) as must the social considerations of c. 1286 on just wages and pensions for those who labor on behalf of the Church. Accountability to the faithful as indicated in c. 1287, § 2 is the responsibility of the pastor in what pertains to him.

The pastor is bound to make the Profession of Faith, as specified in c. 833, no. 6

The pastor is obliged to residence. This is defined in c. 533, § 1 of the revised code: "The pastor is obliged to reside in a parish house close to the church; in particular cases, however, the local ordinary can permit him to live elsewhere, especially in a house shared by several presbyters, provided there is a just cause and suitable and due provision is made for parish functions" (1983 CIC, c. 533, § 1). "To render the care of souls more efficacious, community life for priests is strongly recommended, especially for those attached to the same parish. While this way of living encourages apostolic action, it also affords an example of charity and unity to the faithful" (*Christus Dominus*, no. 30). This norm repeats the norm of the 1917 code with minor changes. In a particular case, the ordinary of the place can permit him to live elsewhere. Particularly recommended is a residence in common with other priests. The condition or caveat imposed in the revised code is not that of distance, as was the case in the 1917 code (1917 CIC, c. 465, § 1), but rather that the carrying out of parish functions can be rightly and aptly provided for from the other residence (presumed to be farther from the church than the parish house). Living in common with other priests cannot, it appears, be imposed on a pastor as an obligation, since it cannot be imposed as such on a parochial vicar. It was proposed to add to canon 550, § 1 a phrase requiring the parochial vicar to live in the parish house. The Commission replied that "even though what is proposed is quite desirable, a strict obligation of residing in the parish house cannot always be carried out." Some things never change: what cannot be imposed on a parochial vicar certainly could not be imposed on a pastor!

Sad news: The 1917 code permitted a pastor to be absent for up to two months' time, taken altogether or in bits, without violating the law of residence. The provision of the revised code is that "A pastor may be absent

190

each year from the parish on vacation for at most one continuous or interrupted month" (c. 533, § 2). The revised code keeps the norm of the 1917 law that retreat time is not counted in as part of a pastor's vacation time. The revised code retains it as an obligation of the pastor to inform the ordinary of the place whenever he is to be absent for more than a week (c. 533, § 2) and to observe the bishop's norms regarding substitutes during his absence (c. 533, § 3).

The pastor has the obligation of offering Mass for the people. The norms of the 1917 code are substantially retained, though simplified (c. 534, § 1); the priest who is the pastor of, or in charge of, more than one community is obliged to offer on the days appointed (Sundays and feasts of precept in his diocese) one Mass for all the people committed to his care (c. 534, § 2); he may entrust this obligation to another (c. 534, § 1); if he omits to do this, he must apply as soon as possible the same number of Masses as were omitted (c. 534, § 3).

Canon 535 speaks of other obligations of the pastor. Section 1 lists the parish registers: baptismal, marriage, death. The conference of bishops may prescribe others. The pastor is urged to diligence in making accurate entries and in keeping the books safe.

Section 2 notes what is to be written in the baptismal book in addition to baptismal entries: what pertains to the canonical status of the Christian faithful because of marriage (except secret marriage, which is recorded in the episcopal curia), adoption, sacred order received, profession made in a religious institute, or change of rite. This information is to be added to baptismal records always.

Section 3 notes that each parish is to have a seal and all official documents issued by the parish are to be impressed with it in addition to bearing the pastor's signature or that of his delegate if they are to have "juridic import."

Section 4 specifies that each parish is to have a cabinet or archive in which the parish books are preserved, together with the letters of bishops and other needful or useful documents. This archive is to be inspected on the occasion of the visitation by the bishop or his delegate, and is to be kept free of alien intruders. Section 5 prescribes that old parish registers are to be carefully preserved according to the particular law.

Several other things are worth noting for the sake of completeness:

—The pastor has all the rights of the *christifideles* and of clerics in general.

—The pastor has the right to due sustenance, as all clerics have. Provision for this is to be made by the bishop in accord with the canons. Specific mention of this is made in c. 281, § 1. In the second section of that canon, priests' pension and social security and health insurance are to be provided.

191

—The pastor has rights in the process of transfer and removal, as outlined in cc. 1740-1752.

—The pastor has the right to preside over the parish council, if there is one (c. 536), and the right to the assistance of the mandatory parish finance council (c. 537).

—Stole fees no longer go by right to the pastor, but to the parish instead (c. 531).

DEGREES OF VOLUNTARY SEPARATION AND CONGREGATIONAL RESPONSIBILTY

ANNE FULWILER, I.H.M.

The new law of the Church has modified the 1917 code in a number of ways and has introduced several innovations, many of which are in the section on consecrated life. The purpose of this paper is to explore briefly the changes in the law which pertain to the voluntary lessening of the bond between a religious and his or her religious institute. Also for our consideration is the question, "What responsibilities does the institute have for the care of these religious?"

Important as it is, this paper will not delve into the history and development of these canons nor will it treat the necessary aspects of theology and pastoral care which are essential elements in the loosening of the religious bond.

In discussing the degrees of separation from a religous institute, it is necessary then to consider canon 665, §1 which pertains to the place of residence for a religious, canon 686 which treats of exclaustration, canon 684 which deals with transfers, and canons 688 and 691 on secularization.[1]

PLACE OF RESIDENCE—CANON 665

Canon 665, §1 is different from 1917 CIC 606 which permitted an absence from community living of six months if the reason was just and grave. If for purposes of study, the time was not specified. This canon hearkens back to days of strict cloisters. The new concepts of canon 665, §1 were introduced by *Cum Admotae* (1964) and by *Religionem Laicalium* (1966).

Many people use the term "leave of absence" in referring to this canon when what they really mean is an "extended absence from community living" and not the meaning used in the business and academic world. Canon 665, §1 clearly states that the proper place of residence for a religious is a house of the institute. If circumstances should warrant it, a religious, with the necessary permission, may live with a religious community other that his or her own. In some instances it may be necessary for a religious to live alone. This canon has come into popular use for discerning one's vocation[2] and for caring for elderly parents. Hence some religious no longer live in community.

With the consent of the council the major superior may grant, for a just cause, the permission for a religious to live apart from community for a year. Three examples of occasions when this permission may extend longer than a year are health, study, and the apostolate exercised in the name of the institute. Note, we called the three instances mentioned in canon 665, §1, examples, for it is believed by some canonists that this list is non-taxative and consequently the

---

[1] Canons are those of the 1983 code unless otherwise indicated.
[2] See David Hynous, O.P., "Leave of Absence," *Angelicum* (1972) 452-462.

two uses of this canon previously mentioned are permitted by proper use of the law.[3]

Confusion has arisen with regard to this canon because it neglects to differentiate between "living outside a community" and "living outside the unity of the institute." It is possible to live apart from one's religious community and yet be an active, participative member. Living outside a community is provided for in canon 665 §1. Living outside the unity of an institute refers to non-members and canon 665 §1 does not apply.

This canon leaves the procedure and the responsibilities of the institute and the religious to the particular law of the intitute. In order to protect the rights of both the religious and the institute, each case should be considered separately. If the rights and obligations of religious are altered by application of this canon through their particular law, then it is strongly recommended that some sort of contract be drawn up by which the rights of all concerned are protected.

The second part of this canon (canon 665, §2) speaks of those religious who leave their institute unlawfully in order to escape the authority of superiors. These religious are to be carefully sought out and helped, not only to return but to persevere. No reference is made to the old harsh term "fugitive" but rather the law speaks of care and assistance being extended to these religious.

With due respect for the fact that whatever a religious earns as a religious belongs to the institute[4] and for the fact that the religious institute must provide for whatever is necessary in order for a religious to carry our his or her vocation,[5] the institute must seriously consider the intention for an "extended absence" and make appropriate adjustments to care for the religious in his or her particular need. Pertinent questions must be asked and answered. For example, some questions pertainng to finance are:

1. Does the institute totally support the religious?
2. Does the religious contribute to support of the institute?
3. Is the religious subject to federal and state income tax?
4. Who pays for medical care and social security benefits during this period?

EXCLAUSTRATION—CANON 686

This canon now permits the supreme moderator with consent of the council to grant an indult of exclaustration, for a grave reason, reserving that authority to the Holy See if the religious is a cloistered nun. The limit of three years may not be extended except by the Holy See in cases pertaining to institutes of pontifical right, and by the diocesan bishop for institutes of diocesan right.

---

[3]See *CLD* 8: 410.
[4]Canon 668, §3.
[5]Canon 670.

Noting the effects of exclaustration a brief comparison of 1917 CIC 639 with c. 687 will give evidence of the Church's concern for the care of religious.

1917 CIC 639	(common to both)	C. 687
	spiritual benefits	
	grave reason	
	remain a religious	
	but dispensed	
	from those obligations	
	which are incompatible	
	with new conditions of life	
	lack active and passive voice	
unless permission to the contrary, the religious habit is to be laid aside		can wear the habit unless specified otherwise in the indult
religious not subject to superiors but to ordinary of place in which he or she resides		remain dependent on and under care of their superiors and of the local ordinary, particularly if religious is a cleric

You will note that the first four effects listed are essentially the same in each law. The difference occurs in two places. First, the emphasis is on the permission for wearing the habit unless the indult states otherwise. Second, the newer canon makes it quite clear that a religious on exclaustration is dependent on the authority of the superior and the superior is obliged to care for the religious.

The practice under the former canon consisted in most cases of merely notifying the local bishop or vicar for religious where the exlaustrated person resided that such a person was now in that diocese. Since Vatican Council II most bishops, through the vicar for religious, make special effort to meet the needs of those on exclaustration.

Let us look briefly at the similarities and differences between an extended absence and exclaustration.

Exclaustration	Extended Absence
C. 686, §1 and 2	C. 665, §1
Granted by supreme moderator with consent of council	Granted by major superior with consent of council
Three-year period for a grave reason	One-year period for a just reason
Legal effects previously noted	No legal effects by general law
Extension beyond three years is reserved to the Holy See	No limit mentioned for health, study apostolate in name of the institute, etc.
Application of the canon for nuns is reserved to the Holy See	Not mentioned here

The granting of exclaustration for nuns is reserved to the Holy See. In all other cases the highest authority in the religious community with the consent of the council may grant exclaustration to one of its members. With regard to an "extended absence" the provincial superior with the consent of his or her council may grant the permission. Absences of a short period of time remain in the domain of the local superior.

Both "extended absence" and "exclaustration" allow the religious to be absent from community life temporarily. It remains to decide which canon is applicable in each case. After considering the "grave" or "just" reasons given, it is the opinion of this writer that before one can make the above decision one must first ask, "What degree of separation from the religious institute does the religious share?" Then one should consider the legal consequences of general and particular law as well as the psychological effects of such a decision.[6]

Canon 686, §3 is a new member of the family. Imposed exclaustration[7] first appeared around 1953. It is a result of the jurisprudence and practice of the Holy See in regard to particular cases.[8] Neither the 1917 code nor the 1983 code states the procedure to be followed. The process used by the Holy See is the same as that given by the canons of dismissal of a perpetually professed member but applied with less rigor.

The general law now permits the supreme moderator acting with consent of the council to request imposed exclaustration from the Holy See for a member of an institute of pontifical right and from a diocesan bishop for a member of a diocesan institute.

Imposed exclaustration is usually initiated by the institute in the form of a request to the Holy See for dismissal of a particular religious. In cases when the religious is in advance age, the Holy See has been known on occasion to deny the request for dismissal and grant "imposed exclaustration" instead. On other occasions the Holy See has imposed exclaustration not as a penalty, even though the cause leading up to it may have been culpable, but for the good of the institute and sometimes for the good of the individual. The legal effects of imposed exclaustration are the same as those for voluntary exclaustration.

The duration of imposed exclaustration is indefinite, yet not strictly perpetual. It varies from case to case. It ceases only with the explicit permission of the Sacred Congregation for Religious and Secular Institutes.[9] The supreme moderator may not readmit such a religious without the necessary permission.[10]

One may argue that imposed exclaustration places the religious institute and in some cases the member at a great disadvantage. Though the situation could be remedied to some degree by a contract between the member on imposed exclaustration and the institute, it does not solve the problem. It is strongly recommended that other means of remedy be sought before invoking the use of this canon.

Not only does the law oblige the institute to provide for its members (c. 670), and those on "leave" or "exclaustration" are members, but canon 686, §3 clearly

---

[6]See James L. O'Connor, "Leave of Absence," *RfR*, July 1971, p. 636.
[7]"Exclaustration ad nutum Sanctae Sedis."
[8]See *CLD* 4: 244.
[9]Hereafter referred to as SCRSI.
[10]See *CLD* 4: 244.

states that "equity and charity are to be observed." As previously noted those on exclaustration "remain dependent on and under the care of their superiors." In the section of the revised code dealing with dismissal,[11] the Church again voices concern for former religious. The religious institute is called to "show equity and evangelical charity" towards its former members.

TRANSFER—CANON 684

Another process for loosening the religious bond is that of transfer. Tranfer is a the process by which a duly incorporated member of a religious institute loses the juridical bond which incorporates him or her in a stable way in that community and becomes subject simultaneously to a new juridical bond which incorporates him or her in another community.[12] The law now states that "perpetually professed members cannot transfer from their own religious institute to another, except by permission of the supreme moderator of both institutes, given with the consent of their respective councils."

The new canons recognize the phenomenon of transfers which have occured since Vatican Council II. No longer is permission from the Holy See required to transfer from one religious institute to another. Only if one desires to transfer from or to another form of consecrated life is permission from the Holy See required. Therefore religious may transfer from an apostolic community to a monastic community of religious life without permission from the Holy See since transfer implies a change in the juridical incorporation and not a change in "state."[13] A "religious passing from one religious institute to another does not cease to be a religious but merely leaves one form of religious life for another form of the same state."[14]

Attention should be given to the required "consent" in canon 684, §1. It does not necessarily mean "approval of the action," but rather that the proper authority have the "knowledge of" and "grants permission for the religious to act lawfully." General law does not require that a religious seek secularization before transferring which has been the practice in some institutes.

The omission of the term "temporarily professed" implies that these religious are able to join another institute in some other way. Consider the complex situation which would arise if a person in temporary vows should attempt to transfer. The general law now requires temporary vows of at least three years and no more than six years. Should a person in temporary vows with less than three years remaining be in a transfer process he or she would be unable to make perpetual vows in that receiving institute when the temporary vows expired

---

[11]Canon 702.

[12]Joseph Konrad, *Transfer of Religious to Another Community,* Canon Law Studies, n. 278 (Washington, D.C.: Catholic University Press, 1949).

[13]Servus Goyeneche, "De transitu ad aliam religionem," *CpR* 1(1920) 219.

[14]T. Lincoln Bouscaren and Adam C. Ellis, *Canon Law, A Text and Commentary* (Milwaukee: Bruce Publishing Co., 1946), p. 303.

because he or she had not completed the three-year probation period in the new institute and, on the other hand, would be unable to renew temporary vows in the former institute since he or she had no intention of remaining in that institute. A person in temporary vows with more than three years remaining of temporary commitment would be an exception. The general law does not and should not provide for all exceptions or for minute details of each individual case.

A most welcome change in the transfer process is the omission of another novitiate period for the transferee. A new novitiate is no longer required of the transferee but instead a period of probation of at least three years is required before the transferee may be fully incorporated in the receiving institute. Thus the law eliminates the dilemma as to whether or not the transferee is a novice.

Both religious institutes, the releasing and receiving one, should care for the transferee. The general practice since Vatican Council II has been that no money is paid, nor patrimony transferred, until the religious is duly incorporated in the new institute.

Many congregations today are not requiring compensation for the tranferees' probation expenses. Instead they are accepting these religious as guests during the probation period. This practice is contrary to previous practice whereby the income from the dowry of the religious was given to the receiving institute for the "novitiate" period. The new institute has the right to the financial goods only from the day on which the profession in made.[15]

A question often arises as to when should the permission for the transfer be given, at the beginning of probation or when the religious is fully incorporated into the receiving institute. There is nothing in the law to prevent superiors of the receiving institute from giving "consent" in two steps. The first step would be the granting of admission to the probation period and the second step, the admission into full incorporation with the notification of that fact being sent to the releasing institute.

INDULT OF DEPARTURE

The indult of departure referred to in canon 688 is the same as the secularization of 1917 CIC 638, that is, definitive separation from the institute. Secularization is a legitimate action and consequently if the person wishes to return to the same institute he or she would qualify for re-admission under the law[16] but must make known the prior commitment should he or she enter another institute. If a person's former incorporation in an institute of consecrated life is concealed, one enters the new institute invalidly.[17]

[15]See Bouscaren and Ellis, p. 304; L. G. Fanfani and K. D. O'Rourke, *Canon Law for Religious Women* (Dubuque, Iowa: Priory Press, 1961), p. 335.
[16]Canon 690.
[17]Canon 643, §5.

Canon 691 clearly states that an indult of departure for a perpetually professed religious of an institute of pontifical right is reserved to the Holy See and to the diocesan bishop for institutes of diocesan right.

According to canon 692, the indult must be refused at the time of notification; otherwise it is valid and becomes effective immediately. This canon also returns us to an earlier practice which was in effect from 1917 to 1953. In 1953 the policy was changed so that a person had to accept the indult within ten days of notification in order for it to become effective.

The revised code continues the practice introduced by the decree, *Cum superiores generales,* which gave authority to the supreme moderator with consent of the council to grant secularization to a temporarily professed religious who requested it. In addition the law requires that an institute of diocesan right and monastaries that have no major superior other than its own moderator must have the indult of departure for temporary professed religious confirmed by the diocesan bishop.[18]

Renovationis causam no. 38 first introduced the possibility for a person to be readmitted to the same institute if he or she had left the insititute prior to perpetual vows without the necessity of repeating the novitiate. It was formerly the practice of the SCRSI to modify the time of novitiate and of temporary vows for those former perpetually professed members who returned to their original institutes.[19] Canon 690 has a broader application. The supreme moderator with the consent of the council can readmit a person who lawfully leaves the institute after completing the novitiate. The same moderator is to determine a suitable probation period prior to temporary vows and the time of vows prior to perpetual profession, cognizant of the fact that the general law requires the period of temporary profession to be not less than three nor longer than six years, at the end of which the religious may freely decide whether to make or renew vows according to law, or to leave the institute.

Should a religious cleric seek an indult of secularization, he must find a bishop who will incardinate him or at least accept him on probation. The term "benevolent bishop" is no longer used. If the probation period has not been terminated by either party, the cleric is incardinated in the diocese after five years by virtue of the law itself.[20] Cases of this type were called "qualified exclaustration." It was thought to be a provisional remedy granted as a favor to religious priests who asked for reduction to the lay state. It is a true exclaustration and has been practiced by SCRSI since 1955. The consequences for such an indult for a religious cleric effect him as a religious and as a cleric.[21]

---

[18]Canon 688.
[19]*CLD* 6: 506.
[20]Canon 693.
[21]For further information see *CLD* 4: 242.

On several occasions SCRSI has spoken to the needs of both men and women who leave their institute and to the corresponding responsibilities of the institute toward these former members.

It has been the law of the Church at least since 1917 that no person can claim recompense from the institute for services rendered while a member. The Church on the other hand is making it quite clear that in charity the religious institute must make some provision for the former members.

Not only does a religious institute have the obligation to provide for the spritual, moral, social and temporal welfare of its own members (c. 670) but the institute also has a duty in charity toward its former members (c. 702, §2). This duty is based on the principles of charity, equity, justice and social responsibility. However, it has been learnedly taught and advocated by SCRSI that a financial subsidy has a temporary character, and is not to have the character of a life pension even if the religious person becomes infirm or grows old. In such a case, the secularized person will have to accept with resignation internment in some appropriate institution.[22]

Religious institutes are in serious difficulties both because of the increased number of those departing and because of the reasons and actions by which those same persons attempt to justify their demands. The amount of financial aid given to former members depends on the capacity of the religious institute itself and the needs of the members. Institutes have been directed by SCRSI to make use of organizations or groups dealing with social security and of national institutes for the infirm and elderly when planning for the care of members and former members.[23]

[22]For further information see *CLD* 7: 562.
[23]*CLD* 8: 424.

ECUMENICAL ASPECTS OF THE REVISED CODE

OTTO L. GARCIA

The purpose of this presentation is to consider some of the ecumenical aspects of the revised Code of Canon Law. It may seem strange to be treating such an aspect of this revised body of ecclesial legislation, especially in view of the juridical principle contained in the opening canon.[1] However, although the legislation contained therein has been promulgated for Latin Catholics, we must keep in mind two aspects of the code which provide a general context for this presentation.

First of all, as we shall see in the course of this presentation, the code contains a number of norms governing the relations of its subjects with other Christians who are, to one degree or another,[2] separated from the Catholic Church. Secondly, it can be said that the code legislates—by way of general inclusion—for other baptized Christians who are separated from the Catholic Church. For example, the definition given to the concept of "person" in the Church by canon 96 of the revised Code,[3] stands as clear evidence of this affirmation.[4] In fact, even in the 1917 Code of Canon Law there was evidence of such "inclusive legislation." As an example, one need only to recall canon 1016.[5]

Keeping in mind these two aspects of the code which provide a general context for this presentation, we can proceed to make four general observations which will be of assistance in our brief study.

I. GENERAL OBSERVATIONS

1. It was the Second Vatican Council which gave the ecumenical movement a renewed impetus in the Catholic Church. The council not only gave special attention to "those activities and enterprises which, according to various needs of the Church and opportune occasions, are started and organized for the fostering of unity among Christians,"[6] but it also had made the restoration of

---

[1]Canon 1: "Canones huius Codicis unam Ecclesiam latinam respiciunt."

[2]For "degrees of communion," cf. the Dogmatic Constitution on the Church *Lumen gentium* (henceforth *LG*) of the Second Vatican Council, nn. 13-15. See also the Decree on Ecumenism *Unitatis redintegratio* (henceforth *UR*), nn. 13-24 and the Decree on Eastern Catholic Churches *Orientalium Ecclesiarum* (henceforth *OE*), nn. 24-29.

[3]The canon reads: "Baptismo homo Ecclesiae Christi incorporatur et in eadem constituitur persona, cum officiis et iuribus quae christianis, attenta quitem eorum condicione, sunt propria, quatenus in ecclesiastica sunt communione et nisi obstet lata legitime sanctio."

[4]Other examples will become evident in the course of this presentation.

[5]Which reads: "*Baptizatorum* matrimonium regitur iure non solum Divino, sed etiam canonico . . . ."

[6]*UR*, n. 3, as translated in *The Documents of Vatican II*, ed. Walter M. Abbott (New York: America Press, 1966).

Christian unity one of its principal concerns.[7]

In his apostolic constitution promulgating the revised Code of Canon Law, Pope John Paul II emphasized that "the council is of supreme importance in regard to (the revised Code of Canon Law) and is closely connected with it."[8] Its revision "had to be based upon the council,"[9] with the result that "the code manifests the spirit of this council,"[10] and thus it is "hoped that the new canonical legislation will prove to be an efficacious means in order that the Church may progress in conformity with the spirit of the Second Vatican Council."[11]

Since this close relationship exists between the council and the revised code, the fact that an ecumenical sensitivity is found in the latter should not come as a surprise to anyone.

2. Even at the present stage in this new era of a still very young canonical tradition, there seems to be sufficient evidence to conclude that specific theological elements in the code, upon which its juridical norms have been based, must be interpreted against the background of the council's doctrine, especially its ecclesiology.

In fact, Pope John Paul II has noted that "what constitutes the substantial 'newness' of the Second Vatican Council, in line with the legislative tradition of the Church, especially in regard to ecclesiology, constitutes likewise the 'newness' of the new code." An example may help illustrate this point. On the one hand, motivated by its concern for Christian unity, the teaching of the council concerning the various degrees of ecclesial communion[13] provided a theological basis for its encouragement of ecumenical activity,[14] as well as for post-conciliar implementation of ecumenical principles.[15]

On the other hand, "among the elements which characterize the true and genuine image of the Church" and which serves as a basis for many of the juridical norms which have come into existence in the revised code, one discovers the conciliar doctrine in which the Church is seen as a "communio."[16] The Holy Father himself has stated that "the code must

---

[7]Cf. John XXIII's apostolic constitution *Humanae Salutis,* December 25, 1961, convoking the Second Vatican Council (*AAS* 54 [1962] 9, 12-13), as well as his opening address at the council on October 11, 1962 (ibid., pp. 793-794). See also *UR,* n. 1.

[8]John Paul II's apostolic constitution *Sacrae discipline leges,* January 25, 1983: *AAS* 75 (1983) vii ff., as translated in *Code of Canon Law, Latin-English Edition* (Washington: CLSA, 1983), p. xi.

[9]*Code of Canon Law,* p. xii.

[10]Ibid.

[11]Ibid., pp. xv-xvi.

[12]Ibid., p. xv.

[13]See note 2, above.

[14]Cf. *UR,* n. 24.

[15]See, for example, the norms contained in the *Ecumenical Directory* issued by the Secretariat for Christian Unity on May 14, 1967; translation in Bouscaren-O'Connor, *Canon Law Digest* [*CLD*] 6:716-734.

[16]Cf. John Paul II, p. xv.

always be referred to [the conciliar image of the Church] as the primary pattern whose outline the code ought to express in so far as it can by its very nature."[17] As a result, it would not be difficult to see how the conciliar doctrine of "communio," so basic to the revised code, would have to be interpreted against the background of the teaching of the council concerning the various degrees of ecclesial communion.

The same would hold true for other basic doctrinal elements of the teaching of the council which have become theological bases for many of the juridical norms of the revised code:[18] they should all be interpreted within the context of the commitment of the Church to ecumenism, keeping in mind the doctrinal contributions made by the council to these elements from the point of view of ecumenism.

3. As has been implied above, the link between the 1917 code and the revised legislation is obviously the Second Vatican Council and its "novus habitus mentis."[19] Thus, as has been often stated by so many canonists, for a correct interpretation of the norms of the revised code it is essential to go back to the documents of the council.

For the proper interpretation of ecumenical aspects of the revised law, *Lumen gentium, Unitatis redintegratio, Orientalium Ecclesiarum* and *Dignitatis humanae* provide much of the proper context. Furthermore, it is my opinion that post-conciliar legislation on ecumenical aspects of the Church's life must also be taken into consideration.[20] After all, at least in a preliminary examination, practically all of the matter contained in those decrees, constitutions, etc., do not appear to fall among the categories of previous legislations abrogated by the revised code.[21] A superficial, though valid, example may help illustrate the point.

Despite the thrust of the council towards Christian unity and the commitment of the Church to ecumenism, no mention is made in the revised code of a "diocesan ecumenical office" among the institutions which are to be found in the diocesan curia.[22] At the same time, we may recall that one of the earliest emphases of the post-conciliar legislation concerning ecumenism at the universal and national levels, involved the establishment of such offices or commissions.[23] Despite their absence from the listing of curial institutions contained in

---

[17]Ibid., p. xiv.

[18]A list of these elements may be found in ibid., p. xv.

[19]That insightful expression of Paul VI has become the goal of so many study sessions on the revised Code (cf. *AAS* 57 [1965] 988).

[20]Most of that legislation may be found in *CLD* 6-9 (cf. index under "Ecumenism" in each volume).

[21]Cf. canon 6.

[22]Cf. canon 469-494.

[23]See, for example, the *Ecumenical Directory*, I, nn. 3-6 (*CLD* 6: 717-718), and the "Interim Guidelines" issued by the United States Bishops' Commission for Ecumenical Affairs, June 18, 1965, I (*CLD* 6: 708-709).

the revised code, one could hardly conclude that such an office would have no place in a diocesan curia!

4. The last general observation which I would like to make is to note that, in reference to norms related to ecumenism, the principle for the revision of the code, approved by the 1967 Synod of Bishops, is very much operative in the revised law. Respecting subsidiarity, much is left to the pastoral discretion of episcopal conferences and/or of the diocesan bishop with regard to the assurance of norms which further specify ecumenical aspects of canonical legislation.[24]

II. SOME ECUMENICAL ASPECTS OF THE REVISED CODE

Although there are numerous canons in the revised code which manifest ecumenical sensitivity, a selection has to be made in view of the limited scope of this presentation. As a result, the canons presented are meant to be illustrative, and will involve principally those ecclesial norms which are of special importance for our praxis of ecumenism.

After an introductory remark concerning ecumenism and the pastoral office in the Church, we will proceed with the presentation of some ecumenical aspects found in books III, "On the Teaching Office of the Church," and IV, "On the Sanctifying Office of the Church." Lastly, I will share some reflections which are the result of this study.

A. Ecumenism and the Pastoral Office in the Church

Unlike the 1917 code, which did not make any specific mention of ecumenical aspects of the episcopal function,[25] bishops are to manifest ecumenical awareness and sensitivity when exercising this pastoral office which has been entrusted to them. As they carry on their function, not only are they expected "to act with kindness and charity toward those who are not in full communion with the Catholic Church,"[26] but they are also actively to "foster ecumenism as it is understood by the Church."[27]

From this specific aspect of the pastoral office of a bishop, an argument could be made by analogy to arrive at the obligation which the pastor of a parish would have to become involved in the quest for Christian unity. In fact, based on solid ecclesiological doctrine concerning the exercise of the sacred ministry in the Church, the revised code defines the pastor as "the proper shepherd of the parish entrusted to him, exercising pastoral care in the community entrusted to him under the authority of the diocesan bishop in whose ministry of Christ he has been called to share."[28]

[24]For example, see canon 844.
[25]Cf. the 1917 code, cc. 335-336.
[26]Canon 383, § 3. See also canon 771, § 2.
[27]Canon 383, § 3.
[28]Canon 519. Cf. also canon 515, § 1.

In the case of ecumenism, what is considered such an important activity in the exercise of the pastoral office of a bishop would have to be considered, by analogy, to be an important part of the ministry of a pastor.

However, the revised code goes beyond this analogy by specifically mentioning ecumenism among the duties of any pastor.[29] As a result, we would have to conclude that in appointing a priest as pastor of a parish, one of the personal "qualities" required by the universal law[30] which the diocesan bishop would have considered before the conferral of the office, would be the candidate's ecumenical sensitivity.

B. Ecumenism and the Teaching Office of the Church

1. While affirming the Church's "innate duty and right to preach the gospel to all nations,"[31] the opening canons of Book III of the revised code add two qualifications which are of importance to us:

a. There must be a respect for the conscience of each individual. This is clearly recognized in the norm which states that "persons cannot ever be forced by anyone to embrace the Catholic faith against their conscience."[32]

Such a statement brings us back to the doctrinal teaching contained in the Decree on Religious Freedom of the Second Vatican Council.[33]

b. The acknowledgement of this basic human right does not in any way exclude promotion of and encouraged participation in ecumenism. In fact, "the special competence of the entire college of bishops and of the Apostolic See to promote and direct the participation of Catholics in the ecumenical movement"[34] ought to be understood within the wider context of the Church's "innate duty and right to preach the gospel to all nations."[35] Furthermore, the affirmation that the Church is bound to promote the restoration of unity among all Christians is based on the will of Christ.[36] Respecting the principle of subsidiarity, the competence of diocesan bishops and of episcopal conferences in issuing practical norms for

[29]See canon 528, § 1.
[30]See canon 521, especially § 2.
[31]Canon 747, § 1.
[32]Canon 742, § 2.
[33]Cf. the Decree on Religious Freedom *Dignitatis humanae* (henceforth referred to as *DH*), nn. 1 ff. It is interesting to note that previous drafts of the decree had appeared as a chapter of *UR* (cf. Abbott, p. 674).
[34]Canon 755, § 1.
[35]Canon 747, § 1.
[36]Canon 755, § 1.

the needs and opportunities which arise in their territory is likewise recognized by the revised code.[37]

Although not explicitly mentioned, the sensitivity of the revised code to ecumenical aspects of the teaching office of the Church is manifested in the section dealing with "Catholic Universities and Other Institutes of Higher Studies."[38] In this section the legislation reminds diocesan bishops of the "serious pastoral concern" they are to have for students, providing "for Catholic university centers in universities, even non-Catholic ones, to give assistance, especially spiritual, to young people."[39] As is well known, the pastoral care exercised in all those centers involves a large amount of ecumenical activity.

3. Another implicit manifestation of ecumenical sensitivity in this area of church life is found in the directives given to directors and professors of ecclesiastical universities and faculties. The revised code instructs them that they are "to see to it that mutual cooperation exists between their own university and faculty and other universities and faculties, even non-ecclesiastical ones," so that "through their combined efforts, meetings, coordinated scientific research and other means, they . . . work together for the greater advance of the sciences."[40]

Likewise, wherever higher institutes for religious sciences are established, not only theological disciplines, but also "other disciplines pertaining to Christian culture" are to be taught.[41]

4. The revised code makes allowances for the possible collaboration between Catholics and other separated brethren for the preparation and publication of translations of the Sacred Scriptures.[42] This opens the way for ecumenical collaboration at the level of biblical scholarship which was nowhere evident in the 1917 code.[43]

5. Concerning seminaries,[44] it is interesting to note that no specific mention is made of "ecumenism" in the listing contained in the revised Code of the disciplines which are to be taught there.[45] However, when treating those "matters"

---

[37]Ibid., § 2. Further on when dealing with "catechesis" the revised code indicates that pastors of souls are to make provision "for the message of the gospel to come to non-believers" (canon 771, § 2). This could very well include ecumenical activity.

[38]Cf. 1983 code, Book III, Title III, Chapter II.

[39]Canon 813.

[40]Canon 820.

[41]Canon 821.

[42]Cf. canon 825, § 2.

[43]See the general prohibition contained in canon 1399 of the 1917 code, which was abrogated by the Decree of the Sacred Congregation for the Doctrine of the Faith dated November 15, 1966: *AAS* 58 (1966) 1186.

[44]Although the revised code treats "seminaries" in Book II ("The People of God"), Title III ("Sacred Ministers or Clerics"), Chapter I ("The Formation of Clerics"), I have included the treatment of these institutions in this section of the presentation for illustrative purposes.

[45]Cf. canon 253, § 2.

in which students are to be diligently instructed because "they have a special relationship to sacred ministry," the code specifically mentions "relationship with people, even non-Catholics or non-believers."[46]

Becoming more specific, the code further establishes that "the students are to be instructed in the needs of the Universal Church so that they have a concern for ecumenical questions."[47] These are considered to be among the "more urgent issues" in the present-day Church.[48]

If a comparison is made of these norms with the corresponding canons in the 1917 code,[49] one cannot help but notice that no mention is made concerning the ecumenical aspects of seminary training. The special sensitivity of the revised legislation in reference to this aspect of seminary training cannot be ignored.

C. Ecumenism and the Sanctifying Office of the Church

Numerous ecumenical aspects are found in book IV of the revised Code of Canon Law. Once again, because of the limited scope of this work, we can only illustrate this by way of the more significant examples. At the same time, some questions which arise from the canonical text will be pointed out with the hope that they might become objects of further study.

1. General Observation

The opening canons of book IV contain a general directive concerning the competent authority for the supervision of the sacred liturgy, as well as for the issuance of liturgical norms.[50] From the canons which follow, it is clear that these two functions of the competent authority would involve ecumenical aspects of church praxis.[51]

2. Sacramental Sharing

While the 1917 code was rather strict in its prohibition of any form of "communicatio in sacris,"[52] the revised code canonizes the limited sacramental sharing which has been admitted in principle by the Second Vatican Council[53] and made possible in post-conciliar legislation.[54] Let us reflect for a few moments on the prescriptions of canon 844.

a. In § 1 of this canon, the general principle concerning the usual administration of sacraments is stated in a more positive fashion than in the 1917 code:[55] "Catholic ministers may licitly administer the sacraments to Catholic

[46]Canon 256, § 1.
[47]Ibid., § 2.
[48]Ibid.
[49]See canons 1352-1371 of the 1917 code.
[50]See canon 838, especially § 1 and § 4.
[51]Cf., for example, canon 844.
[52]Cf. canons 731, § 2 and 1258 of the 1917 code.
[53]See UR, n. 15 and OE, nn. 26-29.
[54]See, for example, the Ecumenical Directory, nn. 38ff. (CLD 6: 782-734) and the "Interim Guidelines" of the United States Bishops, III (ibid., pp. 710-714).
[55]See note 52, above.

members of the Christian faithful only and, likewise, the latter may licitly receive the sacraments only from Catholic ministers." In subsequent paragraphs, this general principle is qualified by the inclusion into the revised code of the limited sacramental sharing which may be allowed by the competent authority.

Reference is made in those subsequent paragraphs to situations involving three sacraments: penance, Eucharist and anointing of the sick. Let us briefly examine the various situations in which the sharing of these three sacraments with other baptized Christians may be possible.

b. § 2 considers the situation of a Catholic who wishes to receive any of the above three sacraments from a non-Catholic minister. For this to happen, the following conditions must be present simultaneously:

> It must be a case of "necessity" (which would seem to narrow greatly the possibilities or of "genuine spiritual benefit" (which considerably widens the possibilities).

> Danger of error or indifferentism is to be avoided. Either of these dangers could exist in the Catholic who wishes to receive the sacraments from a non-Catholic minister or, as a result of his action, in the other members of the Catholic community to which the recipient belongs.

> There exists the physical or moral impossibility of approaching a Catholic minister.

> The non-Catholic minister must belong to a Church in which the three above-mentioned sacraments are recognized as valid. It is understood that such a recognition is to be given *by the Catholic Church*. The doctrinal basis for such a judgment is the possession of a valid priesthood and Eucharist by virtue of the preservation of apostolic succession.[56]

c. § 3 treats the various situations in which a Catholic minister would be allowed to administer the same three sacraments to members of Oriental Churches who are not in full communion with the Catholic Church or to "members of other churches, which in the judgment of the Apostolic See are in the same condition as the Oriental Churches as far as these sacraments are concerned." Although no specific churches are mentioned in the latter group, members of such denominations as the Polish National Church and the Old Catholic Church among others would seem to be included.

Taking into account the close communion which exists between the Catholic Church and the separated Oriental Churches, the code has recognized the fact that there exist "ecclesiological and sacramental grounds for allowing and even at times encouraging some sharing in liturgical worship, even Eucharistic, with these Churches."[57] Based on these principles, requirements are practically

---

[56]Cf. *UR*, n. 15.
[57]*Ecumenical Directory*, n. 40 (*CLD* 6: 728).

minimal for the administration of penance, Eucharist and anointing of the sick to members of these Churches:

> The only condition which appears to go beyond what would be required of Catholics is that members of those Churches are to ask for those sacraments on their own. This requirement seems to imply that, in normal situations, the offer ought not to be made by the Catholic minister.

> The second requirement, that of a proper disposition on the part of the recipient, is nothing more than what is required of Catholics.[58]

d. § 4 considers the various situations in which, in the judgment of the diocesan bishop or the episcopal conference, Catholic ministers may licitly administer penance, Eucharist and anointing of the sick "to other Christians who do not have full communion with the Catholic Church." The "Christians" referred to in this section of canon 844 would be those belonging to separated churches and ecclesial communities "which were separated from the See of Rome during the very serious crisis that began in the West at the end of the Middle Ages, or during later times."[59]

In the case of our relationship with these churches and ecclesial communities, the Catholic Church recognized that where the unity of faith is deficient, the participation of separated brethren with Catholics, especially in the sacraments of the Eucharist, penance and anointing of the sick, is forbidden. Nevertheless, since the sacraments are both signs of unity and sources of grace,[60] the Church can, for adequate reasons, allow access to these sacraments to a separated brethren.[61]

For the administration of any of the three sacraments in these cases, a number of conditions must be present simultaneously. As will be easily seen, these requirements are made more stringent than in the previous two cases:

> The situation of "danger of death" or other "grave necessity" must be present. In post-conciliar legislation, the second situation has been illustrated by such circumstances as "times of persecution" or "imprisonment."[62]

> The separated Christian cannot approach a minister of his own community. It would seem that such an impossibility could be physical or moral ("Ubi lex non distinguit, neque nos debemus").

> The recipient is to ask for the sacrament on his own accord.[63]

> The separated Christian must manifest the Catholic faith in the

---

[58]Cf. canon 843, § 1.

[59]*UR*, n. 19.

[60]Cf. ibid., n. 8.

[61]See *Ecumenical Directory*, n. 55 (*CLD* 6: 732).

[62]Cf. ibid.

[63]Cf. what has been said in the text above, under § 3, with reference to the administration of the three sacraments to separated Orientals.

sacrament which he has requested—a requirement which may be difficult to judge, especially in situations of "persecution" and, at times, "imprisonment."[64]

Finally, the recipient is to be properly disposed, just as in the case of separated Orientals.

What about "reciprocity"? It is interesting to note that § 5 of canon 844 indicates that "neither the diocesan bishop nor the conference of bishops is to enact general norms" for the cases outlined above except "after consultation with the local competent authority of the interested non-Catholic church or community." Note that only "consultation" is required, not "agreement." This brings up the question of the principle of "reciprocity" which should be operative in ecumenical relationships, as indicated in post-conciliar legislation.[65]

We should note that the observance of the principle of "reciprocity" is, by no means, a condition "sine qua non." Were it so, it would not be possible for the competent authority even to issue general norms for sacramental sharing based on the current legislation. Let us analyze this more closely.

The principle involves the concept that one ought not extend an invitation to someone of another communion which one could not accept from the other. Keeping this in mind, the following points ought to be considered.

The Western Communions: When studying the possibility of sacramental sharing with Christians who are members of separated churches and ecclesial communities in the West, it is hard to find a situation in which "reciprocity" would be operative. Although penance, Eucharist and anointing could be administered to such separated Christians, provided that the conditions outlined in "d" above are fulfilled, Catholic participation in those same sacraments in those churches and communities—if they have them at all—mainly would depend on the Catholic Church's recognition of those sacraments as valid as present in those separated churches and communities.[66] Such a recognition is yet to come.

Separated Orientals: It is in our relationship to separated orientals where the principle of "reciprocity" could be most operative. After all, in such cases "the unity of the Church is not jeopardized nor are intolerable risks involved,"[67] for their "entire heritage of spirituality and liturgy, of discipline and theology, in their various traditions, belongs to the full catholic and apostolic character of the Church."[68]

However, even in this case, "reciprocity" cannot be operative at the present time in the implementation of this legislation. Although as Catholics we could

---

[64]"For obvious reasons, this is not a requirement in the cases involving separated Orientals.
[65]Cf. *Ecumenical Directory*, n. 43 (*CLD* 6: 730).
[66]Cf. text above and note 56.
[67]*OE*, n. 26.
[68]*UR*, n. 17. Cf. also ibid., nn. 14-16.

accept from separated Orientals the same invitation which we extend to them,[69] separated Oriental churches do not encourage or even permit any form of sacramental sharing.[70] In fact, even

[69]See canon 844, § 2 and § 3.

[70]The Second Vatican Council took the position that in these cases, "given suitable circumstances and the approval of church authority, some worship in common is not merely possible but is recommended" (*UR,* n. 15). The proper circumstances for the implementation of this ecumenical principle may be found in *OE,* n. 27. These were "canonized" in canon 844 of the revised code.

For the Orthodox position, it may suffice to quote a few pertinent paragraphs from the *Guidelines for Orthodox Christians in Ecumenical Relations* by the Reverend Robert G. Stephanopoulos, Ph.D., approved on March 20, 1973 by the Standing Conference of Canonical Orthodox Bishops of America:

Sacraments and Other Liturgical Services

I. Holy Eucharist

1. Unity in the faith and the active life of the community is a necessary precondition to sharing in the sacraments of the Orthodox Church. The Standing Conference of Canonical Orthodox Bishops in America has expressed the clear position of the Orthodox Church throughout the ages:

"To the Holy Communion the Church admits only her baptized and chrismated children who confess the full Orthodox Faith, pure and entire, and by it she shows forth her oneness with her and with her Divine Spouse. Holy Communion is the sign and evidence of right belief and of incorporation in the Israel of God. Further, the Church teaches that the Eucharist cannot be found, and must not be sought outside the covenanted mysteries. It is the achievement of unity."

"The Standing Conference would at this time remind the children of the Church as they pray, study and work for Christian reunion that the Eucharistic Mystery is the end of unity, not a means to that end, and that therefore, the decisions regarding Holy Communion reached by Christian bodies outside the Orthodox will not be sought by Orthodox Christians outside of the Church, nor will it be offered to those who do not yet confess the Orthodox Church as their mother."

2. This position must be made explicit by the Orthodox pastors whenever a question may arise of a disciplinary or ecumenical nature. It has been solemnly affirmed in the bilateral conversations of the Orthodox representatives with Roman Catholics, Episcopalians, Lutherans, and Reformed Christians, and has been officially promulgated in the findings and statements of these bilaterals. (p.17)

VI. CONFESSION AND HOLY UNCTION

1. The sacraments are a means of divine grace and a sacred activity of the community of faith, celebrated within the community and symbolizing the oneness in faith, worship and life of the community. Where this unity is incomplete, the participation of the non-Orthodox is not permitted. For the same reason, an Orthodox Christian may not participate in the sacraments or ordinances of other communions.

2. In the extreme case that a non-Orthodox person, being without access to the ministrations of his own faith-community, summons an Orthodox priest and declares his faith to be in harmony with that of the Holy Orthodox Church, his or her confession may be heard and the sacraments of Baptism, Chrismation, Holy Unction and/or Holy Communion administered with the understanding that he or she is joining the Orthodox Church. (p.22)

In the extreme case that a non-Orthodox person, being without access to the ministrations of his own faith-community, summons an Orthodox priest and declares his faith to be in harmony with that of the Holy Orthodox Church, his or her own confession may be heard and the sacraments of baptism, confirmation, holy unction and/or Holy Communion administered with the understanding that he or she is joining the Orthodox Church.[71]

Thus it is understandable that "reciprocity" has not been absolutely required by the revised code for the implementation of these ecumenical norms.[72]

3. Conditional Baptism

The sensitivity to ecumenism of the legislation contained in the revised code is manifested in the norms which govern the administration of conditional baptism. A case study may serve to illustrate the point. It is Friday afternoon, and the Chancery receives a call from a priest in one of the parishes of the diocese where the children in the First Communion Program will be receiving First Eucharist the following day. Panic strikes when the Director of Religious Education informs the priest that there is one child who had not presented a Certificate of Baptism.

An interview with the mother reveals that the child was baptized "in a Protestant church" in another state, which a minister visited only on Sundays for services. No information is available concerning the denomination of the church. Then, the purpose of the call: "Can I baptize the child conditionally?"

It would seem that if we examine the prescriptions of the revised law, this may very well be a situation in which the answer given may have to be in the negative. In fact, the celebration of First Eucharist may have to be delayed! Although this may sound a bit difficult to accept, the revised code is rather strict concerning the administration of conditional baptism.

Somehow one gets the impression that a practice has developed in some places where "conditional baptism" was administered without much ecumenical sensitivity. If a certificate was not available, and a person was about to receive confirmation, Eucharist or marriage in the very near future, "conditional baptism" was a convenient way to resolve the situation: "If you are not baptized, you will be after this ceremony. If you are, the ceremony will simply have no effect."

It is known that, due to the unique nature of sacramental celebrations, "both the sacred ministers and the rest of the Christian faithful must employ the *greatest reverence* and the *necessary diligence* in their celebration."[73]

[71]Orthodox Ecumenical Guidelines, VI, 2.
[72]Cf. text above and note 65.
[73]Canon 840. The emphasis is mine.

212

Reverence and diligence on the part of the sacred minister are manifested in ensuring that the Christian faithful "ask for [the sacraments] at appropriate times, are properly disposed and are not prohibited by law from receiving them."[74] Furthermore, the revised code specifies that "the sacraments of baptism, confirmation and orders cannot be repeated since they imprint a character."[75]

Although the last prescription is basically the same as that contained in c. 732, § 1 of the 1917 code, a preliminary condition has been added in the revised code to the corresponding canon of the 1917 code. In the latter, the norm simply stated: "Si vero prudens dubium existat num revera vel num valide collata fuerint, sub conditione iterum conferantur."[76] Perhaps as a result of an abuse of the practice of conditional baptism, the revised code indicates that such a practice is to be followed "if, *after diligent investigation,* there is still a prudent doubt whether these sacraments . . . have been truly or validly conferred."[77] In our opinion, a "diligent investigation" would include: (a) dealing with the question sufficiently in advance in order to make a serious effort to obtain a certificate of baptism; and (b) insofar as it is possible, the prescriptions of c. 869, § 2 ought to be followed, concerning the examination of the matter and form used in the conferral of the sacrament, as well as the intention of an adult baptized person and of the minister of baptism.[78]

Our case study would seem to indicate a situation in which a number of elements needed for a "diligent investigation" were carelessly overlooked. Since "indiscriminate conditional baptism of all who desire full communion with the Catholic Church cannot be approved,"[79] it would seem that from the theological, canonical and ecumenical point of view, it would be best to delay the reception of First Eucharist until such an investigation can be reasonably completed.

In our country, a "prudent doubt" may remain in a number of cases, thus the conditional administration of baptism would be allowed.[80] Think, for example, of the impossibility of carrying on a "diligent investigation" according to the norms found in c. 869, § 2, of a baptism conferred in a store-front church of an unspecified Christian denomination, which is "here today, and gone tomorrow."

Thus, it is evident that the revised legislation is making a serious attempt to sensitize those directly or indirectly involved in the administration of baptism to the fact that

---

[74]Canon 843, § 1.

[75]Canon 845, § 1. See also *Ecumenical Directory,* II, 9 (*CLD* 6: 720).

[76]Canon 732, § 2 of the 1917 code.

[77]Canon 845, § 2. This prescription is repeated in reference to baptism in canon 869, § 1.

[78]This procedure is presented in detail in the *Ecumenical Directory,* II, especially nn. 13-14 (*CLD* 6: 720-723).

[79]*Ecumenical Directory,* n. 14 (*CLD* 6: 722).

[80]If so, then the rather sensible prescriptions of canon 869, § 3 would apply.

Placing a proper value on the baptism conferred by ministers of churches and ecclesial communities separated from us has ecumenical importance. . . . Therefore, it is to be hoped that all Christians will grow continually more reverent and faithful in this regard for what the Lord instituted concerning its celebration.[81]

4. Godparents at Baptism

Since the promulgation of the *Ecumenical Directory* in 1967 there have existed two possibilities of some ecumenical involvement with respect to the role of "godparent" at a Catholic baptism.

The first one involves members of the separated Oriental Churches. In such cases, the *Directory* indicated that,

Because of the close communion between the Catholic Church and the Oriental Churches separated from us . . . it is permissible for a just cause for a member of one of the latter to act as godparent, together with a Catholic godparent, at the baptism of a Catholic infant or adult so long as there is provision for the Catholic education of the person being baptized, and it is clear that the godparent is a suitable one.[82]

This concession was to be considered an exception[83] to the requirement that the godparent be, among other things, a fully initiated member of the Catholic Church.[84] It is evident that such a requirement is based on the understanding which the Church has of the role of a godparent.[85]

In the case of members of other separated churches or ecclesial communities[86],

It is not permissible . . . [for such a person] . . . to act as godparent in the liturgical and canonical sense at baptism. . . . The reason is that a godparent is not merely undertaking his responsibility for the Christian education of the person baptized . . . as a relative or friend; he is also, as a representative of a community of faith, standing as sponsor for the faith of the candidate.[87]

However, since he is a member of such a church or ecclesial community and has faith in Christ, he was permitted to have some ecumenical participation at a Catholic baptism. In such cases, because of ties of blood or friendship, the separated Christian can be admitted with a Catholic godparent as a Christian witness of the baptism.[88]

---

[81]*Ecumenical Directory,* II, n. 18 (*CLD* 6: 722-723).

[82]*Ecumenical Directory,* IV, n. 48 (*CLD* 6: 730).

[83]Cf. *Ecumenical Directory,* VI, n. 57 (*CLD* 6: 732-733).

[84]Cf. *Rite of Baptism of Children and Christian Initiation of Adults,* Praenotanda, n. 10.

[85]Cf. ibid., nn. 8-9.

[86]For an explanation of this term, cf. text above and note 59.

[87]*Ecumenical Directory,* IV, n. 57 (*CLD* 6: 732-733).

[88]Ibid. It goes without saying that based on the principles outlined above, a non-baptized person cannot act as godparent or Christian witness at a Catholic baptism.

Although these ecumenical overtures have improved relations with other Christian churches, some abuses of these permissions have been known to occur. These abuses have had the unfortunate effect of creating tensions in the relationship which exists between the Catholic Church and other Christian churches, as well as confusion and misunderstandings among the members of the Christian faithful.

In a very concise fashion, the above norms have been canonized by the revised code in c. 874, § 2, which states: "A baptized person who belongs to a non-Catholic ecclesial community may not be admitted except as a witness to baptism and together with a Catholic sponsor."

After an initial reading, the legislation may appear to be a step backwards in ecumenical relations. The general character of the statement does not seem to allow for the special exception granted to a separated Oriental permitting the person to act as "godparent" in a Catholic baptism. It is the opinion of this author that this is not the case. The term "communitas ecclesialis," which is used in the canon, does not include "members of Oriental Churches which do not have full communion with the Catholic Church."[89] In ecumenical idiom, that expression is generally used for "the churches and ecclesial communities which were separated from the Apostolic See of Rome during the very serious crisis that began in the West at the end of the Middle Ages, or during later times." At best, we could say that the revised code is silent with respect to the possible role of a separated Oriental at a Catholic baptism. In which case, the legislation found in the *Ecumenical Directory* would fill this "lacuna."

5. Eucharist

Besides what has been indicated above concerning the administration of the Eucharist to non-Catholics, there are few explicit ecumenical aspects to the revised legislation on this sacrament. However, two examples of ecumenical sensitivity may be worth noting.

> a. C. 908 forbids Eucharistic concelebration "with priests or ministers of churches or ecclesial communities which are not in full communion with the Catholic Church." It is clear by the terminology and in the canon that all separated brethren are included and no exception is allowed.[92]

[89]See the specific use of those terms in § 3 and § 4 of canon 844.

[90]*UR*, n. 19. See text above.

[91]See *Ecumenical Directory*, IV, n. 48 (*CLD* 6: 730).

A private response given by the Secretariat for Promoting Christian Unity on December 3, 1970 (*CLD* 7: 597-599) further clarifies the issue providing the proper context for the interpretation of this legislation. Furthermore, indirect proof that our interpretation is correct may be seen in the clarification added to n. 10 of the General "Praenotanda" to Christian Initiation contained in the "Variationes" introduced in the liturgical books by the Sacred Congregation for Sacraments and Divine Worship (cf. *Notitiae* 20 [1983] 545-546). These "variationes" seek to bring liturgical directives into conformity with the revised code.

[92]Cf. the "Declaration on the position of the Catholic Church on the matter of common Eucharist between Christians of different confessions" of the Secretariat for Promoting Christian Unity, *CLD* 7: 796-801.

b. C. 933 allows for the celebration of the Eucharist "in a sacred edifice of another church or ecclesial community that does not have full communion with the Catholic Church." Once again, by the terminology used, one may conclude that all church edifices of separated Christians are included. Only three simple requirements need to be fulfilled: It is to be done for a "just cause, with the permission of the local ordinary, avoiding scandal." Needless to say, this legislation is radically different from the prohibition contained in the corresponding canon of the 1917 code.[93]

6. Marriage

A few examples from the legislation on marriage should illustrate some of the ecumenical aspects contained in this section of the revised Code of Canon Law.

a. Unlike the 1917 code, which states that the marriage of the *baptized* was governed by canon law,[94] the revised code legislates that it is the marriage of *Catholics* which is governed by canon law.[95] Further precision is added when, in the same canon, the revised code indicates that this legal principle holds "even if only one party is baptized."

b. C. 1117 obliges to the observance of the canonical form "whenever at least one of the contactants was baptized in the Catholic Church or was received into it and has not left it by a formal act." As time goes by, the jurisprudential and ecumenical implications of this norm will surely begin to surface.

c. The canonical regulations concerning the place of marriage are more relaxed in c. 1118, §§ 1-2 of the revised code than in the corresponding canon of the 1917 code.[96]

d. Out of respect for separated Orientals, the revised code likewise canonizes the legislation, in effect since 1967,[97] that

If a Catholic party contracts marriage with a non-Catholic of an Oriental Rite, the canonical form of celebration is to be observed only for licitness; for validity, however, the presence of a sacred minister is required along with the observance of the other requirements of law.[98]

e. The faculty granted to local ordinaries to dispense from the canonical form of marriage, a concession which has been in effect since 1970,[99] has also been canonized in the revised code.[100]

[93]See canon 823, § 1 of the 1917 code.
[94]See canon 1016 of the 1917 code.
[95]See canon 1059 of the revised code.
[96]Cf. canon 1109 of the 1917 code.
[97]Cf. the Decree "Crescens matrimoniorum" of the Sacred Congregation for the Oriental Churches, February 22, 1967 (*CLD* 7: 603-605).
[98]Canon 1127, § 1.
[99]Cf. Paul VI's motu proprio *Matrimonia mixta,* March 31, 1970, nn. 9-10 (*CLD* 7: 716).
[100]See canons 1079, § 1 and 1127, § 2.

f. Lastly, the special care which local ordinaries and other pastors of souls are to exercise towards parties involved in mixed marriages,[101] also evidences the ecumenical sensitivity of the revised code.

III. A QUESTION WHICH ARISES

Before concluding this illustrative presentation, I would like to point out a question which has arisen from the general sensitivity towards ecumenism which the revised code manifests in its legislation. There is no doubt that this and many other questions will require answers based on theological and canonical principles which can only be developed in time, thus I will not even make the attempt of providing a response at this time. However, I will try to provide some principles which might be of assistance in the formulation of an answer.

In my opinion, the principal question which arises from an examination of the ecumenical aspects of the revised code is one which has not been treated in this presentation: "Are non-Catholics subjects of obligations and rights within the Catholic Church? and, if so, to what degree?"

1. Let me propose some general canonical principles which must be taken into account in the eventual formulation of an answer.

a. Canon 1 states that the canons of the code affect only the Latin Church.

b. Canon 2 specifies the above principle by establishing that "merely ecclesiastical laws" bind those

baptized in the Catholic Church or received into it;

who enjoy sufficient use of reason;

who, unless the law expressly provides otherwise, have completed seven years of age.

c. Canon 96 defines "personhood" in the Church. It is baptism which incorporates an individual into the Church of Christ, with obligations and rights proper to Christians, qualified by

the condition of each;

the degree of ecclesiastical communion;

any legitimate sanction which may have been incurred.

2. Next let me suggest some theological considerations

a. The wide definition given in c. 204, § 1 of a "Christifidelis" seems to allow for some possibility that the question may be able to be answered, at least in its widest interpretation, in the affirmative. The obligation and right to participate in mission appear to be heavily based on incorporation[102] and communion.[103]

---

[101]Cf. canon 1128.

[102]Cf. canon 849. It is interesting to note that although the basis for incorporation into the Church of Christ, which "subsists in the Catholic Church" (canon 204, § 2), is the sacrament of

b. The Decree on Ecumenism of the Second Vatican Council affirms that

> Baptism . . . constitutes a sacramental bond of unity linking all who have been reborn by means of it. But baptism, of itself, is only a beginning, a point of departure, for it is wholly directed toward the acquiring of fullness of life in Christ. Baptism is thus oriented toward a complete profession of faith, a complete incorporation into the system of salvation such as Christ Himself willed it to be, and finally, toward a complete participation in Eucharistic communion.[104]

c. Likewise, it is true that those "who believe in Christ and have been properly baptized are brought into a certain, though imperfect, communion with the Catholic."[105] However, there is no question that

> The differences that exist in varying degrees between them and the Catholic Church — whether in doctrine and sometimes in discipline — do indeed create many and sometimes serious obstacles to full ecclesiastical communion.[106]

d. Since the participation of the baptized in obligations and rights is related "to the extent that they are in ecclesiastical communion,"[107] the following considerations are also in order.

— There are various degrees of communion.[108]

— Full communion is based on baptism and the union which exists with Christ in the visible structure of the Catholic Church on earth "by the bonds of profession of faith, of the sacraments, and of ecclesiastical governance."[109]

---

baptism, the other sacraments of Christian initiation provide further bases for participation in mission. Confirmation binds the baptized more perfectly to the Church and "obliges them more firmly to be witnesses to Christ by word and deed and to spread and defend the faith" (canon 879). Eucharist is the sacrament to which all exercise of mission is related and directed, be it sacramental or in other works of the apostolate (cf. canon 897).

If the degree of initiation is somehow related to the obligation and right to participate in mission, then there is no doubt that separated Orientals would have a greater "claim" to being subjects of obligations and rights in the Catholic Church than, for example, separated ecclesial communities in the West. Thus, with respect to canon 213, involving the "right to sacraments," one would easily recognize how canon 844, § 3-4 seems to recognize the above proposal (see also *LG*, n. 15). Needless to say, further study must be made of this question by ecumenical theologians and canonists. For a parallel consideration of "communion" as a basis for participation in mission, see text below under "d."

[103]Cf. canon 205 and also canons 96 and 204, § 2.
[104]*UR*, n. 22.
[105]Ibid., n. 3.
[106]Ibid.
[107]See canon 96.
[108]Cf. *LG*, nn. 14-15.
[109]Canon 205.

___ Taking into consideration those bonds, the privileged position of the separated Orientals becomes apparent with respect to their possible participation in obligations and rights.[110]

3. Here are some possible applications.

a. There is no question that some of the obligations and rights of all the Christian faithfull as contained in the revised code could apply to anyone, regardless of religious affiliation.[111]

b. Participation by other baptized non-Catholics in some of the remaining obligations and rights might be possible, but the degrees of participation would appear to have to be regulated by the principle of "communion."[112]

c. There are other important implicit obligations or rights concerning which questions arise.[113]

It is of great importance that the basic question proposed above be clarified. Although little can be done beyond the encouragement of the fulfillment of obligations, the situation is different with rights.

If other baptized non-Catholics are subjects of rights, then it would seem that they would also have the right to vindicate them.[114] In fact, c. 1476 clearly states that "anyone, whether baptized or not, can act in a trial."

To my knowledge, no clear answer to this question is available at this time. Hopefully, further research will continue taking into consideration the ecclesiological principles of the Second Vatican Council as well as the legal principles in the revised code.

IV. FINAL OBSERVATION

As was recalled at the beginning of this presentation, the Second Vatican Council had made the restoration of Christian unity one of its principal concerns.[115] In its work of renewal the council wished to set guidelines, helps and methods which Catholics would employ in order to respond to the "divine summons and grace" of Christian unity.[116]

The code has been presented to the Church as a tool for the implementation of the decrees of the Second Vatican Council, as an instrument to carry on the

[110]See also note 102.
[111]See, for example, canon 220. Likewise see canons 231, § 2 and 793, § 1.
[112]See, for example, canons 213, 214 and 225, § 1.
[113]Cf. for example, canons 805 and 812.
[114]Cf. canon 221, especially § 1. See also the seventh principle of revision approved by the 1967 Synod of Bishops in *AAS* 75 (1983), Part II, p. xxii.
[115]For references, see note 7.
[116]Cf. *UR,* n. 1.

work of renewal.[117] As is known, the new legislation must be interpreted within the context of the doctrinal and juridical legacy of the council.

From this presentation it can be concluded that the very content of the revised code manifests sensitivity to the ecumenical concern of the council and of the Church. In fact, the very promulgation of the revised code brings stability to church discipline and, hopefully, strengthens our fidelity to Christ's calling. This cannot help but have ecumenical implications, for it is hoped that the new legislation will help the Church of Christ to present a clearer "sacramental image"[118] to the world. This manifestation, in turn, may lead all who contemplate this reality with the gift of faith

> Toward a complete profession of faith, a complete incorporation into the system of salvation such as Christ himself willed it, and finally, toward a complete participation in Eucharistic Communion.[119]

[117]Cf. John Paul II's speech at the official presentation of the code on February 3, 1983, in the pamphlet, *Promulgation and Official Presentation of the Code of Canon Law,* n. 9 (Pont. Comm. Codici Iuris Canonici Recognoscendo, Vatican City: Vatican Press, 1983), as well as the apostolic constitution *Sacrae disciplinae leges, AAS* 75 (1983), Part II, pp. vii-ix. Numerous citations from previous popes, beginning with John XXIII, could be presented to support this.

[118]Cf. *LG,* nn. 1 and 8.

[119]*UR.,* n. 22.

AUTHORITY AND OBEDIENCE IN CONSECRATED LIFE

Richard A. Hill, S.J.

The purpose of this presentation is to examine the concepts and their implications of authority and of obedience in religious institutes as they appear in the Revised Code of Canon Law, to which I will add some practical considerations from my own experience with my own religious order and with members of other religious families.

Authority is understood in the Second Vatican Council and therefore in the revised code as the right to give a command or precept or to make a decision and to expect compliance; obedience, the correlative of authority, is understood as compliance with another's command or decision, as submission of will to the will of another. I want to address obedience before turning to authority because its historical evolution as an essential element in religious life sheds some important light on what it is meant to connote and permits us to identify some notions which have attached to it without adequate justification. If we can achieve greater clarity with respect to what obedience is supposed to be, authority and its exercise is easier to describe and understand. I wish to note at the outset my indebtedness to Juan M. Lozano, C.M.F., whose book, *Discipleship: Towards an Understanding of Religious Life,* offers important historical and patristic insights into the evolution of religious obedience and very useful theological reflection on the experience of religious life in the Church.

Etymologically the word, to obey, both in Greek (*hypokouein*) and in Latin (*oboedire*), derive from the verb, to hear or to listen to, but it always means, especially in the New Testament and the patristic literature, to listen to and carry out what is being heard. In NT a different word (*hypotassein*), meaning to submit to, is used, with one exception, if there is question of obedience to another human person. There are some who like to explore a concept of obedience which would connote the obligation of a religious to listen attentively to what the rule or the superior has to say and to admit that in a serious way into his or her ultimate discernment about what to do.

We can distinguish different kinds of obedience depending upon the source of the precept and we can thus speak of obedience to the will of God, especially as revealed in Christ, obedience to the gospel, obedience to one's own vocational gift and to one's own conscience, to ecclesiastical and civil authority, and to religious superiors. All of them, except obedience to religious superiors, are explicit biblical injunctions incumbent upon all Christians; none of them, except religious obedience, implies an obligation arising from a specific or particular vocational gift within the Christian vocation as such. It is necessary, therefore, to approach obedience to religious superiors with a certain caution against generalizations and especially about applying to religious obedience what NT says about other kinds of obedience or submission. There is no scriptural evidence that the following of Christ, even the more literal (*pressius*) following of Christ, suggests obedience or submission to another human person other than civil of hierarchical ecclesiastical authority. Religious institutes do not pertain to the hierarchical structure of the Church.

Of the three counsels called evangelical, obedience is the most remotely rooted in the Gospels. Indeed it was not recognized in the Church for about three hundred years. Chastity or voluntary celibacy and poverty or renunciation of material possessions were obviously highly regarded in the apostolic churches in which the model of Christ's obedience to his Father was preached as applicable to all Christians. Obedience to another human being, however, voluntarily undertaken over and above one's adherence to Christianity, was unheard of and probably would have been met with great suspicion as undermining the submission required to civil and ecclesiastical authorities.

It is traditional and accurate to point to the rise of the eremitical or anchoritic life, which was a more short-lived phenomenon than is commonly supposed before the appearance of monasticism, as the first identifiable form of the way of life which is called religious. In this solitary way of life obedience or submission to another human being was found only during the probationary period prior to undertaking a life which was totally solitary. Obedience to a superior is obviously incompatible with living alone. Nevertheless, it is precisely from the legends of the hermits that all those marvelous, not to say humorous, stories derive, which were so dear to the late medieval and renaissance spititual writers, including St. Ignatius of Loyola, about disciples watering dry sticks, trying to move boulders which many men together could not have budged, and bringing lionesses to the spiritual master. They were stories about neophytes, not about mature and experienced religious. Even when the customs of hermits gathering together from time to time emerged, the presidency of the more senior or more famous fathers implied nothing more than the role of a spiritual director to whom the others deferred.

Obedience as an essential component of religious life develops only with the rather sudden appearance of monasticism in the mid-fourth century in Egypt and in Cappodocia (in modern Turkey) and toward the end of the fourth century in the West in North Africa under St. Augustine. With the virtual disapperance of eremitical life and the ascendancy everywhere of the monastic model of religious life in a community of charity centered on the liturgy, which was abandoned by the hermits along with the cities, obedience to the abbot or abbess came to be recognized as indispensable to religious life in community. This obedience to the monastic superior was principally aimed at observance of the rule as a holy guide for individuals and community in fidelity to their vocation, and the superior from that time on was accepted as the living interpreter of the rule. Obedience to the directives of this superior, moreover, safeguarded the orderly rhythm of community life.

At the same time the monastic community had a continuous task to fulfill, to discern the will of God for it in the light of the gospel, and while this was done in the charitable dialogue of the frequent chapters, the superior alone ratified the communal conclusion and interpreted it for the monastery. From the time of St. Augustine it was the responsibility of the *praepositus,* the one set over the community, "to rebuke those who cause dissension and to strengthen the timid" (*Rule,* 11; cf. c. 619). While the abbot or abbess, as the title implies, was to be and to govern as the spiritual father or mother, they were clearly endowed by the rule with the authority to make decisions and to require that they be implemented.

The monastic understanding of obedience, which was concerned almost exclusively with the religious life within the precincts of the monastery, observance of the holy rule and good order, prevailed as essential to religious life for more than seven hundred years, until the beginning of the thirteenth century, there being no other significant model available until the rise of the apostolic orders. With the founding of the Friars Minor and at almost the same time of the Order of Preachers a new form of religious life seemed a foothold in the Church—a new form which was by its very nature apostolic—and the nature and understanding of obedience was necessarily affected by this change, continuing to exist side by side with the monastic tradition and borrowing from it. For the friars obedience took on an apostolic orientation. The superiors assign the members to apostolic works, to ecclesial mission.

This brought male religious into continuous contact with the Church as a whole. St. Francis of Assisi sought and obtained a close bond with the papacy, which did not hesitate thereafter to employ the friars and later the clerics regular in a wide-ranging mission far exceeding the localized character of a monastery. Religious life was henceforth also urban. The popes of the thirteenth century were confronted with the rapid development of an urban civilization in Europe, of universities and especially of a middle class; later they were challenged by the discovery of whole continents only vaguely suspected. Obedience, while retaining its objective of fidelity to the rule of life and of harmony within the community, embraced readiness for apostolic action, abandoning thereby the stability of monasticism. Nothing substantially different has evolved in religious life during the second seven hundred years.

From the long evolution of the understanding and practice of obedience, what do we find in the revised code? We can respond that, in substance, the code echoes the council. The key passage in the conciliar teaching is found in the decree, *Perfectae caritatis (PC),* 14 which I present here in part in a somewhat rearranged order:

> Under the influence of the Holy Spirit religious submit themselves to their superiors. . .through whom they are guided into the service of all their brothers and sisters in Christ. Through the profession of obedience they offer to God a total dedication of their own wills as a sacrifice of themselves; they thereby unite themselves with greater steadiness and security to the saving will of God. . .and assume a firmer commitment to the service of the Church. . . .

During the post-conciliar period Pope Paul VI restated much of the council's teaching about religious obedience and further elaborated on it in *Evangelica testificatio (ET)* (1971), 25-29, and the Sacred Congregations for Religious and Secular Institutes and for Bishops jointly published *Directions for the Mutual Relations between Bishops and Religious in the Church* (1978), which concerns only apostolic religious institutes. *Mutuae relationes (ME)* presents an interesting analogy between the three-fold ministry of bishops, in which all the baptized share, and the role of religious superiors in their communities. They are said to have an office of teaching and of sanctifying as well as that of governing. ''As to the office of governing, superiors must render the service of ordering the life of the community, of organizing its particular missions and of seeing to it that it be efficiently inserted into ecclesial activity under the leadership of the bishops'' (13).

This brings us to consider briefly the three canons of the revised code which present norms for the observance of the vow of obedience. The first is canon 601 found in the norms common to all institutes of consecrated life. It identifies the object of the counsel of obedience.

> Canon 601 - The evangelical counsel of obedience, undertaken in a spirit of faith and love in the following of Christ who was obedient even unto death, requires a submission of the will to legitimate superiors, who stand in the place of God when they command according to the proper constitutions.

Let us now examine the correlative of obedience, the authority of religious superiors. The ultimate object of religious obedience is to discover the will of God in specific and concrete circumstances. For the religious man or woman the will of God is mediated by the rule or constitutions and by the decisions of chapters, but these, however specific and detailed they may be in some instances, are not adequate for concrete decisions. There is need for a living, human mediation of the will of God with regard to this community in these circumstances. Decisions are always made in community and in a sense by a community. The communal nature of religious life is indispensible to our effort to understand religious authority. However complex or simple the process of descernment may be, the time comes when a definitive decision is needed for the sake of the *communio.* This is the need and role of true authority, the right to command or decide and to expect compliance. The community, life in common, requires that there exist such authority. Without it the community is wounded and could disintegrate.

The authority to decide may rest with the community itself or it may be vested in a single individual. This will depend in large measure on the nature of the religious institute in question and the subject matter of the decision to be made. There never has existed a religious order or congregation in which all decisions and precepts were arrived at by chapters or communities, nor has there ever been an institute in which all decisions were left to the individual religious. The authority to decide in concrete instances is found in the religious superior. It derives from the constitutions approved and guaranteed by the hierarchical authority of the Church. It does not derive from the consent of the governed.

The informed and free religious profession of each individual constitutes him or her as a person henceforth subject to the authority of superiors.

This unique kind of authority limited only by the constitutions, which can be amended within certain bounds, certainly pertains to the realm of faith. It is the result of a tradition of more than sixteen hundred years which has been carefully discerned by the Church to be the gift of God. Authority in religious institutes is truly ecclesial, although not hierarchical, and is conceivable only within a Church which is hierarchically structured and fully endowed with the three-fold role of Christ as prophet, priest and king. The council, the postconciliar magisterium and hence the code unequivocally adhere to this ancient tradition in the Church.

> Not to be weakened, however, is the authority of the superior to decide what is to be done and to require its execution (*PC*, 14).

> The labor of seeking together must end at the appropriate moment with the decision of the superior whose presence and acceptance are indispensable in every community (*ET*, 25).

> Superiors exercise their power, received from God through the ministry of the Church in a spririt of service (canon 618).

This brings us to the second canon which we need to consider. It is canon 619 and is found under the rubric of the governance of religious institutes.

> Canon 619 - Superiors are to devote themselves to their office assiduously and, together with the members entrusted to them, they should be eager to build a community of brothers or sisters in Christ in which God is sought after and loved above all else. Therefore, they are to nourish the members frequently with the food of the word of God and lead them to the celebration of the sacred liturgy. They are to be an example to the members in cultivating virtues and in the observance of the laws and traditions of the particular institute; they are to meet the personal needs of the members in an appropriate fashion, look after solicitously and visit the sick, admonish the restless, console the faint of heart, and be patient toward all.

This canon, of course, is applicable to all religious institutes, whether contemplative or apostolic, and for this reason speaks only to the internal well-being of the community, the observance of the rule and the orderly rhythm of life in communion. The superior is pictured mainly as the designated leader of the community who nurtures, draws and provides the means. The community centers upon the word of God and the Eucharist, and the rule of its life is the virtues and the laws and sound traditions of the institute. Some members require special service by the superior: the sick, the troublemakers and the fainthearted.

In religious institutes committed to the apostolate the superior possesses authority with respect to the apostolic works and the members missioned to them. For such institutes we have to examine canon 678, §2 in conjunction with canon 619.

Canon 678 - §2. In exercising an external apostolate, religious are also subject to their own superiors and must remain faithful to the discipline of the institute, which obligation bishops themselves should not fail to insist upon in cases which warrant it.

In the choice of apostolic works and in the exercise of them religious are subject to the authority of their own superiors in addition to that of the bishops. This is "the appropriate insertion into the ministry of the Church" spoken of in *MR*, 13, the outward thrust and concern which must characterize apostolic institutes.

While the constitutions of each religious family must spell out in sufficient detail the authority and obligations of different superiors, the code itself is by no means silent about these matters, usually speaking of major superiors, and such norms are found throughout the law and not merely in Book II, Part II, Section I. There are literally scores of canons apart from those in the section on institutes of consecrated life which determine norms for the offices of religious superiors. Suffice it to say here that the code requires an immediate superior (c. 608), although only once called a local superior (c. 636, §1), as well as at least one major superior. In institutes divided into provinces or their equivalent there will be two major superiors: the highest moderator or superior general and a provincial superior (c. 620). What this infers—and I believe that this is of great importance for healthy religious life—is that each religious has to have an immediate superior, who is as immediately present and accessible as possible and who has the authority and resources to provide for the needs of individuals and of their communities. It is unhealthy to concentrate all authority in a major superior who is not in immediate and ongoing contact with and involvement in the concerns of the local community, who is not a member of that community. As Pope Paul said in *ET*, each community needs the presence of a designated leader who has the authority to lead effectively (25). Furthermore, inasmuch as every legitimately established house is by the law itself a juridic person, it is the local superior alone who by law represents the interests of that house in the Church (c. 634, §1 and cf. c. 118).

I would like now to allude at least briefly to three issues which always emerge in a discussion about obedience and authority and which often obscure or even inhibit direct discussion of the authority-obedience topic. They are process in decision-making, style of governance, and team governance.

The process employed in arriving at decisions in community should be tailored and proportionate to the importance of the decision to be arrived at. The council says, ". . . a superior should listen willingly to his or her subjects and encourage them to make a personal contribution to the welfare of the community and of the Church" (*PC*, 14). Pope Paul expressed the same thought in a different way, ". . . far from being in opposition to one another, authority and individual liberty go together in the fulfillment of God's will, which is sought . . . through a trustful dialogue between the superior and his or her brother or sister, in the case of a personal matter, or through general agreement regarding what concerns the whole community" (*ET*, 25). And canon 618 states: ". . . promoting their voluntary obedience with reverence for the human person, they are to listen to them willingly and foster their working together for the good of the institute and of the Church...." In other words, the process of decision-making should be as open and as broadly consultative as the matter in question allows or merits.

Style of governance depends very much on the personality and talent of superiors; it is a question of administrative ability rather than of actual authority. Some people are good administrators by nature, it seems, or by training, while others never quite get the knack of it. Some people of the greatest good will and with the very best of intentions seem constitutionally incapable of entering into genuine consultation, of actually hearing what others are saying, or of delegating responsibility to others. While this can make for strained relationships it really has nothing to do with authority.

A great deal is made today of the team governance. This is not alien to canon law as such and is found, for example, in the delegation of two or more persons to exercise executive authority in a strictly collegial manner (c. 140, §2) or in the commitment of a parish to two or more priests *in solidum* with one of them designated as the moderator of team (c. 517, §1). There is, however, only one collegial executive action in a religious institute and that occurs in the dismissal of a professed religious when the highest moderator with his or her council must arrive at a final decision by means of a secret ballot (c. 699, §1). In all other cases the superior acts as an individual by reason of his or her own authority. This is not to say that decisions should not be arrived at in an open and broadly consultative manner whenever possible—Pope Paul's "general agreement regarding what concerns the whole community"—but it is to say that the superior cannot share, except by way of delegation, his or her personal authority with anyone else and constitutions cannot provide for this. The skill again lies in the ability to delegate and to work cooperatively with others. A superior certainly can and commonly does ratify the judgment of a group such as a council, a local community, a province assembly, thereby making it his or her own decision. But a superior cannot be obligated to do this and it would be, in my opinion, very foolish or even reprehensible to commit oneself antecedently to do this. What is seriously lacking in team action is person-to-person dialogue, accountabilty and personal authority. Obedience to a team is excessively contrived.

Why does the issue of authority-obedience become so divisive among religious? Apart from the unbridled pride each of us inherited from Adam, which will go to the grave with us, there are disfiguring scars which so many religious carry with them from the often serious mistakes of the past. I think they were caused by poor spirituality, defective theology and by practices which we have long since recognized as incompatible with gospel simplicity. As I have already noted there crept into a commonly held spirituality of religious life a value of obedience for obedience's sake, watering a dry stick or scrubbing a floor only to have to scrub it again, obedience as self-denial. There can be no doubt that obedience correctly understood and practiced calls for self-denial at the innermost core of our being, our autonomy, but this is neither the nature nor the motive of obedience. We profess obedience in order to enter into and continually create a community of love; it is the unique bond of religious life.

An exaggerated, not to say erroneous, theology of merit deeply infected religious life in recent centuries. This took the form of a principle that only those actions of religious were pleasing in God's sight and meritorious of grace which were done in immediate response to a precept or a permission. Thus an excessive and stifling regimentation entered into religious life and lengthy lists of periodically renewed permissions were drawn up just to be sure that all bases were covered. One needed permission to drink water between meals, to have a fountain pen, to walk around the block and to speak with visitors in the parlor. Religious were encouraged, if not forced, to draw up minutely detailed plans for accomplishing the simplest tasks so that they could be approved by the superior and so have the merit of obedience; bells became the voice of the superior. The council sought to correct this when it said, "Let the superior give the kind of leadership which will encourage religious to bring an active and responsible obedience to the offices they shoulder and the activities they undertake" (*PC*, 14).

Finally, in many, if not practically all, religious institutes the rituals of reverence and deference toward superiors were often worthy of the imperial court of China and certainly at odds with gospel values. Kissing rings, kneeling or bowing, uncovering the head, speaking only when spoken to, inflated titles of address, inappropriate perquisites and the like made it impossible for members or superiors to conceive of themselves as true brothers and sisters, stultified community life, and created a kind of class-system within religious communities. Secrecy was considered of the utmost importance lest religious express their opinions before a decision had been made and thus lose at least some of the merit of obedience or worse, lest the superior lose authority. Fortunately most such practices have long since been set aside, but many religious continue to identify them with authority and obedience.

The final issue I would like to touch upon is the question of obedience and conscience. It is a first principle of Catholic moral teaching that everyone is obliged to follow his or her well-informed conscience when its judgment is that an obligation to act or not to act is certain. This is not the place to discuss conscience with the precision and care it deserves, but it must be affirmed that a directive or decision of a superior can be at odds with a well-formed conscience. Pope Paul addressed this matter in *ET*, 28. A superior is capable of insisting upon an objectively morally evil action such as a clear injustice to another person. What also has to be affirmed, however, it that there is never an obligation of conscience to choose the more perfect of two or more courses of action, provided they are all morally good, or to employ the more effective means. The judgment that this ministry or that place of residence is better for me than some other which does not moral evil can scarcely ever be the imperative of a formed conscience. My discernment about myself, however objectively valid, will only most rarely be so certain or so compelling that to yield to a contrary judgment by my superiors would be sinful. Among the factors entering into judgment of a correct conscience must be the common good of the community or of the the entire institute.

In this presentation I have tried to clarify the understanding of obedience and authority in religious life which underlies the norms concerning religious institutes, to identify the more significant canonical issues which continue to occasion serious difficulties for many religious with respect to obedience and authority. The code does, in my opinion, echo the teaching and the spirit of Vatican II which itself, while trying to correct abuses and defects in the exercise of authority and the understanding of religious obedience, takes its stance squarely in the tradition of the Church on these subjects.

In closing let me offer this insight into obedience as a counsel, for which I am especially endebted to Fr. Juan Lozano. Obedience as an evangelical counsel, as a vocational charism to a particular way of following Christ, is mainly an attitude, an abiding readiness and commitment to seek the will of God in a particular religious community. Obedience becomes active, so to speak, or concrete only when a specific decision is arrived at. Ordinarily such decisions, which should be of some importance and not trivial in order to engage the profession of the counsel of obedience, will be finalized by the religious superior, whose own obligation it is to seek the will of God at this time and in these circumstances for this community or for this brother or sister. This is the nearest we can hope to come to knowing what God wills for us.

PUNISHMENT FOR INDIVIDUAL CRIMES

WILLIAM WOLFE

The second section of Book VI deals with individual penalties. There are seven titles or chapters in this section: (1) delicts against religion and church unity; (2) delicts against ecclesiastical authorities and the freedom of the Church; (3) stealing of and mismanagement of offices in the Church; (4) false denunciation; (5) crime against special obligations; (6) delicts against life and liberty of human beings; and finally, (7) a chapter containing one canon entitled simply "General Norms."

We shall examine the contents of each chapter and comment, where relevant, on the rationale behind the canons.[1]

Title One

Canon 1364 initiates the chapter on delicts against religion and church unity. It states that apostates, heretics, and schismatics incur automatic excommunication. If among these are clerics, they are reminded that they lose their office. They can also be prohibited from staying in the place where the crime occurred. Furthermore, clerics can also be punished for this crime by being stripped of all rights and titles, even honorary titles. For clerics who are guilty of apostasy, heresy, or schism, the ultimate penalty can be dismissal from the clerical state. At one point during the revision process, the *coetus* wanted to drop the automatic excommunication attached to this delict, but the revised code retains the *latae sententiae* penalty of the 1917 code.

A "just penalty" is to meted out to someone who ignores the norms on "communcatio in sacris," according to canon 1365. Just what the penalty is is not specified by the law.

Parents or guardians who allow their children to be baptized or educated as non-Catholics are subject to censure or some other just penalty. Parents can be more easily punished, but the punishment is milder than in the 1917 code.[2]

The crime of desecrating the Eucharist merits automatic excommunication which can only be lifted by the Holy See. If a cleric is found guilty of this, he may be dismissed from the clerical state.

Canon 1368 states that if anyone lies before a priest, they should be punished. There is nothing new about this canon, as the code of 1917 says the same.

The final canon in the first chapter requires that anyone who scandalously denigrates the Church by means of the public media should be punished.

---

[1] I am indebted to Reverend Thomas Green for his two articles on penal reform; cf. "The Future of Penal Law in the Church," *The Jurist* 35(1975) 235-248, and "Penal Law Revisited: The Revision of the Penal Law Schema," *Studia Canonica* 15(1981) 135-198.

[2] Thomas J. Green, "Penal Law Revisted: The Revision of the Penal Law Schema," *Studia Canonica* 15(1981) 174.

In an attempt to summarize the first title or chapter on specific penalties, we should note that desecration of the Eucharist deserves the harshest penalty, inasmuch as only Rome itself can lift the punishment. However, this certainly seems justified, considering the essential sacramental nature of the Church. Thomas Green states that the German canonists apparently prevailed in the writing of canon 1364.[3] Their thinking that apostasy, heresy, and schism attacked the very core of the church community accounts for the *latae sententiae* provision of that canon, even though it was not the *coetus* would have been satisfied to have a *ferendae sententiae* penalty.[4]

The canon on church abuse through the media seems timely, although the vagueness of the wording could spell danger. Local authorities might well invoke canon 1369 to silence theologians with whom they do not agree.

Title Two

Canon 1370 punishes those who physically attack the pope with automatic excommunication reserved to the Holy See. If the culprit is a priest of deacon, a further penalty may be added which might include dismissal from the clerical state. If a bishop is attacked, automatic interdict is the penalty. If the attacker is a cleric, in addition to interdict, suspension is also the penalty. The penalty is not spelled out but left discretionary if a cleric is attacked.

Canon 1371 provides punishment for those who teach doctrines contrary to the Church and do not retract when admonished to do so. If these people persist in being contumacious after having been warned to desist, they are to be further punished by proper authority.

If someone attempts to take a case against the pope to an ecumenical council or to the college of bishops, they are to be punished by interdict or some other just penalty. If someone backs an organization against the Church, they are to be punished.

Canon 1375 provides a penalty for anyone who stands in the way of the Church exercising its public ministry. Anyone who profanes a sacred place should be punished according to canon 1376. Finally, anyone who alienates church property without permission is to be punished.

A look at this section indicates concern that the Church be allowed to act freely and carry out its ministry. Those who would impede this activity are to be censured and otherwise punished. It is really not known why some of these canons exist.[5] For example, canon 1372 seems a relic of a bygone era. By mentioning the episcopal conference, one can only hazard a guess that the *coetus* felt it important to check the strength of such bodies should they become omnipotent.

---

[3]Ibid., p. 175.
[4]Ibid., pp. 175-176.
[5]Ibid., pp. 182-183.

Canon 1378 metes out an automatic excommunication reserved to the Holy See to any priest who absolves an accomplice from a sin against the sixth commandment. Automatic interdict (and suspension, if the offender is a cleric) befall those who simulate the celebration of Mass or hearing of confession. If the gravity of the offense demands it, excommunication may be an added penalty. If anyone simulates any other sacrament, they are to be punished by a "justa poena."

Canon 1380 makes sacramental simony punishable by interdict or suspension. Stealing an ecclesiastical office or holding on to it after being removed deserves a penalty.

Automatic excommunication reserved to the Holy See is the penalty for a bishop who consecrates another bishop without a pontifical mandate. The one who receives the consecration also receives the same penalty. Canon 1383 forbids a bishop to ordain for a year if he ordains someone other than his own subject without proper dimissorial letters. The newly ordained is automatically suspended as soon as he is ordained.

Canon 1384 provides a penalty for anyone who usurps a priestly function or any other sacred ministry over and above those functions listed in the preceding canons.

Money given for Masses must not be misappropriated. Canon 1386 inflicts a penalty for bribery, both on the giver and the recipient.

Solicitation in confession is a serious crime. Depending on the gravity, the penalty can range from suspension to dismissal from the clerical state. Direct violation of the seal of confession is punishable by an automatic excommunication reserved to the Holy See. If the violation is indirect, depending on the gravity of the offense, there is a penalty. If an interpreter is used for confession, this party is also bound by the seal. Excommunication could be a possible penalty.

The final canon in this section punishes those who abuse their office in the Church as well as those who cause damage to others out of culpable negligence (canon 1389).

In the above catalogue, we see a continuation of the same trend, namely the offense is identified and the punishment is left up to the discretion of the proper authority, with a few serious exceptions in which the penalty is specifically spelled out. One feels a certain driftlessness in the wording. Who is to interpret "*justa poena*"? A just penalty in one place may be an unjust penalty in another place. If penal law is to be strictly interpreted, might justice for all be better observed if penalties are specified? The impossibility of legislating for all situations is nowhere more obvious that in Book VI. With few exceptions, one can hardly find fault with the catalogue of offenses, but the lack of specificity regarding penalties leaves much to be desired.

Title Four

The chapter on false denunciation contains only two canons. Canon 1390 deals with the crime of accusing a priest of solicitation. Automatic interdict is the penalty, and suspension is added if the offender is a cleric. Calumny or harming the good name of another can be a punishable offense.

The other canon in this title provides for a penalty if ecclesiastical documents are tampered with in any manner.

Title Five

Depending on the gravity of the delict, clerics engaging in commerce are to be punished.

If obligations accruing from a penalty are not fulfilled, then another penalty can be attached.

Canon 1394 provides for automatic suspension for a cleric who attempts even a civil marriage. If the situation persists, he can eventually be dismissed from the clerical state. A non-clerical religious is automatically interdicted for committing the same crime. The penalty for clerical concubinage is suspension. Once again, if warned to desist and he does not do so, other penalties can be added up to the ultimate penalty of being dismissed from the clerical state. A cleric who commits other grave sins against the sixth commandment, depending on the nature of the circumstances, can also be dismissed from the clerical state if other lesser penalties fail (canon 1395, §2).

Deprivation of office can be the ultimate penalty if all other penalties fail when one is warned to adhere to the requirements of residency which go with ecclesiastical office.

With regard to this chapter, it is interesting to note that the delict of attempted marriage for a cleric is no longer excommunication but suspension.[6] The heavy emphasis on retaining penalties for clerical sins against the sixth commandment continues past tradition. In a certain sense, the penalty section of Book VI seems to inveigh unevenly against clerics, while the non-clerical portion of God's people can do the same things without specific penalties. It may well be that the responsibilty of clergy as leaders in service demands more punitive measures when it comes to accountability of lifestyles.

Title Six

This chapter has to do with offenses against the life and liberty of human beings. It is comprised of two canons. The first has to do with murder or any lesser crime which wounds the body. Murder of a lay person is evidently subject to a lesser ecclesiastical penalty than murder of a cleric.[7]

Canon 1398 certifies that anyone who undergoes abortion is automatically excommunicated from the Church. This is not reserved to the Holy See.

It seems that there is a disparity between penalties for abortion and murder. If both are killing, why not the same penalty?

---

[6]Ibid., pp. 188-189.
[7]See canon 1397.

Title Seven

The last canon of Book VI provides a penalty for any serious violation of ecclesiastical or divine law (canon 1399). While this might seem to cover all the bases, the criticism is that it also leaves the door wide open to arbitrary judgments. The intent of the legislator is well-founded. It is virtually impossible to legislate penalties for all situations. On the other hand, how does one adequately insure justice for all with a canon that knows no bounds?

Conclusion

The remarks that follow are meant to be provocative of further reflection. If we accept the simplification of penalties in the revised code as an improvement over the 1917 code, we should restrain our enthusiasm. We need to continue our reflection on church penalties. There are many who see no need for penal law in a Church that is supposed to be a community of love and service. I feel that this is unrealistic, given the less-than-perfect world we live in. However, if we do accept the fact that punishment is necessary for offenses that harm the well-being of the Church, then how are such penalties to be formulated? The present law does a reasonably good job of stating the case; but, as we have adverted to in this presentation, there are inconsistencies, probably a sign of the world we live in. Canon 1399 allows room for developing penal law. It may also provide an instrument for the abridgment of rights.

There definitely exists a tension between the rigor of the law as it is written and the method by which it may be applied. Some offenses are so grievous that there is no question of delaying penalties. On the other hand, many opportunities exist in the revised code for the proper authority to correct the transgressor without the full brunt of the law. It seems that the fundamental question in the unique community of the Church is not how to punish one for the sake of punishment but rather how best to reconcile the errant.

Often, in Scripture, we see Jesus rebuking those who did wrong. He was firm but compassionate. In no uncertain terms did Jesus tell the Pharisees, the Samaritan woman, Mary Magdalene, and even Judas what was right and what was wrong. But in all things, in all encounters, He hoped that the sinner would open up his or her mind and heart to forgiving grace. We should never forget that the penalties of the Church are not an end in themselves but only means. In this sense, we can see the present penal law of the Church as the sign of Jesus' presence in our time and place and in our less-than-perfect world.

REPORT OF THE PRESIDENT

ROBERT C. BECKER

It is expected that the President report to the annual general meeting on the status of the Society and the activities of his office during the past year. In the interests of keeping to a minimum the length of spoken reports on the opening night of the convention, this report is being made in printed form. Activities will be reported in three major areas: contact with other societies and groups; promulgation-related projects; workshops.

Before beginning, let me say that it has been a rare privilege to serve the Canon Law Society as its President. This has been especially true in this unique time in the history of canon law. In all corners of the country there is an active interest in the content and focus of the revised Code of Canon Law. Because of this, this has been a busy year for the Society as a whole, and for individual canonists all over the country.

CONTACT WITH OTHER GROUPS

The Canon Law Society of America was represented at each of the regional meetings of canon lawyers throughout the country. The President represented the Society at the meeting of the Provinces of New Orleans-Mobile in December, in Birmingham. The President also represented the Society at the Western Regional Conference in Honolulu, and the Texas Conference of Tribunal Officials in San Antonio. The Vice-President, Tony Diacetis, represented the Canon Law Society of America to the Eastern Regional Conference in Wilimington, to the Midwest Canon Law Society in Grand Rapids, and to the Northwest Regional Meeting in Vancouver. The Executive Coordinator, Jim Provost, represented our Society to the annual meeting of the Canon Law Society of Great Britain and Ireland in Dublin.

Each of these meetings was well attended. The presentations were insightful and discussion lively. Clearly, there is keen interest all over the country in the content of the revised code. Canon lawyers are stepping out of the specific areas of concentration demanded by their current assignments and preparing themselves to become familiar with the broad details of the entire revised code. The excitement and hope reflected are contagious.

In addition to regional meetings of canon lawyers, other contacts were made or continued during the past year. The North American Conference of Separated and Divorced Catholics has requested the cooperation of the Canon Law Society in a project aimed at developing a program of preparation for persons about to enter second marriages. The involvement of the Canon Law Society in this project has expanded.

In the spring of the year, all of the constituent based organizations in the American Catholic Church were invited by the Center for Applied Research in the Apostolate to take part in a conference entitled "Toward 2000." The Canon Law Society was represented by the President and the Executive Coordinator. The group met at the headquarters of CARA in Washington. Broadly worded aims and goals were surfaced to address concerns which cut across the specific interests of the individual groups represented. Those groups with headquarters or representatives in the city and area of Washington, D.C. are continuing to meet in alternate months, informally, to maintain contact.

The Canon Law Society worked actively in the past year with the National Federation of Priests' Councils and the National Organization for Continuing Education of Roman Catholic Clergy, to develop a recommended pattern for workshops in the revised Code of Canon Law aimed at clergy and other pastoral ministers. The results of this venture were distributed by NOCERCC to each of their members.

Finally, the Canon Law Society of America cooperated actively with the National Conference of Catholic Bishops. At the request of the NCCB, CLSA drew up a program and provided staff for a series of workshops for bishops in the revised Code of Canon Law. Many of these workshops have already taken place; some will take place in the winter months ahead. Initial reports indicate that there was a warm and appreciative reception on the part of the participant-bishops for these workshops.

Finally, the Canon Law Society of America continues to work actively with the Canonical Affairs Committee of the National Conference of Catholic Bishops, to arrange for an approved translation of the revised Code of Canon Law into the English language in a style based on American usage.

POMULGATION-RELATED PROJECTS

Many of the activities of the Canon Law Society, especially in the winter and spring months, revolved around the then recent promulgation of the revised Code of Canon Law. Through the cooperation of John Hergenrother in Chicago and Ed O'Brien in New York, and associates gathered by them, a press kit was made available to members of the Canon Law Society to ease their contact with the various news-gathering organizations. Royce Thomas of Little Rock, at the request of the Board of Governors, put together a "vacatio survival manual" which was distributed to all the members, containing some preliminary observations and interpretations to ease anxieties during the period of study and preparation for implementation of the revised code.

The President, with the advice of the Board of Governors, has asked Elissa Rinere of Hartford, Connecticut, to pursue the syndication of a column of questions and answers concerning the revised Code of Canon Law. The status of this project is reported elsewhere in the convention packet. We are hopeful that many diocesan and regional as well as national Catholic newspapers will see fit to carry this syndicated column.

In addition to preparing themselves to carry on their normally assigned tasks in canon law, members of the Canon Law Society of America have been participating in and conducting workshops in canon law for a variety of audiences all over the country in the past several months. Several workshops have been sponsored by the Canon Law Society of America. In addition to the workshops for bishops already mentioned, workshops were conducted for tribunal personnel and for chancery personnel in Atlanta and Chicago. A workshop is planned by CLSA, in cooperation with the DePaul University School of Law and the General Counsel's Office of the USCC, and the Diocesan Attorneys Conference. This workshop for civil attorneys will be held in Chicago in December.

It is impossible for the organization of the Canon Law Society to provide programming and staffing for the many specific kinds of workshops which are needed by various audiences in the various areas of the country. Individual members of our Canon Law Society have been extraordinarily generous in their time and efforts in providing competent presentations for these various audiences. The entire American Church is indebted to the generosity of these men and women in the Canon Law Society, as well as the many others who have managed to find the time to work so hard in these many projects, at a time when their own assigned tasks demanded more of their attention than usual.

IN CONCLUSION . . .

This has indeed been a busy year for canon lawyers. In addition to all of the work and effort occasioned by the announcement of the revised code, other work of interest and concern to the members of the Canon Law Society has been continued. Projects and issues which have been part of our agenda for some time, have been furthered. These are reported in appropriate places in your convention packet; some will be reported during presentations at this convention. Fundamental issues on the status of women, on marriage, on diocesan governance and governance in religious life, and the professional responsibility of the canonist, transcend the concern for the revised code. In response to this "life after the revised code," the Board of Governors has outlined for itself a set of goals which are intended to guide our activities for the next five years. While acknowledging the centrality of issues that revolve around the revised code and its promulgation, the Board has refused to allow these issues to act as blinders, narrowing the field of vision unreasonably. The revised code has not precisely changed our agenda, but merely added a series of significant challenges to it. There is every evidence that the members of the Society will continue to respond as men and women of courage and vision.

VICE-PRESIDENT'S ADDRESS

Anthony C. Diacetis

As we celebrate this meal together and enjoy the festivity of a city as beautiful and diverse as San Francisco, I would like to take a few minutes to look into the future.

All of us gathered here are aware of the unique moment which we canonists are sharing in as we prepare for the revised Code of Canon Law to take effect next month. Obviously, a great deal of our time and effort over the past years, and in particular over the last months, has been focused on the possibility, and then the reality, of the revised code. As this period of preparation draws to an end, I would like to suggest that it is time to begin refocusing our energies. Though the actual outline of our daily efforts or the prioritizing of our activities might not change, I do believe that we are in need of beginning a shift in our self-understanding. To that end, I would propose that in the next year, and in the years to come, we canonists should be about four tasks.

The first task is that of continuing education. Now this might not sound like a novel concept. For, in fact, many of us have spent a great deal of time in the last year attending, preparing or giving workshops and study days in the revised code. It is because we have spent so much time and energy in this task that I am concerned that we might come to consider the task of education to be concluded when the revised code takes effect in November. Perhaps an example will help to explain the urgency which I feel on this matter.

Most of us can recall the major effort in education which took place at the time of promulgation of the revised Roman Missal and other post-conciliar liturgical instructions. Many attended these workshops and many went away and did things differently. But in a few years it became apparent to many liturgists that something was wrong. The revisions in the liturgical texts had not achieved the desired effect of a new sense of prayer within the Church. Why was this? Because, though effective for the short term, the real goal of the process of education had not been fully realized. In fact, many people did not come to a new understanding or appreciation of the common prayer of the Church. It is for that reason that many in the liturgical movement of twenty years ago are now involved in spirituality. They have come to see that it is an inner conversion of heart and mind that is necessary if there is to be a renewed sense of prayer in the Church. And at the same time, these same people are concerned that a new rubricism might arise among those who are being trained in liturgy today and who have lost a sense of the profound shift in understanding that the Council mandated.

My concern, my friends, is that the same could well happen to us as canonists. Could it be that we have spent so much time talking about the fact that the revised code incarnates a new sense or a new attitude toward the law, that we have not had time to assist people to effect a change in the interior of their being? Though we will be spending a great deal of time in the days and months ahead explaining the details of the revised code, the truly radical nature of the revised code could get lost if we grow weary or impatient of trying to assist people to come to grips with, and then interiorize, an attitude that sees law as being in service to the community of faith and not as an end in itself. My suggestion is that over the next years we must never lose sight of the fact that we have to continue to educate, or perhaps more appropriately, to assist in the formation of people in a new sense of law and ecclesial service.

The second task is that of implementation. Again, this might seem self-evident. For example, how much time has already been spent by those who are in tribunal work preparing for regional courts and the like. Those engaged in other aspects of canonical service have likewise been involved in trying to calculate how to implement other aspects of the code. My concern here is not that various areas of change in the code will be implemented, but what parts will not be implemented. Again, this is very understandable. Many of us hold a variety of jobs and will find it hard enough to implement those parts of the code for which we are responsible, let alone worry about those areas where some colleague is not aware of the changes that can take place, or is not interested in any change, or where there is no one present to attend implementation. It is this reality of our over-extension and the possible lack of interest or resources that prompts me to suggest that part of our task must be one of advocacy. Namely, we are called to be the devil's advocates within our local church who consistently remind bishops, presbyteral councils, pastoral councils, pastors and the like of the possibilities and exigencies of the revised code. Unfortunately, if we do not take on this responsibility, I am afraid that many of the significant innovations found within the revised code will never be implemented.

The third task I would suggest is a bit more complex than those of continuing formation or advocacy. For lack of a better way of saying it, I will call it the task of attending and assisting. The first aspect of this task is the attending to what will be a reality, and most likely ought to be a reality, in the implementation of any universal code. It is the fact of non-reception. Many sitting here tonight already are aware of some aspects of the code which they believe will not be received in their local church or within the American Church. At times our reaction to such non-reception will be that of a good teacher who will seek to explain the law so that it might be understood and accepted. Such a reaction certainly is proper for one whose ministry to the Church is in and through its law. I would like to suggest, however, that at other times our reaction must be one of attending and monitoring. Because our tradition has affirmed the presence of the Spirit moving within and through the faithful, we must be attentive to how it might be that the Spirit will move people to a legitimate non-reception. We need to stand inside the life of experience of those who are having difficulty with the law and use our expertise to assist them in developing new customs that will better serve a community of charity and justice. To put all of this a bit more simply: non-reception will happen. Though our first task will be that of giving a faithful and positive explanation of a disputed law, our responsibility does not end there. As faithful stewards we should attend to the reason for such non-reception and be of assistance as people of good will seek to find a better way to order their life. We ought to be active participants in the development of good customs that the test of time might affirm and eventually come to call good law.

The fourth task I would lay out for us tonight is that of critique and development. In many ways, this is the other side of the task of attending and assisting. The difference is that this process is not a direct response to the needs of the faithful, but is the faithful execution of our responsibilities as servants of a law that serves the community of faith which is the Church. Tonight I am suggesting that we must avoid the temptation to spend the next years just in education and implementation. And it will be easy to fall prey to that temptation because in many ways this code is our code. We have spent twenty years in dialogue and communication about this code. One of the strengths of this code is that it is the product of a long process of consultation (even though at times we felt the consultation was too little, too late). Will it be easy for us to turn around and begin to critique that which we have helped to develop and which we have spent several years in educating people about its strengths and merits?

No, I do not think it will be easy to return to the role of critic and proposer of change. Some will accuse us of being unfaithful to the Church. Some will accuse us of not giving the law a chance. Others will accuse us of being adolescent in attitude. No matter what the charges or recriminations, we must be about the task of moving beyond this code and preparing for the third code. How many times have we said that this code is the final work of Vatican II? How many times have we said that it is as uneven and inconsistent as was the theology of that council? How many times have we said that this code is the product of compromise and, therefore, is the best that can be had for now? How many times have we answered specific questions and said that there is a better way in which this or that area of church life could be regulated? The answer to these questions is many, many times. My suggestion is that if we are to be true to ourselves and to what we have been as individual canonists and as a society, once again we must return to the task of critique of the law; we must assume the responsibility of assisting in the development that is desperately needed in two areas. I will only mention them tonight, but the need is obvious. I refer to the theological and canonical understanding of marriage and marital failure as well as to the protection of the rights and responsibilities of women, women religious and other minorities within the Church. In both of these areas, the ecclesial practice mandated by the code remains inadequate to the signs of the times. This need for ongoing and faithful critique and for the difficult tasks of struggling with new forms of ecclesial life cannot, and I repeat cannot, be ignored by us individually or as a society.

Well, it is time to draw this to a close. In answer to the question, "Is there life after the code?" my answer is yes. I look forward to a new period of productivity and vitality for the society and for us as canonists. I expect that in one way or another we will be about the four-fold task of formation in the new spirit of the law, of advocacy for the full implementation of the law, of attending to non-reception and assisting in the development of new custom, and finally of being about a faith-filled and loving critique of the code and of proposing new possibilities for church order.

REPORT OF THE EXECUTIVE COORDINATOR

JAMES H. PROVOST

My third year in this office has been an exceptionally busy one, primarily because of the events connected with the promulgation of the revised code but also because of the increased requests for CLSA publications. I will report on my service in terms of the responssibilities outlined in the Constitution.

I. OFFICE

Through the continued generosity of the Catholic University of America the Society's office has remained at Caldwell Hall on the University campus. Full-time office manager, without whose help it would have been impossible to provide service to the members or others interested in the work of the Society, has been Ms. Karen L. Corbett. I wish to express publicly my gratitude to her for her generous service, often beyond the call of the "job description."

We have also received help from various students and part-time employees. I express my gratitude to Ms. Tammy Edgerly-Dowd and Mr. Jeff Finan who served us so well last year, and to those who have helped since the beginning of the summer: Sr. Barbara Anne Cusack, Sr. Nancy Reynolds, Sr. Lynn Jarrell, Mr. Jay Biber and Mr. Brian Abdo. Given the increased activity in the office, the officers have authorized the employment of a second full-time person to assist the office manager.

In preparation for the work connected with the translation of the revised code we purchased a Wang Office Information Systems 105. It has been very helpful in the work of translation and revision, and has also been used for various other functions in the office. Equipment troubles have plagued us which we have brought to the attention of the Wang company repeatedly; recently, we began to receive some attention to our concerns.

Because the Treasurer has the membership list on a computer, it was decided to keep just one list this year, under his supervision. Difficulties have continued, however, in maintaining accurate address lists and in providing materials to all members. I apologize for the delays and difficulties various members have experienced; it is not enough to blame "the computer," I know, and we are taking steps to keep a current list in my office so we can hopefully respond to complaints in a more timely fashion. If any members have failed to receive the 1982 *Proceedings* or other mailings of the Society, please notify me and they will be sent to you right away.

We had hoped to have the Membership Directory in your hands by the time of this convention. Obviously, we didn't make it. The directory proved to be a more complicated project than the group who are putting it together for us first anticipated. They have keyed it onto a computer and are preparing galleys

242

for us to review in light of current positions of members as reported on the dues renewal form. We are now planning to send a first draft of the directory with the post-convention *Newsletter* so that members can provide us with appropriate corrections.

The Society's archives, housed at the office, have been augmented during the year by the addition of some materials from former CLSA committees. If other former committee members have materials they would care to deposit in the Society's archives, we would be very happy to receive them. Please contact me before shipment so we can arrange for their safe arrival.

A final responsibility of the office is to see that timely notice is made of the annual meeting. The local arrangements committee in San Francisco has been prompt in this regard, and I express my appreciation for their service.

II. PUBLICATIONS

We have been quite busy in this regard during the past year. Three newsletters were distributed to the membership, in a more timely fashion as requested by the Board of Governors. Members with information to be included in future newsletters are encouraged to contact me as soon as possible.

The *Proceedings* for 1982 were produced and distributed in the early part of this calendar year. Some confusion surrounding the mailing labels resulted in some members not receiving their copies; those who have not yet requested them are encouraged to contact me at their convenience. This proved to be one of the largest *Proceedings* yet, and the Board has asked that steps be taken to keep the volume to a reasonable size.

At the request of the Vatican Press and with the approval of the Board of Governors, this office became the official distributor for the Latin text of the revised *Codex Iuris Canonici* for the United States and Canada. Initial requests for the code far outstripped the expectations of the Vatican Press, which experienced delays in producing sufficient copies for sale. This was eventually overcome, copies were sent air freight to Washington, and we have attempted to fill all orders as quickly as possible. We still have some copies of both the hardbound and the paperbound editions on stock for immediate delivery.

At the direction of the Board of Governors, I submitted a request to the N.C.C.B. that the C.L.S.A. be authorized to prepare a translation into American usage English of the revised code. Archbishop Roach responded that we could proceed. We drafted a translation and submitted it to the Canonical Affairs Committee of the N.C.C.B. for approval before the end of June. The text was also shared with those writing sections of the C.L.S.A. commentary on the code. The commentators submitted various corrections to the draft which have been incorporated into the translation. The Canonical Affairs Committee members also asked the help of canon lawyers in their areas; these submitted various comments to the Committee, which forwarded them to the C.L.S.A.

on August 29. The translators have corrected the draft and on September 9 it was forwarded to the chairman of the Canonical Affairs Committee for approval. A team of canon lawyers was named by the chairman to assist him in this process, and on September 17 they were provided copies of the corrected draft.

It is not possible to give a precise date when the translation will be available. Much depends on the time it takes for the N.C.C.B. to complete its process of approval. Once approval is obtained, it will take another six weeks to complete production. Pre-publication orders have been received from many people in the United States and abroad, and will be filled according to the order they were received as soon as the books become available. We apologize for any inconvenience this delay may cause, but we are anxious to have a translation that it as accurate as possible, readable in the American idiom, and containing both the official Latin text and our translation. In addition, it will have an analytical index prepared by the C.L.S.A. staff, a glossary of key Latin terms used in the translation, and a translation of the apostolic constitution and preface contained in the Latin text.

The Society was able to provide a useful book of studies on the implications of the revised code for pastoral ministers. *Code, Community, Ministry* proved to be a popular aid for continuing education programs and general readership among pastoral workers. Copies are still available for individual and bulk orders.

Through the generosity of Father Lawrence Wrenn, his popular tribunal aids *Annulments* and *Decisions* have been revised in keeping with the 1983 code and some further jurisprudential developments since the last editions appeared. The first printing of these books was quickly exhausted but a second, larger printing is now complete and ready for delivery.

Drawing on studies produced from the 1982 workshops sponsored by the Society as well as one originally commissioned by the Canon Law Society of Great Britian and Ireland and now further revised, a special volume on *The Art of Interpretation* has been published. It was used in workshops conducted by the Society for bishops in the various regions of the country, and distributed to participants at workshops the Society held in Atlanta and Chicago over the summer. The book is now available for sale.

In preparation for this convention a new collection of *Roman Replies* has been prepared by Father William Schumacher. It is distributed as a benefit of registration at the convention, and is available for sale after the convention through the executive coordinator's office.

In the effort to make C.L.S.A. publications more known and available a printed brochure describing books and tapes available was distributed to the membership and to those placing orders with the Society during the past year. This has proven to be useful, and has been updated for this convention. In addition, several sets of companion publications have been specially priced, bringing additional interest to those works.

We were able to make arrangements with University of Notre Dame Press to purchase the remainder issues of *The Bond of Marriage,* an especially significant collection of studies produced by the C.L.S.A. at a symposium on that topic in 1967. The papers remain of interest to scholars and students of marriage law. The book is available at reduced price through the C.L.S.A. office.

During the past year we have sold approximately 17,167 copies of publications. Of these, 13,000 were C.L.S.A. publications and 4,167 were copies of the Latin code. In 1982 there were 4,296 publications sold, in 1981 sales amounted to 2,903 items, and in 1980 4,268 sales were recorded.

III. Liaison

Collaboration with the N.C.C.B. staff has continued to be an important aspect of the work of this office. Special appreciation is expressed to Father Donald Heintschel, Associate General Secretary of the Conference, for his attention and assistance in a number of matters of mutual concern.

As a consultant to the Canonical Affairs Committee I served as liaison between the Conference and the Society in undertaking a series of workshops for bishops on the revised code as requested by the various N.C.C.B. regions. Together with the president and vice-president of the Society I assisted in developing the program and conducting the training session for those who have been staffing the workshops. I wish to thank Bishop Anthony Bevilacqua who chairs the bishops' Committee for his foresight, encouragement and support in this project.

I have maintained existing contacts with major national Catholic organizations, and have been invited to speak at several of their national meetings. I served on an ad-hoc committee which convened a two day session "Toward 2,000" to explore the interests of various national constituency-based organizations with regard to matters of common concern as we look to the next seventeen years. The staff of those organizations which are located in Washington have a regular informal gathering modeled on the political "taverns" of the late 18th century in this part of the country, and I have been participating in these regular reunions of wine and cheese in the offices of the respective organizations.

Last fall I was elected secretary of the Joint Committee of Catholic Learned Societies and Scholars; Monsignor Frederick McManus, a member of the C.L.S.A. but representing the North American Academy of Liturgy, chairs the group. Efforts are underway to encourage local members of the various societies to convene around the studies already completed by the respective groups on women in the Church as a means of exploring the state of the question today. Other efforts of the joint committee are directed toward building a closer liaison with the bishops through the possible formation of a Bishops and Scholars Committee, similar to the existing committee of bishops and presidents of Catholic colleges and universities.

I have continued contacts from time to time with canon lawyers in other parts of the world and have provided canon law faculties overseas with copies of C.L.S.A. publications. On behalf of the president I represented the Society at the annual meeting of the Canon Law Society of Great Britain and Ireland in Swords, near Dublin, Ireland, in June. I wish to express again my appreciation for the warm welcome and hospitality that was shown to me there.

IV. PUBLICITY AND PUBLIC RELATIONS

The major public relations event of the past year was obviously the promulgation of the revised code. At the direction of the Board I prepared mailings of various materials developed by the Board for the press and for the C.L.S.A. membership. There were numerous inquiries from the secular and religious press about the code at the time of promulgation, and some have continued.

As mentioned earlier, an effort to publicize the C.L.S.A. publications resulted in the printed listing of books and tapes. Brochures describing the summer workshops in Atlanta and Chicago for chancery and tribunal officials were mailed to all dioceses, and brochures providing pre-publication discounts on the C.L.S.A. translation of the revised code were sent to the entire mailing list of the *Official Catholic Directory.*

V. VARIA

After the Hartford convention I contacted the various archdioceses to learn their plans for interdiocesan tribunals. An initial report on these plans, together with copies of materials submitted by several locations, were sent to all metropolitan tribunals and to several others requesting them. A second mailing of follow-up materials was sent later in the spring.

With the continued legal assistance of Mr. Peter Shannon we have resolved technical details for completing the trade-marking of the C.L.S.A. logo, the Society's publications have been copyrighted, and contracts have been completed for the publication of the Society's commentary on the revised code.

Finally, I close with another word of appreciation. The officers and members of the Board have been very supportive and encouraging to me, and have watched lest the office become too great a burden during this year of intense activity. I am grateful for their concern and direction. I also wish to thank the members of the Society for your patience and understanding, and ask your continued help in bringing to my attention any further problems in regard to mailings or materials. It is a pleasure to be of service to such committed and thoughtful persons as make up the Canon Law Society of America.

REPORT OF THE TREASURER

James K. Mallett

The financial statement for fiscal year October 1, 1982, through September 30, 1983 is attached for the consideration of the membership. I offer the following observations on this statement.

First, there has been a large increase in the cash position of the Society. However, total cash of $214,095.99 is offset by liabilities totaling $202,958.68, leaving a balance of $11,137.11 as the cash reserve for the ordinary operating expenses of the Society. Deferred revenues constitute the largest portion of our liabilities: in addition to deferred dues and convention revenue, we have also deferred the pre-publication revenue of our translation which amounts to $129,775.00. In addition to deferred revenues, the Society now manages restricted funds. We received $4,000.00 from the Lilly Endowment, and $7,000.00 from the Raskob Foundation as restricted grants for the Symposium on Diocesan Governance. Of these restricted grants, $8,159.75 remain unspent. The Society also agreed to act as trustee for the assets of the Joint Committee of Catholic Learned Societies and Scholars; the balance in this restricted fund is $230.20. There has been such a large increase in liabilities that the cash reserves of the Society available for ordinary operating expenses has actually decreased by $6,075.00.

Secondly, the revenue from the pre-publication sales of the translation of the Code of Canon Law has been deferred since the publication expenses have not yet been incurred. It is assumed that the net proceeds from the sales of the translation will provide greater financial security for the Society in future years.

Thirdly, the most significant figure on the statement is Total Fund Balances of $45,147.27, an increase of $6,756.58. This figure represents the net worth of the Society; in other words, after all bills have been paid for the fiscal year, and before deferred revenues are made available for the next fiscal year, this amount indicates the fundamental financial position of the Society. However, it is important to realize that the assets corresponding to this net worth include $34,009.96 invested in the publications and postage inventories, leaving a cash reserve of only $11,137.11.

Fourthly, the publications inventory increased by $13,534. This increase was funded by changes in our financial position noted above: a decrease in working capital of $6,075, an increase in fund balances of $6,757, plus a decrease in the postage inventory of $702.

FINANCIAL STATEMENT

September 30, 1983

Assets	*September 30, 1983*	*September 30, 1982*
Cash: First American Bank, Nashville	5,370.10	2,109,75
Cash: Madison National Bank, Washington, D.C.	10,647.52	201.25
Cash, Merrill-Lynch Ready Assets Account	198,078.37	72,267.63
Total Cash	214,095.99	74,578.63
Postage Inventory	198.32	899.89
Publications Inventory	33,811.64	20,278.73
Total Inventory	34,009.96	21,178.62
Total Assets	248,105.95	95,757.25

Liabilities

Deferred Revenues		
Advance Dues Collection	46,782.00	44,029.26
Advance Convention Revenue	18,000.00	13,000.00
Advance Translation Sales	129,775.00	
Total Deferred	194,557.00	57,029.26
Restricted Funds		
Symposium Fund	8,159.75	0
JCCLSS Fund	230.20	0
Total Restricted	8,389.95	0
Accounts Payable		
Employee Taxes Withheld	11.73	337.30
Total Liabilities	202,958.68	57,366.56

Fund Balances

Operating Fund	8,795.80	(13,013.38)
Convention Fund	(1,952.67)	1,278.87
Workshop Fund	17,077.58	26,302.29
Commentary Fund	21,226.56	23,822.91
Total Fund Balances	45,147.27	38,390.69
Total Liabilities and Fund Balances	248,105.95	95,757.25

STATEMENT OF CHANGES IN OPERATING FUND

	Actual 1982-1983	Budget 1982-1983	Actual 1981-1982
Beginning Fund Balance Additions	(13,013.38)	(13,013.38)	26,541.78
Investment Income	3,835.01	5,000.00	6,334.12
Membership Dues	58,308.70	56,000.00	47,056.25
Sales of Publications	31,952.12	40,000.00	7,704.32
Royalties	197.01	400.00	421.69
Donations	65.00	0	365.00
Miscellaneous	0	0	457.33
Transfer from Designated Fund	20,000.00	20,000.00	2,376.90
Total Additions	114,357.84	121,400.00	64,715.61

Deductions			
President			
Travel	4,555.54		3,905.22
Postage	0		25.00
Printing	0		237.00
Telephone	25.06		57.00
Supplies	171.00		0
Total	4,751.60	4,500.00	4,224.22
Board of Governors			
Travel	7,937.73		9,456.54
Postage	0		419.00
Printing	54.87		162.30
Rentals (Housing)	1,918.60		1,756.00
Food Service	0		1,511.33
Supplies	0		26.32
Total	9,911.20	15,000.00	13,331.49
Treasurer			
Professional Services	285.00		745.29
Postage	641.18		451.72
Printing	136.00		496.15
Insurance	0		160.00
Office Supplies	239.60		319.83
Other Expenses	8.71		36.00
Total	1,310.49	1,500.00	2,208.99

	Actual 1982-1983	Budget 1982-1983	Actual 1981-1982
Executive Coordinator			
Wages, Support Staff	12,252.65		12,845.37
Wages, Temporary Employees	270.27		655.25
FICA Tax	838.38		1,272.93
Worker's Compensation	43.07		0
Medical Insurance	865.54		0
Tuition/Fees	217.00		0
Professional Services	280.00		778.00
Travel	284.80		443.00
Postage	4,281.88		3,664.93
Printing	5,401.88		2,490.21
Insurance	478.00		351.00
Telephone	987.91		1,141.83
Repairs/Maintenance	1,085.40		0
Rentals	0		142.50
Office Supplies	2,472.27		793.37
Other Supplies/Materials	2,498.60		68.00
Books/Subscriptions	92.58		69.25
Word Processor & Equipment	14,289.89		147.34
Total	46,640.12	41,900.00	24,862.98
Membership Services			
Postage	3,907.18		1,080.63
Printing	18,299.51		28,196.98
Supplies	0		251.25
Total	22,206.69	15,000.00	29,528.86
Committees			
Research and Discussion	1,614.45	2,500.00	1,376.05
Membership and Nominations	0	100.00	35.15
Resolutions	34.74		0
Marriage	288.00	200.00	0
Religious Affairs	584.50	1,200.00	0
Women in the Church	1,132.55	1,500.00	199.00
Office Automation	919.75	1,000.00	0
Projects			
CTSA/CLSA	1,285.14	1,200.00	3,504.03
Joint Project with Div. Sep. Conf.	526.60	500.00	0
Promulgation Related	1,342.83	5,500.00	0
Transfer to Commentary Fund	0	0	25,000.00
Total Deductions	92,548.66	93,800.00	104,270.77
Ending Fund Balance	8,795.80	145.87	(13,013.38)

Statement of Changes in Commentary Fund

	1982-1983	1981-1982
Beginning Balance	23,822.91	25,000.00
Deductions		
Professional Services	945.00	
Postage	359.64	
Printing	211.85	
Supplies/Other Expenses	1,079.86	1,177.09
Total Deductions	2,596.35	1,177.09
Ending Balance	21,226.56	23,822.91

Statement of Changes in Convention Fund Balances

October 1, 1982 - September 30, 1983

	Hartford	San Francisco	Balance
Balance, October 1, 1982			2,454.37
Additions			
Transfer from Balance			
Registration	20,500.29		
Donations	2,050.00		
Total	22,550.29	0	
Deductions			
Prepaid Expenses	1,175.50		
Professional Services	2,950.00		
Travel	306.31	400.00	
Postage	43.15	2,327.49	
Printing	2,236.88	2,024.53	
Telephone	135.50		
Rentals	13,173.15		
Religious Supplies	29.81		
Food Service	99.63		
Other Supplies/Expenses	1,983.38	72.00	
Transfer to Balance	416.98		416.98
Total	22,550.29	(4,824.02)	(4,824.02)
Balance, September 30, 1983			(1,952.67)

STATEMENT OF CHANGES IN WORKSHOP FUND

October 1, 1982 - September 30, 1983

Balance, October 1, 1982	26,302.29
Transfer to Operating Fund	(20,000.00)
Beginning Balance	6,302.29
Additions (Registration Fees)	41,032.12

Deductions	
Temporary Employees	212.31
Professional Services	4,300.00
Travel	2,734.13
Postage	1,983.48
Printing	6,378.39
Telephone	25.40
Rentals	4,143.96
Food Service	8,012.72
Other Supplies/Expenses	1,511.84
Materials for Meetings	954.60
Total	30,256.83

Balance, September 30, 1983	17,077.58

STATEMENT OF CHANGES IN RESTRICTED FUNDS

1982-1983

Symposium Fund
    Beginning Balance   0
    Additions
        Lilly Endowment Grant   4,000.00
        Raskob Foundation Grant   7,000.00

        Total Additions   11,000.00

    Deductions
        Travel   1,742.25
        Rentals   1,098.00

        Total Deductions   2,840.25

Ending Balance   8,159.75

JCCLSS Fund
(Held in Trust for the Joint
Committee of Catholic Learned
Societies and Scholars)

Beginning Balance   232.00
    Deductions (Postage)   1.80

Ending Balance   230.20

Total Restricted Funds   8,389.95

CODE OF PROFESSIONAL RESPONSIBILITY

The following Code of Professional Responsibility *was adopted by the 41st Annual General Meeting of the Canon Law Society of America for an experimental period of three years. It was revised at the conclusion of that time, and the following revised version was adopted at the 45th Annual General Meeting of the Society.*

PROLOGUE: THE CANONIST IN THE CONTEMPORARY CHURCH

The Church, the people of God, is a community of persons bound together by faith, hope and charity, equal in dignity and freedom, for whom the whole law is fulfilled in one word, "You shall love your neighbor as yourself" (Gal. 5:14). As a community, the Church is a public and visible society, serving the world by witnessing the Good News of salvation. Divine in origin and spirit, the Church is also thoroughly human, sinful as well as virtuous. Because love can be illusory without justice, and justice cruel without love, the members of this pilgrim people commit themselves to constant growth in communion through love and justice.

To promote the unity and mission of this people, God gives charisms of service as gifts to the whole Church. Among these is the charism of the canonical vocation. This charism is to be exercised in mutual collaboration with all members of the Church, including apostolic leadership, so that God's gracious design may be accomplished. Thus canonists, like the law they are skilled in, serve a limited but important function in the Church—to foster and to promote justice and love in the public life of the Church.

I. THE IDEALS TO WHICH THE CANONIST ASPIRES

A. *The Characteristics of the Canonist*

1. Since the legal system of the Church exists within and promotes the pastoral mission of the Church, the canonist is a person firmly committed to Christ and the Church. Through regular prayer, service to the people of God, study and reflection, coupled with openness to the Holy Spirit, canonists strive to deepen their appreciation of the revealed mysteries and transcendent values which are the foundation of the canonist's ministry and to which the canonist gives witness in the public life of the Church. The canonist seeks to grow in Christian virtue so that personal defects may not interfere with the course of justice.

2. The canonist is marked by a zeal for justice in the Church, aware that while each individual must sacrifice for the common good, true communion is

advanced only when the dignity and fundamental rights of each person are held inviolable. The canonist takes as a solemn obligation fidelity to the cause of justice and to the competent fulfillment of one's office, even in the face of misunderstanding or opposition.

3. As servants of the whole Church, canonists are marked by integrity in the pursuit of justice and the fulfillment of their office, scrupulously avoiding partiality—except where a canonist has expressly undertaken to act for a party—and heedless of attempts, from whatever source, to influence them improperly. Moreover, because all offices within the Church exist for the sake of faithful service to God's people, no canonist should ever be swayed by self-interest or egotistical ambition.

4. The canonist is mindful that the integral pursuit of justice must be governed by the spirit of equity. Realizing that the law—a limited human instrument—has no other purpose but to manifest and to serve the life of the Holy Spirit in the Church, the canonist tempers the rigor of the law according to the demands of that Spirit of love in each situation. Since the laws of the Church are to be interpreted and administered in this spirit of justice and equity, issuing in charity, the canonist strives to be a person of compassion, emotional balance and sound judgment, committed to the pastoral care of the people of God.

5. Because compassion without competence can be a cruel hoax, the canonist should take most seriously the obligation to acquire and to develop professional competence. Canonists ought to have a substantive background in Sacred Scripture, theology and church history, and be thoroughly knowledgeable in the law, jurisprudence and the social sciences, particularly within their own areas of specialization. Canonists should further the advance of their knowledge and skills through private study, participation in professional programs, and utilization of existing channels of communication. Furthermore, canonists should support and encourage the efforts of their peers in achieving this purpose.

B. Concerns of the Canonist

1. In order that members of the Church may be aware of their rights and duties, the canonist has a responsibility to educate and to advise the members of the Church as to the substance and procedures of church law, and should make every reasonable effort to correct misinformation. Their dealings with all members of the Church ought to be marked by honesty, integrity and unselfishness. Should the situation seem to call for it, a contractual arrangement between the canonist and the local Church could clarify rights and expectations.

2. In order to advance the protection of human and ecclesial rights in the Church, the canonist has a responsibility to assist in and to support the improvement and development of church law and procedure. Hearing the needs

and concerns of the Christian faithful, especially within the local church wherein they live and minister, canonists bring their particular expertise as skilled servants to the articulation and protection of the rights of all.

3. In order to respond more effectively to the above concerns, and to promote the canonist's own professional development, the canonist should be a member of a professional society of canonists and support its corporate efforts whenever occasion and conscience permit.

4. In order to serve the Christian community most fully, the canonist should cooperate in the pastoral care of persons involved in canonical cases and administrative procedures to the fullest extent consistent with the other provisions of this Code. While the same person should not ordinarily try to serve as pastoral counselor and a canonist in the same matter, the canonist should make known both to pastoral counselors and to concerned parties the pastoral options available under the law in a given case, and should encourage those involved to seek the counseling they need.

Recognizing the import of these aspirations for canonists, we, the Canon Law Society of America, adopt this Code of Professional Responsibility as a guide to ethical judgments, an instrument for individual and mutual professional evaluation, and a standard for accountability of canonists, whether their professional tasks be administrative, executive, judicial or educational.

II. THE DUTIES OF THE CANONIST

CANON ONE
THE SCOPE OF THIS CODE

This Code shall apply to all members of the Canon Law Society of America, and is proposed as a guide to canonists who are not members. The duties delineated in this Code are not a complete list of the responsibilities of the canonist. This Code does, however, identify the principal obligations for which the canonist may be held accountable.

CANON TWO
RESPONSIBILITIES TO REPRESENTED PARTIES

The canonist who undertakes to represent or to advise a party is obliged to investigate carefully and to represent and protect with diligence the rights and remedies to which the party is legally entitled. The canonist is further obliged to avoid undue delays, to seek appropriate consultation as needed, and to employ only such means as are consistent with truth and honor. Furthermore, the canonist is to refrain from unduly influencing the party represented to accept a compromise or informal solution in lieu of the enforcement of legal rights. Pastoral sensitivity to the actual situation and the persons concerned is the best guide in delicate matters.

CANON THREE
RESPONSIBILITIES IN THE JUDICIAL PROCESS

Canonists who undertake the duties of ecclesiastical judges should uphold the integrity of the judiciary, avoid impropriety and perform the duties of their office impartially and diligently. Canonists charged with rendering a decision or recommendation in a case must do so promptly, in accordance with their best professional judgment of the law and the facts, or, if the matter is committed to the canonist's discretion, in accordance with his or her own prudential judgment of how the matter should be disposed of. The canonist should not be deterred from this duty by any personal, pastoral or other consideration extraneous to the applicable law and facts in the case, or by the influence of any person, even one's religious or canonical superior.

CANON FOUR
CONFIDENTIALITY

The canonist should exercise mature professional judgment with respect to confidentiality, exercising due care that any information obtained in the course of any canonical investigation or proceeding is disclosed only to appropriate persons. When a doubt exists as to whether certain information should be disclosed to a specific person, the canonist ought to engage in appropriate consultation to resolve that doubt before revealing such information. This consultation should include the person who has provided the information in question. Furthermore, canonists are not to reveal anything communicated to them in confidence by persons seeking representation or advice except to the extent necessary to prevent the commission of a crime or serious injustice, or to avoid grave public harm.

CANON FIVE
RESPONSIBILITIES AS AN EDUCATOR

a. When requested to do so or when representing a party, the canonist has the obligation of advising as fully as possible the interested parties as to their rights and remedies under the law.

b. The canonist has a continuing duty to advise the ordinary about canonical matters, particularly when the ordinary makes such a request, when the ordinary's action is required, or when the ordinary's view are sought by other authorities in the Church.

c. When assisted by persons who are not professionally trained canonists, the canonist is responsible for their education and supervision.

257

d. The canonist has a duty to advise all engaged in the pastoral ministry about canonical matters which protect the rights of persons, and also those concerned with the good order necessary in the administration of the Church, in matters both spiritual and temporal.

e. Furthermore, canonists have an ongoing obligation to raise the consciousness of others in the Church concerning possible areas of injustice or inequitable practice.

f. Canonists bear a special responsibility for the education of all the Christian faithful concerning their rights and responsibilities in the life and mission of the Church.

CANON SIX
EVALUATIVE RESPONSIBILITY

Canonists have a responsibility to cooperate with reasonable requests from appropriate parties to use their professional expertise in the valuation of canonical and quasi-canonical agencies or structures within the Church, as regards either the design or the functioning of these agencies or structures.

CANON SEVEN
RESPONSIBILITIES TO THE CANONICAL PROFESSION

In order to promote greater understanding of the developmental character of church law, the canonist should cooperate with professional colleagues by sharing insights and experiential knowledge gained as church lawyers, always safeguarding confidentiality in this process. Active participation in interdisciplinary projects with other professionals is another aspect of this responsibility. The canonist should never refuse to respond to reasonable requests for information or for legal opinions, but should so respond only when informed as fully as possible concerning the pertinent law and the facts of the matter.

CANON EIGHT
EVALUATION OF COMPLIANCE WITH PROFESSIONAL STANDARDS

Canonists should meet regularly with colleagues to evaluate their own performance in regard to the professional standards expressed in this Code of Professional Responsibility, and should periodically seek evaluations from those who have used their services. Since the canonical ministry is an enabling one for the life of the Christian faithful, canonists are responsible to them corporately as well as individually.

CANON NINE
ENFORCEMENT OF THIS CODE

a. Canonists are accountable as regards professional competence and performance to their respective ordinaries and to those who share in the ordinary's pastoral ministry within the local church, to their superiors and communities if they be members of a religious institute, to their professional colleagues, and to individuals or groups whom they advise or represent.

b. Should a complaint be made to the Canon Law Society of America by one of the parties to whom a member-canonist is accountable, that the member-canonist has violated duties enumerated in Part II of this Code, that canonist has the right and the duty to submit to a fair hearing by professional peers.

c. (i) The three senior consultors of the Canon Law Society of America's Board of Governors shall constitute a standing Committee on Professional Responsibility.

(ii) The Board of Governors shall appoint three members of the Society to serve staggered three-year terms as Hearing Officers to deal with complaints arising under this Code. Such service may be renewed by consent of the Board of Governors.

(iii) The Board of Governors, by majority vote, shall designate on an *ad hoc* basis at least three of their number to serve as an Appellate Review Panel in any case where a party seeks review of a determination of the Hearing Officer.

d. (i) The functions of the Committee on Professional Responsibility shall be to receive complaints of any party aggrieved with respect to provisions of this Code, to make an initial finding that the complaint is not frivolous, and in the event that a majority of the Committee considers the complaint to be serious in character, to refer the matter to one of the Hearing Officers.

The Committee on Professional Responsibility may issue advisory opinions on the application of this Code or on other questions concerning the professional responsibility of canonists.

The Committee may publish to the members of the Society and to other interested persons those opinions and decisions it considers helpful in developing a general understanding of the professional responsibility of canonists. Except where a public reprimand has been ordered, names and identifying circumstances shall be withheld so as to protect privacy and reputations.

(ii) The functions of the Hearing Officer shall be to attempt wherever possible informal disposition of the complaint by appropriate means of conciliation and mediation, and in the event that informal resolution of the dispute proves unsuccessful, to gather evidence and to conduct hearings, following standard principles and procedures of due process, and to enter appropriate findings of fact.

Among the possible options available to the Hearing Officer are the following:

1. If the Hearing Officer determines that it has not been established by clear and convincing evidence that a canonist has failed to act in accord with the

standards of this Code, the Hearing Officer shall issue a statement to that effect to the parties concerned.

2. If the Hearing Officer determines that it has been established by clear and convincing evidence that a canonist, although acting in good faith, has failed to act in accord with the standards of this Code, the Hearing Officer shall issue a statement to that effect to the parties concerned. The statement shall explain the nature of the violation of this Code. The Hearing Officer may also, in appropriate cases, require the canonist to make good any harm done to individuals, albeit unwittingly, by the violation of this Code.

3. If the Hearing Officer determines that it has been established beyond a reasonable doubt that a canonist has knowingly and willfully violated this Code of Professional Responsibility, the Hearing Officer shall issue an appropriate reprimand. If the violation is extremely grave, bringing into disrepute the canonical profession, the Hearing Officer may recommend to the Board of Governors a penalty as serious as expulsion from the Society. This penalty shall be imposed only by a majority vote of the Board of Governors.

The Hearing Officer may also recommend appropriate remedial actions, and the Board of Governors may require the offender to comply with the recommendations under the sanction of possible expulsion, when fundamental rights of persons require this.

DOCTRINAL RESPONSIBILITIES

PROCEDURES FOR PROMOTING COOPERATION AND RESOLVING DISPUTES BETWEEN BISHOPS AND THEOLOGIANS*

*Joint Committee of the
Canon Law Society of America
and the
Catholic Theological Society of America*

PREFACE

In January 1980, the Catholic Theological Society of America established an "Ad Hoc Committee on Cooperation between Theologians and the Church's Teaching Authority" with Leo J. O'Donovan as the Chair. The Committee reported to the Society in June 1980, and recommended that the Catholic Theological Society of America and the Canon Law Society of America jointly form a committee "to develop a proposed set of norms to guide the resolution of difficulties which may arise between theologians and the magisterium in North America."[1] The two Societies agreed and, in September 1980, they formally constituted "The Joint CLSA-CTSA Committee on Cooperation between Theologians and the Ecclesiastical Magisterium."

The Committee consisted of three members appointed by the CLSA, three members appointed by the CTSA, and a chair jointly appointed by the two Societies. The members were: John A. Alesandro (CLSA), John P. Boyle (CTSA), Robert J. Carlson (CLSA), Patrick Granfield (CTSA), Jon Nilson (CTSA), James H. Provost (CLSA), and Leo J. O'Donovan (CTSA) who chaired the Committee.

*Abbreviations used in this document:

CD	*Christus Dominus* (Vatican II)
CLSA	Canon Law Society of America
CTSA	Catholic Theological Society of America
DH	*Dignitatis humanae* (Vatican II)
DV	*Dei Verbum* (Vatican II)
GS	*Gaudium et spes* (Vatican II)
LG	*Lumen gentium* (Vatican II)
NCCB	National Conference of Catholic Bishops

[1]*Catholic Theological Society of America Proceedings* 35 (1980) 331.

The Committee divided its task into two phases. In the first, the members prepared six background papers dealing with the rights and responsibilities of bishops, the rights and responsibilities of theologians, and an evaluation of current procedures. Each topic was examined from a theological and canonical perspective. The Committee met three times to discuss these papers, and the detailed mutual criticism necessitated several redraftings. The meetings took place at Cathedral College, Douglaston, N.Y. (February 7-8, 1981), The Catholic University of America (May 15-16, 1981), and Georgetown University (September 4-5, 1981). The six background papers together with a consensus statement representing the position of the entire Committee were published in June 1982.[2]

In the second phase, our concern here, the Committee worked to develop procedures. In doing so it acknowledged the significance of earlier efforts by the National Conference of Catholic Bishops which adopted a model for due process in dioceses[3] and issued procedures of its own for conciliation and arbitration.[4] However, those procedures deal with administrative conflicts only. At present, there are no procedural norms in the United States that would forestall and, where necessary, resolve doctrinal disputes between bishops and theologians.

The Committee drafted its proposed norms at four meetings held at the Washington Retreat House (January 29-30, 1982), Cathedral College (May 14, 1982), Georgetown University (September 9-11, 1982), and Immaculate Conception Seminary, Huntington, N.Y. (December 3-5, 1982). Throughout this second phase, the proposed norms were circulated for reaction from representative bishops, canonists, and theologians. Three members of the National Conference of Catholic Bishops—Bishop James R. Hoffman (Toledo), Bishop John F. Kinney (Bismarck), and Archbishop Daniel E. Pilarczyk (Cincinnati)—responded to the invitation to join in the Committee meetings and to participate in the discussions. The Committee appreciated their presence and profited greatly from their suggestions.

The final report of this Joint CLSA/CTSA Committee has three parts.

Part One, "Introduction," presents a general description of the ecclesial framework, the operative principles, and the rights and responsibilities of bishops and theologians. This material presumes the fuller discussion of these issues in the already published background papers. The summary here is intended to provide a context for the rest of the report.

---

[2]Leo J. O'Donovan, S. J., ed., *Cooperation between Theologians and the Ecclesiastical Magisterium* (Washington, D.C.: CLSA, 1982).

[3]*On Due Process,* rev. ed. (Washington, D.C.: NCCB, 1972). In November 1969, the NCCB accepted a report on due process from the Canon Law Society of America and recommended to its members experimentation, adaptation, and implementation of the procedures included therein. In 1971, after a few changes had been made, the Holy See gave the *nihil obstat* to the document.

[4]*Committee on Conciliation and Arbitration* (Washington, D.C.: NCCB, 1979).

Part Two, "Structuring Cooperation," recommends ways in which bishops and theologians can build a spirit of cooperation in their common service of the gospel, especially through personal contacts and informal dialogue. There are also actions by which bishops or theologians might screen complaints from third parties so that unnecessary disputes might be avoided.

Part Three, "Formal Doctrinal Dialogue," sets out a procedure designed specifically to deal with doctrinal disputes between bishops and theologians in dioceses. Since the circumstances in the nearly 200 dioceses of the United States vary widely, the procedures given here are intended to be flexible and adaptable to local needs.

The recommended structures for promoting cooperation and for resolving doctrinal disputes are not so detailed as, for example, *Roberts' Rules of Order*, but they are more than mere exhortation. They draw upon experience already acquired by the church in the United States in building a spirit of collaboration and in resolving conflicts, yet they are designed to address the special problems of a precisely doctrinal dispute.

Appended to the report are two brief statements on the *Ratio agendi* of the Congregation for the Doctrine of the Faith and on the possibility of a National Theological Commission.

The Committee is aware that the resolution of doctrinal disputes is difficult in this time of profound philosophical and theological pluralism. That pluralism makes the task of building cooperation between bishops and theologians more urgent than ever, with a view also towards avoiding intractable disputes. More often now than in the past, however, it may be necessary to acknowledge without rancor that on occasion agreement is not possible.

A common commitment of bishops and theologians to the integrity of the word of God and a common sensitivity to the pastoral implications of theological teaching within the church community can make the structures given here effective both in promoting cooperation and in resolving disputes.

I. INTRODUCTION

A. *Context and Principles*

The ecclesial context is critical for understanding the relationship between bishops and theologians, for encouraging cooperation, and for constructing adequate procedures to prevent or to address doctrinal disputes. In virtue of their faith, baptism, and communion with the church, bishops and theologians alike—however distinct their ministries and charisms—are dedicated to the active proclamation of the gospel and committed to justice and peace. Both participate in the community's experience of faith and, through service to the word of God, they seek to promote its greater understanding. In their common effort, both recognize the importance of communicating the faith with sensitivity to the demands of today's pluralistic world. In their different ways bishops and theologians discharge the mission of the church "to show forth in the world the mystery of the Lord in a faithful though shadowed way, until at last it will be revealed in total splendor" (LG 8).

The ecclesiological principles of shared responsibility, legitimate diversity, and subsidiarity are most important. A reasonable, clear, and fair process must protect the fundamental human and sacramental rights and responsibilities of all parties concerned. The norms should encourage free and responsible theological inquiry in service to the gospel, faithful to Catholic tradition, respectful of the episcopal ministry, and responsive to the needs of the church and the world. The ultimate goal is to foster collaboration between bishops and theologians for the good of the entire church.

The recommendations given in Parts II and III deal with the diocese. It is advisable that attempts to resolve doctrinal disputes be made first at the local level before an appeal is made to Rome. Of course, any bishop or theologian can contact Rome directly; but in terms of subsidiarity, every effort should be made to initiate the process within the local church, before any involvement with the Holy See.[5]

The terms "magisterium," "theologian," "rights and responsibilities," and "interests" are frequently used in this report. There are unresolved questions in the current understanding of these words, but for the sake of clarity, the following specific meanings are stipulated.

"Magisterium" will be used to refer to the ecclesiastical magisterium, i.e., to the teaching authority exercised in the church by the pope and other bishops and persons called to cooperate with them in their doctrinal functions. By their ordination and hierarchical communion, bishops are members of the college of bishops and leaders in their local churches. Aware of the needs of contemporary society, bishops have the pastoral duty of proclaiming the word of God with authority, of teaching the truth of the faith, and of maintaining the authenticity of the word of God as it has been formulated in the course of history.

Theologians have a different function within the church. Prepared by their training in the skills of scholarship, theologians systematically explore the nature and foundations of the church's faith in God's revelation, examine the interrelationships of Christian truths, and interpret the word of God to respond to the challenges of contemporary society. The authority of theologians arises from the scholarly competence they show in discerning and communicating the abiding truth of Christ. The term "theologian" in these pages is used to designate the believer who thus seeks to mediate between faith and

---

[5]This point was also made by the Congregation for the Doctrine of the Faith in a private letter sent to the presidents of episcopal conferences on July 10, 1968. Also see Thesis 12 in the document of the International Theological Commission, *Theses on the Relationship between the Ecclesiastical Magisterium and Theology* (Washington, D.C.: USCC, 1977).

culture through the discipline of scholarship.[6] Although this report is concerned with theologians who are members of the Catholic Church, the procedures could also be used by other theologians in Catholic institutions.

"Rights and responsibilities" and "interests" are used variously in law and ethics. We mean by "right" a moral or legal power to act or to be immune from injury. Rights, and the responsibilities which they imply, have their source in one's human dignity, in one's standing in the church, or from one's function within the Catholic community.[7] Scholars distinguish the possession of a right from its exercise, because the exercise of a right may be circumscribed in order to protect the common good or the rights of others, even though the right itself remains intact.

We use the term "interests" to designate other and more elusive factors in a conflict situation. "Interests" relate to particular and concrete concerns involved in the exercise of personal or official discretion. Interests arise in the pursuit of one's rights or obligations, or more generally, from the freedom appropriate to all the people of God. Procedures designed to resolve conflicts must determine facts, the rights and responsibilities of the parties, and the interests of the parties which are at issue.

B. The Rights and Responsibilities of Bishops

The norms proposed in this report reflect a concern to recognize and foster the rights and responsibilities of both bishops and theologians. Because those rights and responsibilities are set out in detail in the published background papers and consensus statement, they are recalled here only schematically for the convenience of the reader.[8]

The rights and responsibilities of bishops flow from their pastoral office of teaching, sanctifying and ruling in the church. These tasks (*munera*) cannot be fully separated one from the other: they form a single pastoral office. Of the responsibilities and rights of bishops which arise from their pastoral task of authoritative teaching, we call attention to the following.

Preeminent among the responsibilities of bishops is preaching the word of God. In addition, bishops are called upon to preserve and protect the truth of faith, i.e., to transmit the authentic gospel of Christ. Moreover, in the particular church in which he presides, the bishop is to teach in the name of the church; he is to make the pastoral judgment as to how the faith of the com-

---

[6]For more on this matter see John P. Boyle, "The Rights and Responsibilities of Bishops: A Theological Perspective," in O'Donovan, pp. 11-12, and John Nilson, "The Rights and Responsibilities of Theologians: A Theological Perspective," ibid., pp. 53-75.

[7]See the fuller discussion in John A. Alesandro, "The Rights and Responsibilities of Theologians: A Canonical Perspective," in O'Donovan, pp. 82-8.

[8]What follows summarizes material in Boyle's article (see note 6) and in Robert J. Carlson, "The Rights and Responsibilities of Bishops: A Canonical Perspective," in O'Donovan, pp. 31-52.

munity will be publicly expressed at a given time and place. For that reason, the bishop is called upon to judge whether some opinions endanger or are contrary to faith and the Christian life. But it is also the responsibility of bishops to discharge their office so as to respect the gifts imparted by the Holy Spirit to various members of the church. It follows that in the discharge of their pastoral role, bishops should encourage theologians, as well as others, to pursue a deeper understanding of the gospel and its meaning for contemporary life.

In addition to these responsibilities, certain rights of bishops are rooted in their task as teachers. Thus, the bishops of particular churches have the right to exercise their care for the truth of the gospel in the church over which they preside. The bishops teach in the name of the church by reason of their position in the particular church, in union with the head and other members of the episcopal college. What they teach should be received in a way proportionate to the authority with which it is presented. But bishops also have the right to draw upon the contributions and the gifts of all who share the church's saving mission, which includes the heralding of the faith. In their particular church communities bishops have the right to the cooperation and support of the priests who form one presbyterate with the bishop. Bishops also have a right to the collaboration of theologians: bishops draw on their scholarly competence and support; when fidelity to the word of God requires it, bishops expect that their formulation and practice of the faith will be respectfully corrected by theologians. Further, bishops have a right to require in the name of the church that theologians faithfully discharge their own responsibility for the integrity of the gospel. Bishops also have the right to teach without interference from civil authority or exaggerated criticism by theologians or others in the church. Finally, because their solicitude extends to the universal church, diocesan bishops have a right to the church's care for them expressed through existing or potential structures of the episcopal college.

C. The Rights and Responsibilities of Theologians

The rights and responsibilities of theologians may be grouped according to the ways in which theologians participate in the life of the church.[9]

As members of the community of faith, theologians have a fundamental concern for the unity of faith and its promotion of justice and peace throughout the church.

Still, as scholars their first responsibility is a critical fidelity to apostolic faith exercised according to the scholarly principles of that branch of theology in which their work is done. As they discharge that responsibility, theological scholars must expect to give and to receive constructive criticism from other

[9]What follows summarizes materials from the articles by Nilson and Alesandro cited in notes 6 and 7.

scholars, from bishops, from other Christians, and from other interested persons of good will.

As members of particular church communities, theologians should prudently seek more suitable ways of communicating doctrine to people today. They should adapt the presentation of their research findings to the audience of their lectures or publications and use discretion in dealing with the communications media to reduce any harm to the unsophisticated which might result from premature or inappropriate dissemination of their thought.

Finally, to the extent that theologians accept more specifically ecclesiastical activities such as seminary teaching, they must accept reasonable canonical ordering of their work.

Correlative to the responsibilities of theologians in the life of the church are certain rights. Paramount among them is freedom of inquiry and expression of scholarly opinion, even in matters of faith. As they discharge their responsibilities, theologians have the right to support from the community they serve, though they must also welcome objective criticism of their work.

Closely related to that right is another: the right of the theologian to a good reputation and, if needed, the defense of that right by appropriate judicial or administrative processes. In addition, as professional scholars, theologians have the right to employ the usual means of research and publication and to associate freely in private and professional groups.

As members of a particular church, theologians have the right to expect that the pastoral office with which they collaborate will be properly exercised. In cases of dispute, that implies access to due process to protect both substantive and procedural rights. It also implies the right to recognition of contractual and professional agreements into which theologians have entered in accordance with ecclesiastical and civil law.

II. STRUCTURING COOPERATION

A. The Purposes and Climate of Cooperation

Bishops and theologians may cooperate with one another in a variety of ways to enhance the quality of their service to the church. These cooperative efforts may not necessarily serve to resolve doctrinal disputes between bishops and theologians. They are primarily intended to realize the ideals of mutual encouragement, support, and assistance which are proposed by Vatican II, as well as to invigorate the unity without which the church's mission in the world becomes weak and diffuse (LG 4, 13; DV 8; GS 44).

Nonetheless, cooperation between theologians and bishops ought to play a significant, if not indispensable, role as context and prelude to the employment of Formal Doctrinal Dialogue for resolving doctrinal disputes. Bishops and theologians involved in ongoing collaborations are more likely to learn greater respect and trust for one another and thus to assist and support their respective service to the gospel. Appreciating each other as individuals struggling to be faithful to the demands of the gospel for their different functions in the church, their mutual respect and trust may serve to prevent theological disagreements and differences in viewpoint from degenerating to such an extent that Formal Doctrinal Dialogue must be used to resolve the conflict.

Even in cases where Formal Doctrinal Dialogue is employed, structured cooperation will already have established a climate in which all the parties are motivated to act prudently, patiently, and lovingly (DH 14). Regular and meaningful cooperation provides the opportunity for each party to discern and clarify the rights, responsibilities, and interests of the other. Thus, if and when Formal Doctrinal Dialogue is invoked, each party can be aware of the necessary distinctions and of the possibilities and limitations of formal procedures used to deal with them.

Cooperation is not emphasized here as an innovation. Long before Vatican II, there were well established ways for theologians to cooperate with bishops in their tasks of teaching, sanctifying, and governing in the church. In the 1917 Code of Canon Law, theologians (who were, in almost all cases, clerics) were envisaged as members of seminary faculties, as censors of books, as synodal examiners, and as conciliar and curial experts. In the revised Code of Canon Law, even more cooperative roles for theologians are envisaged, at least by implication.[10]

Moreover, it is undeniable that bishops do rely upon theologians, explicitly or implicitly. Every bishop has been educated by theologians. So has every priest who cooperates with him in his ministry. Bishops have been encouraged, even charged, to study theology regularly to inform their preaching and to make their exercise of the pastoral office more effective.[11] So the appropriate questions are: on which theologians do bishops rely? When do they rely upon them? How is that reliance enacted?

A few bishops have appointed theologians as advisors and vicars for theological affairs, or have established boards of theological consultants.[12] The NCCB regularly calls upon theologians to cooperate in its work. Collaborative efforts like these are surely encouraging.[13] Yet instances of structured cooperation between bishops and theologians are still relatively rare. Opportunities for frequent, meaningful collaboration are going largely unrealized.

[10]See Alesandro, p. 101.
[11]LG 25. See also Bishop John Cummins, "The Changing Relationship Between Bishops and Theologians," *Origins* 12 (June 17, 1982) 65-71, and Archbishop James Hickey, "The Bishop as Teacher," *Origins* 12 (July 29, 1982) 140-144.
[12]"One method I find most helpful is to have the assistance of a personal theologian. . . . We would not think of leading a diocese without someone trained in canon law. How much more then the presence of someone well trained in the authentic theology 'of the church'?" Hickey, pp. 141-142.
[13]See Cummins, p. 69, for recent instances of cooperation between bishops and theologians; also, *Catholic Theological Society of America Proceedings* 35 (1980) 332-336.

Theologians, too, could profit from reinvigorated cooperation. Their relationship to the church, which is an essential element in their identity and work as Roman Catholic theologians, may take a further vital form in the course of collaboration with bishops. Cooperation would thus enable theologians better to understand and to fulfill their specific responsibilities in the church.

While the focus of this section of the report is on structured cooperation between bishops and theologians, not all cooperation need or should take place in a formal mode. If bishops and theologians are convinced of the importance of the help they can render one another in carrying out the mission of the church, they will be determined and creative in seeking ways to work together informally. Without the pressure of a crisis, they may find their conversations deeply nourishing and empowering. Together they need to foster regular and personal ways of contact.

The emergence of an important national issue, the promulgation of a papal document, the weeks preceding or following a meeting of the NCCB can be occasions for the bishop and theologians of a diocese jointly to study materials, proposals, or concerns and to discern their local implications and applications. Catholic colleges, universities, and seminaries might make it a practice to invite the bishop to campus events of theological or pastoral significance, such as seminars, lectures, colloquia, and workshops. Catholic scholars at secular institutions could do the same. On such occasions, the bishop need not make any formal statement; he can simply be present as a participant and fellow learner. In some dioceses, it may be feasible for bishops and theologians to meet regularly for informal exploration of mutual concerns or simply for shared prayer.

B. Implementing Structured Cooperation

1. Suggested Areas of Implementation

Initiation and development of collaboration between bishops and theologians will not always require the establishment of new structures. Most dioceses already have offices, departments, and staffs which assist the bishop in meeting his varied and complex responsibilities. The issues and areas delegated to these offices often have important theological dimensions, e.g., health care, ecumenical relations, adult education, catechetics, liturgy, finances, and family life. It would be a relatively simple matter to invite competent theologians to serve as consultants to these offices or even as part-time staff members.

There are also other matters of concern and interest to both bishops and theologians in which a cooperative approach could yield very desirable results. The importance of these matters will motivate joint efforts to establish the appropriate collaborative structures to deal with them. Ways could be developed for theologians and bishops to bring their combined expertise and talent to bear on concerns such as:

- the means and efficacy of the local church's proclamation of the gospel;
- diocesan goals, mission statements, and priorities;
- religious education materials in use or proposed for use in the diocese;
- health care policies and procedures;
- goals and policies of Catholic educational institutions in the diocese;
- policies and guidelines for lectures, conferences, and workshops held in the diocese;
- priorities and policies for the church's charitable endeavors;
- continuing education for priests, religious, deacons, and catechists;
- the theological supports for diocesan statements, position papers, and testimony to be presented in various civic and legal fora;
- the theological background for pastoral letters;
- ecumenical relations
- diocesan employment policies and procedures.

Sometimes a bishop's or a theologian's teaching becomes the target of complaints and charges which have no substance or merit. Although the accuser(s) might be well-intentioned, these situations are potentially volatile and enervating for everyone involved. In some dioceses, it may prove desirable to establish a procedure which prevents groundless delations from occupying more time and attention than they deserve.

An individual or a small committee recognized by the bishop and the theological community for theological expertise, tact, and pastoral sensitivity could be appointed to serve as "gatekeeper." This function is analogous to that of the contact person in Formal Doctrinal Dialogue (see below); all complaints about theological teaching in the diocese would be referred here first. The gatekeeper's task, while respecting and protecting the dignity of the complainant, is to keep a groundless complaint from becoming a dispute which needlessly distracts the bishop and/or the theologian from their more important services to the church.

In the revised Code of Canon Law, canon 812 concerns both bishops and theologians in that it requires theologians teaching in any institutes of higher learning to have (*habeant oportet*) a mandate granted by the competent ecclesiastical authority. Unless an indult or exception from this canon is granted to Catholic colleges and universities in the United States, formal processes will be needed to implement it.[14] The specific elements of these processes must be determined by bishops and theologians together. If they are established unilaterally, it will be extremely difficult, if not impossible, to maintain a climate of cooperation and mutual trust.

[14]See Alesandro, pp. 112-114.

2. Means of Implementation

The first steps toward structured cooperation can be taken by the bishop or by theologians in his diocese. The bishop himself can request the theologians to provide him with the names and areas of expertise of theologians who are willing and competent to offer their services to the local church in a collaborative way. By agreeing to have one's name given to the bishop, a theologian would thereby tentatively agree to serve in this way, if invited by the bishop or by theological colleagues. Theologians themselves could also develop such information and offer it to the bishop. Either way, the local church would have more substantial theological expertise available to it.

With a view to appointing a theological advisor, the bishop could also consult widely with theologians inside and outside the diocese. In larger dioceses, this advisor could become a vicar for theological affairs and serve as the bishop's liaison to the theologians in the diocese. The vicar could facilitate contact between the bishop and the theologians. The vicar should not be the bishop's only spokesperson on theological issues. Nor can the vicar substitute for the personal contact of the bishop with theologians.

Some dioceses in large urban centers have so many theologians that the bishop might well consider establishing a board of theological advisors. Among other functions, the board could serve in cases of dispute as the mediating, screening, or fact-finding body, prior to the initiation of any formal procedures.

Most dioceses in the United States do not have enough theologians to implement structured cooperation very extensively on their own. While this factor presents particular difficulties, it also provides the bishops and theologians of a province or region an opportunity to realize the vision of mutual support and cooperation among dioceses set forth by Vatican II (LG 23; CD 6, 36, 37).

The theologians and bishops of a region could come together informally in the ways suggested above. They could also consider ways in which formal and regular cooperation could be established among them. Some dioceses in Canada have pooled regional resources to develop more effective tribunals. Discussions have been held in the United States with a view to pooling the canonical resources of a region. The document *On Due Process*[15] proposed a regional pooling of resources for more effective resolution of doctrinal conflicts. Some state Catholic conferences have established medical moral commissions.

Granted that the geographical distances involved make such cooperation more difficult to develop and maintain, still the advantages to be gained far outweigh the difficulties involved. Perhaps a grant-funded project in a particular region could develop guidelines to facilitate regional structures for cooperation elsewhere.

---

[15]*On Due Process,* p. 10.

Structured cooperation between bishops and theologians should and, to some extent already does, exist on the national level.[16] Prospects for developing it further, however, deserve serious consideration; one such possibility is discussed in Appendix B of this document.

3. Principles Regarding Theological Consultants

Most theologians hold full-time positions in colleges, universities, or seminaries. As a result, in most instances of structured cooperation their role will be consultative. This means that they will serve in a part-time capacity as regular consultants or advisors to bishops or to departments and staffs which may assist the bishop in carrying out his service to the church.

If this form of structured collaboration is to function effectively and to realize the purposes for which it is established, certain principles should be followed.

First, theologians who serve in any consultative capacity, however they may be chosen, should be recognized by their theological peers as both competent and representative. They should be sensitive to the faith of the universal church and to the ways in which that faith is known and lived in the particular church which they serve as consultants. They should be selected from as many segments as possible on the spectrum of acceptable theological opinion, so that the church can reap the benefits of the fullest range of theological resources available on particular issues or problems.

Second, the names of the consultants and the selection process should normally be known publicly. An air of unnecessary secrecy too easily leads to suspicion and mistrust. An open and careful examination of issues is inhibited when there is evidence suggesting that the discussion process or conclusion is somehow predetermined.

Third, whenever possible there ought to be a staggered rotation among consultants. This will foster the benefits of both continuity and freshness of perspective on the issues. It will also realize the ideal of common effort which is at the heart of authentic unity in the church.

Fourth, everyone involved centrally or marginally in the process should remember that the theological consultant is not exclusively or primarily at the service of the bishop, but of the local church. Otherwise, the complementary but distinct and irreducible roles of the bishop and the theologian may be confused and the anticipated results of real cooperation may not be fully realized.[17]

[16]Ibid.
[17]See International Theological Commission, *Theses on the Relationship Between the Ecclesiastical Magisterium and Theology,* p. 17.

C. Cooperation as Aiding Formal Doctrinal Dialogue

As their conversation and collaboration become more common, bishops and theologians are likely to gain a clearer sense of the distinct yet related services they perform in the one church through, for example, their catechesis, ethical reflection, authoritative teaching, theological education and research, and pastoral leadership.[18] This alone should eliminate many misunderstandings between them.

Regular and active cooperation will also establish a mutual personal knowledge and trust between bishops and theologians which can lessen the occasions when Formal Doctrinal Dialogue is required to resolve a dispute. As bishops and theologians come to know each other not merely in official roles but as faithful persons, recourse to formal procedures to resolve conflicts between them should become less and less frequent.

III. FORMAL DOCTRINAL DIALOGUE

A. Purposes of the Dialogue

Collaboration and structured cooperation help to clarify doctrinal positions. Throughout such contacts there is a presupposition of sound doctrine, a presumption which holds until proven otherwise. Nevertheless, there may be differences of opinion, disagreements, or questions concerning doctrinal matters. If these lead to conflict or dispute, Formal Doctrinal Dialogue may be used.

Such dialogue is not a judicial or administrative proceeding. It is a dialogue about doctrine. Such dialogue should take place before considering any exercise of administrative authority in regard to doctrinal matters.

The purpose of Formal Doctrinal Dialogue is to determine the nature and gravity of the issue at dispute as well as its pastoral significance, and to achieve an agreement between the parties. The process will normally involve meetings, although much can be accomplished by written statements. Such dialogue should be entered in an atmosphere of prayer to emphasize the one faith shared by the parties.

B. Participants

For the purpose of these guidelines, the dispute in need of resolution is presumed to be between a theologian and a bishop, although others involved in theological controversies may find them useful. The theologian or bishop who initiates the use of this formal dialogue is termed the "initiating party." The

---

[18]"The magisterium and theology have two different tasks to perform. That is why neither can be reduced to the other. Yet they serve the one whole. But precisely on account of this configuration they must remain in consultation with one another." John Paul II, *L'Osservatore Romano* [English], no. 50 (662), December 15, 1980, p. 17.

other principal in the dialogue is termed the "second party." Several bishops or several theologians may be acting as initiating party or second party.

Other persons may assist the principals in the formal dialogue. These may be involved in regard to one or more of the following functions.

1. Advice. Advisors assist the initiating party or the second party by their advice and counsel. Advisors are selected freely by the party whom they will be serving as advisor.

2. Expertise. Experts are called upon to assist the parties in reaching mutual understanding about their respective positions, to offer an evaluation of the relationship of theological statements with Catholic tradition, and to give advice about the pastoral effect of such teaching. Experts, therefore, should be knowledgeable about the matter under discussion, should be representative of the variety of views within Catholic tradition, and should participate in the process in a manner acceptable to both parties. Normally such experts will themselves be professional theologians or persons versed in pastoral ministry. While the opinion of experts is not binding, it should be given serious weight in proceeding with the dialogue. If the experts are unanimous in agreement, the parties should not reject their opinion without grave reason.

3. Facilitation. At the request of both parties, a facilitator assists at any of the various stages of formal dialogue. The facilitator helps the process to move forward by bringing the principals to a better understanding of what each means, by settling specific questions for them, and by providing at various stages in the dialogue a "state of the question" to clarify what points are truly at issue at that particular moment.

4. Delegation. Dialogue is carried out most effectively in a face-to-face exchange, through which each party comes to a more personal appreciation of the other's position. Although this is the preferred method, there may be occasions when either party considers it necessary to delegate another person to assist in the various tasks of Formal Doctrinal Dialogue. Even on these occasions, however, the final statement of agreement for each task in the formal dialogue must be signed by the principal parties themselves.

C. Procedures for Formal Doctrinal Dialogue

1. Initiating the Process

Either the theologian or the bishop may be the initiating party. Formal dialogue may begin in one of two ways.

a. Direct contact between the two parties
The initiating party should first have approached the second party in an informal manner to determine whether the apparent dispute may be immediately resolved without formal dialogue.

If formal dialogue is needed, the initiating party shall make a written request to the second party to enter into Formal Doctrinal Dialogue. The written request is to outline the doctrinal points at issue, the manner in which the dispute has arisen, the attempts to resolve the issue which have already been made, the specific request to employ Formal Doctrinal Dialogue to settle the questions, and initial suggestions concerning ways to resolve the doctrinal dispute. The written request is to include the initiating party's name, address, telephone number, the date of the request, and the initiating party's signature.

b. Indirectly, through a contact person

A contact person may be appointed within a diocese to process requests for the use of Formal Doctrinal Dialogue. The first function of the contact person is to determine whether the request for formal dialogue is legitimate. If the request is judged to be inappropriate, the contact person is so to inform the initiating party, indicating the reasons for rejecting the request. If the initiating party then resubmits the request, the contact person is to submit it to the second party for a response.

If the request at the outset is judged to be appropriate, it is to be sent to the second party for a response and the initiating party is to be informed immediately of the date of this action. Rejection of the request by the contact person or submission of the request to the second party for response must take place within one month of the receipt of the request by the contact person.

The contact person is appointed by the bishop. The person should be qualified to evaluate and process such requests, generally acceptable also to the theological community, and easily available for contact.

2. The Response

Acknowledgement of a request for formal dialogue must be given in writing within two weeks of the receipt of the request, and a formal response within one month of the receipt of the request.

a. An affirmative response to the request is to include an explicit commitment to Formal Doctrinal Dialogue, a statement of the points about which both parties seem at the outset to be in agreement, the points which seem to be in dispute, and initial suggestions concerning ways to resolve the doctrinal dispute. The written response is to contain the second party's name, address, telephone number, signature, and the date of the response.

b. A negative response should explicitly refuse to make use of Formal Doctrinal Dialogue and state the reasons for refusal.

c. If, after six weeks from the date on which the formal request was sent to the second party, no response has been received by the initiating party, a second request should be sent to the second party. Failure to respond to this second request within two weeks shall be interpreted as refusal to make use of Formal Doctrinal Dialogue.

3. Agreement on Procedure

The written request for dialogue and the response may have already clarified the disagreement and the desired goal in dialogue. Nevertheless, the next step must be a preliminary agreement on the statement of the issues, on the procedures to be followed, and on the goal to be achieved by their formal dialogue.

In determining procedures, the preliminary agreement should address matters such as the following:

    a. level of confidentiality to be respected;
    b. participation by other persons and how they are to be selected (see above, B, 1-4);
    c. record keeping and, if appropriate, transcripts;
    d. time limits;
    e. responsibility for expenses.

This preliminary agreement, which is to be in writing and signed by both parties, can be modified at any time by their mutual consent.

4. The Dialogue

Disputes between theologians and members of the ecclesiastical magisterium are usually complex and may involve deep feelings. It is not easy to decide a priori on the best or simplest method to resolve the situation. At the beginning, it is essential that both parties be committed to the process. As the dialogue progresses, the parties my find it helpful to alter by mutual consent the process they had agreed upon.

Although disputes may be considerably different, Formal Doctrinal Dialogue will invariably require the completion of four tasks:

    a. gathering data;
    b. clarifying meaning;
    c. determining the relationship of the points at issue to Catholic tradition;
    d. identifying implications in the life of the church.

One of the main instruments for achieving agreement is the formulation of written statements with regard to each of the tasks. These statements, signed by both parties, express points of agreement, clarify reasons for disagreement, and specify further questions to be addressed.

First Task: Gathering the Data

Since doctrinal disputes arise from public utterances or writings, the first task is to agree on what was actually said or written. There may be no disagreement on the facts at all, in which case a statement of agreement should immediately be drawn up and signed by both parties.

If the parties initially disagree about what was said or written, ways should be found to solve this difference of opinion. Examples include:

1. In written matters, copies of the actual materials should be made available to both parties.

2. In spoken matters, tape recordings, written reports and other trustworthy records, if they exist, should be made available to both parties.

3. If no record exists, to settle the question of what was actually said or written it may be necessary to call upon witnesses.

Full access to the record by both parties is essential to effective dialogue. In cases in which a dispute has arisen because of acceptance by one of the parties of complaints or accusations by other persons, the party accused or complained against has the right of access to the materials sent by the other persons. In such situations the burden of proof as to matters of fact rests on those bringing the complaint or accusation.

In determining what was said or written, it is very important to specify the pertinent context, such as:

1. the literary genre: newspaper article, theological study, popular religious work, etc.;

2. The context of spoken communication: lecture, classroom, seminar, radio or television, etc.

3. the audience addressed;

4. the level and extent of publicity.

In especially complicated matters the accomplishment of the task of gathering the data may very well benefit from a facilitator who can settle factual questions to the satisfaction of both parties. The parties may also make use of advisors or, if necessary, delegates to expedite the process.

A written statement of agreement, signed by both parties, completes this task. It specifies the data gathered and the agreement of the parties on the essential points of what was said or written. In some cases agreement on accurate data may itself resolve the dispute and complete the dialogue.

Second Task: Clarifying the Meaning

While completion of the first task may determine clearly *what* was said or written, questions may still exist about the meaning of the data. Since words may admit of varying interpretations, the parties must seek a common understanding of the meaning of what was said or written. The result of this effort will be an agreement on the meaning or differing interpretations.

In reaching this clarification, consideration should be given to various factors, such as:

1. the significance of the words in text and context;
2. the broader corpus of the author's work, philosophical and theological perspective, and method;
3. the author's intention in presenting the material, whether the position was being advocated, defended, described, etc.;
4. the pertinent context of the work at issue as determined in the first task (see above);
5. the degree to which the statement is presented as a personal opinion or as a teaching of the church.

If agreement on meaning is not readily achieved, the parties may find it useful to rely on the advice of others or perhaps to submit the matter to a jointly acceptable facilitator.

This second task is completed with a written statement of agreement, signed by both parties, expressing as clearly as possible the mutually accepted meaning of what was said or written. The statement may also specify any differing interpretations which remain. In some cases, agreement on the meaning may itself resolve the dispute and complete the dialogue.

Third Task Determining the Relationship with Catholic Tradition

Every doctrinal dispute will initially involve at least an apparent divergence of opinion about the consonance of a public utterance or writing with Catholic tradition. The completion of the first two tasks may result in the conclusion that the disagreement was unfounded. Nevertheless, the first two tasks may simply serve to clarify the point at issue; that is, the relationship of what was said or written with Catholic tradition.

This is a very complex matter. It is not a task that can be isolated from the parties themselves. Their personal involvement is especially important at this stage. It is a learning process in which dialogue should assist both parties to grow in their understanding of the fullness of Catholic tradition. Thus, in approaching this task the parties should seek to discover points of agreement, particularly in regard to the questions which must be studied and the appropriate order for addressing those questions.

This stage of dialogue should begin with a written statement by the initiating party outlining the basis on which consonance with Catholic tradition is questioned. The second party should respond to this initial statement in writing. If no agreement is reached, these two documents form the basis for further dialogue.

The term "Catholic tradition" refers to the whole range of church teaching. That teaching is grounded in the word of God, especially in the Scriptures. The magisterium serves the word of God by proposing doctrine in solemn conciliar or papal pronouncements, in ordinary papal and episcopal teaching, and in other activities such as the approval of materials used in the instruction of the faithful and the worship of the church. Catholic tradition is also reflected in the works of approved authors, noted theologians, and in the mainstream of Catholic life and belief. Determining the consonance of a theological view with Catholic tradition will demand a careful consideration of the historical context and development of church teaching, an understanding of the hierarchy of truths, an evaluation of the various levels of teaching authority, appreciation of the distinction between the substance of the faith and its expression, and the degree to which the church has committed itself in this matter.

At this stage in the dialogue the parties may be assisted by a facilitator, by personal advisors, and especially by consultation with theological experts.

This task is completed with a written statement of agreement, signed by both parties. It specifies the steps taken to complete the task, the resulting points of agreement, and any remaining disagreement. Here, too, the written statement of agreement may suffice to resolve the dispute and complete the dialogue.

Fourth Task: Identifying the Implications for the Life of the Church

The previous tasks have resulted in agreements on the public utterances and writings in question, and possibly differing interpretations and disagreements about them. The fourth task is to determine the pastoral implications of these utterances and writings in the life of the church. While actual or apparent implications precipitate most doctrinal disputes, they are frequently the most difficult to sort out and agree upon. This task requires not merely understanding, but prudence; not just learning, but wisdom. Concern for such implications is a responsibility of both bishops and theologians.

To begin this task, the initiating party should state in writing the nature and extent of the implications. The second party should respond to this statement in writing. If no agreement has been reached, these two documents from the basis for further dialogue on this matter.

A discussion about implications cannot be simply an exchange of personal impressions. It should clarify the criteria used by the parties to assess pastoral life. Conclusions should be based on adequate information required for prudential judgments. This may necessitate gathering additional evidence. The discussion might be assisted by the opinion of persons noted for prudence and experience in pastoral and theological matters. The parties may rely on advisors or may mutually agree on a facilitator to assist in this task.

This task is concluded with a written statement of agreement, signed by both parties, specifying the steps taken to determine the implications in the life of the church and their mutual and individual conclusions. It may include actions agreed upon for the future. This written statement may suffice to resolve the dispute and conclude the dialogue, or even provide for continued review of the issue.

D. *Possible Results of Formal Doctrinal Dialogue*

Formal Doctrinal Dialogue may conclude in a variety of ways. It is important to identify the conclusion of the dialogue process and the outcome of the dispute itself. The degree of publicity to be given to the results of the dialogue should be carefully adapted to the particular situation. In every case, even if complete agreement has not been reached, both parties should discuss these matters so that both are aware of proposed actions.

These are some possible results of the dialogue:

1. The theological and pastoral issues may be resolved to the satisfaction of both parties at any stage in the formal dialogue.

2. At the conclusion of the formal dialogue the theological issue may be unresolved, but both parties may agree that the issue may remain so without the need for further action. Agreement to disagree may be a recognition of legitimate pluralism or of a situation in which pastoral responsibility requires no further action.

3. There may be no agreement concerning the theological and pastoral issues nor acceptance of the disagreement as a form of legitimate pluralism. In light of pastoral considerations, various responses on the doctrinal level are then possible. Such responses vary in purpose, intensity, and publicity. They may be mutually agreed upon or may be taken unilaterally by one of the parties. Before any doctrinal response is made, it is desirable that it be discussed between the parties. The following are some examples.

   a. Call for continued critical theological study.
   b. Expand the context of the dialogue to a regional or national level.
   c. Restate in a positive fashion authoritative church teaching.
   d. Issue a doctrinal *monitum,* i.e., a clear statement of concern about what is being taught.
   e. Declare publicly the apparent error of a position.
   f. Classify certain positions as one of the following:
      1) a private position which may be presented by itself, provided it is not represented as official Catholic teaching;
      2) a private opinion which, when presented, must be accompanied by other more acceptable positions;
      3) unsuitable for teaching by a Catholic.
   g. Make an accurate presentation of views to the media.

E. *Subsequent Administrative Action*

The foregoing procedure has been a doctrinal dialogue. The best response to bad teaching is good teaching. A doctrinal response is, therefore, the most desirable response to a doctrinal dispute. Nonetheless, when doctrinal differences begin to affect the common good and doctrinal dialogue has failed to resolve them, administrative action on the part of bishops or recourse on the part of theologians may be appropriate or even necessary.

Administrative procedures do not resolve doctrinal issues; they address pastoral situations. The kind and degree of administrative action should be proportionate to the pastoral requirements of the common good, and should be no more severe than those requirements demand.

The degree of understanding reached in the doctrinal dialogue should help all parties to appreciate their mutual concern for the good of the church and will influence the decision about any subsequent action or resource. In addition, the signed agreements of the Formal Doctrinal Dialogue will provide a valuable record for subsequent action on the part of bishops or recourse on the part of theologians. Differences of responsibility and authority, of course, can become especially apparent at this point. But this should not obscure the fact that doctrinal truth can not be decided or assured simply by juridical decisions. In all cases, bishops and theologians alike should recognize that administrative action is always in service to the truth of a gospel that is meant to set us free.

AFTERWORD

The church's witness and mission in the world are seriously conditioned by its own internal care for truth and justice. Disputes about doctrine and the manner of their resolution seldom remain purely internal affairs. On the contrary, our understanding and practice of faith today concern Christians and non-Christians alike. Publicity is an unavoidable part of modern life, encouraging broad examination of social questions, even though sometimes at the cost of civil courtesy. Our church can still learn much from our nation's civic values of freely expressed public opinion and constructive public debate. Thus, issues that arise in our community should be addressed with prudence and discretion, but also with realism about living in a pluralistic society and learning from it.

We also have much to contribute. We believe that, with the guidance of the Spirit, the many different parts of the body of Christ can be knit together in justice and love and thereby become more truly themselves before God. In seeking clear and equitable ways to resolve disagreements about our faith, we can recommit ourselves to being a church that is one and open, a genuine community of grace sharing the truth freely given to it. Thus we may choose again the life that has been offered to us, that there truly may be "one body and one Spirit, just as you were called to the one hope that belongs to your call, one Lord, one faith, one baptism, one God and Father of all, who is above all and through all and in all" (Eph 4:4-6).

APPENDIX A

Observations on the *Ratio agendi* of the Congregation for the Doctrine of the Faith

The Congregation for the Doctrine of the Faith [CDF] published its procedures for doctrinal investigations (the *"Ratio agendi"*) on January 15, 1971. The official Latin text is found in the *Acta apostolicae sedis* 63 (1971) 234-236 and an English translation in *Origins* 1 (1972) 648.

There are many positive aspects of the *Ratio agendi*. First, the very existence of a published procedure is a definite improvement over past practice of the CDF, which were totally secret. The present norms have been used several times, most notably with Hans Küng and Edward Schillebeeckx. Second, it provides for a thorough discussion of the issues before reaching a final decision. For example, in the initial investigatory phase, there is an elaborate process that involves lengthy deliberation between experts, a *relator pro auctore* (appointed by the Congregation to present the views of the theologian), the consultors, and the members of the CDF. The possibility of a hasty judgment is thus lessened. Third, it allows in its second phase for the theologian to reply in writing and to meet personally at a *colloquium* with representatives of the Congregation. Fourth, it attempts to preserve the principles of confidentiality. Fifth, the CDF itself has acknowledged the changeable nature of the procedures, and recognized the need for greater safeguards to be given to the theologian. Thus, it was announced in December 1982, that the CDF has accepted the proposals made by the West German and Swiss bishops to allow the theologian under examination to be defended by counsel at the hearings held by the Congregation.

The *Ratio agendi,* however, can be improved in several ways. If the procedures proposed in this document are accepted, then the CDF, in accord with the principle of subsidiarity, should refer to the theologian's ordinary any denunciation, delation, complaint, or question it receives concerning the orthodoxy of the theologian's publications or public utterances. A revised *Ratio agendi* should state that the CDF will ordinarily not enter a doctrinal dispute until it has been previously examined at the local level. Every attempt at resolution should be exhausted before the matter is finally brought to the CDF for judgment.

More specifically, any procedure that seeks to prevent or resolve a doctrinal conflict should manifest the principles of subsidiarity, shared responsibility, and legitimate diversity, and should guarantee the fundamental human and sacramental rights of the theologian. Serious consideration should therefore be given to the following recommendations, with a view to incorporating them in a revised version of the *Ratio agendi*.

1. The theologian should be informed of what the charges are and who made them.

2. The theologian should be involved earlier in the process. The present investigatory phase—basically designed to determine probable cause—is long and complicated and should be simplified. It takes place within the Congregation and the theologian is not consulted.

3. The norms should set definite time limits that would apply to both the Congregation and the theologian.

4. The theologian should be granted the right to suggest several names from among which the *relator pro auctore* is selected by the CDF.

5. The theologian should be granted access to all pertinent documentation.

6. The CDF should publish the procedures to be observed during the *colloquium*.

7. The theologian should have the right to know beforehand the names of the persons selected by the CDF to participate in the *colloquium* and to object to their presence for a sufficient reason.

8. The theologian should have the right to call witnesses at the *colloquium.*

9. The CDF should make its decision public, if the case has become public.

10. The CDF should clearly indicate appeal procedures. There are two possibilities:

    a. appeal to the Apostolic Signatura, if the theologian feels the CDF has exceeded its competence or failed to observe its own regulations; or

    b. appeal to the Pope, which would make sense only if prior papal approval of the CDF decisions (which is now mandated) were not required.

A *Ratio agendi* revised in these ways would better serve the church and would strengthen the bonds that already exist between bishops and theologians in their common quest for truth.

APPENDIX B

On the Possibility of a National Theological Commission

Cooperation between Theologians and the Ecclesiastical Magisterium, the Report of the Joint Committee of the Canon Law Society of America and the Catholic Theological Society of America, renewed a recommendation[1] that had previously been made in various quarters,[2] namely, that a National Theological Commission be established in the United States. This Appendix restricts itself to some basic comments on the purpose, constitution, and operation such a Commission might involve. A final paragraph concerns alternative possibilities.

1. *Purpose.* A National Theological Commission in the United States would be analogous in different respects to the International Theological Commission, to the doctrinal committees that have been established in some dioceses, and to the work of theological consultants who have attended meetings of the Bishops' Committee on Doctrine in the United States and elsewhere. The Commission should serve primarily as a consultative and advisory group, promoting theological exchange between bishops and theologians and in the church at large. Since its members would be drawn from different areas of theological study, it could also serve to foster cooperation among the different professional societies. Finally, in cases of doctrinal dispute, the Commission could serve an investigative purpose as well; members of the Commission, or a committee recommended by it, could be asked to assist in resolving theological disagreement through Formal Doctrinal Dialogue.

2. *Constitution.* To serve its purpose, the Commission should genuinely represent the theological community and relate responsibly to the National Conference of Catholic Bishops. It should not be simply a committee of either group, but should serve as a channel between them. This might be accomplished by having members nominated by the boards of the principal theological societies and then appointed by the Bishops'

---

[1]"In Service to the Gospel. A Consensus Statement of the Joint Committee," no. 22, p. 185.
[2]A prominent example: *On Due Process,* p. 10.

Committee on Doctrine or by the General Secretary, through whom the Commission could be related to the Conference. The chair of the Commission should be elected for a specified term by the Commission itself. Competence and representation should be the primary criteria of membership. For greater accountability and effectiveness, members of the Commission should be appointed for a term of some years' length but with a system of rotation within the Commission as a whole.

3. *Operation.* In accord with its purpose, the meetings of the Commission should be regular but not unnecessarily multiplied. Sessions might be held in conjunction with board meetings or annual conventions of the various theological societies or with the meetings of the related Committees of the Conference. The Commission should not be expected to undertake specifically commissioned studies; such long-term work is better left to permanent theological institutions or to the research projects of professional societies and individual theologians. In cases of dispute, when a theological opinion is requested of the Commission or its members, it should seek to offer advice imbued with theological integrity and pastoral sensitivity.

4. *Alternatives.* The needs served by a National Theological Commission might be addressed by alternate means.

a. Consultors for the Committee on Doctrine. In recent years the Bishops' Committee on Doctrine has invited theological consultants to meet with it. This approach has the advantages of efficiency and confidentiality. A disadvantage lies in the fact that the choice of consultants has depended wholly on the Committee on Doctrine, which may weaken the representative quality of the consultation.

b. Advice, on request, from the professional theological societies. When special expertise is needed for the discharge of pastoral responsibility or when coordination of theological research is desired, the boards of the theological societies can be consulted. An advantage here is that committees are not multiplied; a disadvantage is that theologians are selected on an *ad hoc* basis.

c. Referral to the Joint Committee of Catholic Learned Societies and Scholars. The JCCLSS was established precisely to foster communication between bishops and Catholic scholars. It has served this purpose chiefly through colloquia cosponsored with the Bishops' Committee on Doctrine. Such a format, however, facilitates exchange and communication only on a limited basis.

d. List of experts. At the very least, a brief listing of competent and representative experts in the various areas of theology should be available, whether for consultation by bishops or for cooperative work among theologians themselves. This would be advantageous for the purposes of consultation, cooperation, and Formal Doctrinal Dialogue (1, above).

SURVEY ON THE USE OF THE "VETITUM"

CHARLES A. GUARINO
WILLIAM A. VARVARO

On the following pages are the results of a questionnaire sent to every tribunal in the United States this past summer. These statistical results are based on a 77% return (out of 176 questionnaires sent out, 136 responses were received), which seems to indicate sufficient enough interest in the subject for the Canon Law Society of America to pursue the topic further, and perhaps provide national guidelines for a uniform approach throughout the country on the use of the vetitum.

Many tribunals expressed this desire for agreement among dioceses in the country regarding such aspects of the vetitum as:

1. Jurisdiction (i.e., who imposes it and who lifts it);
2. How to make the vetitum an effective instrument of the "healing ministry" that the tribunal seeks to pursue;
3. Guidelines to assist tribunal personnel and parish priests working together to prepare people for second marriages, etc.

While this survey and the presentation at the informal session Tuesday evening, October 11, do not pretend to answer all these questions or exhaust the topic, it is our hope that it will generate enough interest and discussion to provide us all with some direction for the future use of the vetitum and subsequent presentations on this important topic.

May we take this opportunity to thank all who contributed to this investigation by responding to the questionnaire and, in many cases, providing additional information which proved very helpful to our research.

* * * * *

1. In your diocese, when is a "vetitum" imposed on a marriage case (i.e., what are the circumstances or conditions which usually require the placing of the vetitum prior to a second canonical marriage)?

130 responded to the question with 448 responses, which indicates that some tribunals checked off more than one of the following:

a. severe mental illness (e.g., schizophrenia)	122	(27%)
b. personality disorders	100	(22%)
c. alcoholism or drug addiction	97	(22%)
d. physical brutality	84	(19%)
e. non-support of children from 1st marriage	20	(5%)
f. possible scandal arising from 2nd marriage	25	(5%)

Others specified:

    a. Other forms of psychological inability (gross immaturity; lack of competence for marriage, i.e., lack of due discretion, etc.)   21

    b. Intentions against children, fidelity or permanence existed in first marriage and/or presently exists   7

    c. The conditions affecting the civil dissolution still exist (e.g., cruel and inhuman treatment, etc.)   6

    d. As a positive preparation for marriage beyond what the parish priest is providing   5

    e. When the presiding judge deems it warrants the position of the vetitum   5

    f. Vetitum "never" used   4

    g. Repeated "behavioral pattern" which caused the breakdown of *several* previous marriages   3

    h. "Monitum" is used in place of "vetitum" (simply a "caution")   3

    i. Impotence, homosexuality, inhibited sex drive   2

    j. Contempt for tribunal process   2

    k. When a second marriage has already been planned even before the annulment has been decided   2

    l. Lack-of-faith commitment   2

    m. "Vetitum" seldom used   2

    n. In cases of simulation   2

    o. Radical incompatibility   1

    p. Perjury   1

    q. When the Petitioner prevented the respondent from being contacted   1

2. Who imposes the "vetitum"? 130 responded.

    a. The tribunal imposes the vetitum juridically and makes the recommendation to the chancery to enact it administratively.   121   (93%)

    b. The vetitum is imposed directly by the ordinary.   5   (4%)

    c. The vetitum is imposed directly by the chancery.   1   (1%)

    d. Left up to the parish priest or deacon officiant at the subsequent marriage.   1   (1%)

    e. No real way to enforce it.   2   (1%)

3. Who lifts the "vetitum"? 137 responded.

    a. Diocese that imposes the vetitum   81   (60%)

    b. Diocese where 2nd marriage is contemplated   49   (36%)

    c. Coordinated effort of both dioceses   4   (2%)

    d. Left up to parish priest or deacon   3   (2%)

4. Under what conditions is the "vetitum" lifted? 133 responded.

    a. After counseling is completed and report
of the expert received   85 (64%)
    b. Proof that the conditions under which the vetitum
had been imposed, have been fulfilled   35 (26%)
    c. When priest/deacon decides that person is
sufficiently stable to enter new marriage   11 (8%)
    d. Upon request and without question   1 (1%)
    e. Depends upon gravity of situation   1 (1%)

5. How often is a "vetitum" placed on cases in your diocese? 133 responded.

    Frequently   71 (53%)
    Infrequently   57 (43%)
    Never   5 (4%)
    Always   0

6(a) What requirements are made of the petitioner and/or the respondent before a "vetitum" is lifted? (Please explain.) 132 responded.

    1. Counseling has been received and an
evaluative report forwarded   112 (70%)
    2. Conditions under which vetitum had been
imposed are fulfilled   20 (13%)
    3. Positive recommendation by parish priest   17 (10%)
    4. Consult with chancery   6 (4%)
    5. Obstacles to a successful marriage no longer exist   4 (2%)
    6. Faith commitment is restored   1 (1%)

6(b) Do these requirements include the prospective spouse?

    Yes: 51 (62%)   No: 31 (38%)

7. If pre-marital counseling is required of the petitioner and/or the respondent, please describe the requirement.

    a. When does the counseling begin? 128 responded to the question, with 141 responses, which indicates that some tribunals checked off more than one of the following.

    1. When the annulment has been granted   66 (47%)
    2. It is left up to the petitioner and/or the respondent 57 (40%)
    3. After the judicial hearing   17 (12%)
    4. Left up to the judgment of the priest/deacon   1 (1%)

    b. What is the average amount of counseling required? 124 responded.

    1. Varies greatly   104 (84%)
    2. Less than one year   18 (14%)
    3. One year or more   1 (1%)
    4. As much as needed   1 (1%)

    c. In general, how effective is the counseling requirement? 124 responded.

    1. Very effective   63 (51%)

2. No definite results or follow-up	35	(28%)
3. Not very effective	9	(7%)
4. Varies greatly	4	(3%)
5. Depends on personalities	4	(3%)
6. Not effective for respondent	2	(2%)
7. Often ignored by parish priests	2	(2%)
8. Bishop relents under pressure	1	(1%)

  d. Further comments:

1. Counseling requirements should be left up to parish priest/deacon preparing for marriage.	5
2. Practice of requiring counseling should be made standard in country.	3
3. Separate diocesan office should be established to prepare for second marriages.	2
4. Petitioner is more cooperative than respondent regarding counseling.	2

8. If you do not use the "vetitum," what action do you take regarding an intended marriage where potential grave scandal may result? 47 responded.

a. Such concern is left up to the parish level.	19	(41%)
b. No policy exists.	9	(20%)
c. Matter is referred to Chancery or Bishop.	5	(11%)
d. Judge works this out himself.	3	(6%)
e. Scandal is not a problem today.	3	(6%)
f. Change of jurisdiction for new marriage is recommended, if scandal would be local.	2	(4%)
g. Recommend extensive counseling.	2	(4%)
h. Suggest they petition Rome for annulment.	1	(2%)
i. Case is abandoned and remarriage not allowed.	1	(2%)
j. Use appeal process and collegial tribunal.	1	(2%)
k. Correspond with both parties regarding the possibility of scandal, and reconcile the problem with them.	1	(2%)

9. In our presentation of this topic, "the use of the vetitum . . .," what points would you like covered in the discussion?

  a. Provide national guidelines for a uniform approach on the part of all dioceses regarding the use of the vetitum.

  b. Distinguish between a "vetitum" and a "monitum"; what are the criteria that should be applied in imposing a vetitum; what is the efficacy of a vetitum? (Is it a means of punishing uncooperative clients?)

  c. Who has jurisdiction over the imposing and lifting of the vetitum? How long should the vetitum last?

  d. What is the canonical liceity of the vetitum? Should it be the concern of a marriage tribunal to prevent future, possibly scandalous, marriages; or should this not be the concern of the parish level?

e. Stress the "healing" aspect of the tribunal procedure and any counseling recommendations that are made by way of a "vetitum."

f. What effectiveness is there in the counseling recommendation? How do we protect the confidentiality of the acts when sharing this information with third parties such as counselors?

g. Stress greater cooperation and sharing of information between the tribunal and the parish priests/deacons preparing couple for marriage.

h. Establish in every diocese a diocesan office responsible for preparing people for second marriages, coordinating the findings of the tribunal and/or the medical expert and the required counseling and any other conditions that must be fulfilled before another canonical marriage is allowed.

i. How to handle "recidivists"—those who are applying for a second annulment when permission for this second marriage that has ended was based on a counseling evaluation that stated the couple were psychologically capable of entering, validly, a new canonical marriage.

j. Can an "invalidating vetitum" be established as an impediment to marriage?

COMMITTEE REPORTS

Committee: **Commentary on the Code**

Constituted: Board of Governors, February, 1980, implementing initial decision to approve commentary in October, 1979

Charge: To expedite the preparation of commentaries on various schemata of the new law

Membership: James A. Coriden
Thomas J. Green
Donald E. Heintschel

Annual Report

During the past year the committee members have been in continuing contact both with the individual authors working on sections of the commentary and with Paulist Press, which is publishing the commentary. The main thrust of committee activity has been to expedite the preparation of manuscripts for publication, especially after the promulgation of the 1983 Code in January, 1983.

During the year two memoranda were sent to the individual authors by the committee clarifying different aspects of their role in the preparation of the commentary and making available to them certain resources deemed necessary to facilitate their task.

For various reasons several personnel changes had to be made regarding authors involved in the commentary project. However, the respective authors of the various sections of the commentary have generally done their work fairly expeditiously. At present approximately 75% of the final drafts of the commentary has been completed and forwarded to Paulist Press for publication. It is hoped that the rest of the copy will be completed by the end of October.

The members of the committee met twice with representatives of Paulist Press to expedite the process, once in October, 1982 shortly after the convention and again in January, 1983. There has been continuing contact with Ms. Maria Maggi, one of the copy editors at Paulist, especially as regards the preparing of final drafts of manuscripts for publication.

The committee members were also involved in the demanding task of preparing an English translation of the 1983 Code, which was finally approved by the NCCB canonical affairs committee in early October.

The committee members are making every possible effort to see to the speedy publication of the commentary. If all goes well, it should be available in the early spring of 1984.

Committee: **Joint CLSA-CTSA Committee on Cooperation Between Theologians and the Ecclesiastical Magisterium**

Constituted: Board of Governors, 1980

Charge: To research and develop possible norms to assist in the cooperation of theologians and the ecclesiastical magisterium

Membership: John A. Alesandro
John P. Boyle
Robert J. Carlson
Patrick Granfield, O.S.B.
Jon Nilson
Leo J. O'Donovan, S.J., Chairperson
James H. Provost

Annual Report

The Joint Committee completed the first phase of its work with the publication of the research papers and a consensus statement it had developed. These appeared in 1982 under the title of *Cooperation Between Theologians and the Ecclesiastical Magisterium* (Washington, DC: CLSA, 1982; $5.00 each). The second stage of the committee's work was completed during this past year and has resulted in a final report submitted for consideration by the two sponsoring societies.

Entitled *Doctrinal Responsibilities*, the report attempts to summarize the results of the research the committee was commissioned to undertake, and proposes possible norms and procedures to assist in the cooperation of theologians and the ecclesiastical magisterium on doctrinal matters. The report does not address disciplinary or administrative questions, but focuses on the specifically doctrinal relationship and how it can be promoted and supported. The report also suggests a step-by-step approach which can be used in situations of doctrinal disputes. The procedure is one of structured dialogue as recommended by various authorities, including the International Theological Commission.

With the submission of this final report, the committee has completed its charge and goes out of existence.

Committee: **Marriage Research**

Constituted: 35th Annual Meeting, 1973

Charge: To coordinate research into the theology of marriage

Membership: Thomas P. Doyle, O.P., editor
Edward J. Dillon
Ellsworth Kneal
Michael Place

Annual Report

The BOG decided to renew the *Marriage Studies* project for a period of three years. Thomas Doyle, O.P., was retained as editor. Ellsworth Kneal, Edward Dillon and Michael Place were named as members of the editorial board. The editor and members communicated by mail and telephone in the past year but no meetings have been held.

The third edition of *Marriage Studies* is presently under preparation. Thus far nine manuscripts are under consideration for publication in this issue. One is a translation from an article by Tomas Rincon which appeared in *Ius Canonicum*. The others are either talks given at conventions or articles prepared especially for *Marriage Studies*.

Before *Marriage Studies* came into being there was discussion of the mandate of the Marriage Research Committee. One of the areas of projected research was the various implications of the bond of marriage. The second volume contained an historical work on the role of the liturgical celebrant in the formation of the bond. The projected volume will contain two more articles in this area: one on the doctrinal implications of civil marriage between Catholics; the other is a study of Ephesians 5:21-33 and radical indissolubility.

Thus far *Marriage Studies* I and II have been reviewed twice in *Theological Studies* (by Ladislaus Orsy, S.J. and Theodore Mackin, S.J.) and once in *Worship* (by John Huels, O.S.M.)

The members of the CLSA are strongly urged to consider *Marriage Studies* as a possible source for publishing articles which they have written.

Committee: **Meetings and Regional Conferences**

Constituted: C.L.S.A. Constitution, Article X, 1 & 3

Charge: The function of the Committee on Meetings and Regional Conferences shall be:

    a. To choose a place for the Annual General Meeting of the Society, subject to the approval of the Board of Governors; as far as it may be possible, two consecutive meetings shall not be held in the same region.

    b. To promote the formation and continued life of regional conferences.

    c. To act as liaison between existing regional conferences and this Society, especially by the attendance of one or more of its members, whenever possible, at regional meetings.

Membership: Glenn D. Gardner, Chairperson
Bob Cunningham
Ed Holen

Annual Report

The Committee prepared a listing of three possible cities for the 1988 convention of the Canon Law Society. The cities of Cleveland, Cincinnati and Baltimore were submitted; the Board of Governors selected Baltimore as the site. The contact persons in Baltimore are the Reverend Jeremiah Kenney and the Reverend Michael Schleupner.

A report was given to the Board of Governors pertaining to possible changes in the "selection" process in regards to future convention cities. The Board was to discuss this proposal and submit their conclusions to the Chairperson of the Committee.

Committee:	**Membership and Nominations**

Constituted: CLSA Constitution, Article X, 1 & 5.

Charge: The functions of the Committee on Membership and Nominations shall be:

   a. To submit to active members, at least one month prior to the date of election, the names of nominees as provided for in Article IX of this Constitution.

   b. To propose for approval of the Board of Governors applicants for active membership under the exceptive clause of Article III, No. 1 of this Constitution and to propose for honorary membership in the Society those who, in its opinion, qualify according to Article III.

   c. To formulate and recommend to the Board of Governors plans for maintaining and increasing the membership of the Society.

Membership: William V. Sullivan, Chairperson
Harmon D. Skillin
Charles Torpey
James K. Mallett, Treasurer, ex officio non-voting member

Annual Report

As done in prior years, the CLSA membership was requested through the CLSA Newsletter to submit to the committee names for nomination at the 1983 Annual Convention in San Francisco. Over twenty replies were received together with nearly an equal number of suggestions obtained in the course of the committee's consultation.

The committee attempted a geographical balance as well as trying to include among the nominees canonists versed in different aspects of the law and involved in different ministries.

The following slate was completed in August, 1983:

   Vice-President: William A. Logar, Stockton, CA
                    Msgr. William A. Varvaro, Brooklyn, NY
   Secretary: James Parizek, Davenport, IA
                    Robert Fisher, Reno-Las Vegas, NV
   Treasurer: James K. Mallett, Nashville, TN (incumbent)
   Consultor: Richard J. Cunningham, Boston, MA
                    Thomas G. Doran, Rockford, IL
                    Bertram Griffin, Portland, OR
                    John Huels, O.S.M., Chicago, IL
                    Ellen M. O'Hara, C.S.J., Boise, ID
                    Stanley J. Teixeira, Fresno, CA

Article III, No 1 states: "Without prejudice to the status of persons who are members at the time of the adoption of this article, active membership is henceforth restricted to those who have earned at least a Licentiate in Canon Law, unless an applicant shall, in the opinion of the Membership and Nominations Committee, have gained a broadly based competence in canonical issues through work in canonical affairs and/or the projects of the Canon Law Society of America for a significant period of time or who, while being a practitioner of the law in one or more areas for over a year, is sponsored by an active member; application for active status on this latter basis shall in each instance be proposed by the Committee on Membership and Nominations to the Board of Governors for approval of active status."

There were seventeen applications submitted through the office of Executive Coordinator in this past year which were then conveyed to the Board of Governors. The criteria set by the CLSA Constitution for active and associate members have been observed.

The Committee's experience of this past year in inviting members to stand for elective office prompts the additional note that many have either refused or have been unable, because of other duties, to accept nomination. The time commitment of the officers and Board of Governors members as well as the Society's expectation of its officers may need to be addressed in the future.

Charge: To serve CLSA as a resource body in the area of law for religious and to aid the CLSA membership in understanding the law for religious

Membership: Jordan Hite, T.O.R., Chair
Sharon Holland, I.H.M.
Daniel Ward, O.S.B.

Annual Report

The project to publish a practical, pastoral commentary on the section of the 1983 code for institutes of consecrated life and societies of apostolic life is nearing completion. The final editing will be completed from September 30-October 15. There are twelve contributors to the project. The committee members are acting as both contributors and editors. Publication is projected for Spring of 1984.

The committee has submitted a proposal to the Board of Governors that CLSA, CMSM, LCWR and the Vicars for Religious form a committee comprised of a representative of each group to aid religious in understanding the implications of church law in the lives of their institutes.

Committee: **Research and Discussion**

Constituted: CLSA Constitution, Art. X, 1 & 4.

Charge: The functions of the Committee on Research and Discussion shall be:

      a.Above all to work for the attainment of those purpose of the Society stated in Article II of the Constitution.

      b.To submit to the Board of Governors for approval the names of speakers and topics for discussion at the Annual General Meeting.

      c.To initiate or cooperate in all research projects of the Society such as seminars, symposia and special studies relative to research and discussion and to recommend to the Board of Governors honoraria for participants in these studies as well as for speakers at the Annual General Meeting.

      d.To cooperate with the Executive Coordinator in arranging for all publications of the Society.

Membership: John J. Myers, Chairperson
Royce Thomas
Thomas E. Molloy

Annual Report

The R. & D. Committee composed of Otto Garcia (Brooklyn, retiring member), John J. Myers (Peoria) and Royce Thomas (Little Rock) met with the B.O.G. at their Pre-Convention meeting at Hartford. Myers and Thomas attended the Post-Convention B.O.G. meeting at which a preliminary review of the convention was held and further details were determined for the San Francisco Convention in October, 1983.

President Robert Becker appointed Thomas E. Molloy of Rockville Center to the Committee in late 1982. He joined Myers and Thomas at Holy Trinity Seminary in Dallas on January 19 and 20, 1983. Molloy assumed responsibility for completing the Tribunal Statistics to be included in the 1983 Convention Packet. The meeting was to evaluate the Hartford Convention, consider research projects, complete work on the San Francisco Convention and undertake preliminary planning for the 1984 Convention in Milwaukee.

A detailed evaluation of Hartford was prepared for the B.O.G. The Convention was well-received. There was some opinion that the Liturgies should be re-thought. The relatively small number of Critique Forms returned suggested that more attention be given to the evaluation process in the future.

Only one research proposal was received. It called for the CLSA to produce a revised "Practical Formula for Marriage Forms." The Committee sent the proposal to the B.O.G. with recommendations. Since educational efforts are currently taking so much of the attention and energy of members, the Committee initiated no research proposals. They undertook the needed Convention planning. Royce Thomas presented these matters to the Board at their meeting at the same location on January 20-23.

The Committee members met with the "Mini-B.O.G." composed of Anthony Diacetis, Sharon Holland, and James Parizek at the Fullerton Cenacle in Chicago on April 27 and 28. The primary business was to complete detailed planning for the 1984 Convention. Thomas presented the resulting proposals to the B.O.G. which met at the same site from April 28-May 1.

Committee: **Resolutions**

Constituted: CLSA Constitution: Article X, I

Charge: The function of the Committee on Resolutions shall be:

    a.To solicit, develop and draft proposed resolutions which will express the concerns of the Canon Law Society.

    b.To consult with the membership at large and, in particular with the Board of Governors, the standing and ad hoc committees of the Society and the organizers of the convention.

    c.To formulate resolutions on given points in response to requests of the members of the Society.

    d.To compose differences in the formulation of similar proposals and to revise all proposals so that the meaning of each is clear.

    e.To encourage resolutions which authentically express in a positive way the activities and concerns of the Society.

Membership: George E. Mockel, Chairman

                  Jay T. Maddox

                  Adrian Claire Wolfe

Annual Report

The Resolutions Committee requests resolutions from the Chairperson of the Standing and Ad Hoc Committees of the C.L.S.A. making itself available for preparation of resolutions in advance of the coming convention. These resolutions as they were received were forwarded to the general convention chairperson for inclusion in pre-convention mailings to the entire membership. The general membership, through the C.L.S.A. newsletter has been informed of how to submit resolutions for convention consideration. Any resolutions would be included in the convention packet to be mailed and any further resolutions received by Tuesday of the convention week will be distributed for consideration by the general membership.

Resolutions are considered carefully at the business meeting on Tuesday of convention week and then prepared in their final form for presentation and voting on the Wednesday meeting. In this way, the activities and concerns of the Society and all of its members can be positively and authentically expressed.

Committee: **Symposium on Diocesan Governance**
Constituted: B.O.G., Spring, 1982
Director: James K. Mallett

Annual Report

A group designated as the Symposium Leadership met in Cleveland, Ohio on March 11-13, 1983 to discuss the development of a Symposium on Diocesan Governance as commissioned by the Board of Governors of the Canon Law Society of America. The following persons represented the Canon Law Society: James K. Mallett, John J. Myers, Roy M. Klister, and John E. Lynch, (Robert J. Carlson was unable to attend). Rev. Msgr. Francis Barrett represented the National Catholic Education Association. Rev. Thomas J. Harvey represented the National Conference of Catholic Charities. Rev. James Picton represented the National Pastoral Planning Conference. Rev. Msgr. Vincent A. Tartarczuk represented the Diocesan Fiscal Management Conference. Rev. Jerome Thompson represented the National Organization for Continuing Education of Roman Catholic Clergy. Rev. Robert E. Johnson represented the National Federation of Priests' Councils. Sister Barbara Garland represented the National Association of Church Personnel Administrators. Edward M. Sullivan, Ph.D. represented the Center for Applied Research in the Apostolate. The following scholars, invited to participate by the CLSA, were also present: Sister Agnes Cunningham, Rev. George Sarauskus, Rev. Philip Murnion, and Rev. Thomas Curry.

It was decided that three groups would be required to complete the work of the symposium: (a) a group to assume *editorial* responsibilities for various background studies, i.e., historical, theological, canonical studies from which principles and norms can be derived to guide the recommendations made by the symposium; (b) a group to *design* a practical tool for diocesan governance, including organizational charts and models, job descriptions, recommendations for management processes, etc.; (c) a group to develop and promote plans for broader *consultation* with diocesan ordinaries, the leadership of organizations represented in the Symposium Leadership, and other invited persons.

The editorial group is now deciding the topics to be addressed in the background studies. The design group is meeting prior to the San Francisco Convention to begin its work. It is proposed that the consultation group meet in winter of 1984 to discuss processes for broader consultation.

The background studies are scheduled for publication before the end of 1985. The work of the design group should be completed shortly thereafter, and all consultations on this published material should be finalized no later than June 1987.

The Lilly Endowment and the Raskob Foundation have made restricted grants for the symposium totaling $11,000. It is anticipated that the Society will be able to absorb additional costs.

Final approval to the recommendations made by the Symposium Leadership will be given after authorization is received from the Board of Governors prior to the San Francisco Convention.

Committee: **Syndicated Column "New Law and Life"**

Constituted: B.O.G. Spring, 1983

Director: Elissa Rinere, C.P.

Annual Report

Through most of the summer, requests for written contributions for the column were sent out. Twenty-five questions were sent to twenty-five people. Eight responses were received. This 32% return prompted the placing of a "Special Request" in the convention packet. The hope is that self-volunteered writers will be more dependable about deadlines, etc.

Six of the eight responses received were edited and given to Vivian Stephenson, editor of the Connecticut diocesan newspaper, *The Transcript*, whose office is coordinating the syndication process. The first step of this process is the promotion and sale of the column.

The only change suggested by Vivian when we discussed promotion material was that the names and cities of residence of the writers should be used in the column rather than initials, as was originally proposed. She feels that a strong selling point for the column will be the credibility of the writers and for this reason they should be identified for both buyers and readers. Also, rather than setting up a post office box for the receipt of any questions from readers, the mailing address of the Hartford Chancery will be used. Changes in this arrangement can be made later on, if necessary.

As of September 21 *The Transcript* office plans to have a promotional flyer sent out to 150 diocesan and national Catholic newspapers by mid-October, with responses coming back in about two weeks. Publication in those newspapers which purchase the column will begin toward the end of November.

Immediately after the convention, I will begin again to contact writers, hopefully adding to my already existing list of eight "reliables." Assuming that this happens, I do not anticipate any difficulty in preparing one column a week for at least the next six months to a year.

Committee: **Women in the Church**

Constituted: 35th Annual Meeting, 1973

Charge: To continue the study of the status of women and to address itself to the achievement of an equality for women in the Church's law

Membership: Judith A. Barnhiser, Chairperson
Cecilia M. Bennett
Harmon D. Skillen

Annual Report

At the October, 1982 convention, the Committee on Women in the Church met to review its work. The BOG the previous year had endorsed the Committee's proposed educational package as outlined in last year's *Proceedings* (cf. pp. 358-359). By the 1982 convention, the Committee had completed the first two parts of the package: a survey of the CLSA female membership and a description of canonical offices, functions and positions open to women under the revised Code.

With the endorsement of the BOG, preliminary work then was begun on the next parts of the package: an analysis of the survey of CLSA female membership, and proposed models for workshops/seminars on issues regarding women in the Church, vis-a-vis the revised Code of Canon Law.

The Committee met February 1-4, 1983, and completed the following tasks. (1) A complete analysis of the survey was done, which included the history and purpose of the Survey; the population studied; statistical and attitudinal analysis; observations and assumptions drawn from the analysis; and recommendations to the BOG and CLSA membership. (2) The Committee reviewed its October report on the survey of ecclesiastical offices, functions, and ministries open to women in the Church. Later, this was revised according to the promulgated text of the revised code. (3) Models for workshops on issues regarding women in the Church, vis-a-vis the revised code, were prepared. (4) An outline was prepared of the seminar the Committee would be giving at the 1983 national convention. The outline included the title, thrust, and resources to be used. (5) Two resolutions were prepared for the 1983 national convention.

The succeeding months were spent finalizing the above projects. It was decided that the first three parts of the educational package would be distributed at the Committee's seminar as a Learning Handout and later printed in the 1983 *Proceedings*. The Committee will also prepare copies of this package for the BOG with the proposal that the Committee be supported in continuing on to the next phases of the package.

TRIBUNAL STATISTICS—1982

(Arch) Diocese	Formal Cases Presented	Formal Cases Accepted	Formal Cases Decided by Sentence	a) Involving Mixed Marriage	b) Involving 2 non-Catholics	Formal Cases Abandoned by Petitioner	"Informal Negative" Decisions
Albany	537		418	100	75	42	17
Alexandria-Shreveport	135	128	124	43	42	7	5
Allentown	444	370	183	52	31	174	74
Altoona-Johnstown	88	43	29	8	4	4	8
Amarillo	306	304	201	99	56	74	58
Anchorage	105	85	62	28	29	5	5
Arlington	291	261	179	62	45	16	30
Atlanta							
Austin	294	195	165	54	51	4	1
Baker	339	339	177			127	1
Baltimore	606	609	504	201	167	40	86
Baton Rouge							
Beaumont	300	252	251	52	85	1	50
Belleville	296	259	259	66	96	22	34
Biloxi	150	114	20			5	12
Birmingham	138	138	104	38	23	6	0
Bismark	82	82	40	9	10	2	0
Boise	250	210	237	55	75	24	0
Boston	1948	1816	1161			132	663
Bridgeport	350	202	187		8	72	6
Brooklyn	1654	926	703	117	16	728	0
Brownsville							
Buffalo	530	288	238	77	33	3	115
Burlington	206	158	161	32	26	36	0
Camden	322	170	133			12	60
Charleston	187	185	98			6	0
Charlotte	93	79	62	9	31	3	6
Cheyenne	234	234	143	39	58	4	3
Chicago	3232	1872	1763	546	127	1356	69
Cincinnati	813	813	491	145	144	39	25
Cleveland	1008	1170	1022			42	76
Columbus	392	280	265	91	75	116	10

Sentences Appealed	Ligamen Decisions	Defect of Form	Ratum non Consummatum	Privilege of The Faith	Pauline Privilege	2nd Instance Decisions	3rd Instance Decisions	Full Time		Part Time		Total Expenses
								Prof	Secty	Prof	Secty	
3	8	234	0	1	1	0	0					177,834
1	15	82	0	0	0	0	0	3	2	1		95,600
0	7	85	0	0	0	0	0	2	4	14	1	
1	7	57	0	12	3	0	0	4	1	2	1	25,000
0	8	59	0	0	4	0	0	1	0	6	2	30,636
0	7	43	0	0	0	0	0					55,832
6	20	128	0	15	3	0	0	1	2	4	0	65,699
								5	3	2	1	
5	24	125	0	2	2	0	0	1	3	1		
0	16	24	0	2	10	0	0	1	1	1	1	30,000
4	23	328	0	21	3	274	0	5	4	24	1	212,910
								1	1	4	2	
4	24	129	0	0	0	0	0	1	2	2	1	47,000
0	6	96	0	6	5	0	0	3	1	3	1	95,000
0	1	59	0	3	0	0	0	1	1	10	2	
0	9	37	0	0	0	0	0	2	1	8	1	32,961
24	5	39	0	2	0	0	0		1	33	3	11,198
4	34	120	0	8	4	0	0					?
0	8	644	0	5	2	17	0	5	7	0	3	166,859
1	99	0	7	0	0	0						136,000
1	1	590	0	3	1	0	0	12	12	12	1	552,900
0	6	242	0	22	2	0	0	3	3	2	1	72,646
0	10	93	0	2	1	0	0	4	1	3	2	
8	7	13	2	23	3	0	0	2	4	2	0	70,576
95	3	33	0	0	0	0	0	1	2	3	2	21,661
4	11	32	0	0	1	0	0	0	1	0	0	8,793
0	33	73	0	0	2	0	0	1		7	2	34,462
17	34	981	0	87	2	42	2	13	14	10	2	532,643
4	24	288	0	20	13	19	1	7	6			155,000
0	52	514	0	11	5	0	0	8	9	9	0	247,000
12	20	127	0	42	2	0	0	2	3	4	2	

TRIBUNAL STATISTICS—1982

(Arch) Diocese	Formal Cases Presented	Formal Cases Accepted	Formal Cases Decided by Sentence	a) Involving Mixed Marriage	b) Involving 2 non-Catholics	Formal Cases Abandoned by Petitioner	"Informal Negative" Decisions
Corpus Christi	165	165	155	32	35	14	0
Covington	390	371	239	52	86	0	19
Crookston	87	74	65	25	10	11	0
Dallas	450	418	422	120	174	66	70
Davenport	291	188	114	24	37	246	3
Denver	470	375	165	78	28	74	50
Des Moines	145	109	113	22	47	3	5
Detroit	1059	999	984	196	334	80	0
Dodge City	104	104	121	58	20	47	10
Dubuque	674	674	431	?	?	167	57
Duluth	170	152	122			19	0
El Paso	160	142	139	18	21	16	14
Erie	384	217	197	64	18	34	4
Evansville	140	140	122	30	23	18	0
Fairbanks	47	30	11	1	7	5	1
Fall River	130	130	83			13	25
Fargo	253	253	115	48	20	47	118
Fort Wayne-South Bend	212	212	169	40	39	33	25
Fort Worth	328	328	323	69	150	3	0
Fresno	301	301	102	26	27	44	2
Gallup							
Galveston-Houston	621	507	439	117	131	123	0
Gary							
Gaylord	132	125	133	46	28	3	11
Grand Island	162	144	114	27	46	11	10
Grand Rapids	304	292	395	98	82	5	6
Great Falls	172	131	114	35	41	34	41
Green Bay	413	409	343	113	17	5	29
Greensburg	253	218	194	60	68	9	0

Sentences appealed	Ligamen Decisions	Defect of Form	Ratum non Consummatum	Privilege of The Faith	Pauline Privilege	2nd Instance Decisions	3rd Instance Decisions	Full Time Prof	Full Time Secty	Part Time Prof	Part Time Secty	Total Expenses
5	10	115	0	0	0	0	0	0	3	3	0	68,966
0	8	74	0	2	3	0	0	3	2	6	0	50,634
0	5	18	0	0	0	0	0	2	1	7	0	44,210
5	52	195	0	1	0	8	0	4	6	5	2	148,706
0	12	76	0	25	6	0	0	2	3	1	1	90,000
2	10	298	0	18	9	3	0	2	2	1	2	61,034
4	10	52	0	13	0	0	0	2	1	24		43,052
5	51	632	0	33	22	12	1	10	9	28		300,359
1	15	35	0	0	1	0	0	2	2	2	1	9,450
0	15	115	0	4	1	23	0	5	1	1	1	58,617
1	7	56	0	0	0	0	0	2		1	5	53,584
2	2	119	0	0	0	0	0					36,917
5	2	87	0	13	2	0	0	5	3	56	1	92,000
0	11	57	0	33	6	0	0	3	2	3	0	71,695
0	2	21	0	0	0	0	0	2		2	1	18,280
7	3	140	0	1	0	0	0	3	2	22		
2	5	62	0	4	0	0	0	3	1	15	12	27,400
0	14	100	0	27	3	0	0	5	4	32	1	172,078
2	50	124	0	0	3	0	0	2	2		1	40,000
1	6	139	0	4	5	1	0					65,410
7	66	492	0	48	11	0	0	2	2	5	1	84,297
								2	2	2	0	
0	9	47	0	0	4	0	0	0	2	15	0	32,475
0	17	23	0	0	1	0	0	1	1	4		59,983
2	5	144	0	0	2	0	0	3	1	8	2	32,183
1	12	58	0	0	1	0	0	1	1	8	1	32,183
2	0	137	0	0	0	3	0	3	2	3	2	156,000
1	9	114	0	1	1	0	0	2	2	4		57,935

TRIBUNAL STATISTICS—1982

(Arch) Diocese	Formal Cases Presented	Formal Cases Accepted	Formal Cases Decided by Sentence	a) Involving Mixed Marriage	b) Involving 2 non-Catholics	Formal Cases Abandoned by Petitioner	"Informal Negative" Decisions
Harrisburg	523	320	425	124	146	38	40
Hartford	618	475	406			0	26
Helena	143	143	123	35	43	14	0
Honolulu	159	127	108	33	20	3	8
Houma-Thibodaux	93	93	103	20	10	3	1
Indianapolis	137	89	105	31	21	20	0
Jackson	157	98	64	16	30	4	0
Jefferson City	310	185	170	46	58	20	10
Joliet	453	303	237	52	40	2	150
Juneau	8	8	8	3	5	0	0
Kalamazoo	220	204	174	50	76	6	20
Kansas City, KS	205	205	232	32	100	249	0
Kansas City-St. Joseph	148		121	90	4	15	3
La Crosse	356	329	300	67	56	58	27
Lafayette, IN	204	102	69	19	17	7	4
Lafayette, LA							
Lake Charles							
Lansing	675	660	608	154	164	8	37
Lincoln	160	112	94			16	38
Little Rock	200	200	254	39	78	0	0
Los Angeles	978	522	474	120	350	180	151
Louisville	42	42	29	2	9	3	0
Madison	303	303	317	49	45	0	193
Manchester	609	591	546	163	39	35	140
Marquette	190	190	191	58	35	41	10
Memphis	179	179	151	48	87	18	9
Miami							
Military Ordinariate	541	541	314	82	128	107	0

Sentences Appealed	Ligamen Decisions	Defect of Form	Ratum non Consummatum	Privilege of The Faith	Pauline Privilege	2nd Instance Decisions	3rd Instance Decisions	Full Time		Part Time		Total Expenses
								Prof	Secty	Prof	Secty	
1	29	135	0	18	2	0	0	4	5	1	3	152,703
26	11	331	0	9	1	9	0	7	3	30		259,455
2	15	37	0	0	4	0	0	0	1	17	1	28,000
0	3	111	0	0	8	0	0	1	1	7	2	27,669
1	3	68	0	0	0	0	0	11	1	0	0	26,000
2	30	133	0	51	11	0	0	7	4	10	2	214,600
0	8	19	0	3	1	0	0	1	1	1	0	35,535
3	12	39	0	2	2	0	0					40,000
8	7	228	0	6	1	0	0	3	5	2	1	145,557
0	2	2	0	0	0	0	0	0	0	4	2	2,109
0	15	79	0	0	13	0	0					10,000
61	14	68	0	0	2	63	0	2	1		1	37,000
1	37	68	0	5	9	4	0	3	1	0	0	51,900
1	33	76	0	13	0	0	0	3	4	3	1	112,522
10	9	32	0	23	4	0	0	2	3	14	3	
2	40	214	0	0	27	0	0			5	2	30,000
0	11	40	0	2	0	0	0			14	2	
48	19	69	0	0	4	0	0	2	2	0	0	42,911
10	80	973	0	58	26	13	0	6	9	10	6	
3	23	170	1	48	8	0	1	1	3	6	0	
2	7	80	0	3	0	0	0	4	2	2		
10	7	162	0	4	5	0	0	2	3	6	2	
0	3	47	0	0	0	0	0	1		1	1	29,361
1	23	63	0	1	1	0	0	1	1	5	0	32,060
								6	6	2		
1	9	268	0	0	4	0	0	2	4	200-300	0	102,980

TRIBUNAL STATISTICS—1982

(Arch) Diocese	Formal Cases Presented	Formal Cases Accepted	Formal Cases Decided by Sentence	a) Involving Mixed Marriage	b) Involving 2 non-Catholics	Formal Cases Abandoned by Petitioner	"Informal Negative" Decisions
Milwaukee	1178	1180	1276	295	220	65	44
Mobile	230	181	106	27	44	31	0
Monterrey	105	43	19	5	1	6	1
Nashville	275	260	101			48	0
Newark	882	749	583	174	29	60	40
New Orleans	471	368	355	72	49	31	0
Newton (Grk.-Melkite)	15	7		5		8	0
New Ulm	99	99	62	20	13	40	8
New York	628	628	596			32	1
Norwich	221	179	175	40	15	42	4
Oakland	230	170	170	36	36	5	54
Ogdensburg	556	276	136	26	6	99	40
Oklahoma City	346	314	253	75	119	85	28
Omaha	219	210	180	39	42	44	30
Orange	582	578	417	91	103	43	4
Orlando	555	538	419	128	119	86	67
Owensboro	30	1	1			0	20
Parma	18	18	15	4		2	0
Passaic	32	32	16	5	1	1	0
Paterson	252	229	199	50	19	36	6
Pensacola-Tallahassee	83	77	26	13	8	3	6
Peoria	416	109	87	27	23	6	85
Philadelphia							
Philadelphia (Ukr.)	44	22	16	10	3	0	8
Phoenix	612	309	261	74	59	384	16
Pittsburgh	725	503	619	115	73	2	320
Pittsburgh (Byz.-Ruthen.)	16	14	14	0	3	2	0
Portland, ME	555	555	347	84	22	36	30
Portland, OR	297	297	259	58	66	6	25
Providence	498	498	459			11	
Pueblo	118	95	76	15	19	22	7

Sentences Appealed	Ligamen Decisions	Defect of Form	Ratum non Consummatum	Privilege of The Faith	Pauline Privilege	2nd Instance Decisions	3rd Instance Decisions	Full Time Prof	Full Time Secty	Part Time Prof	Part Time Secty	Total Expenses
4	19	434	0	1	1	3	0	5	4	10	1	142,737
1	2	50	0	0	0	0	0	3	2	2	0	
19	4	65	0	1	4	0	0	2	1	8	1	43,131
3	13	71	0	2	0	0	0	3	3	2	0	65,000
2	6	381	0	2	0	13	0	6	6	30	0	237,278
7	7	322	0	3	0	5	0	4	2	11		97,100
0	1	0	0	0	0	0	0					300
0	3	22	0	1	0	0	0		1	5	1	31,000
11	11	564	0	32	3	22	0	11	15	3	4	484,000
0	2	119	0	7	1	0	0	2	1	2	1	
2	16	257	0	16	4	2	0	2	3	4	0	122,375
11	2	75	0	7	0	0	0	2	2	40		52,066
0	8	122	0	3	0	50	0	1	1	2	1	26,106
7	15	114	0	23	4	5	0	3	3	3	1	100,000
1	12	255	0	21	13	12	0	3	3	2	4	131,670
5	46	246	0	0	2	0	0	2	3	2	0	105,927
0	4	33	0	18	1	0	0	2	2	7		1,400
0	1	19	0	0	0	0	0			5	0	
0	2	9	0	0	0	0	0			9	1	4,225
2	4	127	0	1	0	0	0	2	2	6	0	45,000
0	4	62	0	0	0	0	0	1	1	3		38,371
4	15	131	0	64	4	0	0	2	2	2	1	96,255
								5	11	15	2	
0	1	20	0	0	0	0	0	1	0	1	1	1,200
0	25	215	0	0	8	0	0	5	3	9	3	92,261
2	8	427	0	8	4	4	0	3	4	31	0	158,031
0	3	10	0	0	1	0	0	0	0	6	1	
0	16	191	0	31	5	0	0	3	4	6	5	122,000
1	23	146	0	2	10	8	0					
2	5	263	0	5	0	0	0	7	4	1	1	161,433
3	13	59	0	1	1	0	0	1		9	1	14,807

TRIBUNAL STATISTICS—1982

(Arch) Diocese	Formal Cases Presented	Formal Cases Accepted	Formal Cases Decided by Sentence	a) Involving Mixed Marriage	b) Involving 2 non-Catholics	Formal Cases Abandoned by Petitioner	"Informal Negative" Decisions
Raleigh	168	118	64	20	31	6	9
Rapid City	106	99	68	31	37	7	0
Reno- Las Vegas	200	156	164	82	17	4	30
Richmond	625	501	303	90	115	27	124
Rochester	619	619	562	151	98	59	
Rockford	376	382	308	78	72	42	42
Rockville Centre	1560	572	536	124	36	19	988
Sacramento	154	150	127	46	10	39	3
Saginaw	289	289	222	58	47	16	
St. Augustine	206	206	154	40	58	0	0
St. Cloud	182	181	151	38	26	11	7
St. Louis							
St. Maron	50	40	42	8	3	4	2
St. Nicholas (Ukr.)							
St. Paul-Minneapolis	836	700	519	157	74	216	101
St. Petersburg	449	548	566	311	113	15	68
Salina	252	121	46	16	5	25	33
Salt Lake City	118	102	98	25	73	2	18
San Angelo	108	108	79	31	20	2	30
San Antonio	700	590	683	157	396	15	23
San Bernardino	343	308	217	57	56	11	52
San Diego	552	502	379	152	76	10	80
San Francisco	720	720	468			115	191
Santa Fe	167	162	69	32	17	3	5
Santa Rosa							
Savannah	190	71	68	21	32	1	4
Scranton	321	321	185	34	19	17	4
Seattle	689	689	677			49	124
Sioux City	142	124	155	29	47	10	14
Sioux Falls							
Spokane	157	157	175	57	41	22	0
Springfield-Cape G.	166	166	62	16	27	34	2

Sentences Appealed	Ligamen Decisions	Defect of Form	Ratum non Consummatum	Privilege of The Faith	Pauline Privilege	2nd Instance Decisions	3rd Instance Decisions	Full Time Prof	Full Time Secty	Part Time Prof	Part Time Secty	Total Expenses
0	8	57	0	3	0	0	0	1	1	2	1	42,237
0	3	28	0	0	0	0	0		1	4		16,730
1	30	199	0	0	12	0	0	4	2	5		85,000
1	20	176	0	1	0	0	0	3	4	15	1	117,421
0	19	188	0	0	1	0	0	3	1	1	1	73,254
1	23	140	0	13	3	0	0	8	6	5	0	
10	2	452	1	0	2	0	0	7	7		0	240,982
2	9	138	1	19	7	0	0	1	4	3	1	81,381
2	12	97			1	0	0		3	4		87,000
1	16	73	0	0	1	0	0					65,000
8	4	43	0	2	0	0	0	2	2	14	0	23,088
								6	3	30		
0	1	1	0	0	0	0	0					9,350
9	14	398	0	21	2	67	0	1	5	15	2	184,243
0	37	297	0	1	3	0	0	2	4	3		95,000
9	3	44	0	15	1	0	0			7	3	15,707
0	6	78	0	0	9	0	0	1	1	2	1	20,000
1	18	67	0	7	1	0	0					13,315
6	33	361	0	0	0	32	0	4	4	25	0	150,000
0	5	185	0	4	3	0	0	1.5	1.5	3		45,300
0	27	312	0	5	10	0	0	3	2	13	2	57,228
2	19	188	0	6	0	51	0	7	4	2	0	
1	9	154	0	0	1	1	0	2	3	12	0	
								2	1	4	0	
27	6	45	0	3	0	0	0	2	1	1	1	23,184
2	5	161	0	7	0	0	0	2	1	7	6	
0	83	294	0	3	5	0	0					131,493
2	1	54	0	9	1	0	0	1	1	2	1	44,976
0	21	65	0	0	5	0	0		1	3		41,358
5	5	45	0	10	1	0	0	2	1	3	2	45,575

TRIBUNAL STATISTICS—1982

(Arch) Diocese	Formal Cases Presented	Formal Cases Accepted	Formal Cases Decided by Sentence	a) Involving Mixed Marriage	b) Involving 2 non-Catholics	Formal Cases Abandoned by Petitioner	"Informal Negative" Decisions
Springfield, IL	284	284	217	45	48	42	0
Springfield, MA	639	639	590	116	46	3	1
Stamford (Ukr.-Byz.)	8	1	1	0	0	0	0
Steubenville	147	148	136	43	54	1	1
Stockton	92	92	89	27	19	14	0
Superior	80	78	55	24	5	3	2
Syracuse	648	648	583			65	0
Toledo	693	561	519	141	164	13	0
Trenton							
Tucson	139	127	57	34	23	21	33
Tulsa	225	177	121	34	60	0	46
Washington, D.C.	355	253	264			1	14
Wheeling-Charleston	131	103	82	37	16	10	12
Wichita	160	86	63	20	43	16	40
Wilmington	188	179	129	33	30	29	9
Winona	233	233	367	85	72	79	1
Worcester							
Yakima		130	82	15	50	5	45
Youngstown	388	333	350	60	53	20	25

Sentences Appealed	Ligamen Decisions	Defect of Form	Ratum non Consummatum	Privilege of The Faith	Pauline Privilege	2nd Instance Decisions	3rd Instance Decisions	Full Time Prof	Full Time Secty	Part Time Prof	Part Time Secty	Total Expenses
17	16	101	0	24	9	9	0	1	2	26	1	40,745
3	11	240	0	1	0	0	0	4	4	10		80,284
0	0	2	0	0	0	0	0	1	1	3	3	
1	9	64	0	0	3	0	0		1	3		44,866
8	2	0	0	0	2	0	0	0	1	3		30,752
0	4	56	0	2	1	0	0	1	1	1	0	
2	16	234	0	0	0	0	0	6	3	38	0	108,394
4	8	189	0	0	6	0	0	2	7	13	0	180,030
								5	5	4	1	
3	3	143	0	1	2	0	0	1	2	3	4	64,565
0	37	64	0	0	3	0	0	1	0	12	2	13,472
1	16	228	0	23	7	0	0	4	3	9	1	137,302
0	43	80	0	0	31	0	0	2	1	2	1	70,000
63	13	77	0	20	15	0	0			3	2	
2	21	71	0	2	0	0	0	4	2	10	1	
1	4	43	0	1	0	0	0	1	2	11		58,060
0	10	47	0			0	0	2	1	40	1.5	24,800
3	23	160	0	14	9	0	0	4	4	1	1	105,680

THE CANON LAW SOCIETY OF AMERICA
MINUTES OF THE FORTY-FIFTH ANNUAL MEETING

October 10-13, 1983
Golden Gateway Holiday Inn
San Francisco, California

Monday, October 10, 1983

Reception   4:30 p.m.-5:30 p.m.

New members and others interested in the organization and projects of the Canon Law Society of America were welcomed by the President, the Reverend Robert C. Becker. The Vice-President, the Reverend Anthony C. Diacetis, explained to the guests the organization of the CLSA, its structure of committees, and their workings. He invited the new members to active participation in the Society.

Opening Session   8:00 p.m.

The Reverend Robert C. Becker opened the forty-fifth Annual Meeting of the Canon Law Society of America, welcoming the assembled members and guests in the name of the Society. He then introduced the Most Reverend Daniel F. Walsh, Auxiliary Bishop of the Archdiocese of San Francisco. Bishop Walsh welcomed the Convention to San Francisco, expressed greetings from Archbishop John Quinn, and opened the meeting with prayer.

President Becker invited the visiting dignitaries from other canon law societies to be recognized. He explained the format of the meeting, gave a brief report of the work he has done as President during the past year, and spoke of interactions with other English-speaking canon law societies.

The President then presented the keynote speaker, Professor James A. Brundage, who offered the keynote address entitled "Canon Law as an Instrument for Ecclesial Renewal: An Historic Perspective."

Tuesday, October 11, 1983

Major Addresses   9:00 a.m.-10:30 a.m.

"Rights and Duties of Diocesan Bishops." Presented by the Reverend Thomas Green.

"Internal Governance in Consecrated Life." Presented by Sister Sharon Holland.

"Officials of the Tribunal: Terminology, Qualification, Responsibility." Presented by the Reverend Harmon Skillen.

Eucharistic Liturgy   11:00 a.m.

Celebrant and Homilist: The Reverend Robert C. Becker, President, CLSA.

316

Seminars 1:30-2:30 p.m.

1. "Authority and Obedience in Consecrated Life." Presented by the Reverend Richard Hill, S. J.

2. "Deceit/Error of Person as a Caput Nullitatis." Presented by the Reverend J. James Cuneo.

3. "Multiple Marriage." Presented by the Reverend Anthony Diacetis.

4. "Consecrated Life: Dispensations, Exclaustration, including Community Responsibility to Offer Assistance and Support." Presented by Sister Anne Fulwiler.

5. "Punishment for Individual Crimes." Presented by the Reverend William Wolfe.

Seminars 2:45 p.m.-3:45 p.m.

1. "Ecumenical Aspects of the New Law." Presented by the Reverend Otto Garcia.

2. "Confidentiality in Tribunals." Presented by the Reverend Edward Dillon.

3. "Rights and Duties of Pastors." Presented by the Reverend Thomas Doran.

4. "The Canonist: Obstructionist or Enabler for Women in the Church." Presented by the Committee on Women in the Church.

CLSA Open Hearing 4:00-6:00 p.m.

On budget and resolutions.

Informal Discussion 8:00 p.m.-9:00 p.m.

"The Use of the *Vetitum*." Presented by the Reverend Charles A. Guarino and the Reverend Monsignor William A. Varvaro.

Wednesday, October 12, 1983

Major Seminars 9:00 a.m.-10:30 a.m.

1. "Offices of the Diocesan Curia: Interrelationships and Creative Possibilities." Presented by the Reverend Charles Torpey.

2. "The Preliminary Experience of Mandatory Review in Diocesan Tribunals." Presented by the Reverend Daniel J. Murray.

3. "Laws and Non-Laws." Presented by the Reverend James A. Coriden.

4. "Collaboration: Key Concept for Religious and Bishops in the Diocese." Presented by Sister M. Thaddea Kelly.

Eucharistic Liturgy 11:00 a.m.

Celebrant and Homilist: The Reverend Anthony Diacetis, Vice-President, CLSA.

Seminars 1:30 p.m.-2:30 p.m. and 2:45 p.m.-3:45 p.m.

The seminar topics of Tuesday afternoon were repeated by the same presenters.

Business Meeting   4:00 p.m.-6:00 p.m.

The Reverend Robert C. Becker, President of the Canon Law Society of America, called the business meetng to order and led the assembly in praying the Lord's Prayer. The President noted that business would be conducted according to Robert's *Rules of Order,* with The Reverend John Proctor of San Diego acting as parliamentarian. Pointing out the separate seating for active and associate members, the President invited a motion to permit non-voting members the privilege of addressing the assembly. The Reverend Carl Pallasch of Chicago so moved, the motion was seconded and passed unanimously.

Minutes

The President indicated that the minutes of the last business meeting would be read unless he heard a contrary motion. The Reverend James O'Brien of Chicago moved to accept the minutes as published in the 1982 *Proceedings.* The motion was seconded and passed by unanimous vote.

Announcements from the Convention Chairperson

The Reverend James M. Carr, Convention Chairperson, made two announcements. He urged the membership to complete the critique forms for the benefit of the Research and Discussion Committee's use in evaluating the San Francisco Convention and for future planning. He then announced that a second dining room set for 100 persons would be necessary for the Wednesday dinner because of the unexpectedly large number attending the convention. The other dining room would be equipped with audio so that invocations and talks might be heard.

President Becker announced that there is to be a discussion on the *pagella* of faculties prepared by Reverend John Renken of Springfield in Illinois, following the address on Thursday morning. All were invited to the discussion to be led by the Reverend Monsignor John A. Alesandro of Rockville Centre, the Reverend Thomas Doran of Rockford, and Renken.

Election of Officers

The Reverend William V. Sullivan, Chairperson of the Membership and Nominations Committee, presented the slate of officers for election. Sullivan noted that the committee endeavored to reflect in its slate the various regions of the country and the varying canonical interests among the nominees. Recognizing the extra work of competent canonists this year, he encouraged CLSA members to respond positively when invited to stand for office. Finally, Sullivan invited the members to use the sheet provided in the convention packet for suggesting future nominees, which may be given to either the General Convention Chairperson or to the Executive Coordinator.

Sullivan then presented the following slate of nominees for election, asking each nominee to stand.

Office of Vice-President:
The Reverend William A. Logar of Stockton;
The Reverend Monsignor William A. Varvaro of Brooklyn.

318

The President opened the floor for other nominees, and since none were presented, he closed the nominations for the office of Vice-President.

Office of Treasurer

The Reverend James K. Mallett of Nashville.

President Becker closed the nominations for the office of Treasurer, no other nominees having come from the floor.

Office of Secretary

The Reverend James F. Parizek of Davenport;
The Reverend Robert Fisher of Reno-Las Vegas.

There being no other nominations from the floor, the President closed the nominations for the office of Secretary.

Sullivan directed the voting members to vote for one person for each of these three offices. There were six nominees for consultors, and members were to vote for three.

Office of Consultor

The Reverend Richard J. Cunningham of Boston;
The Reverend Thomas G. Doran of Rockford;
The Reverend Bertram F. Griffin of Portland;
The Reverend John Huels, O.S.M., of Chicago;
Sister Ellen M. O'Hara, C.S.J., of Boise;
The Reverend Stanley J. Teixeira of Fresno.

Sister Joan De Lourdes Leonard, C.S.J., of Rockville Center was nominated from the floor by Sister Anne Fulwiler. Her nomination was seconded, and Leonard accepted the nomination. Leonard's name was added to those being considered for the office of consultor. No further nominations being received, the President closed the nominations for this office and balloting began.

Report of the Treasurer

The Reverend James K. Mallett, Treasurer, referred the members to the Treasurer's five-page report contained in the convention packet. The report summarizes the assets, liabilities, and fund balances of the CLSA. He noted that the CLSA has a much greater cash position than last year; however, it is offset by liabilities to be noted below. He called attention to the publications inventory of $34,000, representing the inventory value of the books for sale in the office of the Executive Coordinator.

Total assets are equal to the total liabilities and fund balances: $248,000. Mallett explained the two types of liabilities, deferred revenues and restricted funds. Deferred revenues are those revenues which were received during the fiscal year reported but are deferred until the new fiscal year. The deferred revenues consist of the advanced dues collection ($46,000) which will be used to finance the ordinary operating expenses of the Society, and the advanced convention revenue which will be used to finance the expenses of this convention.

319

Something new this year is the revenue from the prepublication sale of the CLSA translation of the revised code, amounting to nearly $130,000. This revenue is deferred since the translation has not been published yet and the cost of publication has not been incurred.

The other category of liabilities are restricted funds, i.e., funds in which outsiders have vested interests. The Symposium on Diocesan Governance, a project of the CLSA, has received two restricted grants: $4000 from the Lilly foundation and $7000 from the Raskob foundation. A balance of $8,159 remains. The second restricted fund is that belonging to the Joint Committee of Catholic Learned Societies and Scholars. The Reverend James Provost, CLSA Executive Coordinator, is secretary of that group and he has accepted responsibility for managing their modest cash of $230. The other restricted fund is that for withholding employee taxes.

In accord with new guidelines for accounting and reporting issued by the NCCB, restricted funds are deemed liabilities since the CLSA does not have full control over their expenditure.

The most significant information in this report are the fund balances, the changes in which were explained by the Treasurer. The CLSA has five designated funds which are controlled by the Society. The operating fund, which began with a negative balance of $-13,000, now has a balance of $8,795. The convention fund started with a balance of $1,278 and now has a negative balance of $-1,952 because the revenue for this convention has not yet been released from the deferred revenue account. The workshop fund began with a balance of $26,000, from which $20,000 was transferred by the Board of Governors to the operating fund in order to fund the CLSA's operating expenses this year. Left with a new beginning balance of $6,000, the workshops held in Atlanta and Chicago this past Summer profited the Society approximately $11,000, which yields a new ending workshop fund balance of $17,000. Only a modest amount of the commentary fund has been spent. The total fund balances of $45,000 represents the net worth of the CLSA.

Turning to the statement of changes in the operating fund, Mallett noted that the revenue from the sales of publications is much larger than ordinary because of the sales of both the Latin code and the popular volume, *Code, Community, Ministry*. The deductions are largely within budget except for the Executive Coordinator's Office. The increased activity there required the hiring of additional temporary personnel, and so expenditures exceeded budget.

The Treasurer pointed out the two separate fund balances within the convention fund which show that the Hartford Convention profited the society $416. The San Francisco Convention is shown in the red because the deferred revenue has not yet been released from that fund. Deductions in the Workshop Fund represent the expenses of the Summer workshops. On the last page of the Treasurer's report is the statement of changes in restricted funds. The deductions shown represent costs of a three-day meeting in March for 18 persons in Cleveland.

Concluding his report, Treasurer Mallett invited questions from the members. There being none, President Becker commended the Treasurer on the clarity of his report.

Resolutions

The resolutions being the next item of business, the President first determined that there would be no additional resolutions coming from the floor. He then called on the Reverend George E. Mockel of Oakland, Chairperson of the Committee on Resolutions, to report on the resolutions. Copies of seven resolutions, some of which were amended in light of yesterday's hearings, were available at the entrances into the business meeting. Mockel announced that the wording of the entire resolution was open to discussion, but he would read only the dispositive portion of each resolution, that is, the "Be it resolved" clause.

RESOLUTION I

Whereas:

> 1. Bishop Michael F. McAuliffe, S.T.D., then Chairperson of the National Conference of Catholic Bishops' Committee on Women in Society, gave a report to the NCCB at its meeting in January, 1983 and in that report proposed that the NCCB "support an expanded dialogue with women and women's organizations in order to develop a substantive program of pastoral action to deal with issues that are of concern of women"; and
>
> 2. the Canon Law Society of America, principally through the work of its Committee on Women in the Church, is actively involved in developing programs dealing with canonical issues of interest to women;

Be it resolved:

> the Board of Governors of the Canon Law Society of America communicate to the NCCB and the NCCB Adhoc Committee on Women in Society its support of Bishop McAuliffe's proposal; and

Be it further resolved:

> the Board of Governors of the Canon Law Society of America offer the services of the CLSA's Committee on Women in the Church to assist the NCCB's Adhoc Committee on Women in Society in the development of its pastoral action programs dealing with issues of interest to women.

On behalf of the Committee on Resolutions, Mockel moved the acceptance of the resolution. Noting that no second was necessary since the resolution was moved by the Committee, President Becker called for discussion. He requested that participants identify themselves and that they keep their interventions within the established limits: five minutes for the presenters of resolutions; two minutes for those making responses.

321

Cecelia Bennett of Miami spoke for the Committee on Women in the Church and stated that for ten years this committee has been researching canonical issues affecting women in the Church. It produced a learning handout for this convention and this resolution results from the Committee's research into writings by other organizations on issues affecting women. The Committee was impressed by the report of the NCCB's Adhoc Committee on Women in society and by Bishop McAuliffe's address to the bishops, in which he urged the NCCB to expand its dialogue with women and women's organizations and to establish substantial programs of pastoral action to deal with issues of concern to women. In keeping with the educational thrust of the Society, the Committee believes it an opportune moment to continue its educational efforts by asking the CLSA membership to support Bishop McAuliffe's proposal and to offer our Committee's services to the NCCB's Adhoc Committee on Women to develop such pastoral programs.

No discussion followed the presentation and the President called the question. The resolution was *approved* unanimously.

RESOLUTION II

Whereas:

1. The permanent lay ministries of acolyte and lector are open to non-ordained men and closed to women; and

2. the Church since the Second Vatican Council in so many places has promoted the dignity and equality of all members of the Christian faithful; and

3. the revised Code of Canon Law in many places has eliminated discrimination based on gender; and

4. it is the sacrament of baptism and not gender which provides the human person with a status in the Church; and

5. the Canon Law Society of America has constantly supported equality and justice in the legal system of the Church as evidenced by its outstanding work in the areas of due process and the APN;

Be it resolved:

the Board of Governors request the NCCB to petition Rome to open the permanent lay ministries of acolyte and lector to women and that the CLSA offer whatever assistance is necessary to achieve this goal.

Speaking for the Committee on Resolutions, Mockel moved this resolution. Becker invited the committee presenting the resolution to explain it.

Again Cecelia Bennett of Miami spoke, indicating that the resolution derives from the Committee's study of ecclesiastical offices, functions, and ministries open to women in the revised code. The "whereas clauses" present logically a rationale for supporting the resolution and the Committee asks the membership to support it. Bennett noted that the third "whereas clause" was added in light of yesterday's hearing.

322

Again there being no discussion, the Chair called the question. The resolution was *approved*, with a few negative votes heard.

RESOLUTION III

Whereas:

1. Canon 1421 of the revised Code of Canon Law requires judges to have "at least the licentiate";

2. many dioceses in the United States can avail themselves of the services of only one or two persons holding the licentiate (or sometimes of none at all);

3. the licentiate requirement will seriously jeopardize the pastoral efficiency of many diocesan tribunals;

4. past experience has shown that judicial competence can be derived from either experience or programs equivalent to the licentiate;

5. the shortage of licentiates will remain a consistent problem in the foreseeable future;

Be it resolved:

the Board of Governors of the Canon Law Society of America urge the National Conference of Catholic Bishops, through its Canonical Affairs Committee, to petition the Supreme Tribunal of the Apostolic Signatura for an indult that would allow training or experience "equivalent to the licentiate" to fulfill the required canonical qualifications for appointment to judicial office.

The Committee on Resolutions moved this resolution and the President asked for discussion.

The Reverend John Proctor of San Diego provided the genesis of the resolution: the realization by some in moderate and small dioceses that if the revised code's requirement of the licentiate for judges is to be strictly observed, there would be real problems in maintaining adequate numbers of judges. Proctor acknowledged both the Pueblo indult reported in *Roman Replies* and the opinion that the licentiate requirement is necessary for liceity only and not for validity. While this requirement of the JCL could equally well apply to other officers of the court, the most practical need right now is to be able to appoint judges. He noted the two apparent objections which surfaced in the discussions yesterday, one questioning the timeliness and the other urging more creative interpretation. Proctor responded that his proposal is just as timely now as it will be in three or four years since no immediate relief is foreseen for those who have the problem. To the issue of creative interpretation—*nemo tenetur ad impossibile*—Proctor feared that those who appoint judges will not be satisfied with that kind of creative interpretation. Further, professionalism and integrity demand that judicial commissions be legal. Thus on behalf of moderate and small tribunals who face this problem, he urged a positive and affirmative vote on the resolution.

The Reverend Joseph Morrell of Allentown stated that the resolution should designate to whom this privilege would be given, *viz.*, priests who are active in tribunal and chancery work.

The Reverend Thomas Molloy of Rockville Centre spoke against the resolution: since the provision of the new law will not cause anyone presently a judge to lose office, it is a problem regarding the future. If the resolution is passed, it will send wrong signals both to Rome—about the professionalism of the American tribunals—and to our bishops—about the necessity of sending people to study canon law to have educated personnel for tribunals. Further, it is the experience of many in settings where there is a mix of degreed judges with others who have just "experience," that the "equality" spoken of in the resolution is not apparent. Molloy repeated his main concern that the resolution would send the wrong signals.

The Reverend James Provost of Helena also spoke against the resolution for two reasons. The first was procedural: it is not the Canonical Affairs Committee that would petition the Apostolic Signatura; rather it would be up to the Conference itself to make the petition. The second was substantial: a fear of establishing a precedent whereby canonists would immediately seek indults. Contrary to that approach is the canonist's unique characteristic and call to interpret the law creatively. This was the message of the first address at this convention, and taking recourse to an indult is ducking that responsibility.

The Reverend John T. Finnegan of Boston, concurring with the previous speaker, asked if this was not an area of the law in which the bishop himself could dispense. If episcopal dispensation is possible, there is no need for bishops to request indults. The Reverend John E. Fanning of New York also spoke against the resolution, reminding the assembly that ten years ago when the American Procedural Norms were extended, the American bishops specifically told Rome that they would prepare people and have them trained. We should not ask the American bishops to admit that they did not fulfill what they promised.

Proctor offered a friendly amendment to resolve the procedural issue raised by Provost: simply strike the clause "through its Canonical Affairs Committee." The President allowed the presenter of the resolution so to change his resolution.

The Reverend James Coriden challenged the ruling of the Chair to see who would act as parliamentarian. The President quelled the challenge, stating that the Chair rules on such issues. He called the question and following the vote, ruled that the motion was *defeated.*

RESOLUTION IV

Whereas:

1. A significant number of cases involve non-Catholics and even a significant percentage of our Catholic parties are unchurched; thus, the term "annulment" has negative connotations both as a civil

issue and an emotional issue, and is not heard in the ecclesial context in which it is intended;

2. it becomes very difficult for tribunal personnel to develop a spirit of reaching out to these people when using language that immediately alienates;

3. updating our language is nothing new in the Church: what was once the sacrament of confession is now the sacrament of penance and reconciliation, and extreme unction is now the sacrament of the anointing of the Sick and Dying;

4. the members of the Northwestern Regional Canon Law Convention held last April voted unanimously in favor of this action and to support it financially;

Be it resolved:

the Canon Law Society of America appoint a committee to study whether another word or group of words could be used to replace the term "annulment."

The Committee on Resolutions moved this resolution, and the President recognized the presenter, Charlene Cram of Seattle. She noted that pastoral issues historically have been important issues for CLSA members and pastoral sensitivity should be reflected in the language we use. The term *annulment*, once intended to convey a certain ecclesial notion regarding the invalidity of the marriage bond, is not heard by many in this sense at all. It is difficult to be pastorally sensitive and reach out to these people when the language used alienates. Use of this term often provokes negative reactions of the parties towards each other and towards the process itself. Negative reactions are counterproductive of the conversion experience and pastoral healing which, hopefully, are part of the process. The care of souls, conversion, reconciliation and healing are all part of our mission as Church. The way we language what we are doing should help create an atmosphere in which this mission can be accomplished, but this term *annulment* makes it very difficult if not impossible.

Discussion. The Reverend John Huels of the Catholic Theological Union in Chicago simply asked whether this resolution was the same or similar to the resolution which was addressed last year, and was not that resolution defeated. The Chair responded that a very similar one was addressed last year and it was defeated.

The Reverend James Provost of Helena spoke in favor of the resolution. While the body last year precipitously voted down a resolution of similar type, this resolution first of all requests a study; secondly, it addresses the common parlance usage of "annulment," a term that does not appear in the code; thirdly, after the experience of the "60 Minutes" program last year, it is apparent that the terminology used needs refinement to make what we are really doing more understandable to the people.

The Reverend James Coriden of Washington echoed Provost's reasons and urged serious consideration of the resolution. The Reverend Harmon Skillen of Stockton spoke in favor of the motion, citing his experience of speaking to petitioners and respondents about annulments. They have a hard time grasping why the word annulment is used when there was "something" there, some kind of a real relationship. After a wrenching experience of a civil divorce, sensitivity is extremely important and the word *annulment* does not demonstrate that kind of sensitivity.

The Reverend Thomas Molloy of Rockville Centre renewed his opposition presented last year: the drastic change of terminology could be the means of doing an injustice to people. If they knew their marriage was annulled, they might want to appeal the decision. If some generic or more kindly word is used, it may be much later that the person realizes what really happened. Had the person known that the marriage was annulled, there may have been an appeal; and what would the Signatura say about this situation?

The Reverend William A. Logar stressed that the resolution calls for a *study* and does not require the acceptance of a substitute term at this time. The Reverend Thomas Lynch of Hartford stated that when marriage was regarded simply as a contract, then the word annulment was sensible; but now that marriage is understood as an interpersonal covenant, a new term is needed.

There being no further discussion, the Chair called the question. The resolution was *accepted* by the majority voice vote, with some negative votes heard.

Report on the Election

The tellers having returned with the election results, the Reverend William Sullivan, chairman of the nominations committee reported the following votes cast. Upon the request of the Reverend James Provost, the Chair instructed Sullivan to report the number of votes for each nominee.

Office of Vice-President
  260 Votes were cast
  173 William A. Varvaro (elected)
   86 William A. Logar
    1 abstention

Office of Treasurer
  268 Votes were cast
  261 James K. Mallett (elected)
    7 abstentions

Office of Secretary
  259 Votes were cast
  168 James F. Parisek (elected)
   90 Robert Fisher
    1 abstention

Office of Consultor

    257 Votes were cast
      3 Invalid
    177 Bertram Griffin (elected)
    137 Thomas G. Doran (elected)
    131 Richard J. Cunningham (elected)
     95 Stanley J. Teixeira
     87 John Huels
     86 Ellen M. O'Hara
     40 Joan De Lourdes Leonard

President Becker thanked the 3 voting members and the ex-officio member of the Committee on Membership and Nominations for the arduous task of assembling a ballot and conducting the election. Also he expressed gratitude on behalf of the membership to those members who stood for office, whether elected or not, as a mark of their commitment and service.

The President allowed the Committee to complete its final item of business. Sullivan announced that by the suggestion of a CLSA member and in accord with Article 3, Section 3, of the CLSA Constitution, the Committee was placing before the membership a nominee for honorary membership: the Reverend Monsignor John S. Quinn of Chicago. He informed the assembly that Monsignor Quinn served as President of the Canon Law Society of America in 1957-1958. Under his leadership the Metropolitan Tribunal of Chicago has taken a lead in service to the Christian faithful by means of the Church's judicial system. He served as a *peritus* at the Second Vatican Council and was instrumental in its work on the "Declaration on Religious Freedom." As a member of the Code Commission *coetus* on marriage, he is regarded as the "father" of Canon 1095 concerning the capacity to contract a valid marriage. Father Sullivan concluded by stating: "The Committee, in recommending this, seeks to honor one of our own members who 'summarizes' the service of so many in these final years of the Church's first code of canon law and who calls us to a broad range of canonical service under the Church's second code. We place his name before you for honorary membership and ask the Society so to vote."

The President asked Monsignor Quinn to rise and be recognized. The question was called and Monsignor John Quinn was unanimously voted honorary membership.

The President asked the Vice-President, the Reverend Anthony Diacetis to chair this portion of the meeting. The Vice-President requested George Mockel to resume with his presentation of the resolutions.

RESOLUTION V

Whereas:

1. At its 41st Annual General Meeting in 1979, the Canon Law Society of America adopted the *Code of Professional Responsibility* under these

327

terms (*Proceedings*, 1979, pp. 153-154):

1) The *Code of Professional Responsibility* shall go into effect on January 1, 1980, for an experimental period of three (3) calendar years.

2) At the end of this period, the Board of Governors shall be responsible for an evaluation of the *Code of Professional Responsibility* for consideration by the membership of the Society at its 45th Annual General Meeting in 1983; and

2. the Board of Governors has completed this evaluation and mandated the appended revisions of the *Code of Professional Responsibility* which is presented for the consideration of the membership for adoption at its 45th Annual General Meeting;

Be it resolved:

the Canon Law Society of America adopt the amended text of the *Code of Professional Responsibility* as its statement of policy.

The Committee on Resolutions moved the resolution. Vice-President Diacetis reminded the assembly that no second is needed; and he called upon the presenter to speak to the issue.

On behalf of the Board of Governors, President Becker urged the adoption of the resolution, the result of the reflection by the Board of Governors and the Society based on the experience of this code in the past three years. It results also from the Society's commitment to express rights and responsibilities in the Church. This commitment has been reinforced by the text of the revised code of canon law in its section on the obligations and rights of the Christian faithful people. The *Code of Professional Responsibility* is an attempt on the part of the CLSA to sensitize its members and those who look upon our work to the need for going beyond the mere letter of the law and for administering dioceses, tribunals, religious communities, and other interests in the Church in ways which are not simply legal, but fair and in the best interests of the people of God. On behalf of the Board Governors he urged the adoption of this resolution.

Seeing no others wanting to address the issue, Diacetis called for a vote. The resolution *carried* by unanimous vote.

RESOLUTION VI

Whereas:

1. The Joint Committee of the Canon Law Society of America and the Catholic Theological Society of America have prepared procedures for promoting cooperation and resolving disputes between bishops and theologians, entitled *Doctrinal Responsibilities*; and

2. the Catholic Theological Society of America, meeting in June 1983, endorsed the *Doctrinal Responsibilities* paper as a working document to be recommended to the N.C.C.B.;

Be it resolved:

the Canon Law Society of America endorse the final report of the Joint CLSA-CTSA Committee, *Doctrinal Responsibilities*, as a working document to be recommended to the National Conference of Catholic Bishops for promoting cooperation and resolving doctrinal disputes between bishops and theologians.

The Vice-President asked the presenter to speak to the resolution. President Becker spoke on behalf of the Board of Governors. The document *Doctrinal Responsibilities* was distributed prior to the Convention. It is the result of some three or more years of dialogue between the canon lawyers of the CLSA and some members of the CTSA, in consultation with at least three members of the NCCB. It is an attempt to provide a framework in which theologians and bishops can address questions on which there is disagreement, with a view towards resolving those questions amicably and in the best interests of the people of God in the local and national Church. It is a document which has been supported unanimously by an identical resolution passed by the CTSA in its meeting last June. On behalf of the Board and the members of the joint committee who worked toward this great service to the Church in this area, he urged this resolution's adoption.

Seeing no others who wished to speak, Diacetis called for a vote. The resolution *carried unanimously.* The Vice-President relinquished the Chair to the President.

RESOLUTION VII

Whereas:

1. The members of our Church need and deserve better procedures for the redress of grievances occasionally caused by administrative actions; and,

2. the provisions for administrative tribunals, which might have met these needs, were not included in the code when promulgated in January, 1983;

Be it resolved:

the Board of Governors establish a task force to investigate possible options for diocesan, regional and national procedures for the redress of grievances and report to next year's annual convention.

The Committee on Resolutions moved this resolution.

As presenter of the resolution, the Reverend James Coriden of the Washington Theological Union urged its support by the membership. In continuity with the resolution passed last year on the implementation of administrative tribunals, which at that time was thought to be possible, the resolution keeps the matter on our agenda since the revised code does not provide for administrative tribunals. At the hearing yesterday the resolution was expanded to include diocesan level procedures; however, he sees a priority for a study of the supra-diocesan structures because of the jurisdictional problems. Any estimate on funding depends on many factors, but the Treasurer has assured that the projected budget of the Society could afford a modest task force of five to seven members.

The Reverend John Fanning of New York proposed amendment to change the phrase from "redress of grievances" to "protection of rights of persons in Church." Coriden accepted this as a friendly amendment, and not hearing any request for further discussion, President Becker called the question. The motion *passed*, with no opposition.

Old Business

The President mentioned that this completed the agenda, and nothing else was proposed as old business.

New Business

President Becker inquired whether there was any new business, reminding the membership that any new business which needed discussion required the house's permission to engage in that discussion.

The Reverend Edward Weist of Cleveland offered a comment on the growing awareness of issues affecting women in the Church. Citing the Synod of Bishops, which is open to major superiors of clerical religious institutes but not to women's religious institutes, he asked that the Committee on Women in the Church look into this as a real possibility for women's participation. The Holy Father is looking for feedback from the entire Church on issues that pertain to the universal Church, and women should be participating in this area which does not require orders or jurisdiction.

Monsignor John S. Quinn, recipient of the honorary membership in the CLSA, thanked the Chairman, the Committee, and the members of the Society for his nomination as an honorary member. Monsignor Quinn stated that he has always enjoyed attending the Society's meeting every year and meeting so many wonderful people. His honorary membership comes to him as a great and wonderful surprise.

President Becker closed the meeting and reminded the membership of the reception and banquet. Morning prayer Thursday at 9 a.m. precedes the major address by the Reverend Bertram Griffin at 9:30. The meeting was adjourned at 5:15 p.m.

Reception 7:00 p.m.-8:00 p.m.

Host: The Most Reverend John R. Quinn, Archbishop of San Francisco.

Dinner 8:00 p.m.-10:00 p.m.

During the dinner, President Becker introduced the newly elected officers of the Canon Law Society of America, and he expressed his gratitude for the confidence and support he has received from the membership. Then the Vice-President, the Reverend Anthony Diacetis, was called upon to speak. He commended President Becker on his leadership and dedication to the CLSA, and he challenged the membership to continued growth and vitality with ever greater cooperation and collaboration.

President Becker introduced The Reverend James E. Risk, S.J., J.C.D., the recipient of the "Role of Law Award." Father Risk offered his response, reflecting his many years of service as a canon lawyer and educator.

Thursday, October 13, 1983

Morning Prayer 9:00 a.m.

Major Address 9:30 a.m.-11:00 a.m.

"The Role of the Canonist in the Contemporary Church," by the Reverend Bertram Griffin.

Post-Convention Meeting

The President invited all interested to a discussion on the faculties a diocesan bishop may choose to grant to priests and deacons serving within his diocese. The discussion is in response to the paper "Diocesan Faculties" prepared by The Reverend John A. Renken of Springfield-in-Illinois, which was distributed in the convention packet.

The Reverend James F. Parizek
Secretary

CITATION FOR THE ROLE OF LAW AWARD

ROBERT C. BECKER

The City of San Francisco has given us much, from the Golden Gate to C.P. Huntington's railroad to Willie Mays. For our own Society, San Francisco has a special meaning. It was here in 1964 that the members of the CLSA, meeting in Convention, chose to shift the direction, the purpose, the focus of the Society. In the comparatively few years that I have been involved in the Society, the San Francisco Convention has usually been referred to in terms of awe and mystery by those who were there. One gets the sense that the shift was not only dramatic, but also, unfortunately, painful.

What motivated that shift? Innocent of any direct knowledge, but having come to know many who were there on the famous occasion, let me suggest some answers.

It seems, in retrospect, improbable that any meanness of spirit was significant in the motivation. Rather more prominent, judging from the events of the years which followed, were a deep commitment to gospel values, a deep sense of the dignity of the baptized in God's Church. Clearly there was a resonance with the work of the Council which was just drawing to a close.

The years following the San Francisco experience saw the Society address in rapid succession such issues as due process, procedures in marriage nullity actions and selection of bishops. CLSA sponsored symposia on the *Bond of Marriage*, church governance, and *Sexism in the Church*. For us who have become active more recently this is a part of our heritage which we dare not lose sight of.

Whence the energy, the vision, the stamina? Those then involved were, surely, caught up in the times. They were also men who had studied the law. We must dwell on this last point. Without the learning which had been afforded through study, the technical application of law, the discovery of new forms faithful to canonical tradition simply would not have been possible. More—without a vision of the role of law as service to God's people, there would have been no impetus to take bold steps.

The technical details and the vision which breathes life are the province of the canonical schools, and the canonists who teach there. Is it unreasonable to think that much of the energy and dedication of the members of the CLSA has at its root the talent and vision of their teachers?

It seems, then, extraordinarily appropriate that as we return here to San Francisco, we should present the Society's highest accolade to a man who inspired so many. As a technician of the law, a support in studies, a role-model for the canonist in service, he was central to the formation of a whole generation of American canonists. It is an honor to me to present this year's Role of Law Award to Father James Risk.

Many of you may not know Jim Risk, or be aware of his work. Let me tell you about him.

It was over 60 years ago, in 1923, that Jim first professed vows in the Society of Jesus. Ordained in 1933, he completed the course in canon law at the Pontifical Gregorian University in 1939. For eleven years he taught Canon Law and Ethics to Jesuit students. In 1952 he began what was to be a sixteen year career in the School of Canon Law at the Gregorian University. In the course of those sixteen years he directed the theses of scores of English-speaking canonists. In addition to that invaluable service, he served as counsellor, support and friend. His gentle wisdom and quiet inspiration have never been forgotten.

On his return from the Greg in 1968, at the age of 65, Jim was in no way content to sit back. He made himself available to the bishop of Bridgeport for service in the tribunal of that Diocese, as an advocate, defender of the bond, auditor, and then for nine years as officialis. Having inspired the men who moved the American Procedural Norms, he had the personal satisfaction of being able to apply them to God's people.

Through all of this time, Jim remained available for retreats, spiritual direction, and canonical assistance. His time was yours, because his time was the Church's.

Eighty years of age last month, he has not yet stopped. Having studied the code of 1917 with Vidal, Capello and Creusen, he has now written a significant part of the commentary on the code of 1983 for the CLSA.

The criteria for determining the recipient of the role of law award are five: pastoral attitude, commitment to research and study, participation in the revision of law, response to needs for practical assistance, and facilitation of dialogue and interchange of ideas within the Society and with other groups. In the opinion of the Board of Governors, Father James Risk of the Society of Jesus meets these criteria in a preeminent manner. In the name of the Board and the Society it is my privilege to present the Role of Law Award to Father James Risk.

RESPONSE TO THE ROLE OF LAW AWARD

JAMES RISK, S.J.

It is with deep appreciation that I appear before you, expressing my gratitude for the treasured honor you have given me today. I mention a few members of the Canon Law Society who have been especially helpful, such as Fathers Robert Becker, Anthony Diacetis, James Cuneo, James Provost, Thomas Green, each of whom was helpful in a particular way. Many others have been generous to me over the years I have spent as a member of the CLSA. To name them would sound like a litany. Special mention should be made of Bishop Walter Curtis of the Diocese of Bridgeport who gave me the opportunity to become better acquainted with the actual operations of a tribunal, after leaving the teaching staff of the Gregorian.

Some fifteen years ago, at a convention of canonists in Rome, over which His Eminence Cardinal Pericle Felici presided, it became clear that some of the members became more and more conscious of their didactic capacity. One repeater was given the minimum advice by His Eminence, "Esto brevis," which in the vernacular may be translated as "Make it fast." And so he did and so shall I. Commenting on the transition period preceding the promulgation of the new code, it seems that we may liken ourselves to the scribe mentioned by Our Lord in the parable of the Kingdom, who brought forth from his treasury the old and the new, the *nova* et *vetera*. The reform of the code meant retaining what was valuable in the old code and adopting prescriptions meeting the needs of the present day, producing a happy blending of the old and the new.

Cautiously picking my steps over Memory Lane, which takes me back over 40 years, when I joined the Canon Law Society of America, I find a number of fugitive impressions returning from time to time. The CLSA was founded in 1939 and the first convention was attended by 60 persons. From those early days, the Society has continued to attract in increasing numbers those who are interested in the law of the Church and what its rich heritage means to all Christians. Several of the Founding Fathers of the CLSA, so prominent for their scholarship, were professors of Canon Law at the Catholic University of America. Reverend Jerome Hannan, later Bishop of Scranton, in addition to his duties as lecturer also served as the first managing editor of *The Jurist*. Reverend Clement Bastnagel was the recording secretary and for many years treasurer of the Society. His impeccable penmanship seems to have made for him the use of a typewriter unnecessary. Monsignor Motry, Dean of the School of Canon Law, once coyly remarked at a convention meeting that even some Jesuits were in attendance. Among the earliest members of the CLSA was Dr. Stephan Kuttner, the internationally renowned scholar in the field of medieval Canon Law. Other prominent figures at the conventions were Msgrs.

Edward Dargin of New York and James Griffiths of Brooklyn, and Father Frank Reh of New York, who later became bishops. Father Eugene Dooley was recognized among others for his talented contributions from the very beginning of the Society.

Many of the pioneer members of the CLSA have, in the words of St. Paul, "fallen" asleep, while others are "wayfarers from the Lord." Recalling some of the earlier conventions, it seems that a tone of formality was observed, even in the discussion of contemporary canonical issues. For example, "I would like to comment on Dr. Smith's remark about the *aut-aut* cases," or, "Dr. Jones is referring to the exclusion of a culpable party from attacking the validity of his marriage," or, "We shall now hear from Dr. Gratian, J.C.D., who will summarize his position on the *matrimonium ratum.*" While such highly proper formalities are not noticeable at present day conventions, neither the professional expertise nor the administrative efficiency have suffered thereby and the scholarly productivity of the Society has reached a new high. Did women take part in the conventions? *Nec nominetur in vobis!*

In the first issue of *The Jurist*, Monsignor Motry composed an article entitled "Cannotative Value of the 'Sacred Canons,'" in which he brought out with clarity and conviction the relationship between theology and canon law and its vital role in the plan of man's salvation. With the evolution and the clarification of the law, this intimate connection becomes more and more apparent.

The well-known axiom of St. Paul (2 Cor. 3:6), "The written law kills, but the spirit gives life," cannot be applied to canon law, since it is fundamentally a science that traces its spiritual lineage back to apostolic times. Its roots cannot be torn from Catholic doctrine nor dissociated from the moral teaching of the Church. The very heart or spirit of canon law differs greatly from the purely positive secular law, which prescinds from the supernatural and almost resentfully declares its independence from any relationship to religion. The law of the Church recognizes, for example, the sublime reflection of the marriage covenant as the image of Christ's union with the Church, while the State regards the bond, whether sacramental or natural, as a contract regulated by purely human discipline. The other sacraments, quite obviously, are of no interest to the secular power. The somewhat complex judicial structure, while reflecting the general outlines of its Roman counterpart, is rooted in the natural law and has been traditionally sustained under the vigilant eye of the Catholic Church as the guardian of justice. The teaching office of the Church, coming from the mandate of Jesus, the teacher of mankind, finds its clear delineation in the Code of Canon Law. Worship, church government and even sanctions never lose sight of the supreme law which is the salvation of souls. The canonist recognizes the doctrinal continuity beginning in the early Christian era and reaching into the latest formulation of church law, the pulsating heart of which derives ultimately from the will of God. "Love is the fulfillment of the law" says St. Paul (Romans 13:6).

In an allocution to the professors and students of the University of Vienna Law School on June 3, 1956, Pope Pius XII made the following appropriate remarks. "Church law is not an end in itself. It is a means to an end. Like everything else in the Church, it is at the service of the *salus animarum* and therefore is a matter of pastoral care. It should assist in opening and smoothing ways into the hearts of men for the truth and grace of Jesus Christ." Many canons, to be sure, are only protective norms, such as those which guard the faith from decay and keep the dignity of grace and the sacraments from sacrilege. But in addition to these, there are canons which are built into the very structure of the Church by her divine founder and which are indeed in direct accordance with her nature. These include such forms of organization of the Mystical Body of Christ as the laws regulating the constitution of the Church and those defining the powers of the pope and of the bishops. Christ founded his Church not as a formless spiritual movement but as a strongly organized association.

"Certainly church law must not stifle the spiritual and supernatural virtues it is intended to serve. The accusation has indeed been made that this is just what it does and there has been talk of the 'excessive legalization' of the Church. Thus the voice of accusation is too often raised against the inflexibility with which the Church holds fast to the indissolubility of a consummated Christian marriage. And yet she treats this problem not with legalistic heartlessness and harshness, as though she does not perceive the tragedy which is often present in such cases, but simply with regard to the faithful administration of the marriage laws, which her divine founder himself has laid down and upon which the Church is not competent to pass judgment. . . . We must also keep in mind the operation of Providence in the formation of the Code of Canon Law, etc." (Reported in *Canon Law Digest* 5:3-4.) The life stream of Canon Law pours forth "e fontibus Salvatoris" (Is. 12:3).

At the 1980 Synod of Bishops, Cardinal Felici presented his observations regarding the operation of church tribunals. At the same time, however, he commented on the pastoral dimension of canon law, stating that "Sometimes it is asserted that canon law is something separate from theology and pastoral ministry. This is not true, as long as one clearly appreciates what canon law is, and knows its history and nature, as well as the work done by the Commission for the Revision of the Code of Canon Law, about which I have several times given reports in this Hall, and which is clearly available in the Schemata already submitted to the episcopal conferences and in the magazine *Communicationes*. In the application of canon law it can happen that some people separate law from pastoral ministry and indulge in a certain juridicism. But this is against the mind of the legislator and is not in accordance with sound doctrine. Not only is canon law by its very nature pastoral; it should proceed not only in parallel with pastoral action, but join forces with it."

That canon law should not remain a subject restricted to a few specialists but should be, as it were, the common patrimony of the people of God, seems to follow from the emphasis given its pastoral significance by Pope Pius XII and

Cardinal Felici. We are reminded by Pope Celestine, as reported in the Decretals and quoted by Pope Benedict XV, that no priest should be ignorant of the sacred canons nor should he contravene any of the rules enacted by the Fathers. It is to be hoped that with the re-birth of the code many priests will avail themselves of the opportunities for refreshing their knowledge of canon law and so prepare themselves for the frequent questions proposed by the faithful relating to the law of the Church as it affects their personal spiritual lives, or at least suggests questions regarding its purpose and practical significance. By way of example, television productions featuring roundtable discussions on annulments or clerical celibacy stimulated an interest in these issues and suggested questions from many of the viewers. Any one expected to be informed on such subjects could be approached for an answer, and this could mean any priest or sister or educated Catholic layman. Teachers of courses in religion or religious studies are approached by their students as are priests and religious engaged in campus ministry, and the parish priest by members of his parish. Some of the answers are, or should be, easy, while others can be more complicated and require some research or at least consultation with one supposed to know.

Like any truly professional organization, the Society has gained international prominence by the merit of its publications as well as by its influence exercised throughout the Catholic world. To mention some of these influential publications, there are the following: *Marriage Studies; Code, Community, Ministry; The ERA in Debate,* which indicate the sensitivity of the authors to contemporary issues relating in a special way to the People of God. Other publications include *Decisions, Annulments,* the annual *Proceedings* of the CLSA, *Roman Replies* and the *Newsletter,* a quarterly bulletin issued to members and containing all up-to-the-minute items of importance, whether communicated from Rome or from other quarters. Issued at the present convention was a four page informational list containing the titles of books and tapes available for members. In addition to all these sources of canonical information produced by the Society, studies published by the Canon Law Faculty of St. Paul's University of Ottawa and contained in *Studia Canonica, Handbook for Marriage Nullity Cases,* etc., serve to amplify the range of canonical scholarship produced in North America. The *Canon Law Digest,* now in the 50th year of its publication, remains the outstanding documentary source of contemporary canon law. *Canon Law Abstracts,* compiled by members of the Canon Law Society of Great Britain and Ireland, provides us with a quick survey of the articles written or translated by canonists of the English speaking world. The entire aggregate of canonical productions just mentioned represents a treasury of church law from which all may profit directly or indirectly, due consideration being given to the intellectual receptivity of the person seeking a knowledge of the law. The educational program expands beyond the range of formal studies and may include well-balanced articles in Catholic magazines, question and answer columns, continuing educational programs for the Roman Catholic clergy, developed by the CLSA.

From all levels of the Catholic community come questions prompted by statements made in the Catholic or secular press relating to Church law, such as marriage, clerical celibacy, the observance of days of penance and of feast days and even excommunications. It is quite clear then that canon law is not a severely sequestered arcanum to be revealed only to a chosen few.

The educational function of the CLSA has not only fulfilled, but has, it would seem, transcended the ambitious objectives of its founders. With the unremitting industry of its writers and its administrative units, it has become an ever expanding center of learning, extending its inspirational influence on ever widening areas of the people of God. Even parish centers have sponsored lectures on choice aspects of the new code. All such programs, if efficiently and patiently conducted, will contribute to the dissemination of the knowledge of the Church's law.

To the canonist of the contemporary era a rich opportunity has been offered for deepening his or her knowledge of the code of 1983. Happily, the many writers among the members of the CLSA have been aware of this opportunity and have supplied all members with the fruits of their scholarly research. From the very birth of the Society and antedating by two decades the decision of Pope John XXIII to convoke Vatican Council II and to update the Code of Canon Law, *The Jurist* has been the principal publication relating to the Society. Its first issue appeared in 1941 and since that year has continued to flourish with its scholarly articles, studies, reports of decrees ecclesiastical and civil. As its sub-title indicates, *The Jurist* now includes within its sphere of interest church ministry as well as church law. By way of digression, a companion publication, known as *The Seminar,* under the sponsorship of the CLSA, appeared for the first time in 1943 and continued its publication until 1956, after which it was discontinued. It provided civil as well as church jurists with a wealth of profoundly researched studies covering questions relating to Roman and medieval law as well as questions more appropriate to a later era. "Punishment in Ancient Rome for Cattle Stealing" was an amusing article appearing in the first issue of *The Seminar.*

Promulgating the new code, Pope John Paul II stated that among the elements which express the true and authentic nature of the Church is the "doctrine whereby all members of the people of God, each in a manner proper to him, share in Christ's threefold office of priest, prophet and king. To this doctrine is also connected that which looks to the duties and the rights of the Christian faithful, particularly the laity." "Hence it is of the greatest importance that the norms shall be carefully expounded on the basis of solid juridical, canonical and theological foundations."

Finally, I am convinced that our Canon Law Society has, from its very beginning lived up to the noble ideals envisioned by its founders. Its spiritual motivation, its scholarship and devotion to the service of the Church over four decades have been truly admirable. May the Holy Spirit continue to inspire all its members to love the law as an instrument in spreading the Kingdom of Christ. Again, hoping that I have not exceeded the brevity recommended by Cardinal Felici, my deep gratitude I express once again to all.

SUGGESTED DIOCESAN FACULTIES

This paper presents faculties which the diocesan bishop may decide to grant to the priests and deacons serving within the diocese. Several observations are to be made from the outset.

First, these faculties are concerned with subjects treated in the 1983 Code of Canon Law. Reference is not made, for instance, to liturgical matters not treated in the code (e.g., the faculty to celebrate a second Mass on Holy Thursday).

The faculties deal with privileges able to be given to priests and deacons. It is not suggested that every diocesan bishop necessarily grant all the faculties mentioned in this paper. A diocesan bishop may wish to restrict, amplify or in some other way modify these suggested faculties. This paper hopes to serve as a model to assist each diocese in developing its own pagella. It may happen, too, that a diocese may wish to develop two sets of faculties: one for priests and another for deacons.

In this paper, the faculties given to priests and deacons are valid within the confines of the parish to which they are assigned, unless otherwise stated. Other approaches could provide faculties valid within the confines of the diocese unless otherwise stated. Faculties granted to "pastors" are understood in this paper as being given also to the "parochial administrator" (c. 540) and to the members of a "parish team" (c. 517, § 1; cf. c. 543, § 1). Moreover, a priest who resides in a parish without being assigned as a parochial vicar would need special permission to enjoy the same faculties as a parochial vicar. This could be done by the faculties themselves; or, perhaps more easily, priests in residence could be assigned as parochial vicars only for the purpose of exercising the faculties restricted to parochial vicars. The law (c. 545, § 2) does permit the assignment of parochial vicars for limited purposes.

Finally, the following faculties do not mention the rights and privileges which are granted by universal law itself to priests and deacons, an example of which is the faculty to preach. Canon 764 gives priests and deacons the faculty to preach everywhere in the world with at least the presumed consent of the rector of the church and without prejudice to the norm of canon 765. (The local ordinary, however, can restrict or remove this faculty.)

A special word of thanks for their assistance in the composition of this paper is due to Monsignor John A. Alesandro, S.T.L., J.C.D., of Rockville Centre; Reverend Thomas G. Doran, J.C.D., of Rockford; and Reverend James H. Provost, J.C.D., of the Catholic University of America.

Reverend John A. Renken, J.C.D., S.T.D.
Diocese of Springfield in Illinois

In addition to the rights and privileges granted to priests and deacons by reason of the universal law of the Church, the following faculties are granted to the priests and deacons serving this diocese:

1. **The faculty is granted to pastors and parochial vicars to baptize one who has completed the fourteenth year, without previously referring the matter to the diocesan bishop.**

Canon 863 requires that the baptism of persons fourteen years of age and older be referred to the diocesan bishop, so he himself may confer baptism if he so decide. This faculty allows pastors and parochial vicars to baptize such a person without previous recourse to the diocesan bishop.

Canon 866 says that unless a grave reason to the contrary exists, an adult should be immediately confirmed after the reception of baptism. Since a deacon cannot administer confirmation, the above faculty does not give him the permission to baptize a person fourteen years of age and older.

2. **The faculty is granted to parochial vicars to administer the sacrament of confirmation to those persons who have attained the use of reason and whom they baptize. Pastors and parochial vicars are also given the faculty to confirm those persons who have attained the use of reason and are already baptized in another church or ecclesial communion, when they are received by them into full communion with the Church.**

Canon 883, 2° gives by law the faculty to confirm to the priest who by virtue of office or episcopal mandate baptizes an adult or admits a baptized adult into full communion with the Church. Canon 530, 1° says pastors have by office the right to baptize. Canon 866 says that when an adult is baptized, unless a grave reason prevents it, the person should be immediately confirmed. Thus, pastors have the rights to confirm those adults whom they baptize. The above faculty gives pastors, in addition, the mandate to confirm those baptized persons with the use of reason whom they receive into full communion with the Church. It also gives parochial vicars the mandate to confirm those with the use of reason whom they baptize or receive into full communion.

It can happen that an individual who was baptized a Catholic as an infant but never reared in the faith would as an adult seek to be reconciled to the Church. In a certain sense, this situation is similar to receiving a baptized non-Catholic into full communion. Therefore, a diocesan bishop may decide, in view of canon 884, § 1, to allow pastors and parochial vicars to administer confirmation to such an adult when he or she is reconciled to the Church. Should the diocesan bishop so choose, the following would be added to the above faculty:

Pastors and parochial vicars also enjoy the faculty to confirm Catholics who, although baptized earlier, have not been reared in the Church, on the occasion of their being reconciled to the Church.

3. **The faculty is granted to priests, for a good reason, to celebrate the Eucharist twice on weekdays and, if a pastoral necessity requires it, three times on Sundays and holydays of obligation.**

Canon 905, § 1 states that a priest may not celebrate the Eucharist more than once a day, except on those occasions when the law permits him to celebrate or concelebrate a number of times on the same day. Canon 905, § 2 adds, moreover, that if there is a shortage of priests the local ordinary may permit a priest for a just cause to celebrate two times on weekdays and, if pastoral need requires it, three times on Sundays and holydays of obligation. The above faculty grants this permission.

Canon 1248, § 1 says the faithful fulfill their obligation of assisting at Mass on a day of precept by attending Mass either on the day itself or on the evening of the preceding day. Since the obligation is fulfilled on the evening preceding the day of precept, and since canon 905, § 2 is a disciplinary law of the Church, it would appear in view of canon 87, § 1 that the diocesan bishop may permit priests to celebrate Mass three times on the day preceding a day of precept, provided the third Mass that day was for the day of precept and provided the provisions of canon 87, § 1 were fulfilled.

4. **The habitual faculty to hear confession is granted to priests.**

Canon 968, § 1 says that by virtue of his office and within the confines of his territory, the faculty to hear confessions is granted by the law to the local ordinary, the canon penitentiary (cf. c. 508, § 2), the pastor and those who take the place of the pastor. Canon 969, § 1 says all other priests must receive the faculty to hear confessions from the local ordinary (and religious priests are to use this faculty only with the permission, at least presumed, of their superior).

The faculty to hear confessions may be granted by the local ordinary either temporarily or habitually. In the latter case, the grant must be made in writing (c. 973), as is done by means of the diocesan pagella.

Canon 967, § 2 states that those who have the habitual faculty to hear confessions from the local ordinary either of the place of incardination or of the place of domicile may exercise that faculty anywhere in the world, unless in a particular case the local ordinary has refused, without prejudice to the provisions of canon 974, §§ 2 and 3. The above faculty gives to priests within the diocese the habitual faculty to hear confessions within the diocese. In other words, any priests to whom the above faculty is granted have the faculty to hear confessions within the confines of the diocese. If the diocese is that of the priests' incardination or domicile, they then may hear confessions throughout the world, in accord with canon 967, § 2.

5. **The faculty is granted to confessors to dispense from irregularities for the exercise of orders already received, provided their dispensation is not reserved to the Apostolic See. This faculty can be exercised in the internal or external forum, within the confines of the diocese, and on behalf of any person regardless of the person's residence or the place where the penalty was incurred.**

Canon 1047, § 4 gives to the ordinary the power to dispense from irregularities and impediments not reserved to the Apostolic See. Canon 1047, § 1 says that if the fact on which they are based has been brought into the judicial forum, the dispensation from all irregularities is reserved to the Apostolic See. In addition, canon 1047, § 3 lists those irregularities whose dispensation is reserved to the Apostolic See. In view of that canon, the following irregularities may be dispensed by the ordinary (cf. c. 1044, § 1):

1. the irregularity incurred by one who, while bound to an irregularity for the reception of orders, unlawfully received orders;

2. the irregularity incurred by one who publicly committed the offense of apostasy, heresy or schism;

3. the irregularity incurred by one who has attempted an occult marriage, even civil, either while himself prevented from marrying because of an existing marriage bond, or a sacred order, or a public and perpetual vow of chastity, or with a woman prevented from marrying because of an existing marriage bond or a public and perpetual vow of chastity;

4. the irregularity incurred by one who has gravely and maliciously mutilated himself or another, or who has attempted to kill himself;

5. the irregularity incurred by one who has carried out an act or an order reserved to those in the presbyterate or episcopate, either while himself not being in that order or while being prevented from its exercise by a declared or imposed penalty.

This faculty gives to the confessor the power to dispense from these irregularities. It may be exercised in the internal or external forum, within the confines of the diocese, and on behalf of any cleric regardless of his residence or the place where the irregularity was incurred.

6. **The faculty is granted to confessors to remit in the internal or external forum a *latae sententiae* penalty established by the law but not yet declared, provided the remission is not reserved to the Apostolic See. This faculty may be exercised only within the confines of the diocese, and on behalf of any person regardless of the person's residence or the place where the penalty was incurred.**

Canon 1355, § 2 states: "If it has not been reserved to the Apostolic See a *latae sententiae* penalty established by the law but not yet declared can be remitted by the ordinary on behalf of his own subjects, of those who are actually within his territory, and of those who committed the crime in his territory. Any bishop has this power within the act of sacramental confession." By reason of canon 1357, § 1 confessors can remit in the internal sacramental forum a non-declared excommunication or interdict, provided it is difficult for the person to remain in a state of grave sin for the time necessary for the proper superior to provide. Canon 1357, § 2, however, requires that the confessor impose upon the person the obligation to have recourse within a month to the competent superior, under the pain of incurring the censure once again;

such recourse can be made, of course, through the confessor.

The above faculty gives to confessors the ability to remit *latae sententiae* penalties established by the law but not yet declared, provided these are not reserved to the Apostolic See. The faculty may be exercised anywhere within the confines of the diocese, and may benefit anyone regardless of the person's residence or the place where the penalty was incurred. By reason of this faculty, no recourse to a competent superior is required, before or after the remission of the penalty: hence, the contrast with the norm of canon 1357, §§ 1 and 2.

Special consideration must be given to the *latae sententiae* excommunication, not reserved to the Apostolic See, stemming from apostasy, heresy or schism (canon 1364, § 1). Should a person by a formal act leave the Catholic Church (and thereby enter a state of apostasy, heresy or schism), he or she is not bound by the canonical form for a subsequent marriage (canon 1117). Should this same person then seek to be reconciled with the Church (by reason of the remission of the *latae sententiae* excommunication), he or she would again be bound to canonical form for marriage. In view of all this, it would seem most appropriate that the remission of the *latae sententiae* excommunication from apostasy, heresy or schism be given in the external forum (and perhaps even with an entry made into the baptismal register?).

7. **The faculty is granted to parochial vicars and deacons to assist at marriages within the boundaries of the parish to which they are assigned.**

Canon 1111, § 1 says that the local ordinary and the pastor, as long as they validly hold office, can delegate priests and deacons the faculty, even in a general fashion, to assist at marriages within the confines of their territory. Canon 1111, § 2 requires that general delegation be in writing. This faculty gives such written general delegation to parochial vicars and deacons; the faculty is valid within the confines of the parish to which they are assigned. In light of canon 137, § 3 the delegated parochial vicar and deacon can subdelegate this faculty in individual instances.

Some dioceses may favor granting the general faculty to priests and deacons to assist at marriages throughout the entire diocese. In this instance, the faculty may state:

> **The faculty is granted to priests and deacons to assist at marriages within the confines of this diocese.**

8. **The faculty is granted to those able to assist at marriages to dispense from the canonical form for marriage and from all the impediments to marriage which may be dispensed by the local ordinary, when everything has been prepared for the marriage and when the marriage cannot be delayed without the probable danger of grave harm until the dispensation can be obtained from the competent authority.**

Canon 1080, § 1 says that whenever an impediment is discovered after everything is prepared for the wedding and the marriage cannot be delayed without the probable danger of grave harm until a dispensation is obtained from the competent authority, the local ordinary may dispense from all impediments of ecclesiastical origin except the impediment arising from sacred orders and the impediment coming from a public perpetual vow of chastity in a religious institute of pontifical right. Moreover, in occult cases, these same ecclesiastical impediments may be dispensed by a minister as defined in canon 1079, §§ 2 and 3.

This faculty gives to those able to assist at marriages the ability to dispense from the canonical form of marriage and from all ecclesiastical impediments which may be dispensed by the local ordinary, when everything is prepared for the wedding and when the marriage cannot be delayed without probable danger of grave harm until the dispensation can be obtained from the competent authority. It is an extension of the instances mentioned in canon 1080, § 1 inasmuch as it permits a dispensation from canonical form and a dispensation from non-occult ecclesiastical law impediments from which the local ordinary can dispense.

9.   **The faculty is granted to pastors, parochial vicars and deacons assigned to a parish, to permit the marriage between two baptized persons, one of whom was baptized in the Catholic Church or received into it after baptism and who has not departed from the Church by a formal act, and the other of whom belongs to a church or ecclesial community not in full communion with the Catholic Church. This permission is not to be given unless the conditions mentioned in canon 1125 are fulfilled.**

Canon 1124 says that without the express permission of the competent authority, marriage is prohibited between two baptized persons, one of whom was baptized in the Catholic Church or received into it after baptism and who has not departed from the Church by a formal act, and the other of whom belongs to a church or ecclesial community not in full communion with the Catholic Church. The above faculty gives the ability to permit such a "mixed marriage" to pastors, parochial vicars, and deacons assigned to a parish. Before the permission is given, however, the conditions mentioned in canon 1125 concerning the affirmation and promises by the Catholic and the education of both parties concerning marriage must be fulfilled.

In addition to this faculty which concerns canon 1124, another faculty may be granted by the diocesan bishop whereby pastors, parochial vicars and deacons assigned to a parish would be permitted to allow some or all of the marriages which, by reasons of canon 1071, may not be celebrated without the permission of the local ordinary.

10.   **The faculty is granted to pastors, parochial vicars and deacons assigned to a parish, to dispense from the impediment of disparity of cult, provided the conditions of canon 1125 have been fulfilled.**

By reason of canon 1078, § 1 the local ordinary can dispense from the impediment of disparity of cult (c. 1086). This faculty gives to pastors, parochial vicars and deacons assigned to a parish the ability to grant the same dispensation. The conditions of canon 1125, however, must be met.

11. **The faculty is granted to parochial vicars and deacons assigned to a parish, to allow the marriage of a Catholic and a baptized non-Catholic to be celebrated outside the parish church but in another Catholic church or oratory.**

Canon 1118, § 1 gives the local ordinary and the pastor the ability to permit the marriage of a Catholic and a baptized non-Catholic to be celebrated outside the parish church but in another Catholic church or oratory. This faculty gives to parochial vicars and deacons assigned to a parish the same ability.

12. **The faculty is granted to pastors, parochial vicars and deacons assigned to a parish, to permit the marriage of two Catholics or of a Catholic and a baptized non-Catholic to be celebrated in some suitable place other than a church or oratory.**

Canon 1118, § 2 says that the local ordinary can allow a marriage to be celebrated in a suitable place other than a church or oratory. This faculty gives pastors, parochial vicars and deacons assigned to a parish the ability to allow marriages between two Catholics or between a Catholic and a baptized non-Catholic to be celebrated outside a church or oratory but in some other suitable place. It should be noted that by reason of canon 1118, § 3 no special permission is needed for a marriage between a Catholic and a non-baptized person to be celebrated in some appropriate place other than a church.

13. **The faculty is granted to pastors, parochial vicars and deacons assigned to a parish, to allow church funeral rites for an unbaptized child, if the parents had intended to have the child baptized.**

Canon 1183, § 2 states that the local ordinary may allow church funeral rites to be celebrated for children whose parents had intended to have them baptized but who died before baptism. This faculty gives the ability to permit such funerals to the pastor, the parochial vicar and deacons assigned to a parish.

14. **The faculty is granted to pastors, parochial vicars and deacons assigned to a parish to allow church funeral rites for a baptized person belonging to a non-Catholic church or ecclesial community, provided this is not clearly contrary to the wishes of the deceased and provided a minister of the faith of the deceased is not available.**

Canon 1183, § 3 says that, in accordance with the prudent judgment of the local ordinary and provided the deceased's own minister is unavailable, a baptized but who died before baptism. This faculty gives the ability to permit such funerals to the pastor, the parochial vicar and deacons assigned to a parish. wishes. This faculty gives the ability to allow such funerals to pastors, parochial vicars and deacons assigned to a parish, who must first make a prudent judgment concerning the matter.

15. **The faculty is given to priests and deacons to dispense, in individual cases and for a just reason, from the Eucharistic abstinence.**

Canon 919, § 1 requires that anyone receiving the Eucharist abstain for at least one hour before Holy Communion from all food and drink, except water and medicine. This faculty allows priests and deacons to dispense from this Eucharistic abstinence, in individual cases and for a just reason.

16. **The faculty is given to parochial vicars and deacons assigned to a parish to dispense, in individual cases and for a just reason, from the obligation of observing a day of precept or a day of penance, or to commute the obligation into other pious works. This faculty may be exercised on behalf of a parishioner and a person visiting within the boundaries of the parish.**

Canon 1245 gives the pastor the ability, for a just cause and according to the prescriptions of the diocesan bishop, to dispense from the obligation of observing a day of precept or a day of penance, or to commute the obligation into some other work. This power can be exercised on behalf of the pastor's parishioners and those visiting within the confines of the parish (cf. canon 91). This faculty gives to parochial vicars and deacons assigned to a parish the same ability to dispense or commute. This power can be exercised on behalf of parishioners and persons visiting within the confines of the parish to which the parochial vicars and deacons are assigned.

17. **The faculty is granted to parochial vicars and deacons assigned to a parish to dispense from private vows made by a person belonging to the parish to which they are assigned and also by a visitor within the territory of the parish. This dispensation may be granted only if no injury is done to the acquired rights of others.**

Canon 1196, 1° gives to the local ordinary and the pastor the ability to dispense their own subjects and visitors from private vows, provided no injury is done to the acquired rights of others. Canon 1196, 3° indicates that the Apostolic See and the local ordinary may delegate the faculty of dispensing to others. This faculty grants this delegation.

18. **The faculty is granted to parochial vicars and deacons assigned to a parish to commute to a lesser good what has been promised by a private vow made by a person belonging to the parish to which they are assigned and also by a visitor within the territory of the parish.**

Canon 1197 says that what has been promised by a private vow can be commuted into something better or equally good by the person who made the vow. It can be commuted into something less good by the one who has the authority to dispense in virtue of canon 1196. This faculty is the logical sequel to the preceding one, which gives parochial vicars and deacons assigned to a parish the ability to dispense from private vows.

19. **The faculty is granted to parochial vicars and deacons assigned to a parish to suspend, dispense or commute a promissory oath. This faculty may not be exercised if the dispensation from the oath would tend to prejudice those who refuse to remit its obligation.**

Canon 1203 provides that those who can suspend, dispense or commute a vow have, in the same manner, the same power over a promissory oath. However, if the dispensation from the oath would tend to prejudice others who refuse to remit the obligation of the oath, only the Apostolic See can dispense the oath. According to canons 1196 and 1197, the local ordinary and the pastor have the ability to dispense from private vows and to commute what has been promised by a private vow to a lesser good. In view of canon 1203, the local ordinary and the pastor can also dispense from promissory oaths.

The two preceding faculties give to parochial vicars and deacons the ability to dispense from a private vow and to commute what has been promised by a private vow to a lesser good; this faculty grants to parochial vicars and deacons the ability to suspend, dispense or commute a promissory oath.

FACULTIES FOR JUDICIAL VICAR

The 1983 Code of Canon Law describes the power of the judicial vicar (or officialis) as ordinary, vicarious power (canon 1420, § 1). Since it is ordinary power the judicial vicar's authority comes from the office to which the bishop appoints him, and its nature and extent are delineated in Book VII, *De Processibus.*

The extent of this power is carefully circumscribed by the code. It should be noted, first of all, that the exercise of judicial power is restricted to acts involving the prosecution or vindication of rights of physical or juridical persons, declaring juridical facts, and imposing or declaring penalties for delicts (canon 1400, § 1). Excluded from the judicial authority of the diocesan officialis are acts or controversies arising from the exercise of administrative power (canon 1400, § 2) and cases reserved to the tribunals of the Apostolic See (canons 1404-1406).

Judicial power is further restricted in virtue of its vicarious nature. The judicial vicar constitutes one tribunal with the diocesan bishop (canon 1420, § 2). The code prescribes that the bishop may reserve to himself certain cases or classes of cases, and such reservation prevents the judicial vicar from rendering a decision (canon 1420, § 2). The code specifies a few areas where the judicial power rests with the diocesan bishop himself, not the judicial vicar unless specifically mandated by the bishop. Such a mandate from the bishop may take the form of "faculties" granted the judicial vicar; these are described in this paper.

These faculties are presented for consideration by individual dioceses. As "faculties" they are facultative; i.e., the bishop may or may not decide to grant them. The purpose for this paper is to assist dioceses in understanding the options that are available.

This paper was prepared for distribution at the 1983 Annual Meeting of the Canon Law Society of America, and has been revised in light of comments received since then.

Reverend Ronald J. Bowers, J.C.L.
Archdiocese of Saint Paul and Minneapolis

***

1. Canon 1425, § 1 prescribes that a collegiate tribunal decide contentious cases involving the bonds of holy orders and matrimony, and penal cases involving either the penalty of dismissal from the clerical state or the imposition or declaration of an excommunication. Canon 1425, § 4 determines that if the National Conference of Catholic Bishops permits a derogation from the law, the bishop is able to commit such cases to a single, clerical judge, who may be

assisted in rendering a decision by an assessor and auditor if that is possible, when establishing a collegiate tribunal is impossible. It is presumed the N.C.C.B. will decide to permit such a derogation. If it does, the bishop can authorize the judicial vicar to make this assignment, provided the single judges he selects are clerics. Since the text does not speak of "single cases" or "each case," such a faculty can be given in a general fashion. Here is a proposed reading of the faculty:

In accord with the prescriptions of canon 1425, § 4 and the provisions of the National Conference of Catholic Bishops, you are hereby authorized to assign cases to a single clerical judge.

2. Canon 1430 describes the function of the promoter of justice, which focuses on protecting the public good wherever it may be affected by contentious or penal cases. Canon 1431, § 1 states that the bishop is responsible for deciding whether the promoter of justice ought to intervene in a contentious case. Because the officialis is involved in the day-to-day exercise of judicial power and thus has a more immediate awareness of cases coming before the tribunal, the bishop may choose to authorize him to decide the need for the promoter's intervention. Here is a proposed reading of the faculty:

In those contentious cases where you judge the intervention of the promoter of justice to be necessary and neither the law nor the nature of the case provide for it, you are hereby authorized to order the promoter of justice to intervene.

3. Canon 1469, § 2 permits judges, for a just cause, to acquire proofs outside their own jurisdiction, provided they have the permission of the diocesan bishop within whose jurisdiction the proofs are to be found. The canon indicates the bishop is to designate the place (or places) where the judges are to conduct their work. The bishop may choose to delegate the officialis to grant such permission. Here is a proposed reading of the faculty:

You are hereby authorized to permit judges from other ecclesiastical tribunals to gather evidence for their own cases within this diocese, when the need arises and such proofs are to be found within this diocese. You are to designate where they are to conduct their investigation within this diocese.

4. Canon 1653, § 1 prescribes that the diocesan bishop or his delegate mandate the execution of a definitive sentence in accord with the norms of law. The bishop may choose to delegate this executive function to the chancellor or vicar general; or, he may decide to delegate the judicial vicar for this purpose. In which case, here is a suggested reading of the faculty:

You are hereby authorized to mandate the execution of definitive sentences rendered in contentious and penal cases, in accord with the norms of law.

5. Canon 1700, § 1 permits the bishop to commit in a stable manner (*stabiliter*) the instruction of cases petitioning a dispensation from a ratified

but non-consummated marriage. The judicial vicar could be so designated. Here is a suggested reading of the faculty:

You are hereby authorized to instruct the process for petitioning a dispensation from a ratified but non-consummated marriage, according to the norms of law.

6. Canon 1717, § 1 decrees that the ordinary, either personally or through a delegate, is to investigate cautiously the facts, circumstances and possible imputability whenever he receives notice of a delict, unless the investigation appears superfluous. The delegate has the same authority and function as an auditor, but is prohibited from serving as judge in the same case should a judicial procedure follow (§ 3). With this prohibition in mind, the bishop may still choose to have the judicial vicar conduct this investigation. Here is a suggested reading of the faculty:

You are hereby authorized to conduct, in accord with the norms of law, the investigation of the facts, circumstances and possible imputability in cases alleging the commission of a delict to which an ecclesiastical penalty is attached, with due regard for the prohibition stated in canon 1717, § 3.

7. In cases of presumed death, canon 1707 provides for the diocesan bishop to issue a decree after appropriate investigation. Conduct of the investigation and even the issuance of the decree could be delegated to the judicial vicar. Here is a suggested reading of the faculty:

You are hereby authorized to conduct investigations in cases of presumed death and, if warranted, to issue the necessary decree in accord with canon 1707.

8. Although not mentioned in the new Code, there is a probable opinion that the administrative process remains in effect for declaring the nullity of lack of form marriages (i.e., marriages in which a Catholic bound by the canonical form of marriage did not observe that form, and was not dispensed from it). This is in addition to the documentary process (canons 1686-1688) in which the new code authorizes the judicial vicar to decide defect of form cases. The bishop could decide to delegate the judicial vicar to process such cases rather than the administrative agencies of the diocese or parishes. Here is a suggested reading of the faculty:

You are hereby authorized to investigate cases of lack of canonical form in which a Catholic was clearly bound by the form of the Church and no semblance of that form was observed, and if warranted by the facts to issue an administrative decree declaring nullity.

POSTSCRIPT. Although no granting of faculties is involved, it may be helpful to make special reference to the provisions of canon 1673, § 4 governing competence for marriage cases based on the fact that the tribunal is the one in which most of the depositions or proofs have to be collected. The new code represents a simplification of preceding law. Both the *motu proprio Causas matrimoniales* (art. IV, 1, c) and the American Procedural Norms (norm 7) required the consent of both the ordinary and the officialis in order to establish competence in this situation. Canon 1673, § 4 requires the consent of only the respondent's judicial vicar, given after consultation with the respondent.

Appendix to
Faculties for Judicial Vicar and Adjutant Judicial Vicars

The following is a restatement of and additions to the above listing of faculties which can be committed to the judicial vicar (officialis) and adjutant judicial vicars (vice-officiales). The list has been developed by Reverend Edward J. Dillon, J.C.D. and Reverend Monsignor Ellsworth Kneal, J.C.D., based on the initial paper above submitted to the Convention by Reverend Ronald J. Bowers, J.C.L.

As above the listing in this "Appendix" is drawn primarily from canons in the 1983 Code of Canon Law, where provision is made for the diocesan bishop to act in various circumstances relative to the tribunal and which therefore require special delegation (faculties) for the judicial vicar or his adjutant to perform. The faculties are also based on the opinion that those provisions of *Provida Mater* remain in effect which are not changed by the 1983 code or which concern matters not totally reorganized by the provisions of the code.

***

Faculties Relative to the Discipline and Functioning of the Tribunal

1. To substitute judges according to norm 19, § 1 of *Provida Mater*.
2. To appoint judges out of turn (c. 1425, § 3).
3. To commit cases to judgment by one judge (c. 1425, § 4).
4. To appoint auditors (c. 1428, § 2).
5. To direct the intervention of the promoter of justice in contentious cases (c. 1431, § 1).
6. To appoint and to substitute the promoter of justice in individual cases and for a grave cause (cc. 1430, 1435).
7. To appoint and to substitute the defender of the bond in individual cases and for a grave cause (cc. 1432, 1435).
8. To administer the oath of office to officials of the tribunal (c. 1454) and all others associated in the tribunal process.
9. To approve advocates (c. 1483).
10. To appoint individuals as necessary to fulfill the various offices and functions in tribunal processes in accordance with the norms of law.

11. To permit judges from other ecclesiastical jurisdictions to gather evidence in the territory of the diocese and to designate the place where this is to be done (c. 1469, § 2).

12. To execute sentences (c. 1653, § 1).

Faculties Relative to Specific Types of Cases

1. To issue a declaration of nullity in lack of form cases (cc. 1066 and 1085, § 2).

2. To instruct the process for petitioning a dispensation from a ratified but not consummated marriage (c. 1700, § 1).

3. To conduct investigations in cases of presumed death and, if warranted, to issue the necessary decree (c. 1707).

CONTRIBUTORS TO *PROCEEDINGS*

Judith Barnhiser, J.C.D., J.D., is an advocate with the State Advocacy Office in Richmond, Virginia.

Robert C. Becker, J.C.L., President of the Canon Law Society of America, is Judicial Vicar of the Archdiocese of Chicago, Illinois.

Cecelia Bennett, J.C.L., is Director of Campus Ministry at Biscayne College, Miami, Florida.

Ronald J. Bowers, J.C.L., is Judicial Vicar of the Archdiocese of Saint Paul and Minneapolis, Minnesota.

James A. Brundage, Ph.D., is Professor of History at the University of Wisconsin-Milwaukee, Milwaukee, Wisconsin.

James A. Coriden, J.C.D., J.D., is Academic Dean of the Washington Theological Union, Silver Spring, Maryland.

J. James Cuneo, J.C.D., is Judicial Vicar of the Diocese of Bridgeport, Connecticut.

Anthony C. Diacetis, J.C.D., Vice-President and President-Elect of the Canon Law Society of America, is Judicial Vicar of the Diocese of Albany, New York.

Edward J. Dillon, J.C.D., is Judicial Vicar of the Archdiocese of Atlanta, Georgia.

Thomas G. Doran, J.C.D., is Chancellor and Judicial Vicar of the Diocese of Rockford, Illinois.

Anne Fulwiler, I.H.M., J.C.L., is advocate and canonical consultant on the Tribunal of the Archdiocese of Washington, D.C.

Otto Garcia, J.C.D., is Chancellor of the Diocese of Brooklyn, New York.

Thomas J. Green, J.C.D., is Associate Professor of Canon Law at The Catholic University of America, Washington, D.C.

Bertram F. Griffin, J.C.D., is a pastor in the Archdiocese of Portland-in-Oregon, and is Judicial Vicar for the Interprovincial Tribunal of Anchorage, Portland and Seattle.

Charles A. Guarino, J.C.D., is Adjutant Judicial Vicar for the Diocese of Rockville Centre, New York.

Richard A. Hill, S.J., J.C.D., is Associate Professor of Canon Law at the Jesuit School of Theology in Berkeley, California.

Sharon Holland, I.H.M., J.C.D., serves in the office of the Delegate for Religious and on the Tribunal of the Archdiocese of Detroit, Michigan, and is a Provincial Councillor for her community in Monroe, Michigan.

M. Thaddea Kelly, P.B.V.M., is Associate Vicar for Religious in the Archdiocese of San Francisco, California.

James K. Mallett, M.Ch.A., Treasurer of the Canon Law Society of America, is Vicar for Administration and Chancellor in the Diocese of Nashville, Tennessee.

Daniel J. Murray, J.C.L., is Secretary to the Chancery and Adjutant Judicial Vicar in the Diocese of Orange, California.

James H. Provost, J.C.D., Executive Coordinator of the Canon Law Society of America, is Associate Professor of Canon Law at The Catholic University of America, Washington, D.C.

John A. Renken, J.C.D., is Assistant Chancellor and Coordinator of the Tribunal in the Diocese of Springfield-in-Illinois.

James Risk, S.J., J.C.D., is retired as Professor of Canon Law at the Gregorian University, Rome, and as Judicial Vicar of the Diocese of Bridgeport, Connecticut.

Harmon Skillen, J.C.D., is Judicial Vicar in the Diocese of Stockton, California.

Charles Torpey, J.C.L., is Chancellor and Judicial Vicar in the Diocese of Grand Island, Nebraska.

William A. Varvaro, J.C.L., is Judicial Vicar of the Diocese of Brooklyn, New York and J.C.D. candidate at the Gregorian University, Rome.

William P. Wolfe, J.C.L., is Associate Director of the Tribunal in the Archdiocese of Los Angeles, California.